THE SUBJECT APPROACH
TO
INFORMATION

THE SUBJECT APPROACH
TO
INFORMATION

THIRD EDITION BY

A C FOSKETT
MA FLA ALAA
Principal Lecturer, Library Studies
South Australian Institute of Technology

CLIVE BINGLEY
LONDON

LINNET BOOKS
HAMDEN · CONN

Publishing history

FIRST PUBLISHED 1969
REPRINTED 1970
SECOND EDITION 1971
REPRINTED 1973, 1975, 1976

THIS THIRD EDITION PUBLISHED 1977
BY CLIVE BINGLEY LTD 16 PEMBRIDGE ROAD LONDON WII UK
SIMULTANEOUSLY PUBLISHED IN THE USA BY
LINNET BOOKS THE SHOE STRING PRESS INC
995 SHERMAN AVENUE HAMDEN CONNECTICUT 06514

PHOTOSET IN 10 ON 11 POINT PLANTIN
AND PRINTED AND BOUND IN GREAT BRITAIN BY
REDWOOD BURN LIMITED TROWBRIDGE & ESHER

BINGLEY ISBN: 0-85157-238-3
LINNET ISBN: 0-208-01546-9

Contents

Illustrations

Author's preface

The first edition of this book, published in 1969, was prompted by changes in the Library Association syllabus which for the first time enabled lecturers to treat classification and subject cataloguing as different aspects of the same topic. These changes coincided with the publication of the results of the Cranfield project, which showed clearly that all indexing languages are basically the same. However, although it was possible to teach these new approaches, there was no one textbook which covered the subject approach in the way that I felt was needed. The first edition was intended to fill this gap, and its reception, both in Britain and abroad, showed that it did indeed fulfil a real need. It met with a very positive welcome from lecturers and—more importantly—from students, particularly in the United States, where British textbooks on classification had previously been regarded with something akin to suspicion. (As the Dean of one American library school is alleged to have remarked, '*What* theory of classification?')

The first edition was quickly sold out, and I decided to revise it in the light of comments by colleagues and reviewers, and of developments in my own thinking. My experience in teaching at the University of Maryland during 1968–1969 and summer 1970 was another important factor influencing my decision to revise rather than reprint. I was thus able to include such important developments as the adoption of PRECIS by BNB with the introduction of MARC at the beginning of 1971, and it was a matter of some small pride that my account of the eighteenth edition of Dewey appeared at about the same time as the official publication of the scheme itself, thanks to the cooperation of the editor, Mr Ben Custer, and of BNB, which had started to use DC18 at the beginning of the year, in advance of publication.

The second edition was also well received all over the world, and was accorded the singular honour of translation into Portuguese for use in library schools in Brazil. In due course, the question of whether to revise or reprint arose again. The timing of a work such as this presents some difficulties; if one delays revision, the text gradually becomes more and more out of date, until it lapses into a state of desuetude, but if one rushes into print one is sure to find within the year that some new development has occurred which simply cries out—too late—for inclusion. My first intention was to prepare the third edition for publication in 1976, to celebrate the centenary of Dewey and Cutter, but a stroke in June 1975 put this out of the question; the delay did however have one valuable bonus in the publication of the PRECIS Manual, that invaluable contribution to indexing thought. It has not yet brought before me any of the schedules of the new edition of the Bibliographic Classification, much to my regret; this has had to be described at secondhand. Swings and roundabouts!

This third edition contains a number of quite important changes. In 1969 it seemed legitimate to place the computer in a section called 'The future'; by 1971 this was already beginning to look a little out of place, and in 1977 it is plainly ridiculous. The computer is with us here and now, and on the grand scale; one reads of on-line access via international telephone lines from the National Library of Australia to the Lockheed Corporation's DIALOG system containing a total of some twelve million references from a variety of data bases, and accepts this as part of our present way of life. I have therefore brought forward the chapter on the computer to chapter 3, which has enabled me to refer to its use wherever appropriate in the later chapters. I have dropped the chapter on edge-notched cards, which can no longer be regarded as a significant form of retrieval device, and substituted a chapter on computer-based services, much of which is new. Much of what I previously included under the heading 'Research' is now practice, and has been transferred to appropriate places in the earlier sections; the rest forms the basis of an expanded chapter on evaluation. The chapter on subject analysis has been expanded into two chapters, on semantic and syntactic analysis respectively; this has given me the opportunity to tidy up some material previously scattered and to include the results of some more recent research. PRECIS, which in 1971 was just making its appearance in its first version, is now well established in its second version. In view of its origins in the work of the CRG towards a new general classification, I have included it in a separate chapter after the section on classification. Chapter 1 now includes a section on information retrieval as a form of communication, which I hope will illuminate the whole of the rest of the book; information retrieval systems have no existence in their own right, but only insofar as they enable communication to be maintained between authors and readers, and we overlook this at our peril. It is all too easy to become wrapped up in the intricacies of this or that system to such an extent that we forget their basic purpose. In chapter 2, I have enlarged the discussion of recall and relevance by using set theory and notation. Having myself been brought up on classical maths, I used to believe that set theory was something only to be studied at university level, but I have now learnt enough about it from my children at secondary (and primary!) school to believe that most students will be able to take this section in their stride, and welcome the clarification it affords. Lecturers of course I cannot vouch for. The chapters on classification schemes have been brought up to date where necessary, and in some cases amended to reflect the fact that different schemes are now available to me for first-hand comment. Every chapter has been scanned to identify sections needing alteration, and in fact the only chapter to escape amendment entirely is that on Sears' List; with no new edition to comment on at the time of writing, I found no reason for change. I hope that I have not committed too many sins of commission; of sins of omission I am well aware there are many. This edition is larger than the second, which was larger than the first; if the book was to remain within tolerable limits of size (and price) it was necessary to leave out many items that I would have liked to include. I hope that what *is* included will serve as a firm basis for the study of other areas and other schemes.

As this is a textbook intended to be used by students following courses in library schools, I have tried to devote particular attention to topics such as the Principle of Inversion which, though relatively unimportant in the overall scheme of things, seem to cause students a disproportionate amount of difficulty. I have concentrated everywhere on the modern approach, including terminology; I have never found it particularly useful for students trying to see the wood of classification to be distracted by the Tree of Porphyry. Existing schemes are judged by their ability to function well in present day libraries exploiting (and that is an important word) present day literature. A scheme may well have been very satisfactory in, say, 1910, or it may still appear to function adequately today, so long as nobody actually tries to *use* it; but today's libraries must be prepared to take an active part in seeing that information reaches those to whom it will be of value, and this requires tools which match today's needs, not yesterday's. I would also like to emphasize a point made in the text; it is not possible to study a scheme of classification, subject headings or coordinate indexing descriptors *at second hand*. Students should study *all* the schemes referred to for themselves, preferably under the direction of a tutor, with a certain amount of practical work. For this reason I have tried to concentrate on explaining why schemes are what they are and how their background and history affect their use today, rather than go into a lot of detail on their content.

Many of my examples are taken from science and technology. This is to some extent the reflection of a personal predilection, but I make no apology for it. Many library school students have a non-scientific background (to put it charitably) and may find some of the terms used in the examples unfamiliar—but they will also find this situation repeated very frequently once they start practising their profession. I have tried to show that subject knowledge or the lack of it is not necessarily an important factor in the ability to index and retrieve information, a point first shown clearly by the Cranfield Project. Terminology and subject structure are usually reasonably well defined in science and technology, a state of affairs which does not always hold good in other subject areas, and examples taken from these other areas might well prove a great deal more difficult for students to grasp, even if the words used were more familiar (or perhaps *because* of this!). A final, and very significant, reason is that until quite recently most of the examples of modern indexing techniques had to be taken from the scientific and technical literature, since only there were they to be found. Anyone finding an example with unfamiliar words in it should not despair; in the first place, the examples demonstrate *structure* rather than terminology, and in the second—most of us have access to dictionaries.

In one of his perceptive articles on citation indexing, John Martyn refers to 'Alice in Wonderland' citations: irrelevant allusions included by authors to 'add artistic verisimilitude to a bald and otherwise unconvincing narrative' (Pooh-Bah, in 'The Mikado'). This text contains its share of such allusions: to those who recognize them, I hope they will provide those brief moments of relaxation which enable us to continue our studies refreshed. One of the greatest sources of satisfaction I have gained from the first two editions is the frequent comments received from both students and lecturers that they found the book *readable*; if I have maintained the same degree of readability in this edition, I will have achieved one of the primary objectives of good technical writing. One point is perhaps worth mentioning here. The text is intended to be read straight through; as the King of Hearts advised Alice, 'Begin at the beginning, and go on till you come to the end: then stop'. However, I realize that this may not fit some teaching programmes, and I have therefore included a certain amount of repetition to enable those who follow a different route to do so with a minimum of inconvenience. For those who *do* follow the pattern of the text, I hope that any repetition will serve as reinforcement of points I believe to be of particular importance.

My thoughts have obviously been influenced by many previous writers, as well as by comments from colleagues at Loughborough Technical College, the College of Librarianship Wales, University of Maryland and South Australian Institute of Technology; so many, in fact, that to name them all would be to repeat a substantial proportion of the citations in the book, while to select a few would be invidious. I hope that they will all accept my grateful thanks for their help; for the deficiencies and errors that remain, I must accept full responsibility, and plead, with Dr Johnson, 'Ignorance, madam, pure ignorance'. One acknowledgement must however be made. Without the constant help and encouragement of my wife, who alternately cajoled and bullied me out of the Slough of Despond into which my unexpected illness in 1975 cast me, this new edition would never have seen the light of day.

A C FOSKETT
January 1977

List of abbreviations

ACS	American Chemical Society
ADI	American Documentation Institute (now ASIS)
AERE	Atomic Energy Research Establishment
AIM/TWX	Abridged Index Medicus/Telex
ALA	American Library Association
ALMS	Automated Library Management System
AMRS	Australian Marc Record Service
ANB	Australian National Bibliography
API	American Petroleum Institute
ASCA	Automatic Subject Citation Alert
ASCII	American Standard Code for Information Interchange
ASIS	American Society for Information Science (previously ADI)
ASSASSIN	Agricultural System for Storage And Subsequent Selection of INformation
ASTIA	Armed Services Technical Information Agency (now DDC)
BC	Bibliographic Classification (Bliss)
BCM	British Catalogue of Music
BLLD	British Library Lending Division (previously NLLST)
BM	British Museum
BNB	British National Bibliography
BS	British Standard
BSI	British Standards Institution
BSO	Broad System of Ordering
BTI	British Technology Index
CA	Chemical Abstracts
CAC	Chemical Abstracts Condensates
CAS	Chemical Abstracts Service
CASIA	Chemical Abstracts Subject Information Alert
CC	Colon Classification
CDU	Classification Décimale Universelle (= UDC)
CFSTI	Clearinghouse for Federal Scientific and Technical Information (now NTIS)
CLIR	Clearinghouse for Library and Information Resources
CLIS	Clearinghouse for Library and Information Science (now incorporated in CLIR)
CLRU	Cambridge Language Research Unit

xiv

CLW	College of Librarianship Wales
CNRS	Centre Nationale pour la Recherche Scientifique
COM	Computer Output Micro-form/film/fiche
COSATI	Committee On Scientific And Technical Information
CRG	Classification Research Group
CSIRO	Commonwealth Scientific and Industrial Research Organisation
DC	Decimal Classification (Dewey)
DC&	Decimal Classification Additions, Notes, Decisions
DCD	Decimal Classification Division (Library of Congress)
DDC	Defense Documentation Center
DK	Dezimal Klassifikation (=UDC)
DRTC	Documentation Research and Training Centre
EBCDIC	Extended Binary Coded Decimal Interchange Code
ED	ERIC Document
EE	English Electric Company Limited (now part of GEC)
EJ	ERIC Journal abstract number
EJC	Engineers Joint Council
EURATOM	European Atomic Energy Community
ERIC	Educational Resources Information Center
FID	Fédération Internationale de Documentation
FID/CCC	FID Central Classification Committee
GRACE	GRaphic Arts Composing Equipment
IBM	International Business Machines Corporation
ICI	Imperial Chemical Industries Limited
IEE	Institution of Electrical Engineers
IIB	Institut International de Bibliographie (later IID)
IID	Institut International de Documentation (now FID)
IM	Index Medicus
INSPEC	INformation Service in Physics, Electrotechnology and Control
INTREX	INformation TRansfer EXperiments
IR	Information Retrieval
IRE	Institute of Radio Engineers (now Institute of Electrical and Electronic Engineers)
ISBN	International Standard Book Number
ISI	Institute for Scientific Information
KWIC	KeyWord In Context
KWOC	KeyWord Out of Context
LA	[British] Library Association
LC	Library of Congress classification
LCSH	Subject Headings used in . . . the Library of Congress
LISA	Library and Information Science Abstracts
MARC	MAchine Readable Cataloguing
MEDLARS	MEDical Literature Analysis and Retrieval System

MeSH	Medical Subject Headings
MIT	Massachusetts Institute of Technology
NASA	National Aeronautics and Space Administration
NIH	National Institute of Health
NLL	National Lending Library for Science and Technology (also NLLST; now BLLD)
NLM	National Library of Medicine
NSA	Nuclear Science Abstracts
NTIS	National Technical Information Service
OCLC	Ohio College Library Center
OECD	Organisation for Economic Cooperation and Development
OSTI	Office for Scientific and Technical Information (now British Library Research Division)
OTS	Office of Technical Services (later CFSTI, now NTIS)
P-Note	Provisional extension to UDC
PCMI	Photo-Chromic Micro-Image
PMEST	Personality, Matter, Energy, Space, Time
PRECIS	PREserved Context Indexing System
SC	Subject Classification (Brown)
SCI	Science Citation Index
SDI	Selective Dissemination of Information
SHARP	Ships Analysis And Retrieval Project
SLIC	Selective Listing In Combination
SMART	Salton's automatic retrieval system
SRC	Standard Reference Code/Standard Roof Classification (BSO)
SSCI	Social Science Citation Index
STAR	Scientific and Technical Aerospace Reports
SYNTOL	SYNTagmatic Organisation Language
TEST	Thesaurus of Engineering and Scientific Terms
TIP	MIT Technical Information Project
UCLA	University of California at Los Angeles
UDC	Universal Decimal Classification
UKAEA	United Kingdom Atomic Energy Authority
UKCIS	United Kingdom Chemical Information Service
UNISIST	United Nations Information System In Science and Technology
USEAC	United States Atomic Energy Commission
VDU	Visual Display Unit
WRU	Case Western Reserve University

PART I: THEORY OF
INFORMATION RETRIEVAL SYSTEMS

CHAPTER 1

Introduction

Libraries form an essential part of the chain of human communication. Before knowledge was recorded (and even to this day in very primitive societies), individuals formed the repository of knowledge, the bridge between successive generations and between those who generated new information and those who required to use it. The amount of information that can be passed on in this way is limited, and society began to move forward when information of various kinds began to be recorded in relatively permanent forms which could serve as a substitute for the 'wise man' in person.

Nowadays, the quantity of new information being generated is such that no individual can hope to keep pace with even a small fraction of it, and the problem that we have to face is that of ensuring that individuals who need information can obtain it with the minimum of cost (both in time and in money), and without being overwhelmed by large amounts of irrelevant matter. Instead of the individual store of knowledge, we have the corporate store: the library; instead of the individual memory, we have the corporate memory: library catalogues and bibliographical tools. And just as the individual whose memory fails him cannot pass on wanted information when it is wanted, so a library whose corporate memory is inadequate will fail in its purpose.

THE IMPORTANCE OF CATALOGUES AND BIBLIOGRAPHIES
Libraries contain information in many different physical forms. While for many the book is still the major vehicle for the communication of information, for others the periodical or the technical report have taken its place; for yet others, newer forms such as films or gramophone records are the significant items. It is clear that the same work can appear in several different physical forms: for example, we may have Shakespeare's play *Hamlet* in book form, as a film, or on a record. The intellectual content will be the same in each case, but obviously it is not always practical to try to arrange the different physical forms together. Although it is possible to obtain shelving which does permit this, it is not economical of shelf space, and in some libraries might well be regarded as more of a hindrance than a help.

We cannot therefore rely on the physical arrangement of the items in a library to gather together different versions of the same work; we have to rely on a substitute—a set of records (surrogates) of the content of the library. In addition to the physical form, other factors may influence the place where we choose to keep any given item: we may decide that it should not be removed from the building, so it is placed in the reference section; or it may be suitable for children rather than adults, so it is placed in the children's section; or it may be a rarely used work which is placed in the stack rather than in the section open to the public. All of these factors emphasize the importance of the records, as opposed to the items themselves, for we can gather together in one place the records of items which themselves must perforce be scattered.

Suppose that our library only contains items of one kind, *eg* books. We can now attempt to arrange these in a way that will be useful, but we still cannot dispense with the records. For any particular book there will be several ways in which we might wish to find it: we may know the author, or the title, or we may need to find it because of its subject. The arrangement of books on our shelves may be by author, in which case we shall be able to find the required book if we know the author, but not if we only know the title or subject; equally, it may be by subject, in which case we shall not be able to find a book if we only know the author. But there is no such restriction when we consider the records we may make, for we can record a book by any and every factor which we think may prove to be of use when we are later searching for it. All we need is a fixed address to which each of these factors will lead us, so that we can locate the physical item no matter how we approach it. Once again, it is the records of the contents of our library which are the essential keys: the corporate memory.

The library's catalogue, however, is only one of the tools which serve as the corporate memory. A library containing large numbers of periodicals will not attempt to list every article in every issue it receives; instead, we rely on indexes, abstracts and similar bibliographical tools, which present the same kind of opportunity—and the same problems—as the library's catalogue, by enabling us to obtain access to any particular item through a number of different approaches.

FACTORS WHICH IDENTIFY

Some of these approaches *identify* the items they refer to. For example, if we state the number of a patent specification, there will only be one item corresponding to that description; if we name an author, we immediately limit severely the number of works which will satisfy us. Title, edition, date of publication, publisher, are all factors of this kind. We can therefore give a definite yes/no answer to an enquiry regarding one of these factors; either we can supply what our reader wants, or we cannot. A reader who asks for a copy of *Hamlet* may not mind very much which edition we give him, but he will certainly object if he is given *The alchemist*. An enquiry for AERE Inf/Bib 132 will not be satisfied by AERE Inf/Bib 125. Provided we have entries in our records which will lead us to the place where we can find these items, our search is straightforward.

FACTORS WHICH DO NOT IDENTIFY

There are, however, other approaches which do not identify the items which will answer them. If we are asked for a 'nice detective' we have a wide choice of answers, any one of which may satisfy the enquirer. More seriously, if we are asked for something on a particular subject, we may be able to find a number of potential answers from which we shall have to ask our reader to make his own selection. Because authors write from within their own individual nexus of experiences, and readers read within their limits, there will seldom be the exact correspondence that we have with factors which identify; instead, we shall have to try to get as good a match as we can between our reader's needs and what we can supply, accepting that it is unlikely that we shall immediately find the same kind of yes/no answer as is possible when we can identify.

INFORMATION RETRIEVAL AS A FORM OF COMMUNICATION

We may consider information retrieval processes as part of the overall pattern of communication.[1] The most commonly used model of the communication process is that devised by Shannon and Weaver, shown in figure 1a. In this model, we see that a *source* has a *message* which is to be transmitted to a *receiver*; before it can be transmitted, the message must be *encoded* for transmission along the selected *channel*, to be *decoded* before it can be understood by the receiver. In information retrieval, the sources are the originators of the documents we handle; the encoding process includes the choice of the appropriate words and their translation into print (or whatever medium is used); the channel is the document and its progress from originator to user; and the decoding process involves the user and his ability to comprehend the message in the form in which it is presented to him. The final element in the model is *noise*. Noise may be defined as anything which detracts from the fidelity of the transmission of the message from source to receiver. Shannon and Weaver were concerned with the transmission of messages over telephone wires, but the concept of noise, which is obviously relevant to that situation, can be generalised to cover all kinds of interference with communication—for example, unwanted documents retrieved in answer to a request.

If we consider normal verbal communication, we can see that the model (figure 1b) is in fact that of figure 1a doubled, so that the original source functions also as a receiver and vice versa. In this situation, a further important element enters the picture: the idea of *feedback*. If

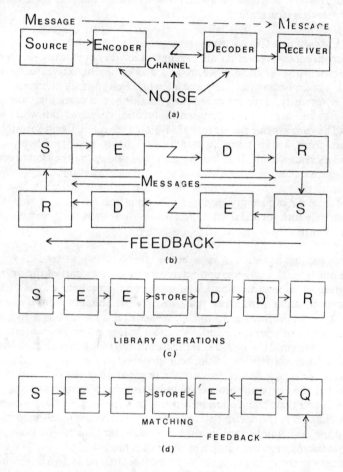

FIGURE I: Models of the communication process.
(a) The Shannon-Weaver model.
(b) Verbal (two-way) communication; involves feedback.
(c) The effect of library operations.
(d) The query situation: feedback through the matching process.

the message becomes distorted on its way from source to receiver, the receiver can immediately query it (I didn't quite catch that? or, Could you explain that again, please? or, *What?*) Feedback can thus reduce the effect of noise and improve the fidelity of communication.

Unfortunately, when we are dealing with documents, there can be little, if any, feedback from user to originator, and any that does take place is usually at a distance, for example through correspondence. The source has no control over who receives his messages, and cannot therefore direct them to a specific audience, though he may well have a fair idea of the *likely* audience. The receivers in their turn cannot be certain that they have understood the messages correctly, or that they have located the messages they are looking for. Librarians are all too familiar with the user who returns a book with the comment that it was not quite what they wanted. Indeed, the situation is in some ways made more difficult by the interposition of additional encoding processes in the library, which then require further decoding processes on the part of the user. We normally arrange books by putting a code on the spine: a class mark; and we identify them in our catalogues by a further series of codes: catalogue entries (figure 1c). Many readers have difficulty in comprehending these codes; some indeed regard them as a barrier imposed by librarians to prevent the users from obtaining easy access to the items they want and thus ensuring a measure of job security. Catalogue entries and class marks can in fact give a great deal of information, but there is no doubt that they do form an additional complication in the chain of communication, and as such are an additional source of noise.

Furthermore, as may be seen from the diagram, we have introduced yet another complication. Not only is transmission of the message indirect; it is also *delayed* by being placed in a *store* of some kind. A book may be regarded as such a store, as may any kind of document, but we are primarily concerned here with the library, as represented in catalogues and bibliographies, as our store. In this context, such relatively trivial matters as misshelving of documents or misfiling of catalogue cards all add their quota of noise to the communication process.

SEARCHING

So far we have considered the passive approach: the library provides material, which the readers select in a fairly indeterminate way. However, much of the use made of libraries is active: readers come to the library seeking information on particular subjects, and expect our systems to be able to provide the answers. In this situation, the receiver becomes a source, encoding a message in the form of an enquiry. We now have to discover any messages in our store which appear to match the enquiry; having found some, we can pass them on to the enquirer, who can decide whether they match his needs. In the light of our response, the enquirer may modify his message in an attempt to achieve a closer match with his requirements; in other words, we have a degree of feedback in the system, which may enable us eventually to satisfy a request despite an initial failure. This failure may arise from a variety of causes: the enquirer may not be able to express himself clearly, or he may not be very sure exactly what it is he needs (if he knew the answer he would not need to ask the question!); or our encoding processes may be inadequate; or the original source (the author) may not have made his message clear, or may even have had some quite different message in mind (for example, the answer to a question from a librarian on the optimum number of staff required to man the circulation desk may be found in a book on supermarket management). The significance of this feedback mechanism is discussed further in chapter 2 in relation to iterative and heuristic searching.

It is helpful to bear this model in mind when considering any information retrieval system. Are there any factors which tend to increase noise? Which is the most appropriate channel for any particular message? Libraries now take the whole of recorded knowledge as their province, not merely the more conventional books and periodicals; perhaps a tape-slide presentation or a videotape may be the best answer to an enquiry. How accurate are our encoding and decoding processes? How much feedback can be built into the system? With these points in mind we can be more confident of our ability to achieve the match between our readers' needs and what we can supply which we have already referred to. The study of communication has shown that it is quite rare for 100% success to be obtained even under optimum conditions, while the plays of such authors as Harold Pinter show all too clearly the extent to which we all too often fail to achieve any kind of communication at all. With this in mind, we should strive to optimize our information retrieval systems, while recognizing that they are always likely to remain imperfect.

SOME FURTHER FACTORS TO BE CONSIDERED
There is a further set of factors which do not identify particular documents but which are very important in selecting once we have identified potentially useful items. These include physical form—we may have the very thing, but only as a microfiche, useless without a reader; language—just what is wanted, but in Russian; level—we want an elementary introduction, but only have a doctoral thesis; intented audience—a book intended for one particular group of people (*eg* fluid mechanics for civil engineers) may not be well suited to the needs of another group; author's viewpoint—a Marxist history of Christianity may offend the practising churchgoer. It will be clear that we can only consider these factors when we have selected a set of documents which appear to match the reader's needs as far as their subject content is

concerned.

This book is concerned with a discussion of the problems of optimizing our responses to requests for information on subjects. This is not to suggest that identifying factors such as authors' names do not present any problems; the fact that it took some twenty years of discussions to produce a new edition of the Anglo-American code,[2] which has since been the subject of continuous further discussion, shows very plainly that they do! The problems of the subject approach to information, however, are more severe because they are more indeterminate; we never reach the stage of being able to say we have finished a search conclusively. A great deal of research has been done on these problems; much more remains to be done. This book is an attempt to show the present state of the art, in a way which will be acceptable as an elementary textbook; it does not pretend to be an advanced study, of which there are many, but rather to give beginners some understanding of present theories and ideas.[3]

BIBLIOGRAPHY

1 Berlo, D K: *The process of communication: an introduction to theory and practice.* Holt, Rinehart and Winston, 1960. There are a number of works on communication, but Berlo's approach is peculiarly well suited to many of the problems of information retrieval; chapters 1, 2, 3, 7 and 8 are particularly useful.

2 *Anglo-American cataloguing rules;* prepared by the American Library Association, the Library of Congress, the Library Association and Canadian Library Association. British text published by the Library Association, 1967. North American text published by the American Library Association, 1967. Since AACR67 was published, we have seen the introduction of the International Standard Bibliographical Description for monographs and serials, and notable revisions in the practice of cataloguing non-book materials. A new edition of AACR is to be published in 1978.

3 Of the making of many books on information retrieval there is no end. The following selection is listed alphabetically by author; 'elementary' indicates a work that can be read with profit by the novice; 'intermediate' indicates a work which should be read, but preferably after some preliminary grounding has been obtained; 'advanced', works which may be read by the student wishing to pursue the subject beyond the level of this text.

Artandi, S ed: 'Rutgers series on systems for the intellectual organization of information'. This series includes volumes on UDC, SYNTOL, CC, faceted classification, coordinate indexing, and the alphabetical approach; all of them are of high standard and contain much original material. Advanced.

Austin, D: *PRECIS: a manual of concept analysis and subject indexing*. Council of the British National Bibliography, 1974. Intermediate.

Brown, A G: *An introduction to subject indexing*. 2v. Bingley, 1976. Elementary. (Programmed text)

Coates, E J: *Subject catalogues: headings and structure*. Library Association, 1960. One of the few worthwhile books on the alphabetical approach. Unfortunately, this excellent work is now out of print, and it does not of course include recent developments such as PRECIS.

Foskett, D J: 'Classification'. (Chapter in Batten, W E *ed*: *Handbook of special librarianship*. Aslib, fourth edition 1975). A concise but useful summary. Intermediate.

Foskett, D J: *Classification and indexing in the social sciences*. Butterworths, second edition, 1975. Discusses many general problems as well as those specific to the social sciences. Intermediate.

Foskett, D J: *Classification for a general index language*. Library Association, 1970. (LA Research pamphlet no 2.) An exposition of the theoretical development of the new general classification scheme being prepared by the CRG, this is of wider interest also as a statement of the problems to be dealt with. Elementary.

Hutchins, W J: *Languages of indexing and classification*. Peter Peregrinus, 1975. A linguistic study. Advanced.

International study conference on classification research, Dorking, 1957: *Proceedings*. Aslib, 1958. Advanced.

International study conference on classification research, second, Elsinore, 1964. *Proceedings*. Copenhagen, Munksgaard, 1965. Advanced. (In general, the papers are beyond the scope of the student, but specific chapters, *eg* those on LC and UDC, are of value.)

Kochen, M: *Principles of information retrieval*. Melville, 1974. Advanced.

Lancaster, F W: *Information retrieval systems: characteristics, testing and evaluation*. Wiley, 1968. A valuable textbook by one of the Cranfield workers. Intermediate.

Lancaster, F W: *Vocabulary control for information retrieval*. Information Resources Press, 1972. Intermediate.

Langridge, D: *Approach to classification*. Bingley, 1973. Elementary.

Langridge, D: *Classification and indexing in the humanities*. Butterworths, 1976. Intermediate.

Library Association: *Some problems of a general classification scheme: report of a conference held in London, June 1963*. Library Association, 1964. Intermediate.

Maltby, A: *Classification in the 1970's: a second look*. Bingley, 1976. A revision of a useful work, giving a variety of opinions on current developments. Intermediate.

Needham, C D: *Organizing knowledge in libraries: an introduction to cataloguing and classification*. Deutsch, second edition 1971. Useful though most of the emphasis is on cataloguing. Elementary.

Palmer, B I: *Itself an education*. Library Association, second edition 1971. The six lectures on various aspects of classification which formed the first edition published in 1962 are reprinted, together with a valuable new chapter on PRECIS by Derek Austin. Elementary.

Sayers, W C Berwick: *Manual of library classification*. Fifth edition revised by A Maltby, Deutsch, 1975. The best presentation of the traditional approach to classification, this edition has been thoroughly revised to introduce modern theory. Elementary.

The Sayers memorial volume, edited by D J Foskett and B I Palmer. Library Association, 1961. A festschrift in honour of Sayers, who died before it could be published. Contains several chapters on modern developments of importance. Intermediate.

Sharp, J: *Some fundamentals of information retrieval*. Deutsch, 1965. Demonstrates the ways in which classification can cause difficulties in retrieval, and the methods which may be used to overcome these. Intermediate.

Sharp, J: 'Information retrieval'. (Chapter in Batten, W E, *ed: Handbook of special librarianship*. Aslib, fourth edition 1975.) Like the chapter on classification, this is a concise but valuable summary. Intermediate.

Vickery, B C: *Classification and indexing in science and technology*. Butterworths, third edition 1975. Of more general scope than its title implies, this work, like Coates, is not easy, but is essential reading.

Vickery, B C: *Information systems*. Butterworths, 1973. Advanced. (In effect, this might be regarded as the third edition of *On retrieval system theory*, in that it attempts to set out a unified theory of information retrieval, taking account of developments since the second edition in 1965.)

Vickery, B C: *On retrieval system theory*. Butterworths, second edition 1965. One of the most satisfactory attempts to present a unified theory covering all IR methods. Advanced.

Vickery, B C: *Techniques of information retrieval*. Butterworths, 1970. Emphasizes the relationship between information retrieval and other aspects of library science, particularly bibliography. Intended as a textbook, it contains many valuable examples. Intermediate.

Wellisch, H: *Subject retrieval in the seventies: new directions*. Proceedings of an international symposium . . . 1971, edited by Hans Wellisch and T D Wilson. Greenwood Publishing company, 1972 (University of Maryland School of Library and Information Services: Contributions in librarianship and information science number 3). Intermediate.

For developments over the past few years it is helpful to consult the chapters on classification in *Five years' work in librarianship; 1956–1960* by J Mills, *1961–1965* by A C Foskett: and in *British librarianship and information science, 1966–1970*, by K G B Bakewell. These chapters also have comprehensive bibliographies. Students should also note the series 'Progress in documentation' which now appears regularly in the *Journal of documentation* since 1969. This consists of a series of 'state-of-the-art' reviews covering, for example, 'Classification', and 'The automatic generation of indexing languages'. The relevant chapters in the *Annual review of information science and technology* are also valuable for the student wishing to pursue the subject in some depth.

CHAPTER 2

Features of an information retrieval system

Authors generate large quantities of information every day. Estimates suggest that the number of useful (*ie* not merely repetitive) periodical articles published each year in science and technology alone is in excess of one million[1]; in Britain over 25,000 books are published every year. Libraries acquire a selection of this enormous output for the immediate use of their readers, and through the various schemes of inter-library cooperation they have access to a very much wider choice.

At the other end of the chain of communication we have readers, each with his own individual need for information which has to be selected from the mass available. The reader's appproach may be purposive, that is, he may be seeking the answer to a specific question, which may be more or less clearly formulated in his mind. This is the situation that we shall consider first, but we must not overlook the browser, who is looking for something to catch his interest.

CURRENT SCANNING AND RETROSPECTIVE SEARCHING

Our reader may be mainly interested in keeping up to date with current publications in his subject. In this case, our retrieval system must also be up to date; however, because the items referred to are usually easily available, our system need only be a fairly simple guide; if an item looks interesting, the reader can obtain the original without much trouble. On the other hand, the reader may need as much information as can be found regardless of date; in this case, much of the material may be difficult and therefore expensive to obtain, and we need to be much more certain that it will be of use before we attempt to follow up a reader's request. Our information retrieval system must give us enough information about a document for us to be able to decide whether to pursue it or not. Since this second situation is the more demanding, it is the one on which we shall be concentrating in this book, but the more straightforward current scanning should not be forgotten. The contrast between the two approaches is well illustrated by such works as *Current papers in electrical and electronic engineering* and *Electrical and electronics abstracts*, both of which cover the same groups of documents but with the two different purposes in mind. There are a number of similar publications covering various subject fields; within the library, current scanning needs are often met by current accessions lists, while the catalogue serves the major function of the retrospective searching tool as far as the library's own stock is concerned.

SELECTIVE DISSEMINATION OF INFORMATION

In addition to providing facilities for current scanning and retrospective searching, both of which imply that the user takes the initiative, for many years now libraries have themselves taken the initiative by endeavouring to see that readers are kept informed of new materials in their fields of interest. In the public library, this might be on a haphazard, 'old boy', basis, but in the special library it has always been regarded as an important part of the library's function. There are, however, certain difficulties in the way of running such a service successfully, some intellectual, some clerical. The use of a computer can solve many of these problems and enable us to give a more complete and accurate service to our readers.[2]

A system for computer operation was developed by H P Luhn of IBM and is still valid today, though it has been modified in some respects. In effect, it involves each reader in stating his requirements in the same method of subject description as is used in indexing the library's holdings. If the library uses a thesaurus, then terms will be chosen from this; if a classification scheme, this will be used. These reader 'profiles' are fed into the computer together with the similar profiles for new accessions; when the computer finds a match between the two, it prints out a notification.

Clerical problems are thus fairly easily solved. The intellectual problems are rather more intractable. A research project begun by the National Electronics Research Council and later taken over by the Institution of Electrical Engineers with support from OSTI showed that perhaps the most pressing difficulty in setting up a viable SDI system was to obtain a valid statement of readers' needs. Users were asked to state their interest profiles, and were sent a selection of articles on the strength of this. At the end of the month they were asked to state which of the articles had been of use, and which article they had read during the month had proved most interesting to them. While the majority of the references notified by the SDI systems were of some value, the 'most interesting articles' were often found to bear little relation to the reader's profile! By asking readers to return the notification form, indicating whether the reference had been of interest or not, a degree of feedback can be obtained which can be used to modify their profiles, but there will never be any means of foretelling the 'wayout' article which may prove of interest.

Despite the difficulties, the IEE has developed this work into a satisfactory integrated system, INSPEC, in which all the operations involved in the SDI service and the production of the various parts of

Science abstracts, including *Electrical and electronics abstracts*, and *Current papers . . .* are integrated.[3] This is only one of many such services, discussed in more detail in Chapter 25.

While SDI systems may not be able to achieve the impossible, they can function very effectively within a particular organization, and computer processing enables us to extend the benefits to a larger audience. The success of the many services now available has shown that provided the users do their part by stating their needs precisely, a very effective service can be given on a nation wide scale.

In sum, readers will need all the information that we can collect (at least that is the hope of the authors!), but we cannot tell in advance what items of information we are likely to acquire that will be of value to any particular reader. What we have to do is organize our library in such a way that when we search for information for a reader we do not have to scan the whole contents in order to find what he wants, but can go with the minimum of delay to those items which will be of use. To look at it from another angle, our organization must permit us to eliminate what is *not* wanted. This idea introduces three very important concepts: recall, relevance and precision.

RECALL, RELEVANCE AND PRECISION

For any particular reader who comes to the library with a need for information, there will be certain items in our collection which will be relevant. Among these it will be possible to establish some sort of precedence order; some will be definitely relevant, others will be useful, but less so, while others will be only marginally relevant. To take an example, a reader might want information on Siamese cats: in our collections we may have items dealing specifically with Siamese cats, and these will probably be highly relevant. There are however factors other than the subject alone which will influence this; these items may be too detailed, or not detailed enough; they may be written at the wrong level, or in a language which the reader does not understand. The reader's background will inevitably affect his decision as to which items he finds most relevant. To find more information we may broaden our search: that is, present to our reader those items which, though they do not deal specifically with the subject he is interested in, do include it as part of a broader subject. In our example, we may find items which deal with cats in general, not just with Siamese cats; or with pets in general, not just with cats. However, we must accept that the more we broaden our search—the more material we *recall*—the less likely it is that any given item will be *relevant*. At the extreme, we will find relevant information in a general encyclopedia, but it will only form a very small proportion of the total information therein. There is thus an inverse relationship between *recall*—the number of additional items we find in broadening our search—and *relevance*—the likelihood of

13

their matching our reader's requirements.

Normally, a reader will be satisfied with a few items, so long as they contain the kind of information he wants; that is to say, we need a system which will give us high relevance, even though recall will be low. But there will be situations when the reader will require high recall—as much information as possible—even though this means that he will have to look through a lot of items which will turn out to be of little or no value to him. We need to be able to vary the response of our system to cater for the kind of demand. It is also clear that relevance is a subjective factor depending on the individual; the same question, posed by two different readers, may well require two different answers. Indeed, we may carry the argument further. Each document revealed by our search may change a reader's view of what is relevant, as we have already mentioned in chapter 1, so that even a single individual's decisions on relevance may vary from time to time.

The problem arises from the fact that readers seek information which they can build into their own corpus of knowledge with the minimum of difficulty, whereas authors present information in a context dictated by *their* own background; the two will not necessarily coincide exactly. We must design our system to make the likelihood of achieving a match between reader's need and author's offering as high as possible, but we have to accept the fact that the match will not always be an exact one.

In an experimental situation, such as those studied in the various research projects concerned with the evaluation of indexing systems described in chapter 28, it is possible to establish which documents are to be considered as relevant to a particular question *in advance,* and we can thus arrive at an objective judgment of the success of the system. In this case, it is usual to refer to precision rather than relevance.[4]

We may use Venn diagrams and set notation to examine these concepts further. If we take as our universe a set of documents L, then in response to any given question there should be a set A of documents which are relevant, where A is a subset of L (A ⊂ L). If we use our information retrieval system to try to find these documents, we shall actually retrieve a rather different set B (B ⊂ L), of which only the subset forming the intersection of A and B (A ∩ B) will be relevant. We may now define the two terms recall ratio and precision ratio:

$$\text{Recall ratio} = \frac{(A \cap B)}{A} \qquad \frac{\text{(relevant documents retrieved)}}{\text{(total of relevant documents)}}$$

$$\text{Precision ratio} = \frac{(A \cap B)}{B} \qquad \frac{\text{(relevant documents retrieved)}}{\text{(total of documents retrieved)}}$$

These are usually expressed as percentages by multiplying by 100. Another term which is sometimes used is fall-out ratio, defined as:

Fallout ratio $= \dfrac{A-B}{B'}$ (relevant documents not retrieved)

(all documents not retrieved)

The set B—A consisting of documents retrieved but not relevant, may be regarded as noise, while the set $(A \cup B)'$, documents neither retrieved nor relevant, may be thought of as *dodged*, to use Vickery's term.

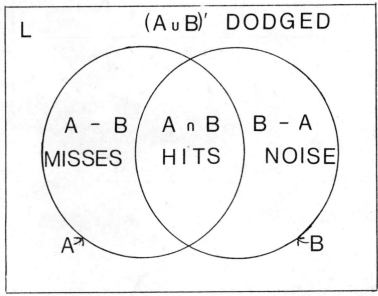

FIGURE 2: Venn diagram of the retrieval process.

Unfortunately, the set A is rarely clearly defined; in fact, probably only in the experimental situation can we delineate A precisely. In real life there is a grey area, consisting of those documents which *may* be relevant. If we draw a cross-section through A, and plot this on a graph showing degree of relevance, we get the result denoted APUPA by Ranganathan: U denotes the *umbra, ie* those documents which are clearly relevant (within the *shadow* of the subject); P denotes the *penumbra* (the 'twilight zone'); and A denotes *alien, ie* those documents which are clearly *not* relevant. It is the penumbra which makes it impossible to define A clearly, and this means that we cannot use the term precision in this situation. In this text, *relevance* is used to refer to the real-life situation, *precision* to refer to the experimental situation where the set A can be predetermined.

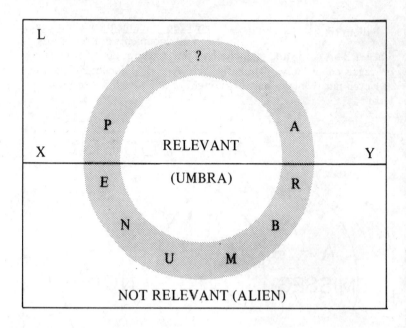

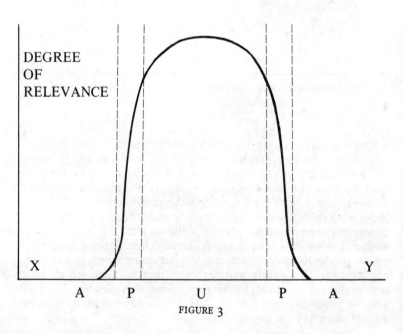

FIGURE 3

We can display the four classes of document A ∩ B, A − B, B − A and (A ∪ B)′ in the form of a matrix:

	Retrieved	Not retrieved	Total
Relevant	A ∩ B	A − B	A
Not relevant	B − A	(A ∪ B)′	A′
	B	B′	L

We can take the results of a number of tests and use these to plot a graph of recall ratio against precision ratio. Ideally, of course, our graph would be concentrated into the 100% recall and 100% precision corner, but in practice we obtain a curve of the kind shown in figure 4.

The implication of this curve is that if we try to improve recall, we can only do so at the expense of precision, and conversely that if we try to improve precision, we can only do so at the expense of recall. We owe the terms recall, relevance and precision to the Cranfield Project, but the same idea was expressed some years earlier by Fairthorne in the phrases 'All but not only' (ABNO) and 'Only but not all' (OBNA).[5] One measure of the effectiveness of an information retrieval system is the freedom with which one may move from one part of the recall-precision curve to another; for example, if our first search does not reveal all the information we want, can we increase recall by moving up the curve (and thereby sacrificing a degree of precision)? If our first search reveals an overwhelming amount of information, can we increase precision and thus reformulate our search strategy to give lower recall? Ways of altering our search strategies to give such changes will be discussed in due course, when it will become apparent that not all systems have the same degree of flexibility in this respect.

We should be cautious about accepting the recall-precision curve unquestioningly. As Cleverdon himself has pointed out, it represents the *average* performance of any given system, and this may vary quite considerably in particular situations. For example, in the MEDLARS evaluation study (chapter 28) Lancaster found that the system was operating on average at about 58% recall and 50% precision, retrieving an average of 175 documents per search. To achieve 85% to 95% recall would have meant retrieving an average of some 500 to 600 documents per search, with a precision ratio of about 20%. However, if we examine the results of individual searches, we find that in some cases 100% recall was achieved with 100% precision, while in others both recall and relevance were zero! Furthermore, while it may not be possible to alter the response of a system to a particular request—if we try to improve recall or precision we can only do so at the expense of the other—in practice, once we start to obtain documents from the system in response to a request we may well be able to modify the request in such a way as to improve both recall and precision.

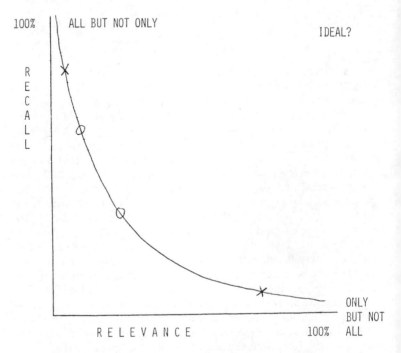

FLEXIBILITY OF SYSTEM: ABILITY TO SELECT THE APPROPRIATE OPERATING POINT ON THE RECALL-RELEVANCE CURVE SYSTEM X-X IS MORE FLEXIBLE THAN SYSTEM 0-0 (X AND 0 MARK LIMITS OF OPERATING PARAMETERS)

FIGURE 4: The recall-relevance/precision curve.

From the point of view of the user, it is usually relevance rather than recall which is desirable. The majority of enquiries can be satisfied by providing no more than half a dozen documents, providing they are all useful, and it is only in the minority of cases that a high recall figure is necessary. For example, the Patent Examiner needs to be sure that he has found every relevant document, but the casual enquirer would almost certainly not wish to be presented with an enormous pile of documents in response to his request. There is also the point that many

18

documents are repetitive: they do not add anything significant to our knowledge. R Shaw examined a collection of documents on milkweed in detail, and came to the conclusion that all the information to be found was contained in 96 of the total of four thousand![6] Of course, we must be able to identify the ninety-six, and this may be impossible without looking at the four thousand, but this example does tend to re-inforce the point of view held by many writers that what we are facing is a publication explosion rather than an information explosion. Per-haps librarians could solve some of the problems of recall and rele-vance by encouraging some kind of literary contraception.

Recall, precision and relevance are valuable concepts in the study of any information retrieval system. They are however not the only cri-teria by which a system may be judged. We can now move forward to consider some of the factors affecting recall and precision, and some of the other important aspects of IR systems.

PROBABILITY OF ERROR

Indexers are human; so are users. Both are thus liable to make mis-takes. Our system should be one which reduces the probability of error as far as possible. For example, research by Post Office engineers some years ago showed that the probability of incorrect dialling began to rise steeply if the length of the number increased to nine or more digits. (It is perhaps depressing to realize that most of us now have 9 or 10 digit telephone numbers.) If a system uses numbers for coding, mistakes may arise and probably will arise if the numbers grow beyond the limit indicated above; even if we use words, the likelihood of error still exists.[7]

Errors will have an effect on relevance, in that we shall get answers which are wrong; they will also affect recall, in that we shall miss items which we ought to find. We should therefore make sure that the system we use does not have a built in tendency to increase human error. Just as faults in a telephone line introduce audible noise and thus interfere with our reception of a message, so human errors in an information re-trieval system introduce their own particular kind of noise. The fewer the errors, the less will be the noise from this source; there are however other sources of noise to be considered, most of them less amenable to straightforward improvement than this one.

SPECIFICITY AND EXHAUSTIVITY

There are several other factors which affect the overall performance of an information retrieval system and its potential in terms of recall and relevance. First, we may consider *specificity*: the extent to which the system permits us to be precise when specifying the subject of a docu-ment we are processing. The higher the specificity, the more likely we are to be able to achieve high relevance, and conversely, with a system that permits us only limited precision we are likely to achieve reasonably high recall but correspondingly low relevance. In the previous example, if our system did not permit us to specify *Siamese* cats, we should have to look through all the items about cats before we could find out whether we had anything on that particular breed. Further, if the second item we found did relate to Siamese cats, there would be no guarantee that this would be the only one, or that any others would be found alongside it. If specificity is lacking, we are in fact reduced to the kind of sequential scanning that is necessary if our collections are not organized at all—though of course we have reduced the amount of material that we have to scan by partially specifying its subject content. If we are to obtain the maximum amount of control over our searching, the system must permit us to be precise in our specification of subjects; in fact, our specification should in every case be coextensive with the subject of the document. If we need to increase recall, we can always ignore part of our specification, but we cannot increase relevance by adding to it *at the search stage*. It is very important to keep clear the distinction between the INPUT to our system (*ie* the specifications of the documents we are adding), and the OUTPUT (*ie* the results of the searches we perform among these specifications). We cannot add to the input at the output stage; anything omitted at the input stage will remain outside the system, and will have to be replaced by sequential scanning of an unnecessarily large output. (We may however be able to use a systematic approach to help us formulate our search strategy, even though it is not part of the system used to specify the input.)

Specificity is a function of the system, but another important factor, *exhaustivity*, is the result of a management decision. This is the extent to which we analyse any given document to establish exactly what subject content we have to specify. We may distinguish between the overall theme of a document, and the subthemes which it may contain; for example, a description of a scientific experiment may be concerned overall with the purpose and results, but it will probably also contain a description of the apparatus used. In a large general library we may content ourselves with specifying the overall themes, giving perhaps an average of one to one and a half specifications per document, whereas in a small special library, anxious to exploit the stock to the maximum advantage, we may wish to index subthemes as well, giving perhaps dozens of specifications for every document. This is known as *depth indexing*, as opposed to the *summarization* of the first method. Depth indexing might indicate that a book is about Dryden, Wycherley, Congreve, Vanbrugh and Farquhar, while summarization might say that it was about Restoration drama. It would clearly be very difficult if not impossible to index *all* the subthemes in a document in a library catalogue or a bibliography (the index to the present work contains nearly

1,000 entries), so depth indexing is usually carried out in libraries where the needs of the readers can be foreseen fairly clearly; often depth indexing is applied to technical reports and similar documents which are relatively short and are therefore manageable. It involves the indexer in the exercise of judgment as to which themes and sub-themes are worth noting. In choosing between depth indexing and summarization, the decision is ours and is not a function of the system. Recent research has shown, however, that there is a link between exhaustivity and specificity, in that there is little point in increasing exhaustivity unless the system being used has adequate specificity; depth indexing will not give improved access to the contents of a document unless the additional entries are specific.

A moment's thought should show that whereas specificity is a device to increase relevance at the cost of recall, exhaustivity works in the opposite direction, by increasing recall, but at the expense of relevance. A device which we may use to counteract this effect to some extent is *weighting*. In this, we try to show the significance of any particular specification by giving it a weight on a pre-established scale. For example, if we had a book on pets which dealt largely with dogs, we might give PETS a weight of 10/10, and DOGS, a weight of 8/10 or less. If it gave some information about dogs, but not much, we might give DOGS a low weighting of 2/10. The reader wanting high relevance now knows that this particular item can be ignored, at least for the time being, while the reader wanting high recall will have no difficulty in finding it.

EASE OF USE

Whatever system we choose to use, there are two persons who must find it usable: the person responsible for the input, *ie* the *indexer*, and the person trying to obtain an output, *ie* the *user*. At the input stage, how much skill does the indexer need to be able to use the system? Does it help to overcome deficiencies in his appreciation of the subjects he is dealing with? *Non omnia omnes possumus:* we cannot all be omniscient! Users often find it difficult to express exactly their needs; does the system help them to formulate a satisfactory search despite this? Is the physical form of the output acceptable? A system which presents the user with a set of documents, or at least abstracts, is likely to be more popular than one which gives merely a string of numbers.

TIME

Indexing takes time; searching takes time. By increasing our effort at the indexing stage—the input—we may well be able to reduce the amount of time we have to spend at the output stage in searching. On the other hand, in any given library situation, a proportion (which may be high) of the documents indexed will never be sought, and the effort used to index them will be wasted; if we concentrate our effort at the output stage by keeping our indexing to a minimum (for example by using abstracts or even whole texts for the input instead of subject specifications) and then perform complex searches to find relevant items, we can argue that we are eliminating a large amount of unnecessary work. As has already been mentioned, users cannot always specify exactly what it is they want, so any search will be a dialogue between the user and the system; the results of a first search will be used to modify or refine the question so that further searches can be performed until such time as a satisfactory end point is reached. By concentrating our efforts on the searching rather than the indexing, we do not hamper this dialogue in any way, but we can very easily make use of such feedback in planning future search strategies. In a system where the effort is concentrated on the input, this may not be quite so easy, as the output cannot affect the input retrospectively; to take account of experience gained in searching we may have to re-index some items— *ie* increase the input effort still further.

At present, nearly all systems involve large amounts of input effort rather than transfer this to the output stage. As yet, the complicated search strategies necessary with the latter technique, together with the large amount of input information required, make it impractical in the normal library situation, though this is changing as more powerful computers become widely available. Some of the SDI services referred to earlier rely on the abstracts or even the titles alone, and the consequences of this in terms of search strategy or profile construction are discussed in more detail later. Searching of full texts is likely to be too costly to be adopted widely for some years yet, and is in any case likely to present problems in terms of relevance, since exhaustivity of indexing will obviously be 100%.

ITERATIVE AND HEURISTIC SEARCHING

The idea of a dialogue between the user and the system is worthy of further examination. As has been pointed out above, users often find it difficult to express their needs precisely. In a conventional library, searches may be carried out by the user, or by the librarian acting for the user. When they are carried out by the user himself, the search will usually be modified as it progresses; each relevant document found tends to influence the user's decision as to what further information he requires. In many cases the clarification that results as the search is pursued leads to a situation where the user finishes up with an objective rather different from the one he started out with. Such a search, where the course of events is modified continuously in the light of knowledge being gained, may be described as *heuristic*. If on the other hand the search is carried out by the librarian, this continuous modification is not possible, since modifications of the librarian's knowledge do not affect the user. For this reason it is usual for the librarian to perform a first search and present the results to the user; the search strategy may then be modified in the light of the proportion of relevant documents among those resulting from this search. A second search may then be performed, and the process repeated until the user has what he wants. This kind of search, which is modified not continuously but at intervals, may be described as *iterative*. Both heuristic and iterative searches require interaction between user and results, but heuristic searching eliminates the time delay between receiving the result of a search operation and using it to modify the search procedure.

Many information retrieval systems do not permit heuristic searching, for example most of those described in Part IV of this book, whereas the conventional library card catalogue does. The importance of this should not be overestimated, but it is obviously a point to be considered when we are trying to estimate the relative value of different systems.[8]

BROWSING

We have assumed so far that the purpose of our system is to make it possible to find information on demand—that the users will approach it with some definite objective in mind, even though they may not, to begin with, have clarified this. However, this is by no means always the case; there will be many occasions when readers will approach the collection without any particular need in mind but wishing instead to be able to select items at random. To help in this situation, our system should permit *browsing;* a reader should be able to follow a casual train of thought as well as a planned search. As was pointed out in the discussion of SDI, it is often an item which does *not* fit our existing patterns of interest which proves to be the most interesting; many of the most significant scientific discoveries have arisen as the result of *serendipity*—'the faculty of making happy and unexpected discoveries by accident'[9]—and a system which excludes this possibility might prove to be *too* successful in matching readers' expressed needs!

COST

Many of the factors affecting information retrieval systems are cost factors. We have to balance the cost of so organizing our libraries that we can find information when it is required, against the cost of not finding it at all, or finding it too late for it to be of use. In libraries serving industrial firms, for example, the cost of not finding information may be high; this is why 'hard headed businessmen' add to their overheads by paying for extensive library services. (The term 'library services' is here taken to include those denoted by the more elite term 'information services'.) On the other hand, public libraries have in the past tended to regard the exploitation of the information in their stocks as very much less important than its provision, because the cost to the community at large if one of its individual members fails to find information he requires is considerably less than the cost of organizing the material adequately. However, it is now being realized that the cost to the community of wasted information is in fact very high in terms of international competition, and more effort is being devoted to providing adequate services. We still have to find out a great deal about the cost effectiveness of various methods of organizing information, though we are beginning to learn something about their comparative efficiencies as systems. Despite our relative ignorance we must not ignore cost factors altogether, but they can usually only be studied in detail in a particular set of circumstances, and will therefore only be indicated in general terms in this text.

Modern trends in the evaluation of cost significance have been towards the idea of cost effectiveness. Most of the sophisticated devices developed in recent years have been aimed at improving relevance: reducing the number of unwanted documents revealed by a search, and thus reducing also the time taken to scan through the results and select those which are of use to us. However, if it costs more to use a sophisticated system for indexing than it would cost to look through the output of an unsophisticated system, there is no point in using the more advanced system. We have also to bear in mind that a relevance level which might be tolerable in a small system might well be quite unacceptable in a large nationwide mechanized system. If a search reveals ten documents, four of which are useful, this is not too bad; but if we have the same level with a collection a hundred times as large, we might well boggle at the thought of discarding six hundred documents from a total of a thousand. As yet only a limited amount of research has been carried out into this aspect of information retrieval, but it is obviously a field that is likely to be explored in more depth in the future, particularly with the development of the mechanized systems described in chapter 25.

PROBLEMS OF LINEAR ORDER

Knowledge is multi-dimensional: that is to say, subjects are related one to another in many different ways. In the example quoted earlier, it was assumed that Siamese cats were to be considered as pets, but it is obvious that they can be regarded in many other ways—as a branch of the zoological class *felidae*, or as originating in a particular part of the world, to name but two approaches. However, when we try to arrange items in our library or catalogue, we find that we are restricted to a linear, unidimensional, sequence, just as we are if we are reading a book. We cannot *display* multiple relationships and must therefore find some other means of showing them. If we have a book with no contents list and no index, the only way we can find a given item in it is to read it through. We have only one means of access: sequential scanning. However, we can overcome this problem by providing multiple access through the contents list and index, which permit us to go direct to the information we require; but the text of the book continues to display its information unidimensionally. The sequence in the book is chosen for us by the author and we cannot alter it, though we may to a large extent minimize the effect by adequate sign posting in the form of indexes and guiding.

We face exactly the same problem in organizing the information in our libraries. We can provide a sequence which we hope will be helpful to our readers, just as an author does, but we must recognize the need to cater for other modes of access. We must also realize that without these secondary modes of access we can only find information in one way, unless we are prepared to revert to sequential scanning. A simple example will demonstrate this in relation to a familiar tool, the telephone directory. These directories are arranged according to the surnames of the subscribers, set out in alphabetical order. Provided we know the subscriber's name, we can find his telephone number without much trouble, but we cannot perform the operation in reverse; we cannot find out the name of a subscriber whose number we know, unless we are prepared to look through the directory until we find it. To overcome this we can have a second sequence, arranged this time by number; but we still cannot find the number of a friend if we only know his forename and his address.

The problem is of course largely an economic one. We do not set up multiple sequences of books and other items in our libraries because it would cost too much to try to arrange a copy of a book at every point in the library where it might be related to other items. Nor can we afford to make multiple sequences in bibliographical tools which have to be printed and distributed. We might perhaps make several sequences in our records within the library, but even this will prove very expensive if we are to be consistent and comprehensive. However, just as we can overcome the problem in a book by providing multiple access through subsidiary sequences which lead us to the required points in our main sequence, so we can do the same thing in our information retrieval system. Different systems will permit us differing degrees of multiple access; the more flexible a system is in this respect, the more likely it is to be of value.

LITERARY WARRANT

No matter what our system may be, the information in it must be a function of the input; that is to say, our systems must take account of the relationships between subjects shown in the items we are indexing. We may in addition build into it relationships between subjects of which we are aware *a priori*, through a study of knowledge *per se*, but if we restrict ourselves to a study of knowledge alone without taking into account knowledge as it is presented in recorded form, we shall find ourselves unable to specify subjects precisely. In other words, we are concerned with the organization of knowledge in libraries rather than the organization of knowledge on its own. The term *literary warrant* is used here to denote that our system must be based on the material we put into it rather than on purely theoretical considerations.

There is another aspect to this particular question. It is the output of the system which is important, since this is the whole purpose of the system. But we cannot know in advance what output will be required, at least not with any degree of precision, though we may be able to form an intelligent guess on the basis of past experience. So although it would be desirable to build up our system in such a way that it matched the required output, we are unable to do this since we do not know what the required output will be. We are obliged to use the input as our basis for building up the system, adding to this whatever is suggested by studies of knowledge outside the system. If we restrict ourselves to studies of knowledge outside the system we shall, by ignoring the input, be removing our system one stage further from the required output. In any subject area there will be an accepted corpus of knowledge, but each document we index may modify this; literary warrant implies a system that is able to accept this kind of change.

There is perhaps a danger that we may take a negative attitude to literary warrant: exclude from our system the possibility of catering for subjects which have not as yet appeared in our collections. This danger is usually associated with the older kind of enumerative system described below, but there have been more recent examples to demonstrate the problems that arise if we deliberately make our system a static one. Hospitality to new concepts as they are revealed by our collections is vital if we are to maintain the desired level of specificity.

The term literary warrant was used by Wyndham Hulme to denote a rather different kind of idea, though one basically similar. He considered that if we have a document entitled, say, *Heat, light and sound*, then that represents a subject for which we should make provision in our system. However, most of these are not genuine subjects but aggregates of subjects resulting from the bibliographical accident of being bound within the same pair of covers. They are better treated as separate topics and indexed as such. This situation should not be confused with that of a genuine interaction between subjects, *eg* the effect of heat on sound (discussed in more detail on p 91—); this is a different kind of situation for which we do have to make provision. Hulme's use of the term is rarely found now, though his ideas were largely reflected in the practice of the Library of Congress, and have indeed developed into the modern theory already outlined.[10]

HEADING AND DESCRIPTION

We use the terms in our indexing system to name the subjects of the documents in our collection, but obviously a user who has found the correct subject description will require in addition some details of the documents to which that description applies. We can therefore divide an entry in the system into two parts, the heading and the description.

The *heading* is the subject description which determines whereabouts in the sequence we shall find any given entry. (The present work is restricted to considerations of the subject approach; in a full catalogue, headings will include names of authors and titles as well as subjects.) In an alphabetical system, headings will consist of words, while in a systematic arrangement it is the notation that is used for the headings. The *description* is the part of an entry which gives us information about a document, and will therefore contain all those factors which serve to *identify*. There are various sets of rules for the compilation of document descriptions, *eg* those in the Anglo-American code, or the International Standard Bibliographical Descriptions, but for our purposes here we need only note their existence. The presence of a document description enables us to make a useful distinction: a *subject entry* consists of a heading from the index vocabulary together with a document description, while an *index entry* or *cross-reference* leads us from a heading with no document description to an entry. The heading from which we make a cross-reference may be one which appears only in the entry vocabulary, in which case the reference is a *see* reference, leading us from a heading not used to one which is used; or it may appear in both entry and index vocabulary, in which case the reference is a *see also* reference linking two headings which are both used, in order to show some kind of relationship.

It should be noted that in some systems the descriptions may be in the form of a number (an accessions number or document number) rather than the detailed information about author, title, imprint and so on which we find in, for example, a library card catalogue. The links between related headings may form an integral part of the main sequence of entries, as in the dictionary catalogue; part of a subsidiary sequence, as in the classified catalogue; or quite separate, as is usual in post-coordinate systems. These points will be clarified in due course; at this stage it is important to realize that these features, like the others in this chapter, are common to all information retrieval systems. Their presence or absence can make a great deal of difference to the ease with which we can retrieve information.

TERM ENTRY AND ITEM ENTRY

The preceding section implies that we make entries for a document (which we identify by its description) under each of the appropriate headings, and file these in the correct place in our alphabetical or classified sequence. A system which works in this way is called a *term entry* system, and nearly all manual systems are of this kind, for example the conventional card catalogue, particularly if unit cards are used, and the peek-a-boo and Uniterm systems described in chapter 24. However, it is possible to adopt the opposite approach, and make a single entry for each item, using some physical form which permits access to the entry from all the necessary headings. Such a system is known as an *item entry* system; examples are edge-notched cards, used in manual systems, and many computer-based systems. Edge-notched cards are not considered in this book, as their value in information retrieval is limited to very small collections; for a reasonably full description the reader is referred to this author's work on personal indexes.[11] Computer-based systems are of course becoming rapidly more significant, and the implications of item entry are discussed in chapter 3.

There is some confusion in the literature over this distinction; Uniterm and peek-a-boo are frequently contrasted, as term entry systems, with conventional catalogues as item entry systems, and it is not uncommon to find them described as 'inverted indexes' to emphasize the difference. Though a difference exists, it lies in the use of single concepts which are coordinated at the search stage, rather than being stored as composite headings, not in the use of term as opposed to item entry.

SEPARATION OF INTELLECTUAL AND CLERICAL EFFORT
In any system, part of the work involved will be intellectual and part will be clerical. Deciding which headings a document should be entered under is an intellectual operation, but the actual mechanics of placing an entry in a file is not. Similarly, in searching, we need to make an intellectual decision as to which headings are likely to reveal the answers to an enquiry, but the task of displaying the entries under those headings does not involve intellectual effort. Conventional forms of catalogue, which give document descriptions, tend to blur these distinctions; although filing is a routine operation, it is usual for it to be checked before cards are finally accepted into the catalogue (a junior assistant files 'on the rods'), and at the search stage we tend to perform a subsearch at any given heading by looking at the document descriptions and estimating relevance from these.

The distinction becomes important when we are considering the use of computers. Computers can perform clerical operations very well: they are more accurate, and much faster, than their human counterparts, provided that they are given the correct instructions. At present we do not know nearly enough about the way in which the human mind works to be able to give computers the right instructions to enable them to perform intellectual operations; these must still be done by human effort. However, careful studies such as those made by E J Coates in connection with the use of a computer in the production of

BTI have shown that many of the operations which have in the past been thought of as essentially intellectual can in fact be reduced to a set of rules (algorithm) which can be mechanized. It is clearly advantageous to transfer as much routine work to machines as we can, to enable us to concentrate on the intellectual tasks; by doing so, we can only improve our service to readers.

BIBLIOGRAPHY

1 Vickery, B C: *Techniques of information retrieval.* Chapters 1 and 2.

2 East, H: 'The development of SDI services'. *Aslib proceedings,* 20 (11) 1968, 482–491.

Hall, J L and Terry, J E: 'Development of mechanized current awareness services at Culham and Harwell.' (*in Handling of nuclear information.* International Atomic Energy Agency, 1970. 201–209).

Three recent reviews of the whole topic will be found in: Housman, E M: 'Selective dissemination of information.' *Annual review of information science and technology, 8* 1973, 221–241.

Mauerhoff, G R: 'Selective dissemination of information.' *Advances in librarianship, 4* 1974, 25–62.

Leggate, P: 'Computer-based current awareness services.' *Journal of documentation, 31* (2) 1975, 93–115.

3 Clague, P: 'The SDI study in electronics.' (*In* Houghton, B, *ed: Computer based information retrieval systems.* Bingley, 1968.)

4 Cleverdon, C W, Mills, J, and Keen, M. *Factors determining the performance of indexing systems.* Cranfield, Aslib-Cranfield Research Project, 1966. 2v in 3.

5 Fairthorne, R: 'Automatic retrieval of recorded information'. *Computer journal, 1,* 1958, 36–41.

6 Shaw, R: *Private communication,* quoted by Cleverdon in *Journal of documentation, 30* (2) June 1974, 174.

7 Conrad, R and Hille, B A: 'Memory for long telephone numbers'. *Post Office telecommunications journal, 10,* 1957, 37–39.

8 Lancaster, F W: 'Interaction between requesters and a large mechanized retrieval system'. *Information storage and retrieval, 4* (2) 1968, 239–252. The development of this idea arose during the survey carried out by Lancaster of the working of the MEDLARS project, discussed in chapter 28.

9 *The concise Oxford dictionary.* Clarendon press, sixth edition, 1976.

10 Hulme, E Wyndham: *Principles of book classification.* Association of Assistant Librarians, 1950 (AAL Reprints no 1). Originally published in the *Library Association record,* 1911–1912.

11 Foskett, A C: *A guide to personal indexes.* Bingley, second edition, 1970.

CHAPTER 3

The computer

As we have indicated in chapter 1, the quantity of information that we have to handle nowadays is one of the main reasons why we have had to develop new techniques of information handling. One other reason is that the tempo of life generally is faster, and techniques which were adequate in a more leisurely age are so no longer. Computers offer a means of processing large quantities of data at very high speeds, and it is therefore obvious that we have to consider their relevance to information retrieval; we should however be on our guard against the assumption that the use of these machines will solve all our problems without any further intellectual effort on our part. This is not the case; although some recent work has shown that computers can be programmed to retrieve information by processing texts in natural language, with results comparable with intellectual indexing, there remains a great deal of work to be done, for example in such areas as linguistic analysis, before such systems can be regarded as universally acceptable. Much of the experimental work has also been limited to small collections of a few hundred documents in a relatively small subject area. Nevertheless, this does not mean that computers cannot usefully be employed now to facilitate the non-intellectual aspects of information retrieval systems. As we have seen, any system is a mixture of intellectual and clerical operations, and if we can clearly distinguish the two we may well be able to use a computer for the latter. Indeed, the computer's high speed may enable us to undertake operations which we *can* perform manually, but usually do not for lack of time.[1]

Costs are an important factor in any library operation. In the past, costs of using computers have been such as to prohibit their use in libraries on a large scale, but new developments in computer technology have reduced costs to the level where they are competitive with clerical effort, at least in highly developed countries. However, it seems likely that the advantage in turning to computers does not lie in a reduction of costs, but in the fact that for about the same cost we can get a great deal more output; in other words, we spend no less but we get more for our money.

It is not necessary for librarians to know the technical details of how computers work, but it is helpful to have some overall understanding of computer processing if we are to be able to judge what is required of us before we can use the machine, and what the machine can give us in return. For this purpose it is helpful to regard the computer as a set of 'black boxes'; we can then consider the functions of these without having to know how they are performed. The heart of the computer is the core store; this is where information in the form of machine-readable signals is kept while it is actually being processed. Core stores are expensive units, and in older computers they were usually quite small. The amount of information that the computer can process at one time depends on the size of the core store, so older computers (first generation, using electronic valves (tubes) and second generation, using transistors and similar devices) were best suited to the handling of relatively small amounts of information because of their relatively slow speeds. Information retrieval systems involve the handling of large amounts of information, on which basically only one operation is performed, that of matching. With the development of third generation computers, using integrated circuits, we now have machines which can handle much larger quantities of information at much higher speeds than before. In addition to making the computer more suitable for the kind of requirement found in library operations, this has other consequences of value which will be discussed later under the heading Time-sharing and multi-programming.

The core store may receive information from a variety of input devices, all of which must have one thing in common: they *must* present the information in machine-readable form, and in the vast majority of cases at present this involves some form of conversion of the original text. The most commonly used form of input is 80-column punched cards, which have to be prepared by a key-punch operator. Another common form is punched paper tape, which may be prepared specially or may arise as a by-product of some other operation, for example typing on a tape typewriter. Magnetic tape may be used, in fact large scale computers often convert all forms of input to magnetic tape as an intermediate step; its advantage is that it can be 'read' into the machine at very high speeds, much higher than those possible with cards or tape. Magnetic tape may also be available as a by-product of some forms of typesetting, for example using the Photon filmsetting machine; thus the production of the text in conventional book form may at the same time make it possible to process the text in a computer without any additional input effort.

It would be very convenient if we could simply use normal text and some sort of reading device. Such *optical scanners*, as they are known, do indeed exist, but as yet they can read only certain varieties of type face; the stylized figures found along the bottom edges of cheques can be read by machine, and IBM have developed a typewriter type face which can be used as input to a scanner. We are a long way from a

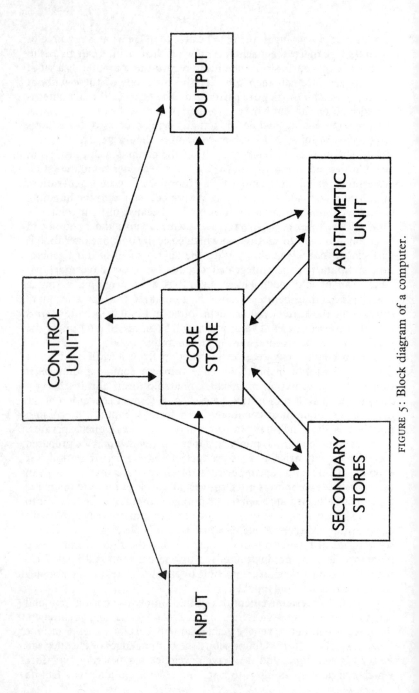

FIGURE 5: Block diagram of a computer.

device that can interpret the many varieties of type face found in even a modest library, while the ability of the human eye to read handwriting is well beyond the capability of any existing machine even in the laboratory. Such machines will come eventually, but in the meantime we shall have to make do with other forms of input!

For library housekeeping routines, two devices have been introduced which should prove very useful. One of these is a strip of magnetic tape inserted into the cover of the book, which can be 'read' by a scanner built into the issue desk. The other is the light pen, which can scan information printed in the form of vertical stripes. As yet, it is difficult to see any application of these devices to information retrieval, but the principles involved may well prove to be of value in the future.

Information can be transmitted to a computer directly from a *terminal*, which acts in a similar way to an electric typewriter. It may be a 'hard copy' unit, in which case anything typed for input to the computer is printed out at the same time; output from the computer to the terminal will also be typed out. The usual speed of this kind of terminal is of the order of 14 characters per second. A terminal may also be linked to a television-type screen to give a *visual display unit* (VDU), also known as a console. This form of input/output device may be said to have transformed the prospects for information retrieval using computers, and has also proved its value in other library activities, for example cataloguing and acquisitions.

As the core store is limited in size, even in the largest computers, it has to be supplemented by secondary storage, usually in the form of magnetic disks or tapes. Magnetic tapes are normally loaded on to the computer as required, since each user will have his files stored on his own magnetic tape reel. Disks may be left permanently connected to the computer; this has the advantage that we may call on the stored information at any time, without having to perform any external physical activity such as mounting a tape, but this convenience has of course to be paid for by a corresponding increase in cost.

Another important factor, particularly with regard to secondary storage, is the question of random as opposed to serial access. Information on a magnetic tape can only be utilized by passing the tape through a reader until the required section is reached; we have serial access only—sequential scanning. In contrast, we may utilize information stored on a magnetic disk almost instantaneously; we have random access to any part of the storage. A parallel may be found in the fact that we can select any band on a record simply by moving the pickup to the required spot before setting it down, whereas with a tape recording we have to run the tape through the deck until we find what we want, often by trial and error. (A similar parallel may be seen between the book and the papyrus roll.) The significance of this for libraries is considerable. With information stored on tape, we may have to search the whole tape to find what we want, and if we want to add further items we must usually be prepared to copy the whole tape, including any additional items, on to a new tape. This is normally associated with batch processing. With the random access given by disk storage, we can go at once to those items to the items we require, and updating the file can be done *in situ*. This is often associated with on-line processing; for example, a cataloguer may update the catalogue as each book is added. Disk files may also be updated by batch processing, of course, as for example when a library updates its loan records at the end of the day.

STORAGE TERMINOLOGY

The terminology of computer storage is confusing to the uninitiated, and the situation is not made any easier by the fact that different manufacturers use different methods of coding. The basic unit of coding is the *bit* (binary digit): a switch is either on or off, or a memory unit in the core store is magnetized clockwise or anticlockwise. All processing within the computer is carried out in binary arithmetic, using base 2 rather than the base 10 that we are accustomed to in everyday life decimal numbers. In order to be able to represent characters, *ie* letters as well as numbers, six bits are used in one method of coding to represent one character; this permits us to code up to sixtyfour symbols (2^6).

One form of coding of this kind is called EBCDIC—Extended Binary Coded Decimal Interchange Code. 64 characters will give the alphabet as well as the numbers 0 to 9 and some punctuation symbols, but as the use of computers was extended into the field of printing, it became necessary to extend the base even further to accommodate upper and lower case letters and a variety of other symbols, for example accents. This has been done in two different ways.

In the first method, six bits are still used, but two particular six-bit codes may precede them to serve as 'shift keys', comparable with the shift key on a typewriter. (Early model typewriters c1920 did have two shift keys). For convenience, the six bits are grouped into two sets of three, and the result written in octal notation (base 8). Thus the figure 4 in decimal notation is represented by 24 in octal coding, or 010100 in binary coding. In the second method, eight bits are used, split into two groups of four, each of which is represented by a hexadecimal digit. In this form of coding, the figure 4 decimal is represented by 34 in hexadecimal notation, or 0011 0100 in binary. One version used by the Library of Congress in its MARC records is known as expanded ASCII (American Standard Code for Information Exchange). With this form of coding it is possible to represent 256 symbols: upper and lower case alphabets, decimal digits, punctuation marks, some mathematical symbols, accents, and computer instructions such as 'carriage return'

34

and 'backspace'. However, it is possible that for some special purposes even 256 will not suffice, and forms of coding using more than 8 bits may have to be introduced. The exact method of coding information in a computer is of little or no concern to the librarian. What *is* of concern is that different methods of coding give different filing orders, and sorting a set of catalogue entries into alphabetical order using one coding may give a different result from that obtained with another. Considerable care must be taken in programming to take account of these differences, and this has the unfortunate effect that programs written for one computer can only rarely be used on another computer without modification.

The group of bits used to represent an alphanumeric character is called a *byte*. A 6-bit byte may represent two characters, depending on the use of the shift code; an 8-bit byte represents one character. In the computer, bits are grouped into *words*; these are not words in the usual sense, but convenient blocks of information which can be manipulated by the machine. The size of a word may vary; for example, one may find words of 16, 24, 32, 36 or even 60 bits, depending on the size of the computer and on the manufacturer's choice. The size of the core store is usually expressed as, *eg* 60k words, where k denotes 1024 (2 to the tenth power). The size of secondary stores is usually expressed in terms of characters or bytes, depending on which system of nomenclature and coding is in use by the manufacturer. Thus a disk pack may have a storage capacity of 220,000,000 characters; this would be a large capacity pack, and smaller units might have capacities ranging from 2 million to 8 million bytes.

It is important to realize that libraries do make significant demands on computer storage—considerably larger than most scientific users, for example. To take two instances will demonstrate this quite effectively. One Government special library in Australia allows an average of 600 characters per catalogue record (the Library of Congress MARC record allows a maximum of 2048), with an annual input of about 50,000 records, or 30 Megabytes; to sort these entries requires approximately 75 Megabytes, or the whole of a disc unit. In five years, there will be 250,000 records in the system . . . Our second example comes from the National Library of Australia, which in 1976 installed an IBM System/3 computer, the largest of its kind in Australia, with 128k bytes of main storage and 200 Megabytes of disk units, in addition to three high-speed tape units. If the proposed BIBDATA network goes ahead, it is assumed that further substantial computing power will be needed, at a cost of several million dollars.[2] It is clear that the average library will have to think carefully before launching out into computer-based information retrieval on its own, and the idea of networks of cooperating libraries, with central libraries acting as nodes, is now widely accepted. Some examples will be described later.

We have now considered some of the mechanics of what goes on inside the computer, and this leads us on to a discussion of the output. Again, in practice certain kinds of output are more commonly found than others, the most common being the line printer. This is a device which prints a line at a time at high speeds, present limits being of the order of 1200 lines per minute. Quality is not particularly high and is often restricted to a limited range of characters; most line printers will only give upper case letters, for example, though models are now available which will give a full range of characters. Magnetic tape is a useful form of output, as it may be used to store information for future use; it can also be copied very easily, so that information from a data base generated by a computer in one country can very conveniently be distributed on a world-wide basis. A very considerable number of bibliographical tools is now available in this form,[3] which has other advantages. It can be used in computer-controlled typesetting, as already mentioned, and it makes practical the cumulation of successive issues. To quote only one example among many, the weekly issues of the *British national bibliography* are produced in this way, as are the various cumulations, while copies of the tapes are available as part of the MARC programme, discussed in more detail later, together with other examples.

As mentioned earlier, the console is a very significant factor in the use of computers for information retrieval. We can of course use consoles to search our own local files, but it is perfectly feasible to connect a console to a computer hundreds or even thousands of miles away and have in effect instant access on-line to material stored in disk packs. In fact, the limiting factor may well be the telephone link and its cost rather than the capacity of the computer. In a country such as Australia, where distances between the major centres of population are very large, this may prove to be a significant factor, since although computer costs are falling steadily in relation to computing power, telecommunication costs are not following a similar pattern.

THE CONTROL UNIT
Brooding over the whole assembly is the control unit, which is the part of the computer which controls all the rest. The control unit switches on the input and output, it initiates the transfer of information to the arithmetic unit and its return, and it governs the transfer of information from and to the secondary stores. However, like all the rest of the computer, it is simply a set of electronic circuits, and it functions as it does because it is in its turn controlled by a set of instructions which we feed into it via the core store. This set of instructions is the program.

So far we have been considering the physical units which together form the computer; these are known as the hardware. The core store, the arithmetic unit and the control unit together are known as the central processing unit, while the rest of the equipment is known as the peripherals. We now have to consider programs, which form part of the computer *software*. Computers can only respond to machine-readable signals: we have to make sure that we feed in the right set of signals for them to respond to, that is, we must feed in the correct data; but we must also feed into them instructions which cause the control unit to operate in the right way. It has to switch on the input at the right time, to recognize the information we are feeding in, to see that the correct transformations are performed by the arithmetic unit, and that the output reaches us in the form that we want. Since the computer does not 'know' anything that we have not told it, we have to make quite sure that our instructions are complete down to the last detail. For example, if we tell somebody to look something up in a book, we do not normally find it necessary to tell him to open the book first; we assume that he will do this without having to be told. No such assumptions can be made with computer programs; in effect, we have to tell the machine to fetch the book, open it and turn to the required page, then read what is on the page and record it in some form.

To write such a set of instructions we have to have a very clear idea of what we are trying to do; the first stage of writing a program is thus the analysis of the operation that we wish to transfer to the computer. This kind of rigorous analysis can often have a beneficial effect in itself, for it leads us to question the established routines that have grown up over the years. Indeed, it has in some instances led to such an improvement in the library's functioning that it has not proved necessary to take the next step and computerize the operations!

Programs may be written at three levels. The basic level is in binary form so that the instructions can be used directly by the machine, and eventually all programs have to be converted into this *machine language*. However, only an expert programmer who is familiar with the exact mode of functioning of the machine can write programs in machine language, and a more easily used form of language soon came into use, known as *assembly language*. This uses a few simple words (*eg* ADD), but is still only suitable for the skilled programmer. A further disadvantage for the ordinary user (as well as the skilled programmer) is the fact that the machine language and the assembly language are unique to a particular computer, so that if a program is to be used on a different computer it must be completely rewritten. This led to the development of what are known as *high-level languages*; these use a stylized form of English, which can be learnt relatively easily, and are designed to be used on any computer. Since the machine can use only its own machine language, these high-level languages must be 'translated' into this by an additional program known as a *compiler*.

There are now a number of widely used high-level languages, such as FORTRAN and ALGOL (both mainly intended for scientific purposes), COBOL (COmmon Business Oriented Language), and BASIC, intended particularly for on-line use. There are also many other specialized languages for particular purposes, but the details of these are not normally of interest to the librarian. What *is* of interest and concern is that although these languages have been standardized, in fact every manufacturer introduces a few additional facilities. These are usually of value, of course, but once again they have the effect that a program written in a version that will work on one machine may have to be modified before it can be used on another.

In fact, it is not unknown for a program that will work on a computer used in 'batch' mode (explained in a later paragraph) not to work on the same computer used 'on-line'! What all this means to the librarian is that the interchange of programs between libraries is fraught with difficulties, and the fact that a colleague has a system working and is willing to make the programs available does *not* necessarily mean that it will work in another library without modification. No doubt computer programmers are as concerned with job security as librarians.

It is not necessary for the librarian to be a skilled programmer himself, but he should be aware of the kind of problem outlined above in order to be able to appreciate the problems of the programmer and to be able to prepare an adequate brief for him. There is however one particular aspect of programming which should be mentioned before we move on to consider other aspects of modern computer use. This is the question of *field length*. A field is a set of characters representing a single unit of information. For example, in a catalogue entry, we may refer to the author field, title field, date field, and so on. The simplest mode of operation is to use fixed fields; on a punched card, for example, we might always use the first six columns for accession number, the next twelve for author's name, then four ten-column fields for subjects. We can then instruct the computer that the information it finds in those positions will always be that particular kind of information, and this simplifies programming. However, suppose that we want to include titles or abstracts? We have no idea how long to make the field (one field may occupy more than one 80-column card), and if we make it long enough to cover the worst possible case, most of that field will be unused for most of the time.

The solution is to use variable fields: to make each field as long as we need it for the particular document we are dealing with. What we must do if we adopt this procedure is to instruct the computer how to recognize a new field; we have to label each field with its own identifying tag and include in our program the information that tells the computer that, *eg*, when it meets the tag for 'title' it goes to the next line and indents four spaces. It is of course possible to use a combination of fixed and variable fields, provided the instructions take account of this. Most modern computer-based information systems use variable fields, but this does mean that programming is made more complicated.

TIME-SHARING AND MULTIPROGRAMMING
First and second generation computers only had room in the core store for one program, together with the information it was processing. They could also only accept one input at the time. The new models have much larger core stores and can thus find room for more than one program *and* the input information for them. To make it possible for the computer to work on more than one program at the time, a sort of super-program, known as director or supervisor, is necessary, to control the way in which the computer handles all the different sets of information. It would not do if the input intended to be processed according to one program were in fact processed according to another! This method of operating a computer is called multiprogramming, and is usually associated with another development found with third generation machines, time-sharing.

Electrical signals travel with the speed of light, and their transit from one part of a computer to another is very nearly instantaneous, particularly in recent models using integrated circuits which enable the whole machine to be built on a much smaller scale than was possible with circuits using conventional components. Operating speeds have thus increased as the size of computer units has diminished so that we now have computers which can complete one operation in a matter of a fraction of a micro-second, *ie* less than one millionth of a second. To perform some meaningful process may take hundreds or even thousands of operations, but even so it is obvious that the machine is working at a very high speed. Compare this with a typist working at a rate of 600 characters a minute (100 words, average length 6 characters); this is not a bad speed for a typist, yet it only represents 10 operations a second—each operation takes 100,000 microseconds! In fact, only a tape typewriter could keep up this speed for any length of time, yet between each keystroke a computer could perform tens of thousands of operations. This difference between input speeds and computing speeds is the basis of time sharing, which consists of connecting up several separate input devices to the same computer at the same time.

ON-LINE OPERATION (REAL-TIME OPERATION)
Older computers could only accept one input at a time, and in conse-

quence a particular job had to wait its turn in the queue to be fed into the machine. This mode of working is known as *batch* operation, and it means that the response to a particular input may not be available until some time later—often the next day. This may not be particularly important for some library operations, but for information retrieval it can be very unsatisfactory. For example, it means that searching must be iterative; we must wait until the results of a search become available before we can judge whether we need to modify our request to try to obtain better results. Time sharing means that a terminal or console can be left permanently connected and used whenever the need arises. Multiprogramming means that the terminals do not all have to use the same program, though they will always need to identify the program they wish to use. This kind of flexible, direct access, use is known as on-line operation, and is one of the most significant developments as far as library needs are concerned. No longer do we have to wait until it is convenient to run our program; we can use the computer at any time we want to. In particular, on-line operation means that we can conduct heuristic searches, modifying our request in the light of material found, just as we can in a card catalogue or abstracting journal. VDUs can present their response at high speed (for example 70 characters per second), while the computer can also give other information, for example the number of references which we will retrieve by following a particular search pattern. The news that the question we have put to the system will retrieve over 3000 references may well make us think again about just what it is we want! The computer can provide this kind of information immediately; using conventional means we find out the hard way.[4]

One problem that is being overcome is that computers are incapable of thought; the slightest mistake, which the human mind could take in its stride, will result in failure when processed by the computer. However, programs are being written which take account of the average individual's typing problems, so that if a minor mistake occurs the computer either corrects it or sends back an error message with a suggested amendment. There is also a valuable trend towards helping the user by simplifying the instructions he is required to give, and in effect conducting a dialogue with him. There is no doubt that on-line operation is a highly significant development for the librarian; it is perhaps an indication of how quickly we may become blasé about such things that after a period of wonder at the speed of retrieval, one begins to feel that delays of as long as ten seconds seem interminable!

LIBRARY APPLICATIONS
Computers have been used in libraries for two rather different purposes. The first of these, and the more straightforward, is the

mechanization of clerical and accounting operations such as book ordering and circulation. We are not concerned here with this side of library science, but with the second, which is information retrieval.

In this chapter, we have tried to set out some of the technical factors which affect the way in which librarians can make use of computers; in subsequent chapters we shall be looking at some of the systems which have been, or are being, developed. Whatever our attitude towards the machine, it is pointless to ignore the enormous impact it is having on information retrieval techniques and theory.

BIBLIOGRAPHY
There is now a plethora of books on 'the computer', and the following is a very limited selection. In many cases students will have access to other works of equal value, and should read whatever is available at a suitable level.

1 Artandi, S: *An introduction to computers in information science.* Metuchen, NJ, Scarecrow Press, second edition, 1972.

Hayes, R M and Becker, J: *Handbook of data processing for libraries.* NY, Wiley, second edition, 1970.

Henley, J P: *Computer based library and information systems.* Mac-Donald, 1970.

Houghton, B, ed: *Computer based information retrieval systems.* Bingley, 1968.

Kent, A: *Information analysis and retrieval.* NY, Interscience Publishers, 1971. (A revised version of the author's earlier *Textbook of mechanized information retrieval*, 1962.)

Kimber, R T: *Automation in libraries.* Pergamon Press, second edition, 1974.

Laver, M: *Computers, communications and society.* OUP, 1975.

Program, published quarterly by Aslib, includes reports on much of the work that is going on in the United Kingdom; the *Journal of library automation* and *Journal of the American Society for Information Science (JASIS)* cover the United States, and *LASIE* (Library Automated Systems Information Exchange) reports work being done in Australia.

2 National Library of Australia. *Bibdata network: draft proposal for an Australian national shared cataloguing system.* Canberra, NLA, 1976.

3 Williams, M E and Rouse, S H: *Computer-readable bibliographic data bases: a directory and data sourcebook.* Washington DC, ASIS, 1976. (Lists 301 services from the USA and Europe.)

4 Lancaster, F W, and Fayen, E G: *Information retrieval on-line.* Los Angeles, Melville, 1973.

CHAPTER 4

Derived indexing

As we have seen in chapter 1, we have to encode the subject of the document in order to be able to place the document itself or our records of it in our store. This means that we must in some way be able to specify the subject. How can we establish the subject of a document so that we can specify it? The obvious answer is to read it, but this is not always as helpful as it might be. We do not have time to read the whole of every item we add to our stock, and even if we did we might not understand it. There are certain short cuts we may take; we may read the contents list, or the preface or introduction, or the publisher's blurb on the dustjacket; the author may have prepared an abstract if the item in question is a periodical article or technical report; we may turn to the claims in a patent specification. All of these will give some indication of the subject and will suggest certain lines of thought if we want to pursue the matter further, for example in a technical dictionary.

We may decide that in the interests of economy we will rely solely on information which is *manifest* in the document; that is to say, we will make no attempt to use our own knowledge of the subject, or other guides, but will use only the contents of the document to provide our encoding system. In this case, we are said to be using *derived indexing*, *ie* indexing derived directly from the document. This chapter is devoted to the study of those parts of the document which may be used in this way.

There is of course one part of the book in which the author himself usually tries to define the subject: the title. In many cases this will give us a very clear indication of what a book is about; however, there are also cases in which the title will not be of any great help, and some in which it is of no help at all because it has been chosen to attract attention rather than state subject coverage. In the first category we might place: *The heat treatment of metals*, and, *High-speed analogue computers*; in the second: *The teaching of commercial subjects in secondary schools* (what are 'commercial subjects'?), and *The opening of the Canadian West* (pioneering? transport?); and in the third: *Supper in the evening*, and *One pair of hands*, neither of which gives us any clue at all as to the nature of the subject. Authors often try to generalize in the titles they select, so that the subject area covered by the document may in fact be rather narrower than is implied by its title. So titles may be of help in tracing particular documents if the user remembers them, but are of more limited help as the basis of a complete system; they can suggest what subject it is we are trying to specify, but lack precision as specifications themselves. In addition, if we have two items on the same subject, the authors will almost certainly have tried to find two different titles, so any system based on their use is bound to have low recall, though it may give us high relevance.

However, though different authors may try to select different groups of words to name their books on the same subject, these different groups of words may well contain the same significant words. Consider the following titles:

Manual of library classification
Library classification on the march
Introduction to library classification
Prolegomena to library classification
A modern outline of library classification.

It is clear that the significant words in each title are the same, and might be used as the basis of a retrieval system. There are various methods of using the key words in titles for indexing, all of which depend on manipulation of the title to give multiple entries, one for each significant word.

CATCHWORD TITLE INDEXING

Catchword indexing has been used for many years in such bibliographical tools as *British books in print* and in the indexes issued by periodicals, for example *Nature*. The method may be rather haphazard if rules are not set down first; the title *Field plotting by Fourier synthesis and digital computation* needs careful manipulation if all the concepts present are to be used as index entry points:

Field plotting by Fourier synthesis and digital computation
Plotting, field, by Fourier synthesis and digital computation
Fourier synthesis and digital computation, field plotting by
Synthesis, Fourier, and digital computation, field plotting by
Digital computation and Fourier synthesis, field plotting by
Computation, digital, and Fourier synthesis, field plotting by.

It is clear that this requires rather more than a purely clerical operation, but gives a reasonable statement of the sense at each entry. Straightforward rearrangement would give the following:

Field plotting by Fourier synthesis and digital computation
Plotting by Fourier synthesis and digital computation, Field
Fourier synthesis and digital computation, Field plotting by
Synthesis and digital computation, Field plotting by Fourier
Digital computation, Field plotting by Fourier synthesis and
Computation, Field plotting by Fourier synthesis and digital.

Because this splits pairs of words like *field plotting* and *Fourier synthesis* when the second becomes the entry word, it gives entries which may be rather less helpful than the previous example, but this method does not require any intellectual effort.

KEY-WORD IN CONTEXT(KWIC) INDEXING

A method which does not require any intellectual effort may be used on a machine, and one particular development of catchword indexing is now widely used to produce title indexes on computers. The method was used by Crestadoro to compile a catalogue of the Manchester Public Library during the nineteenth century, but its value for computer manipulation was established by H P Luhn of IBM.[1] Each significant word in a title becomes an entry point, as in catchword indexing, but instead of appearing at the left hand side of the page the entry word appears in the middle, with the rest of the title on either side. A long title may have to be split, so that it appears with the end preceding the beginning, but having the filing word in the middle of the page helps to keep down the number of times this happens. The title used in the previous example will give rise to the following entries:

digital computation/ **Field** plotting by Fourier synthesis and
computation/ Field **plotting** by Fourier synthesis and digital
Field plotting by **Fourier** synthesis and digital computation/
plotting by Fourier **synthesis** and digital computation/ Field
Fourier synthesis and **digital** computation/ Field plotting by
synthesis and digital **computation**/ Field plotting by Fourier.

As with catchword indexing, the entries resulting from the manipulation of the title are filed in alphabetical sequence of filing word. Insignificant words are ignored and do not give rise to index entries. A good example of a computer-produced KWIC index is *Chemical titles*, which indexes several hundred periodicals within a few weeks of publication.

KEY-WORD OUT OF CONTEXT (KWOC) INDEXING

Because the filing word is not in the normal place, KWIC indexing seems unfamiliar, and a further development of this kind of title manipulation is to move the key-word back to its normal place at the beginning of the line, but to follow it by the complete title, rather than by some altered form as in catchword indexing. This gives the advantage of having a familiar appearance—filing word at left—and also of presenting the whole title as it stands, but to set against this it is not so effective as KWIC indexing in bringing together titles which contains the same *pairs* of words. Consider the following titles:

Manual of library classification
Library classification on the march
Introduction to library classification

Prolegomena to library classification
A modern outline of library classification
The hospital library service in Lincoln
The National Library of Canada
Mechanized acquisition procedures in the University of Maryland Library
The King's Library in the British Museum
Library education
Public library administration

If we use catchword indexing and edit the titles, the five items on library classification will appear together under both library and classification; if we do not edit the titles, they will appear together under library but not under classification. If we use KWIC indexing, they will appear together under both; if we use KWOC, they will be scattered under both.

The following table sets out the index entries for these items that will appear at the word 'library':

1) *Unmanipulated catchword indexing*
   Library administration, Public
   Library classification, Introduction to
   Library classification, Manual of
   Library classification, A modern outline of
   Library classification on the march
   Library classification, Prolegomena to
   Library education
   Library in the British Museum, The King's
   Library, Mechanized acquisition procedures in the University of Maryland
   Library of Canada, The National
   Library service in Lincoln, The hospital.

2) *Manipulated catchword indexing*
   Library classification, Introduction to
   Library classification, Manual of
   Library classification, A modern outline of
   Library classification on the march
   Library classification, Prolegomena to
   Library education
   Library, The King's, in the British Museum
   Library, National, of Canada
   Library, Public, administration
   Library service, hospital, in Lincoln
   Library, University of Maryland, mechanized acquisition procedures in.

3) *KWIC indexing*

University of Maryland library/ Mechanized acquisition procedures
Public library administration/
Introduction to library classification/
Manual of library classification/
A modern outline of library classification/
Prolegomena to library classification/
Library classification on the march/
Library education/
The King's Library in the British Museum/
The National Library of Canada/
The hospital library service in Lincoln/.

(NB When using a computer it is usual to restrict entries to one line only; long titles may lose some words, as seen above and below.)

4) *KWOC indexing*

Library A modern outline of library classification
Library Introduction to library classification
Library Library classification on the march
Library Library education
Library Manual of library classification
Library Mechanized acquisition procedures in the University of
Library Prolegomena to library classification
Library Public library administration
Library The hospital library service in Lincoln
Library The King's Library in the British Museum
Library The National Library of Canada.

Using these systems, each title is liable to give rise to a number of entries: as many as there are significant terms, in fact. For this reason, they are normally used as indexes, *ie* guides leading to entries in a separate list, rather than as methods of arrangement of items or full entries.

Looked at according to the criteria established for information systems in general, those using titles for their sole source of information do not stand up very well. Though relevance may be high, in that a title found by looking for a particular word is likely to be useful, we may have to look through a number of entries at that word before finding a title that looks like the topic we want; in other words, once we have selected a set of titles, we are likely to find that a good proportion of them are useful, but we will probably have to search through quite a number of entries before we can select our set. Recall, however, is certain to be low; we have no means of linking related topics (other than our own knowledge, which is outside the system), and as we have

46

already seen, in describing the same subjects, authors are likely to go out of their way to use different terms. We can only be as specific as the author permits, and in many cases a title gives only a broad description of the subject matter in an article. Similarly, we are limited as far as exhaustivity is concerned by the extent to which the author thinks it necessary to include detail in his title.

The major advantage of indexing systems based on titles is that, as in all derived indexing systems, little or no intellectual effort is involved in putting items into the system. Indeed, KWIC and KWOC were specifically intended for machine manipulation; all that is necessary is for the titles to be produced in machine-readable form, *eg* punched cards, and the computer can then generate the appropriate entries and print them out very speedily (KWIC is an unusually apposite homophonic acronym), without any of the delays associated with normal indexing processes. This does however raise a point which can be of some importance: how are the significant words selected? The discussion and examples cited earlier assumed that entry would be made under each significant word, but obviously a computer cannot select particular words unless it is previously programmed to do so. In practice, the method is inverted; instead of significant words being selected, non-significant words are rejected. A *stop list* is compiled of words which are of no value as indexing terms, *eg* a, the, and, very; the computer is then programmed to delete any entries which might arise under these terms. IBM has a standard stop list containing 17 such terms, which is supplied as part of the program. All other words will give rise to index entries, which may lead to a situation where useful entries are swamped by a mass of entries under terms which are of very dubious value; it is therefore usual to compile a second stop list, based on experience, of words unlikely to be useful in a particular subject area or library, and this can reduce substantially the number of unwanted entries in the index.

This secondary stop list can be varied to take account of changes in terminology (science and technology have their 'fashions', which may date as quickly as other fashions) and in subject coverage of the input of documents to the system. There will also be words which occur so rarely that it is not thought necessary to include them in the stop list even though they are not useful; in such cases, one must be prepared to accept that there will be entries in the index which no one will find useful, but as a general rule we may accept that it is better to have a few entries which are not useful than to delete some which are.

The problems of exhaustivity and specificity can be overcome to some extent by using what is called *enriched* KWIC or KWOC. Additional terms are inserted into the title or added at the end to give further index entries. This method obviously involves intellectual effort in the selection of the additional terms and thus may be said to negate the advantage of speed.

Within a particular organization, it is possible to introduce a degree of sophistication into KWIC indexing that is not possible if straightforward titles are being used. For example, ICI has developed a suite of programs which will give several different types of KWIC index, adapted to the kind of input.[2] Correspondence contains several elements—writer, addressee, address, date, subject content—which may be fitted into columns of fixed field length. An accessions list can be produced, and the various elements then used to produce a series of KWIC indexes which between them give complete access to the files. When one considers the effort involved in indexing correspondence files by conventional methods, this approach looks extremely attractive! Other company information may also be processed in a similar columnar fashion. With the increasing availability of computer facilities in the form of on-line terminals, it also becomes feasible to maintain personal indexes in KWIC form. Personal indexes maintained by manual methods can take more effort than many scientists and engineers are able or willing to devote to them. If all that is necessary is to write out the required entry in KWIC format and send this to the computer centre, a whole new range of possibilities is opened up. The items included need not be published; a piece of information learnt over lunch may be included if it is written down in the prescribed format. The user can gain access to his personal file through a terminal at any time; the fact that the indexing may not be particularly good is far outweighed by the fact that one nearly always can remember something about an item that one has personally dealt with. Again, this looks very attractive compared with manual methods, and is likely to become available to large numbers of people in the next few years.

There are occasions when a reader can *identify* a document by its title; there are in fact indications that in many situations a reader is likely to remember a title more accurately than an author's correct name.[3] In such cases KWIC and similar indexes can serve both for subject information retrieval and document retrieval. The index entries, which are *headings*, must of course be linked to *descriptions* of the appropriate documents; this is usually done by means of a number which leads to a separate file of full entries. A typical KWIC index will thus consist of three parts: an accessions file, in which each item is given its identifying number; the keyword index based on the titles; and an author index. (In the case of a periodical, the page number might take the place of the accessions number.)

In recent years there has been considerable pressure on authors to give their papers meaningful titles which can be used in KWIC indexes. This has mainly been in the United States, where the lead was taken by the Engineering Societies and the American Chemical Society, and has been followed by the US Government. In science and technology

13927	JAPANESE MEDICAL	LIBRARIES*
13918	BRITISH MEDICAL	LIBRARIES 1953–1962*
13930	TITUTE OF ARCTIC AND ALPINE RESEARCH* THE	LIBRARIES AND LITERATURE OF C
13931	EARCH CENTER, UNIVERSITY OF WISCONSIN* THE	LIBRARIES AND LITERATURE OF C
13936	PUBLIC	LIBRARIES IN CZECHOSLOVAKIA*
13920	MEDICAL	LIBRARIES IN HOSPITALS*
13921	SCHOOLS*	LIBRARIES IN NURSE-TRAINING
13916	LITTLE BROTHER TO	LIBRAROCRAT*
13933	LANGUAGE AND THE LAW	LIBRARY*
13919	THE GENRAL HOSPITAL	LIBRARY*
13935	THE YOUNG STUDENT AND THE SCIENTIFIC	LIBRARY*
13932	SPECIAL LIBRARY SERVICES* THE JOHN CRERAR	LIBRARY, A COMPLEX OF SPECIAL
13934	RICAN MEDICAL ASSOCIATION* THE ARCHIVE	LIBRARY DEPARTMENT OF THE AME
13929	DAPRATO	LIBRARY OF ECCLESIASTICAL ART
13944	ING RURAL COMMUNITY*	LIBRARY SERVICE FOR THE CHANG
13926	TIONS* A	LIBRARY SURVEY OF 117 CORPORA

Example of a section of a KWIC index to 16 items taken from *Library and information science abstracts* generally it would seem that indexes using titles are likely to be more widely used in the future, because of the very large numbers of documents to be dealt with, though it is perhaps worth noting that KWIC indexes are rather unsuccessful with patents, where the title is often deliberately vague or misleading. In other subject areas, such as the social sciences, indexes based on titles are likely to be less useful because of the problems of terminology. They are also of very limited value if foreign language material is included in the collection, unless the titles are first translated.

The above discussion suggests that title-based indexes are better suited to *current notification*, *ie* informing readers of what is being published now and thus covering relatively small numbers of documents, than to *retrospective searching* among large collections, for which more tightly organized systems are probably more effective.[4]

CITATION INDEXING

Documents of value are likely to contain bibliographies; this is the way in which the author shows the foundations on which he has built. There is a link between the document and each item cited in its bibliography; we can invert this, and say that there is a link between the original item and the document citing it. By scanning a large number of documents we could establish a much larger number of such inverted links (since documents normally cite more than one item in their bibliographies). If we now file these according to the items cited, we shall bring together all the documents which have included a given item in their list of references. This is the basic principle of citation indexing.

Once again, though the idea itself is not new—it has been used in legal literature for many years—the use of computer techniques has led to the development of an important new service, Science Citation Index, and, more recently, Social Science Citation Index. Between them, these two indexes now cover well over 3000 periodicals; these are scanned, and all the bibliographic links found are fed into a computer. This then generates a citation index, corporate index, and source index. The stored information is also used for an SDI service, ASCA (Automatic Subject Citation Alert) and a subject index, the Permuterm index, which enters each item under pairs of significant words found in the title.[5]

To use a citation index it is necessary to have the reference of a relevant document, but it is often the case that a search starts from such a basis. From the citation index we can find which more recent articles have cited the one we already know (assuming that it is not too recent to have been cited by others). We can then turn to the articles we have found; if they are not relevant we can discard them, but if they are relevant we can look to see what other articles they cite. With these citations we can go back to the citation index and continue to expand the search. By this process of re-cycling we can compile a large bibliography from our single starting point.

Since every item in the periodicals covered is entered, we can follow up corrections and amendments to previously published articles. These often contain important information, but tend to be ignored by conventional abstracting and indexing services. This advantage is of course not inherent in citation indexing, but reflects the cost of SCI when compared with conventional services in its field.

Compiling a bibliography manually using the re-cycling technique described above can be tedious, but it can of course be done quite simply by the computer. A development which is of interest is the idea of *bibliographic coupling*. Two articles which both cite another earlier article must have something in common; if they both cite two earlier articles, the linking is increased; while if their bibliographies had half a dozen earlier articles in common we should be justified in assuming that they covered very much the same subject. In other words, the articles cited by an author are to a considerable extent a reflection of the subject he is writing about. The idea of bibliographic coupling has been developed at MIT (Massachusetts Institute of Technology) in Project TIP.[6] In this, some 1,200 articles a month are entered; the information given for each includes author, author's affiliation, title, citations, and bibliographic reference. The system has been shown to give good results, relying on bibliographic coupling to reveal articles on the same subject.

Another approach which has been suggested is the study of *co-citation, ie* the citation together of two or more items in more than one paper.[7] To take a concrete example, if we are studying 'Bradford's law of scattering', we would expect to find Bradford's book *Documentation* cited, since it was in this work that he first published the idea to a wide audience. However, if we look carefully, we find that nearly all the articles on the subject also quote Vickery's article in the *Journal of documentation* 4, (3) 1948, 198–203. Even if we did not have the title of the article (which is in fact 'Bradford's law of scattering') we could be reasonably confident that Vickery's article was on the same subject because of this pattern of co-citation. As the study of Bradford's law has developed, its relationship to the ideas on the frequency of occurrence of words formulated by G K Zipf was noted, and Zipf's work *Human behavior and the principle of least effort*[8] began to be quoted regularly along with Bradford and Vickery. Although the study of such patterns would be tedious using manual methods, the availability of large computerized data bases such as that forming the basis of SCI and SSCI means that we can examine them more easily, and even follow the pattern of development of an idea through its various stages.

In an interesting project, the Institute for Scientific Information, which produces SCI and SSCI, took all the links found in the last quarterly issue of 1969 SCI, and used these to give comparative rankings of all the periodicals covered, showing how often each was cited and by which journals. The straightforward rankings ignored the fact that some journals are much larger than others, and are thus likely to be cited more frequently on that account; a further ranking was therefore calculated showing the *impact factor*, *ie* the number of times a journal was cited as a function of the total number of articles it contained. These rankings have been put forward as a basis for journal selection, on the grounds that the journals most frequently cited, or having the highest impact factor, must therefore be the most important in their subject field.[9] This conclusion has been questioned by a study carried out at the NLL (now BLLD), which compared the ISI rankings with the statistics of loans for the same period, and found very little correlation.[10] Despite this, it is clear that citation counting can be of help at least in the difficult task of journal selection, even if it is not the only factor to be taken into account.

Derived indexes such as SCI and Project TIP require no intellectual effort at the input stage, because in effect they assume that the author has done the intellectual work for us. They assume that an author is familiar with the literature of his subject, and will quote the appropriate sources, correctly and fully. They assume that an author does not indulge in unjustified self-citation, and does not ignore documents which put forward relevant but opposing views, while quoting articles of marginal relevance by his friends. They assume that authors are conscientious enough to check all of the items they cite, and do not cite them merely because it is 'the done thing' to do so in that subject field (as one might pay homage to Bradford by citing *Documentation* without really considering its significance to the subject in hand). All of these assumptions are by and large justified, but it would be a mistake to accept without question that authors are not just as liable to commit sins of omission and commission as anyone else. Nevertheless, although one may not share the unbounded enthusiasm of the publishers of SCI and SSCI for their product, there is no doubt that these tools are an extremely valuable addition to the range of bibliographical services available to the librarian, and that they fit in well with the kind of approach to a literature search common among users, who start with an article which has aroused their interest and which can be used as the starting point for a search in a citation index—to 'prime the pump'.

AUTOMATIC INDEXING AND EXTRACTING
If we have the text of a document in machine-readable form, is there any way in which we could use the computer to derive suitable indexing terms, to produce a conventional type of index of the kind found in

books? To take the idea a stage further, could we program a computer to select sentences from a document which would form an *auto-extract* sufficiently good to be an adequate substitute for a normally produced *abstract*? In view of the ever-increasing costs of intellectual indexing and abstracting, and the world-wide shortage of skilled indexers and abstractors, both ideas are attractive, and a steady stream of research projects have been carried out to explore the possibilities.

The first attempts at computer indexing were based on word counts. It was assumed that a word which occurred frequently in a document (excluding of course common words) would bear a significant relationship to its subject content, and—*vice versa*—that the most significant words would be those which occurred most frequently. This is too much of a simplification; an index to the proceedings of the Washington Scientific Information Conference, 1958, was produced in this way, and a study by Vickery revealed that it was defective on a number of counts.[11] A much more effective method is to count the number of occurrences of a word *in relation to the expected number*. This involves the establishment of a frequency norm by compiling a dictionary of words in a large body of text and finding out how often each occurs in relation to the total number of words in the documents studied. Using this criterion, a word which occurs only a few times in a particular document may nevertheless be shown to be significant, because its expected frequency as indicated by the dictionary is lower than is actually found. Other more useful results were obtained when the co-occurrence of terms was measured; if two words were frequently found together, the significance of their joint occurrence was likely to be a great deal higher than that of their occurrences measured in isolation. A technique for automatic abstracting was developed, which involved selecting and printing out those sentences of the original which contained the most significant word pairs, but this proved to be inadequate and was abandoned.[12]

Recent work has been in the direction of refining the criteria for selection of sentences. Instead of a simple statistical criterion, one may introduce four measures of significance, and give each sentence a weight according to these. Sentences with the highest weights are likely to be those which best summarize the content of the document, and it is possible to program the computer to extract all sentences with weights above a predetermined level, which will depend on the subject matter, kind of literature and so on. The four measures proposed are based on 1) keywords determined statistically, using the expected frequency of occurrence technique; 2) cue words, *eg* significant, important, which indicate that the author wishes to emphasize a statement; 3) title and heading words, which may be assumed to have particular weight; and 4) position of the sentence in the overall structure—for example, the first sentence in a paragraph is often a 'topic' sentence and would thus be useful as an indication of the content of the paragraph. The overall result compares reasonably well with an abstract prepared by a skilled abstracter, who will of course be basing his own summary on a similar analysis. The preferred term for this technique is now 'autoextracting' rather than 'autoabstracting', to emphasize the fact that it is essentially based on the existing content of the document and can only extract from it.[13]

COMPUTER SEARCHING OF TEXT

If we knew that some information we wanted was to be found in a particular document, but there was no contents list or index, we could find what we wanted by reading through the whole of the document, looking for the words we were interested in. To use the term that we have used previously, we would be trying to *match* our requirements, as expressed in certain words, against the words to be found in the document. Now we may be prepared to do this for one document, but when we start to think in terms of a whole library the process clearly becomes impractical. Even to look through a lengthy list of titles can be very time-consuming, as many librarians know from scanning booksellers' lists and similar publications. However, as we have seen in the previous chapter, we have in the computer a device that can perform this kind of matching operation at high speed; if the titles or other parts of the text that we wish to scan are in machine-readable form, we can program the computer to carry out the matching process and identify the documents likely to be useful for us. All that we have to do is to feed into the computer the words that we want it to match.

This makes it sound very simple, but in practice it turns out to be rather more complex. Suppose we that are interested in classification; we may find documents using the word *classifying* just as useful. Again, suppose that our interest is in *pollution*—a topic which is very much in the public mind. We could program the computer to search for *pollution*, but we should then miss documents which only use the word *pollutant*, or *polluting*. The solution is relatively simple, and is available in most computer-based systems; we can see that all of the words we are interested in have the same stem, so we *truncate* our search term, and program the computer to search for *pollut*. Our search will now pick out all of the terms we are interested in. Similarly, a search for *classif* will pick out all the various forms of the key word in that example. The exact way in which we indicate truncation will depend on the program we are using; for convenience, an asterisk will be used here, as it is one of the most commonly used methods. (We must indicate somehow that we want the computer to look for the word stem *plus*, otherwise it will perform a fruitless search for *pollut* or *classif*, rejecting any words which do not match this exactly.)

Truncation is a very convenient device, but must be used with care.

We can use *forward truncation*, as in POLLUT*, or *backward truncation*, as in *CLASSIF*; the latter will now match *reclassification* in addition to all the other words. However, it will also match *declassification*, the term used to denote the process of making a secret document more widely available. Suppose we are studying the role of the *parent* in the family; the words that might be of value include *parents*, *parental* and *parenthood*, and if we think carefully we may conclude that it would be useful to find anything containing the word *grandparent* as well. So we cheerfully program the computer to search for *PARENT* and sit back expectantly, only to find that we are retrieving documents using the words *parenthesis*, *parenteral* and *transparent*! In some systems we can include an extra instruction telling the computer to ignore certain ways of extending the word stem, but of course we have to think out in advance what the undesirable extensions might be, which may not be particularly easy if we are not familiar with the subject, or are not accustomed to using computer-based systems.

So far, we have assumed that our search is for a single word, but in practice we would normally be thinking of more than one word to describe the subject we are interested in. For example, we might be concerned with *water pollution* rather than just pollution. In this situation we can use the ability of the computer to handle 'logical' statements; the logic referred to is Boolean rather than Aristotelean, and it means that we can link the words we are searching for by means of the operators AND, OR and NOT. So our search formulation becomes:

'WATER' AND 'POLLUT*'.

However, we would quickly realise that *water* includes *rivers* and *seas*; we can use the operator OR to take care of this:

'POLLUT*' AND ('WATER' OR 'SEA*' OR 'RIVER*').

We may be interested in all forms of pollution other than that from *sewage*; here we can exclude the unwanted term by using NOT:

'POLLUT*' AND ('WATER' OR 'SEA*' OR 'RIVER*') AND NOT 'SEWAGE'.

There is an order of precedence among these operators, which is usually NOT, AND, OR. Thus

'POLLUT*' AND 'WATER' OR 'SEA*'

will be taken to mean a search for *pollut** in association with *water*, *or* for *sea** on its own. The use of parentheses as in the example above is necessary to override this precedence order, and is often recommended as a useful way of clarifying the search formulation anyway.

Further refinements are sometimes available. For example, it may be possible to specify that two words which are of interest must occur within the same sentence, or within so many words of each other. It is also possible to *weight* important words heavily and less important ones more lightly, and then set a limit below which a document will not be retrieved even if it contains *some* of the less important words.

For example, if we were looking for information about the use of computers for information retrieval we might formulate a search:

INFORMATION (3)
RETRIEVAL (3)
COMPUT* (1)
MACHINE (1)
AUTOMAT* (1)
MINIMUM WEIGHT 7

This search would not retrieve a document on information processing by computer even if the words *machine* and *automat** were present.

One method, used by IBM in their Advanced Text Management System (ATMS), is to create a second file in which each term in the text (other than those in the stop list) acts as an index entry. In conjunction with STAIRS (STorage And Information Retrieval System) this gives very fast access to any part of the file; the penalty to be paid for this is that the whole file is slightly more than twice the size of the data base, and the large files described in chapter 25 would thus require very large disk storage units to make them available on-line.

There are a number of computer-based information retrieval systems now available, and examples are described in chapter 25. Most of them use limited amounts of information, for example the author, title and bibliographical reference, while some include abstracts. Full texts are normally only used for special purposes, since not only would their use increase costs by a large factor, but also it seems likely that relevance would be poor, because exhaustivity of indexing would—as has already been pointed out—be 100%.[14]

BIBLIOGRAPHY

1 Luhn, H P: *Keyword in context index for technical literature.* IBM, 1959. See also ref 12 for the collected works of H P Luhn.

2 Matthews, F W and Shillingford, A D: 'Variations on KWIC.' *Aslib proceedings,* 25 (4) April 1973, 140–152.

3 Ayres, F H: 'Authors versus title: a comparative study of the accuracy of the information which the user brings to the library catalogue'. *Journal of documentation,* 24 (4) December 1968, 266–272.

4 The BLLD publishes a regular KWIC index to conference proceedings received, and there are other published services, *eg Chemical titles.* Students should scan one or more of these carefully to evaluate it. See also Vickery, B C: *Techniques of information retrieval,* p 188+.

5 Garfield, E: *'Science citation index*: a new dimension in indexing'. *Science, 144* (3619) 1964, 649–654.

Garfield, E: 'Primordial concepts, citation indexing, and historiobibliography'. *Journal of library history,* 2 (3) 1967, 235–249.

Cawkell, A E: 'Citations in chemistry'. *Chemistry in Britain,* 6 (10) 1970, 414–416.

Keen, E M: 'Citation indexes'. *Aslib proceedings, 16* (8) 1964, 246–251.

Martyn, J: 'An examination of citation indexes'. *Aslib proceedings, 17* (6) 1965, 184–196.
Students should see either a set of SCI or SSCI or (with caution) the publicity matter distributed by the Institute for Scientific Information.

6 Kessler, M M: 'The MIT technical information project'. *Physics today, 18* (3) 1965, 28–36.

7 Small, H: 'Co-citation in the scientific literature: a new measure of the relationship between two documents.' *Journal of the American Society for Information Science, 24* (4) 1973, 265–269.

8 Zipf, G K: *Human behavior and the principle of least effort.* NY, Stechert-Hafner, 1949.

9 Garfield, E: 'Citation analysis as a tool in journal evaluation.' *Science, 178,* 1972, 471–479.

Scales, P A: 'Citation analyses as indicators of the use of serials: a comparison of ranked title lists produced by citation counting and from use data.' *Journal of documentation, 32* (1) 1976, 17–25.

Martyn, J: 'Citation analysis'. *Journal of documentation, 31* (4) 1975, 290–297 (Progress in documentation).

10 Wade, N: 'Citation analysis: a new tool for science administrators.' *Science, 188,* May 2 1975, 429–432.

11 Vickery, B C: 'The statistical method in indexing.' *Revue de la documentation, 28,* 1961, 56–62.

12 Luhn, H P: *H P Luhn: pioneer of information science. Selected works,* edited by Claire K Schultz. Macmillan, 1968. Luhn wrote several articles on statistical encoding and auto-abstracting, which will be found in this memorial volume.

13 Edmundson, H P: 'New methods in automatic extracting'. *Journal of the Association for Computing Machinery, 16* (2) 1969, 264–285.

14 Lynch, M F: *Computer-based information services in science and technology—principles and techniques.* Peter Peregrinus, 1974.

Doyle, L B: *Information retrieval and processing.* Los Angeles, Melville, 1975. (A completely revised edition of the work of the same title by J Becker and R Hayes, 1963.)

CHAPTER 5

Assigned indexing 1: semantics

In the previous chapter, we looked at ways in which we could derive indexes from information manifest in the document. However, the discussion indicated some problems that we are likely to meet in doing this.

Firstly, we have to choose the words which we will use in a search of the system by trying to think of all of the words that the authors of the documents we have indexed might have used to describe the topic that we are interested in, and, having chosen the words, we have to think of the various forms in which they might occur. Truncation serves as a means of merging different word forms, but not always; TEACH* will retrieve *teaching* and *teacher* but not *taught*. Secondly, we often need to search for combinations of terms; word pairs are more significant than the individual words on their own, but we often find ourselves wanting to associate more than two words. This process of *coordination* is in effect a process of class intersection. To use one of our previous examples, our collection of documents (the universe of discourse) contains a group of documents to which the word *water* is relevant, and another group to which the word *pollution* is relevant; each of these groups forms a class, and if we are searching for documents on *water pollution* we are looking for the intersection of these two classes.

We also noted that *water* on its own might not retrieve all the documents of interest, because they might use different but related terms: *sea* and *river*; in order to carry out an adequate search of our collection of documents, we had to think up not only the words in which we were interested, and all of the forms in which they might be used, but also all of the alternative or related terms. We then had to decide on just how we were going to coordinate these words in order to retrieve relevant documents, while at the same time excluding words or combinations of words which would retrieve irrelevant material. This is obviously quite a complex operation, and if we are to do it well we need some guidance: a list of words showing their relationships and indicating ways in which they may usefully be combined to give the class intersections we are interested in. However, in chapter 1 we pointed out that what we are actually trying to do is carry out a matching operation between the messages which in their encoded form are the input to our system and the messages—again in their encoded form—which represent the questions we put to the system. This concept of matching is of course strongly reinforced by our examination of computer-based systems, which depend on the computer to match the words of our question against the words in the documents.

Now if we are to use a list of words to help us in our searching, it would appear that we would increase the chances of achieving successful matches if in fact we used the same list of words to encode the documents at the input stage, and *assigned* the appropriate words to each document ourselves rather than rely on the authors' choice. In other words, if we devise an *indexing language*, and use this for both encoding operations: input and question. Such systems are referred to as *assigned indexing* systems, and most of the rest of this book is devoted to the problems of constructing and using such systems. In this chapter we shall examine some of the basic theoretical problems.[1]

CHOICE OF TERMS

Assigned indexing is also known as *concept indexing*, because what we are trying to do is to identify the concepts involved in each document. (Concept: idea of a class of objects; general notion).[2]

Recent work by the Classification Research Group suggests that there are five categories of concept: entities; activities; abstracts; properties; heterogeneous. A concept is denoted by a *term*, which may consist of more than one word. (Term: a word or expression that has a precise meaning in some uses, or is peculiar to a science, art, profession or subject).[3] We may examine each of these categories in more detail. *Entities* are things which may be given a denotative meaning,[4] *ie* we can identify them by pointing at them. They may be physical, *eg* matter, or physical phenomena; chemical, *eg* molecular states, minerals; biological, *ie* living beings; or artefacts, *ie* manufactured items. *Activities* are usually denoted by verbal nouns, *eg* building, lubricating, though in some cases we may find the passive rather than the active form, *eg* lubrication. *Abstracts* usually refer to qualities or states, and are given connotative meanings, *ie* each of us may attribute a different meaning to them depending on our particular corpus of experience. They may be physical, *eg* energy; symbolic, *eg* Justice (as a blindfolded figure); and behavioural, *eg* truth (the definition of which was questioned on at least one notable occasion). *Properties* are of two kinds, which are distinguished by their grammatical form. Adjectival forms can only be used in conjunction with a noun, which they qualify in a subjective or attributive way, once again giving a connotative meaning. They may relate to sight, *eg* dull, shiny, symmetrical; sound, *eg* loud, musical; or to the other three senses, touch, taste and smell. They may also relate to mechanical properties, *eg* loose, rigid. Noun forms describe physical properties which may be measured, *eg* rigidity, reflectivity, loudness. It will be clear at once that there will in many cases be a definite relationship between the two kinds. We may refer to the rigidity of an iron bar, for example, in which case we are thinking of the property; or we may refer to a rigid bar, in which case we are using the property to define the kind of entity that we are considering.

Heterogeneous concepts form a very mixed bag, in that they usually represent concepts which might be further analyzed into two or more simpler concepts which would fit into the other four categories, but are nevertheless usually regarded as unitary concepts and treated as such. The problem arises from the fact that it is very difficult to fix an absolute level of analysis; there is nearly always the possibility of carrying our analysis one stage further. We cannot use the criterion of 'one word or more'; some single concepts can only be denoted by more than one word, *eg* mother of pearl, moment of truth, while composite concepts may often be denoted by a single word, *eg* demography (statistics of population). Willetts[5] has suggested some types:

Roles of man (Entity + Activity, Entity + Property) *eg* teacher, landlord

Groups of man (Entity + Abstract) *eg* society, conference

Types of building (Entity + Activity + Property) *eg* library, theatre

Discipline (all four) *eg* Physics, Medicine

Groups of chemicals (Entity + Activity, Entity + Property) *eg* catalysts, polymers.

During the 1950s a team at Case Western Reserve University worked on a system of this kind known as *semantic factoring*. The objective of the method was to break down every concept into a set of fundamental concepts called semantic factors. Because of their fundamental nature, there would be only a limited number of these factors, and concepts would be specified by coding them to show the semantic factors involved and also the specific concept. For example, the generalized concept metals is coded M TL; metal is coded MATL; and aluminium, a particular metal, is coded MATL. I. ⌐AQL, where I is a role indicator and the ⌐ Q is a special code into which can be fitted the chemical symbol, in this case AL for aluminium. Thermometer is coded MACH.MUSR.RWHT.4X.002, where MACH = device, MUSR = measurement, RWHT.4X = heat, and .002 indicates the second use of this code. By the use of a complex set of roles and links, codes for the concepts involved in a document can be strung together to form a 'telegraphic abstract'—a detailed subject specification which forms the input to the computer-based system.

The method is clearly a powerful one, but is open to some doubts and objections. Exactly how far does one carry such an analysis? Heat and temperature, for example, could be specified as *movement* of *molecules*. Again, it is possible to specify a concept by using only some of its attributes; or perhaps more significantly, is it ever possible to specify *all* the attributes for a given concept? For example, thermometer may be specified as above, instrument: measuring: temperature; and barometer may be specified as instrument: measuring: pressure. Neither reveals the fact that both of these may have other factors in common, for example the fact that they may be mercury-in-glass devices. Certainly for most purposes a mercury barometer has more in common with an aneroid barometer than it does with a thermometer, but this may not be the case if we are thinking of the instrument maker. If we think of a particular individual, we may have no difficulty in putting a name to the object of our thoughts; we may find it impossible in practical terms to think of all the possible terms that might be needed to denote that individual without naming him or her. Sex, age, nationality, family status, marital status, height, weight, occupation, language,—the list is almost endless. Furthermore, we may find ourselves in the position of not knowing all of the information we require; we have to remember that we are dealing with the information in our collection of documents, and this will often be incomplete. The problem has no easy solution, as can be seen from the fact that it is still being actively discussed by the CRG: to what extent is it permissible to 'telescope' concepts from different facets when their combination is itself a wellknown isolate? When is it legitimate to decide that one will carry one's analysis no further? We still have some way to go in terms of linguistic and semantic analysis before we can have any confidence in our answers to these questions.[6]

CHOICE OF FORM OF WORD

During the above discussion of categories of concept it should have become apparent that—with the sole exception of adjectival properties, which cannot stand alone—all of the concepts involved were denoted by nouns. Even activities are denoted by verbal nouns, active or passive, *eg* cataloguing and classification. In fact, it is the norm in indexing languages to use nouns as far as possible, and various sets of rules have been drawn up to give guidance on the use of singular and plural. Figure 6 is based on the rules given in the EJC *Thesaurus of engineering and scientific terms,* described in Chapter 26; both the American National Standards Institute[7] and the British Standards[8] Institution have published guidelines, as has Unesco.[9]

HOMOGRAPHS

The same spelling is sometimes used for different words, which may or may not be pronounced the same, *eg* sow and sow, China and china. This may arise by a figure of speech such as metonymy, in which we use part of a description to mean the whole; it may be through analogy, for example when terms such as 'filter' from hydraulic engineering are used by electrical engineers; or it may be simply an etymological accident. Whatever the cause, there is likely to be confusion if we do

TYPE OF TERM	USE SINGULAR	USE PLURAL
MATERIALS PROPERTIES	WHEN SPECIFIC EG. POLYTHENE DENSITY	WHEN GENERIC EG. PLASTICS CHEMICAL PROPERTIES
OBJECTS EVENTS OBJECTS SPECIFIED BY PURPOSE		CARS LAWS WARS LUBRICANTS
PROCESSES PROPER NAMES DISCIPLINES, SUBJECT AREAS	LUBRICATING EARTH (THE PLANET) LAW WAR	

FIGURE 6: Choice of singular or plural form of noun.

nothing to distinguish such words. One way of doing this is to qualify each by another word in parenthesis to show the context and thus the meaning, *eg*

PITCH (Bitumen)
PITCH (Music)
PITCH (Football)
PITCH (Slope)

If we do not distinguish homographs we shall get reduced relevance; the seriousness of this will depend on the coverage of our system. For example, if our collection only covers music there will be no problem with the word Pitch, since other meanings than the musical are unlikely to arise at the input stage.

RELATIONSHIPS

We have seen that in addition to the choice of terms and the form in which they should be used, there are two kinds of relationship between terms that we have to take account of: the recognition of terms denoting related subjects such as water, sea and river, and the association or coordination of otherwise unrelated terms to represent composite subjects. If we study Table 1 carefully, we can identify these two different kinds of relationship, and it will be seen that the first kind are permanent, and arise from the definitions of the subjects involved (aluminium is always a non-ferrous metal; polyethylene is always a plastic), whereas the second kind arise from the subjects we have to deal with in documents, and represent temporary, *ad hoc*, associations. The first

1 Metals	10 Plastics
2 Ferrous metals	11 Plastic films
3 Iron	12 Polyethylene
4 Non-ferrous metals	13 Polyethylene films
5 Aluminium	14 Plastic bags
6 Heat treatment of metals	15 Polyethylene bags
7 Heat treatment of non-ferrous metals	16 Welding of plastics
	17 Welding of plastic bags
8 Heat treatment of aluminium	18 Welding of polyethylene bags
9 Aluminium windows	

TABLE I: *Related subjects*

kind are known as *semantic* relationships, while the second are called *syntactic*. Thus heat treatment is an activity performed on aluminium, an entity; windows are a product made from aluminium, the raw material, both being entities; in both instances the concepts are linked in a manner corresponding to the syntax of a normal sentence. This suggests that our indexing language must contain the equivalents of both a dictionary, to show semantic relationships, and a grammar, to cater for syntactic relationships.

SEMANTIC RELATIONSHIPS

We find that these may be considered in three groups: equivalence, hierarchical, and affinitive/associative. The first two groups are reasonably straightforward, but the third is much less clearly defined, and is the group which causes most problems in practice. Table 2 lists the specific kinds of relationship falling into each group, and we may examine these in more detail.

EQUIVALENCE

The English language is rich in synonyms and near-synonyms, because it has roots in both Teutonic and Romance languages. While it is true that Wordsworth's ode would sound less impressive as *Hints of death-lessness* than it does as *Intimations of immortality*, the former is as correct a formulation of the subject as the latter. Should we try to eliminate synonyms and thus achieve a higher degree of consistency?

There are many situations where we have to make this decision; for example, many subjects have both a common name and a scientific one, American terminology differs from English, authors differ in their usage. For example, a technical article will use technical terms, whereas a popular article on the same subject will use popular terminology; by not merging synonyms, we will in effect be keeping these two papers on the same subject apart. A search based on the technical terms will retrieve technical papers only, while one based on popular terms will retrieve only those using that set of terms. If we do not

Equivalence
   Synonyms and antonyms
   Quasi–synonyms
     Same continuum
     Overlapping
   Preferred spelling
   Acronyms, abbreviations
   Current and established terms
   Translations

Hierarchical
   Genus–species
   Whole–part

Affinitive/Associative
   Coordination
   Genetic
   Concurrent
   Cause and effect
   Instruments
   Materials
   Similarity

TABLE 2: *Semantic relationships*

merge the various synonyms into one preferred form, we shall lower the recall of our system, though we will probably get high relevance.

It may seem a little odd to place synonyms and antonyms together, yet in trying to retrieve information we may often find it useful to treat them in the same way. The temperance worker may well require a work on alcoholism! In practice, we find that antonyms often fall into the next category, of quasi-synonyms which represent points on the same continuum, *eg* roughness—smoothness. One could regard these as antonyms, yet actually they represent a subjective judgement; what one person might think rough could appear smooth to another, and it is clear that there is no hard and fast dividing line between them. The other kind of quasi-synonym arises from the overlapping of two concepts, *eg* distance and length. (The distance between two points is a length, and vice versa).

The other four instances of equivalence quoted in table 2 are self-explanatory. Preferred spellings: *eg* Labour, Labor; acronyms: *eg* STAR, Scientific and technical aerospace reports; current and established terms: *eg* Third World, Developing countries, Underdeveloped countries; and translations.

The equivalence relationship implies that there will be more than one term denoting the same concept. In an indexing language, it is usual to introduce a measure of control over this situation by choosing

64

one of the terms as the *preferred term*, and using only that term in our index. We must of course make provision for those users who look for information under one of the other terms, and this is discussed below in the section on showing semantic relationships.

HIERARCHICAL

The usual kind of hierarchical relationship is that of genus to species, which represents class inclusion (all A is B; some B is A). It is seen most clearly in the biological sciences (all mammals are vertebrates; some vertebrates are mammals), but is also found in other subject fields; indeed, much of classification is concerned with the establishment of hierarchies. Austin[10] distinguishes what he calls quasi-generic relationships from true generic, using the criterion of permanence. For example, a rabbit is *always* a mammal of a particular species (oryctolagus cuniculus); it is *sometimes* a pest, a pet, or the basis of a stew. So it will always appear in the appropriate zoological hierarchy, but its appearance in the other hierarchies will depend on the context (a matter of taste, one might say).

Whole-part relationships are not generic. A wheel is not a species of bicycle, nor is a door a species of house. However, it is convenient to regard whole-part relationships as hierarchical, and it has been suggested that the two kinds should be distinguished as Generic and Partitive.[8]

AFFINITIVE/ASSOCIATIVE RELATIONSHIPS

Because these are the least well-defined, and often are not immediately obvious, they are the group likely to cause most problems in an indexing language. Indeed, Coates has criticized the Library of Congress list of headings for including these relationships in what appears to be a quite haphazard way. Despite the difficulties, we should make some attempt to cater for these relationships by first of all recognizing that they exist and then trying to identify them systematically.

Some present fewer problems than others. Coordination is in fact a by-product of the generic relationship: species of the same genus are coordinate. Thus the brown hare, the blue hare, the Arctic hare, and the jackrabbit are all coordinate species of the genus *leporidae*. Proton, neutron and electron are all coordinate species of sub-atomic particle. Coordination can obviously also arise from the whole-part relationship; doors, windows and floors are coordinate parts of the whole house, and root, stem, leaf and flower are coordinate parts of the whole plant. It is worth noting that if division of this kind is *dichotomous*, *ie* into A and A', the result is to give two concepts which are antonyms, *eg* male and female, poetry and prose. For this reason antonyms are sometimes considered to fall within the associative rather than the equivalence group.

Genetic relationships is also straightforward, *eg* Mother—son; here again we may note that the first level of genetic division will give coordinate concepts, *eg* son—daughter. Concurrent refers to two activities taking place at the same time in association, and is thus open to much broader interpretation; an example is education—teaching. Cause and effect are rather easier to identify, though of course they have been the subject of much philosophical discourse; an optimistic example from the draft British Standard is teaching—learning. Instruments, *eg* teaching—overhead projectors; and materials, *eg* plastic film—transparencies; are usually fairly obvious. The final category, similarity, however, is perhaps the most difficult of the affinitive relationships, in that it necessarily implies a subjective judgement; how similar do two concepts have to be for us to include the relationship in our indexing language? At present, the only answer to this question lies in the judgement of the index language compiler, and we should not expect any great degree of consistency between different indexing languages.

THE NEED TO RECOGNIZE SEMANTIC RELATIONSHIPS
At the beginning of this chapter we saw how the need to identify semantic relationships could arise, but in view of the fairly detailed analysis that we have just carried out, it is worth restating the problem, from two rather different points of view. We started off from the viewpoint of the searcher trying to carry out a search in a computer-based system using the texts, or parts of the texts, of the documents in our collection. Just which collection of terms do we have to use in order to make sure that we have covered all the possible approaches to a concept? To put it another way: if the term we first think of does not retrieve the documents we want (or perhaps does not retrieve any documents at all!) *what other terms can we substitute?* It is obviously of help in this situation if we have some kind of list of terms showing the relationships between them, to suggest substitute terms.

This list of terms—our indexing language—is equally obviously of value to the indexer who is trying to encode the document in such a way that it will be found by searchers who are likely to deem it useful. The concept the indexer is trying to encode may be unfamiliar, in which case it is useful to be able to follow a path through a network of related subjects until we find the most appropriate term. It will also indicate the terms we are likely to have used in encoding previous documents dealing with the same concept.

However, it is worth noting that if the concept we are dealing with has a clearly defined name known to both indexer and searcher, the need for an indexing language with its network of relationships disappears; we will do perfectly well using a computer to match the term the searcher first thinks of with the corresponding term in the documents.

This point is sometimes overlooked by enthusiastic indexers, and we shall have occasion to return to it in discussing evaluation tests in chapter 28. For the time being, we shall assume that the pessimistic view is the correct one, and that indexing languages do serve a useful purpose; to put it another way, we shall often need help in conducting a search, whether it be in a computer search of texts, relying on the words used in them, or in a highly controlled file using a complex indexing language, while the indexer constructing such a file needs the detailed help that an indexing language can give.

SHOWING SEMANTIC RELATIONSHIPS

So far, we have seen that our indexing language will consist of a list of terms denoting the concepts we wish to include, together with a set of relationships linking various sets of terms. We now have to consider the question of how to arrange our terms, and how to show the relationships which exist among them.

The simplest way to arrange our terms is alphabetically, as in a dictionary; one example of this kind of arrangement in use is the dictionary catalogue, in which entries for authors, titles and subjects are all arranged in one alphabetical sequence. However, it is obvious that alphabetical arrangement cannot show any kind of relationship except the accidental one of bringing together words which have the same stem, which at best can only cater for a very small part of the problem. The answer is to insert a series of *linkages*, usually called *cross-references*, which serve to bring semantic relationships to the attention of the user.

Equivalence relationships normally imply the selection of one form as the preferred term, as we have seen, so we make a cross-reference pointing from the non-preferred term to the preferred term:

Footpaths *See* Trails (LCSH)

Bovines USE Cattle (TEST)

In the indexing language, we need to show the inverse of these directions to help the indexer, once again using various conventions:

Trails
  x Footpaths (LCSH)
  CATTLE
  UF [*ie* Use For] Cattle

These inverse directions do not normally appear in the index itself, but this is more a matter of historical practice than of any theoretical consideration.

HIERARCHICAL AND AFFINITIVE/ASSOCIATIVE RELATIONSHIPS

As we have seen, equivalence relationships are essentially one-way, taking us from non-preferred terms to preferred. By contrast, the other two categories of relationship are two-way, and this implies slightly different treatment. We shall need cross-references in both directions. To take some examples of the hierarchical relationship, if we have material in our catalogue on both the sun and the solar system, we need to draw the attention of the user to this:

Solar system	Inverse:	Sun
See also Sun		xx Solar system
Sun		Solar system
See also Solar system		xx Sun (LCSH)

Again, it is historical practice, mainly for economic reasons, not to include the second in the catalogue, but only in the indexing language used to construct the catalogue. A rather different convention is used in many indexing languages:

CATTLE	Inverse:	**BEEF CATTLE**
NT Beef cattle		BT Cattle (TEST)

where NT stands for Narrower term and BT for Broader term. It will be seen that this convention indicates the kind of relationship, whereas the earlier *See also* and xx merely show a relationship. This point becomes clearer if we consider the affinitive and associative relationships, where the earlier system uses the same convention, but the more modern approach uses RT, indicating Related Term:

Forging	Inverse:	**Blacksmithing**
See also Blacksmithing		xx Forging
Blacksmithing		**Forging**
See also Forging		xx Blacksmithing (LCSH)
CATTLE		**HIDES**
RT Hides		RT Cattle (TEST)

In the examples from LCSH, the symbols x and xx are of course found only in the indexing language, not in the catalogue, and serve as aids to the indexer.

COMPARISON OF LINKAGES IN DIFFERENT INDEXING LANGUAGES

It can be both interesting and constructive to compare the networks of cross-references in two indexing languages, and Kochen and Tagliocozzo have proposed two measures for this purpose.[11] The first of these is the *correctedness ratio*:

the number of terms linked to other terms as a proportion of the total number of terms in the vocabulary.

The second is *accessibility*:

the average number of terms leading to any given term.

Accessibility is related to the density of the cross-reference network, while the connectedness ratio is a measure of the number of *orphans*, a term coined by Daily to denote terms which have no linkages.[12] Such terms can of course only be found if we think of them for ourselves, since by definition no other term that we think of will lead us to them. Of the 36,000 entries in the 7th edition of LCSH, some 7,000 are orphans, which seems a rather high proportion; however, Austin has found a somewhat similar proportion in PRECIS, which is a much more tightly controlled system than LCSH.

ENTRY VOCABULARY AND INDEX VOCABULARY

From the above discussion it should be clear that terms linked by equivalence relationships are rather different from the other two, in that we select one preferred term and use only that one in our index, whereas the other two kinds of relationship occur between terms which are both used in the index. For example, if we choose CATTLE as our preferred term, rather than BOVINES, then all the information that we have in our collection on this subject will be indexed by the term CATTLE, and none by the term bovines; users who think of the latter term will find the instruction Use Cattle. But we *will* index any relevant information by the term HIDES, since this is linked to CATTLE by a Related term reference. In our indexing language we will therefore have both preferred terms, which are used for indexing, and nonpreferred terms, which are not. The preferred terms on their own form the *index vocabulary*, while the preferred terms and non-preferred terms together form the *entry vocabulary*. The entry vocabulary is very important; there will be many occasions on which we decide for one reason or another not to use a particular term, but to use one already in our index vocabulary instead, and it is essential that both indexers and searchers know what decisions of this kind we have made. For the indexer, there is the question of consistency: using the same preferred term every time. For the searcher, there is the question of which is the right term to substitute for the one he cannot find in the index. The MEDLARS evaluation project, discussed in detail in chapter 28, showed very clearly that an inadequate entry vocabulary led to failures in both recall and relevance, and all of us must have experienced the frustration of trying to find information on a specific topic in a book with an inadequate index, or—worse still—with no index at all.

SYSTEMATIC ARRANGEMENT

The above discussion on showing semantic relationships related to one method of arrangement, the alphabetical. There is another way of showing relationships, *juxtaposition*, ie grouping together related concepts in a systematic arrangement to form a classification scheme. Such a scheme will show hierarchical relationships and whole-part relationships as well as coordinate relationships, and may well show others such as instruments and materials. In this way, a substantial part of the cross-reference structure required by an alphabetical arrangement is eliminated, because the relationships are shown by the way concepts are grouped. We normally arrange books on the shelves of a library in this way in order to help the users, who will, we hope, find all the books they are interested in shelved in the same area.

There is however a price to be paid for this advantage. If we group our preferred terms systematically, then the order in which they occur is no longer self-evident, and we are forced to introduce a *notation*, or *code vocabulary*, to show the order and enable us to find particular concepts among the systematic arrangement. The entry vocabulary now becomes doubly important, because not only does it include all the non-preferred terms but, being arranged alphabetically, it forms our only means of access to the systematic arrangement, via the code vocabulary. We need to decide what terms denote the concepts we are interested in, then look them up in the entry vocabulary, which will tell us what codes have been used to denote them:

Electronics	621.381
Cyclotrons	621.384.61
Preaching	PXP
Disease (Medicine)	L:491
Amplifiers	TK6565.A55

Equivalence relationships are catered for by simply showing the same code for each; in fact, all of the entries in the entry vocabulary are equivalence relationships, in that they show the preferred heading (in this case a piece of notation) for both non-preferred and preferred terms. In the *schedules* of the scheme, *ie* the list of index vocabulary terms in systematic order, we shall normally find only the preferred terms.

A further problem arises because, as we have seen already, a concept may appear in more than one hierarchy, where one represents a permanent, generic, relationship, while the others are quasi-generic. So the same basic concept may well be represented by more than one code, depending on the context in which it appears:

Tobacco	
botany	583.79
hygiene	613.8
social customs	394.1

Systematic arrangement can show many of the categories of relationship we have identified, either by juxtaposition in the schedules or by the complementary juxtaposition of entries in the alphabetical sequence of the entry vocabulary. However, this does not cover all of the affinitive/associative group, some of which may actually be hidden by the arrangement. The only way in which these may be drawn to the attention of indexer and searcher is through cross-references in the schedules or in the entry vocabulary. Unfortunately, such cross-references are the exception rather than the rule in most classification schemes; this may well be a reflection of the fact that it is only in recent years that we have begun to clarify the nature of the various relationships that may occur between concepts. To conclude this chapter, it may be instructive to compare the categories of relationship we have been considering with a similar categorization of relationships revealed by psychological word association tests.[13] It may be that a study of such associations might throw further light on the kinds of relationship we need to cater for in our index vocabularies.

Relationships discussed	Word associations
Word forms	Word derivative
synonyms	similar
antonyms	contrast
hierarchical	superordinate
	subordinate
coordinate	coordinate
whole–part	whole–part
concurrent	contiguity
cause and effect	cause and effect
instruments	verb-object
materials	material
similarity	similarity
genetic	—
—	assonance

TABLE 3: *Relationships and associations*

THE FUNCTION OF SEMANTIC RELATIONSHIPS

As we have seen, the inclusion of a network of semantic relationships in our index vocabulary enables us to increase the range of a search, by suggesting substitute or additional terms that we can use in trying to achieve a match between our formulation of a question and the codings of the concepts in the documents in our system. In other words, the function of this kind of relationship is to enable us to improve recall. This may however be at the expense of relevance. If we have to substitute a term for the one we first thought of, it *may* be an inferior substitute, though not necessarily; the term we first thought of may in fact itself have been wide of the mark, since it is often difficult to state precisely what it is that we want to find out. If however we *are* quite certain of the objective of our search, then even a synonym may be less acceptable; it can be argued that in the case of words having connotative meanings there cannot be any exact synonyms. The merging of synonyms and other equivalence relationships, the grouping achieved by hierarchical and affinitive/associative relationships, are both means of retrieving more documents then we would have done by using only our original terms; *ie* they are devices to improve recall for the searcher. The only way in which they may improve relevance is by enabling the indexer to do his work more effectively by suggesting the most appropriate terms to use in indexing a particular document.

BIBLIOGRAPHY

1 Cleverdon, C W, Mills, J and Keen, E M: *Factors determining the performance of indexing systems*. Cranfield, Aslib-Cranfield Research Project, 1966. 2v in 3.

2 *The concise Oxford dictionary*. OUP, 6th edition, 1976.

3 *Webster's seventh new collegiate dictionary*. Springfield, Mass, Merriam, 1971.

4 Berlo, D K: *The process of communication*. 1960. Chapter 8.

5 Willetts, M: 'An investigation of the nature of the relation between terms in thesauri.' *Journal of documentation*, 31 (3) 1975, 158-184.

6 Perry, J W and Kent, A: *Tools for machine literature searching: semantic code dictionary: equipment: procedures*. New York, Interscience Publishers Inc, 1958. 972 p.

7 American National Standards Institute: *American national standard guidelines for thesaurus structure, construction and use*. ANS Z.39.19. 1974.

8 British Standards Institution: *Guidelines for the establishment and development of monolingual thesauri for information retrieval*. (Notes for a draft standard). BSI, 1972.

9 Unesco: *Guidelines for the establishment and development of monolingual thesauri*. Paris, Unesco, 2nd revised edition, 1973.

10 Austin, D: *PRECIS: a manual of concept analysis and subject indexing*. Council of the British National Bibliography, 1974. Many of the ideas discussed in this and the next chapter arose from the development of PRECIS and the work by Cleverdon and his fellow-workers at Cranfield (ref 1 above).

11 Kochen, M and Tagliacozzo, R: 'A study of cross-referencing'. *Journal of documentation*, 24 (3) September 1968, 173-191.

12 Daily, J: *LC and Sears: their adequacy for today's library needs*. ALA Pre-conference Institute on Subject Analysis, Atlantic City, June 19–21, 1969.

13 Miller, G A: *Language and communication*. McGraw-Hill, 1951. Chapter 9.

CHAPTER 6

Assigned indexing 2: syntax

In the opening sections of the previous chapter we saw that two kinds of relationship were involved in searching: semantic, arising from the need to be able to search for alternative or substitute terms; and syntactic, arising out of the need to be able to search for the intersection of two or more classes defined by terms denoting distinct concepts. In this chapter we shall mainly be concerned with the ways in which we can carry out this process of coordination.

The first point to note is that we can approach the problem in two quite different ways. In the first, we can index documents by terms denoting all the individual concepts present, but use a physical form that permits us to coordinate terms at the moment of searching. Forms that permit us to do this include the computer and the manual methods described in Part IV, and the method is known as *post-coordinate indexing*, to emphasize the fact that coordination takes place *after* we have stored the encoded documents. In the second, the indexer coordinates the appropriate terms at the time of indexing; this method is known as *pre-coordinate indexing*, and is treated first in this book, in Part II, for historical reasons. In both cases we have to decide how we are to show syntactic relationships, or if we are to show them at all. The fact that pre-coordinate indexing involves more problems is a further reason for treating it first, since the problems of post-coordinate indexing may then be resolved relatively easily. However, we may first consider some quite general questions concerning relationships between concepts.

In figure 7, we see that all relationships between concepts may be regarded as basically dyadic; that is to say that even if we have several concepts involved in a *composite subject* such as 'the manufacture of multi-wall kraft paper sacks for the packaging of cement' (a real example taken from BTI), we may regard it as a series of *pairs* of concepts linked together. There are three ways in which we can express such a relationship. The first is simply to say that a relationship exists, without specifying what kind of relationship is involved; this is the kind of coordination we shall get from a simple computer search for the co-occurrence of two terms. The second method is to define the kind of relationship that exists between the two concepts by using a *relational operator* to link them. There are two systems of some significance using relational operators, devised respectively by J E L Farradane and J C Gardin.

COORDINATION

DYADIC RELATIONSHIP

FIGURE 7: Coordination—methods of showing dyadic relationships.

FARRADANE[1]

Farradane has based his system on a study of the development of the learning process. By studying the psychology of childhood we can begin to understand how children, and thus all human beings, learn by developing powers of discrimination in time and space; we can then establish stages of discrimination in each of these areas. In time, the first stage is 'non-time'—the co-occurrence of two ideas without reference to time; the second stage is 'temporary'—the co-occurrence from time to time, but not permanently, of two ideas; and the third is 'fixed'—the permanent co-occurrence of two ideas. In space, the stages of discrimination are: first, 'concurrent'—two concepts which it is hard to distinguish; second, 'not-distinct'—two concepts which have much in common; and third, 'distinct'—two concepts which can be completely

74

distinguished. These two sets of gradations can be used to form a matrix, the points of intersection denoting nine different kinds of relationship. Concepts may be joined by operators to give *analets*, which from the simplest form involving only two concepts can be built up, if necessary in two dimensions, to represent extremely complex composite subjects.

INCREASING ASSOCIATION $\longrightarrow$

		COGNITION (AWARENESS)	MEMORY (TEMPORARY)	EVALUATION (FIXED MEMORY)
P E R C E P T I O N	RECOGNITION (CONCURRENT)	CONCURRENCE /θ	SELF-ACTIVITY /*	ASSOCIATION /;
	CONVERGENT THINKING (NOT DISTINCT)	EQUIVALENCE /=	DIMENSIONAL (TIME, SPACE, STATE) /+	APPURTENANCE /(
	DIVERGENT THINKING (DISTINCT)	DISTINCTNESS /)	REACTION /-	FUNCTIONAL DEPENDENCE (CAUSATION) /:

(Left margin: INCREASING CLARITY OF)

FIGURE 8: Farradane's operators.

Farradane has claimed that his system gives very good results in terms of recall and relevance, and that once the basic theory underlying the system is grasped, it can be applied very easily; an average of two minutes to construct the analet once the subject of the document has been determined is suggested[2]. This claim is not borne out by other workers; in the CLW project, discussed in chapter 28, it was found that even after a fair amount of experience had been gained, the amount of time taken to index a document using this system was such as to make it highly uneconomic, while the results obtained were no better than with other systems. Willetts[3] points out that two of the relationships, concurrence and association, are ill-defined and need clarification and possibly further analysis. However, in support of the system, Neill[4] has pointed out that we should regard Farradane's system as relating to *percepts* (objects of perception) rather than *concepts* (abstractions), and that if we do this, his operators appear to correspond to fundamental ideas which are independent of any particular language, and could thus form the basis of an internationally acceptable indexing method.

Unfortunately, much of Farradane's own work has remained unpublished, but the following are some examples of analets constructed using the system:

Authors/: Books
  /θ   *ie* Books by English authors
Nationality/= English

Steel/: Plates/—Clamping
  /;   *ie* Clamping of hardened steel plates
Hardening

Engineering/; Special libraries/(Staff
                    /+
                    United States

Aerospace engineering/ Reports/—Accuisition
                        /;   /—
                        Publishing Special
                        /=   Libraries
                        Publishers
                        /=   /+
                        Government
                          Agencies/+ United States

Libraries/— Using/; Users/— Surveying/; Surveys (*ie* the activity)
Libraries/— Using/; Users/; Surveying/; Surveys (*ie* the result)

SYNTOL[5]

The Cranfield project, discussed in chapter 28, showed that all indexing languages are fundamentally similar, in that they consist basically of an index vocabulary together with means of showing semantic relationships (to help improve recall) and syntactic devices (to help improve precision). This suggested that it might be feasible to develop a 'meta-language' which would form a common ground between various other systems. This would be particularly useful in computer-based systems, which tend to use specially designed indexing languages. A contract was awarded by EURATOM in 1960 to a team headed by J C Gardin, Director of the Section on Automatic Documentation of the CNRS (the French national centre for scientific research). Certain assumptions formed the basis of the project: that there *is* an information explosion requiring new methods to solve new problems; that indexing is still a valid method of storing and retrieving information, as opposed to searching of natural language texts; that intellectual

$/\theta$	Concurrence
	1. Mental juxtaposition of two concepts.
	2. Bibliographic form.

$/\theta$ Concurrence
     1. Mental juxtaposition of two concepts.
     2. Bibliographic form.

$/;$ Association
     1. Unspecified
     2. Agent
     3. Abstract, indirect or calculated properties
     4. Part or potential process
     5. Thing/application
     6. Discipline (subject study)
     7. "Dependent on. . ."

$/*$ Self-activity
     1. Intransitive verb
     2. Dative case
     3. "Through. . ."

$/=$ Equivalence
     1. Synonyms, quasi-synonyms
     2. Use

$/+$ Dimensional
     1. Position in time and space
     2. Temporary state
     3. Temporary or variable properties

$/($ Appurtenance
     1. Whole-part
     2. Genus-species
     3. Physical or intrinsic properties

$/)$ Distinctness
     1. Awareness of a difference
     2. Substitutes or imitations

$/-$ Reaction
     1. Action of a thing or process on another thing or process

$/:$ Causation
     1. One thing caused by another
     2. Product from a raw material or process

TABLE 4: *Farradane's operators and their applications*

effort is involved in indexing; and that a computer-based system should be the objective.

The most significant feature of SYNTOL, the SYNTagmatic Organization Language developed by the team, is its explicit differentiation between *a priori* relationships, *ie* those that are known in advance of scanning any particular document, and *a posteriori* relationships, *ie* those which are found only be scanning a particular document.

We have used the term semantic to denote *a priori* relationships, *ie* those depending on definitions of terms, and syntactic to denote the *a posteriori* relationships arising out of the association of terms in particular documents. Gardin coined the terms paradigmatic and syntagmatic to denote these two kinds of relationship, but he emphasizes that the distinction he has in mind is an operational one; the relationship between two concepts may be either, depending on how we build it into the system.

Any meta-language must be simple if it is to be able to accept a wide variety of inputs. In SYNTOL, this simplification has led to a basic unit consisting of two terms plus a relationship: a 'dyadic string' in the form (R, a, b) is called a *syntagma*; in one format, there are four such relationships, which are thus even more generalized than Farradane's relational operators. The four are:

R_1 predicative, usually exemplified by an adjective plus a noun, *eg* close, classification

R_2 associative, often shown by noun plus noun, *eg* information, retrieval

R_3 consecutive, involving the concept of dependence or sequence, *eg* economic crises (due to) wars

R_4 co-ordinative, involving the idea of comparison, *eg* treatments using drugs (or) surgery

It is admitted that these relationships are ill-defined, but to offset this it is claimed that in practice the context shows exactly what significance we should read into the syntagma.

So far experimental work and use of the system has been confined to some of the social sciences, in particular physiology and psychology, sociology, and cultural anthropology. The team felt that if the problems could be solved for these fields, where terminology tends to be ill defined, it would almost certainly prove successful if the system were applied to other fields where terminology is used more precisely, *eg* the physical sciences.

For the student, perhaps the main value of the SYNTOL project is the emphasis it places on the fundamental similarity of all information retrieval systems, and its formalization of syntactical relations. If Farradane is correct, it is in this direction that most progress is to be made, and SYNTOL may be regarded as one step in this direction.

Relational operators are necessarily associated with precoordinate indexing, since they permanently link the concepts involved. Role indicators are linked to the concepts to which they refer, and can thus be used in both precoordinate or postcoordinate indexing. They are however most commonly found in precoordinate indexing, where they may be either explicit, as in PRECIS, or implicit, as in DC. But before launching into a discussion of how they may be used, we must first define what we mean by the word *role*.

In the previous chapter, we saw that it was possible to identify five broad categories of concept, and this analysis was of value in demonstrating that, apart from adjectival properties, all of the concepts were denoted by nouns. However, for most practical purposes analysis into these five categories is only helpful up to a point, and we need to identify more specific categories. We can do this at the general level, to give categories of wide application, *eg* raw material, product; or we can devise categories which fall into one of these general groups but can be given specific names because they relate to specific subject fields, *eg* crops (the *product* in the specific subject field Agriculture). By placing a concept in one of these categories, we are in effect defining its *role* in relation to concepts in other categories.

We can illustrate the point by considering some of the examples from table 1. 'Heat treatment of metals' involves an *operation* on a *patient* metals by an *agent* heat; 'heat treatment of aluminium' gives us exactly the same categories. 'Aluminium windows' involve a *product* windows made from a *raw material* aluminium: 'plastic bags' give the same categories. 'Heat treatment of non-ferrous metals', 'welding of plastic bags', 'polyethylene films', may all be analyzed in the same way to fit into categories which define their role in relation to the other concepts involved. A particular concept may not always fit into the same category, depending on its role in the subject we wish to represent; for example, in the subject 'extraction of aluminium from bauxite', aluminium is the *end product* and bauxite the *raw material*, with extraction as the *operation*.

Various systems of categories have been devised by different indexers, and these will be discussed in detail as each system is described. The point at issue here is that all of these categories represent roles, and are shown as such either explicitly, by the use of some kind of symbol, or implicitly, by their relative position. In precoordinate systems we may find either method used; for example, in the heading from BTI 'BOTTLES; polyethylene, blow moulded' the semicolon before polythylene indicates that it is a *material*, while the comma before blow moulded indicates that this is a *kind* of polyethylene, whereas in the Dewey Decimal Classification notation 823 we know from a study of the structure of this section of the scheme that 2 indicates a *language* (English) and 3 a *literary form* within the class Literature denoted by 8. In the first example the role indicators are explicit: they appear in the form of additional symbols. In the second case, the role indicators are implicit in the form of the notation. In postcoordinate systems, if role indicators are used at all, they must be explicit; for example, we may find Paint (B) in an index using the American Petroleum Institute list of terms, where (B) indicates *product*, or Penicillins—therapeutic use and Penicillins—analysis in *Index medicus*, where the roles are spelt out in the form of subheadings.

COMBINATION ORDER

Although we can, obviously, use role indicators with single concepts, we are normally concerned with composite subjects, *ie* those involving two or more concepts. In precoordinate systems we assemble these into a *string* of terms corresponding to phrases or sentences in natural language. The question must therefore arise: why do we not use phrases from natural language as they stand? Why go to all the trouble of constructing an artificial syntax as well as an artificial vocabulary? (Artificial in the sense that we control the form of words, using only nouns or adjectives, and select preferred terms where natural language gives us a free choice.) The reason lies in the flexibility of natural language; just as we may have more than one word denoting the same concept, so we may have more than one grammatical construction to express the same subject. For example, we may say 'manufacture of paper sacks' or 'paper sack manufacture'; 'the process of communication' or 'the communication process'. Clearly we may have a form of equivalence relationship arising not from the semantic associations between words but from their syntactic association. Just as we find it advantageous to control semantic equivalents, so we shall achieve consistency only if we control syntactic equivalents in the same way. What this means is that we must decide on the order in which we shall assemble the terms in a particular string, so that we retain the correct sense but eliminate alternative possibilities.

In all precoordinate systems, combination order is a major feature, though not always under that name. In classification schemes it is usually known as *citation order*, while Coates uses *significance order* to stress the principle on which he constructs his strings of terms. Whatever the name, the principle remains the same: to ensure that the same composite subject is always treated in the same way, no matter how it may be expressed in natural language.

This element of consistency is extremely important, not only from the point of view of the indexer seeking guidance on how to treat a particular subject, but also from the point of view of the user. For the indexer, it is obviously important that he should not index a document in one way if a colleague has already indexed a similar document another way; even the same indexer may well treat similar documents differently on different occasions unless he has clear rules to guide him. For the user, the effect is two-fold. In the first place, it means that once he has found out how a subject has been indexed, he will find all similar documents, which will presumably also be relevant, indexed in the same way; in the second place, it means *predictability*: the ability to foresee how documents involving other concepts, but in the same way, will be indexed. Some examples will make this clear.

One of the rules used by Coates is that when we have a *thing* defined by the *material* of which it is made, the thing precedes the material, which is introduced by the role operator;. The user finding the heading Tanks; Aluminium, and learning its meaning, will know on another occasion that the heading he wants is Bridges; Concrete. No such rules are apparent in the Library of Congress Subject Headings; what then is the geographer to make of the sequence under the word Geographical in Table 5 (Preferred terms are in bold type)?

Geographical distribution of animals and plants
Geographical distribution of fossil animals and plants
   See Paleobiogeography
Geographical distribution of plants
   See Phytogeography
Geographical location codes
Geographical models
   See Geography – mathematical models
Geographical photography
   See Photography in geography
Geographical pathology
   See Medical geography
Geographical names
   See Names, geographical

TABLE 5: *LCSH inconsistent forms of heading*

Where is he to look for the correct heading for Geographical features? Such examples are to be found time and time again in LCSH, and the psychological effect on the user must be devastating. The fact that there is usually a cross-reference to the correct heading can only lessen, not eliminate, his annoyance at not being able to guess right first time, and on the all too frequent occasions when there is no cross-reference to guide him to the 'correct' heading, what is he to do? Consistency is a key feature of a sound indexing language.

The first writer to discuss the order in which terms should appear in a heading was Cutter, who recommended the use of natural language order 'unless some word other than the first is decidedly more significant'. The consequences of this somewhat inadequate rule are discussed in chapter 7, and it has led to the organized chaos that we find in LCSH.

Kaiser (chapter 7) proposed the simple formula Concrete-Process, which is basically sound, and is still used by most modern systems, but does not go far enough. Ranganathan postulated five fundamental categories: Personality; Matter; Energy; Space; Time (cf of the five basic categories proposed by the CRG and discussed in the last chapter) and laid down the most famous (or notorious, depending on one's point of view) combination order PMEST for systematic arrangement, or EMPST for alphabetical headings. Coates (chapter 7) developed Kaiser's order further to give Thing-Part-Material-Action-Agent, while Vickery (chapter 8) has proposed Substance (Product)-Organ-Constituent-Structure-Shape-Property-Patient (Raw material)-Action-Operation-Process-Agent-Space-Time.

Fortunately, we do not have to remember all of these different answers—and the above is not a complete list—to the same problem. In analyzing a particular subject field, a combination order can often be found in the structure of the subject itself, but these generalized proposals serve to remind us of the kind of categories to look for and ways in which they may usefully be combined. We should also point out that a fixed combination order can present problems, especially in systematic arrangement, where the groupings resulting from the combination order we choose may not suit all of our users. These problems are discussed further in chapter 8. In postcoordinate indexing, where terms are combined at the moment of searching, there are no problems of combination order, but on the other hand we lose the element of meaning provided by the syntax of the string of precoordinated terms.

PROBLEMS OF PRECOORDINATION

What are the problems referred to in the previous paragraphs, and what general solutions can we find for them? As with the problems discussed so far, we can then measure the particular solutions found in various indexing languages against these criteria.

There are two fundamental problems. The first is that our choice of combination order may not suit all our readers, who may find that we have scattered on the shelves or in our catalogues the concepts that are of interest to them; the second is that, as we saw in chapter 2, any linear representation of multi-dimensional knowledge can only give us access to *one* term, the one that comes first in our combination order and therefore forms the filing element. In effect, both of these are different aspects of the same problem: the fact that any term after the first is hidden, and cannot be found directly. It should be noted that the problems are the same, whether our chosen indexing language gives us alphabetical or systematic arrangement; however, they are perhaps more acute with systematic order, since the major objective of this is to show relationships by grouping together related subjects. If our groupings do not show the relationships that are of interest to our users, they will more of a hindrance than a help: unfortunately, we have to accept the fact that we can rarely find a combination order that will give groupings of related subjects which will satisfy all of our readers, and we must normally be content to please *some* of the people all of the time.

There are two different approaches to these problems. The first is to make one *entry* (*ie* heading plus document details) and then give access to this through cross-references. The second is to enter the document under as many different headings as are thought necessary. The first method is economical, in that one cross-reference will serve no matter how many entries are involved, but the second method is more satisfactory from the reader's point of view, since it means that he is not referred from the heading he first thinks of to one filed somewhere else. It is important to distinguish between an entry and a cross-reference, since the difference can be quite significant economically. Suppose that we have one document, and we are faced with the choice of making one entry and four cross-references or five entries; either way will give us the same number of cards in the catalogue (assuming that physical form is used). But if we should add to the collection another nine documents on the same subject, the first method would give us ten entries and four cross-references (the same four, of course) while the second would give fifty entries. If we now think in terms of twenty similar subjects, the first method would give us 200 entries and eighty cross-references, but the second would give us 1,000 entries. The distinction is that an entry contains information about a document, and can therefore relate only to that one document, whereas a cross-reference links related headings and thus relates to everything filed at those headings. Both are, however, entry points into the sequence, and we have to provide an entry point under each term that the user is likely to use in his search, insofar as we can establish this in advance.

CROSS-REFERENCES
In table 1, we mentioned the subject 'Heat treatment of aluminium'; in most indexing languages this would be entered as
Aluminium: heat treatment
using the generally accepted principle that Thing (Concrete) is more

significant than Action (Process), and should therefore precede it in the combination order which determines the form of the string of terms we construct. For this particular heading, one method of constructing a cross-reference suggests itself:

Heat treatment *see also* Aluminium: Heat treatment (Related terms) Alternatively, we may make a cross-reference from the inverted heading:

Heat treatment: Aluminium *see* Aluminium: heat treatment (Equivalence) But what are we to make of the much more complex subject mentioned earlier: 'the manufacture of multi-wall kraft paper sacks for the packaging of cement'? Coates' heading for this, based on his ideas on significance order, is (using commas only, to simplify matters):

CEMENT, packaging, sacks, paper, kraft, multiwall, manufacture. Such a heading, though it denotes the subject fully and unambiguously, raises in an acute form the problems we are considering. In the first place, although we hope that our significance order will enable users to find this straight away, there is no guarantee that this will succeed every time, and we therefore must cater for the user who looks under one of the hidden words. In the second place, users who are primarily interested in paper sacks may very well wish to know of the existence of at least one document on their use in the packaging of cement.

PERMUTATION
There are various ways in which we might approach this problem. One would be to *permute* the terms in the heading, that is, to make a cross-reference to the chosen heading from every possible arrangement of the terms. To give an example in symbolic form, if we chose a heading ABCD we would make references to it from

ABDC	BCDA	CDAB	DABC
ACBD	BCAD	CDBA	DACB
ACDB	BACD	CABD	DBCA
ADBC	BADC	CADB	DBAC
ADCB	BDAC	CBDA	DCAB
	BDCA	CBAD	DCBA

Twenty three cross-references in all! The number of permutations that can be made of n things is n! (factorial n) or

$$n \times (n-1) \times (n-2) \times \ldots \times 3 \times 2 \times 1.$$

For our symbolic heading containing 4 elements, n! is 24 ($4 \times 3 \times 2 \times 1$), giving us one heading and twenty three cross-references; but the example we are looking at from BTI contains seven elements, which would give us one entry and no less than 5,039 cross-references! This is obviously impractical, so we are faced with the problem of selecting which of these entries and cross-references we are to make.

84

A moment's thought should show that if there are n significant elements in a given heading, then $(n-1)$ of them will be 'hidden' and ought to form additional entry points. Obviously, we must then make at least $(n-1)$ cross-references, for if we make fewer than this we must be overlooking one of the hidden elements. We have already seen that if we permute we have to make $(n!-1)$ if we wish to cover every possible variation, so there will be a wide margin between the minimum and the maximum as n increases; but when $n = 2$, $(n-1)$ and $(n!-1)$ are both the same: 1. The problem of having to find an economic means of selecting which cross-references to make only becomes acute when we use composite headings with more than two elements.

CHAIN PROCEDURE

Ranganathan has suggested a method whereby we can make the minimum number of cross-references, yet still be sure that readers will find an entry point under every significant term in a composite heading. We begin by writing down the 'chain' of terms:

CEMENT, packaging, sacks, paper, kraft, multiwall, manufacture.

We now write down the last term in the chain, following it by each of the preceding terms in turn; this forms the entry point under that word, and refers us to the full heading in its preferred order:

MANUFACTURE, multiwall, kraft, paper, sacks, packaging, cement
   see
CEMENT, packaging, sacks, paper, kraft, multiwall, manufacture.

We have now covered the approach through this word, and can move on to the next-to-last, following exactly the same procedure for this:

MULTIWALL, kraft, paper, sacks, packaging, cement
   see
CEMENT, packaging, sacks, paper, kraft, multiwall.

We follow this procedure through until we have made the necessary $(n-1)$ cross-references, in this case six:

KRAFT, paper, sacks, packaging, cement
   see
CEMENT, packaging, sacks, paper, kraft
PAPER, sacks, packaging, cement
   see
CEMENT, packaging, sacks, paper
SACKS, packaging, cement
   see
CEMENT, packaging, sacks
PACKAGING, cement
   see
CEMENT, packaging.

Every hidden term now forms an entry point which will lead us to the correct part of the catalogue, *ie* the preferred heading. Note also that if we next have to deal with a document on Plastic sacks for the packaging of cement, we shall make an entry for this

CEMENT, packaging, sacks, plastic

but we shall only need *one* more cross-reference because the network we built up for the similar subject earlier will serve for the rest:

PLASTICS, sacks, packaging, cement

   see

CEMENT, packaging, sacks, plastic.

This method of compiling a network of cross-references is called *chain procedure;* we make a cross-reference from each link in the chain. It is a very economical method; we can in effect make fewer than the minimum number (n−1) of cross-references because some will serve for more than one heading. To set against this is the disadvantage that only the first is specific; the others do not lead us to the full heading we have used.

The point is shown by the sample references already worked out; for example, the word SACKS does not lead us to the specific subject

CEMENT, packaging, sacks, paper, kraft, multiwall, manufacture

but to the much broader heading

CEMENT, packaging, sacks.

We have seen that the entry vocabulary to a classification scheme is in effect a series of equivalence relationships, so it is not surprising to find that chain procedure can be used for this purpose, and has in fact been used ever since Dewey introduced his 'relative index' in 1876. The following example, taken from BNB (1970) shows how the method works in this situation. The subject involved is 'the electrical conductivity of metal films' and in DDC it falls into the discipline Physics, giving a class number (from the *code vocabulary*) 537.62(1); in words, this represents the string of terms:

Physics: Electricity: Conductivity: Metals: Films

(NB: The DDC is not specific enough to denote this subject fully, so the last two terms are not represented in its code vocabulary; BNB uses (1) to indicate an extension beyond the 'official' notation.) Using chain procedure, we can very easily generate the set of index entries:

Films: metals: conductivity: electricity: physics	537.62(1)
Metals: conductivity: electricity: physics	537.62(1)
Conductivity: electricity: physics	537.62
Electricity: physics	537
Physics	530

Again we find that only the first entry leads us to the specific subject, and the others may in fact lead us to 'vacant' headings, *ie* headings under which no entries are filed. In both alphabetical and classified files it *should* be possible to get from such a heading to the one we want without much difficulty, but the reader who does not understand the mechanics of the system may find it less than helpful.

86

Chain procedure is straightforward, and can be successfully computerized, even in a modified form, as Coates has shown (chapter 7). It also maintains the relationships between terms in the string being processed, but at the expense of steadily decreasing specificity. Permutation retains specificity, in that all the terms remain in each entry, but at the expense of the syntactic relationships between the terms in the string. For instance, using the above example, permutation would give us headings:

Conductivity: films: metals: electricity: physics
Conductivity: electricity: films: metals: physics

In the first of these we lose the link between Electricity and Conductivity, while in the second we lose the link between Electricity and Physics, and gain a false link between Physics and Metals. These are only two out of a possible 119 permutations (120 if we include the original string), and many of the others will be even less helpful. Are there any methods which enable us to select a limited number of these permutations, particularly those which retain at least most of the syntactic relationships?

CYCLING

One method of keeping the number of possible forms down and preserving most of the syntactic structure is to treat the string of terms as a sort of endless belt, *cycling* them to bring each to the front in turn. (cf a bicycle chain). The entries for the previous example would then be:

Physics: electricity: conductivity: metals: films (main string)
Electricity: conductivity: metals: films: physics ⎫
Conductivity: metals: films: physics: electricity ⎬ cycled
Metals: films: physics: electricity: conductivity ⎪ headings
Films: physics: electricity: conductivity: metals ⎭

Each term forms an access point, but the sense of the whole string is somewhat clouded. A further problem arises if we add a document on the conductivity of metals, since this will give the following headings:

Physics: electricity: conductivity: metals (main string)
Electricity: conductivity: metals: physics ⎫
Conductivity: metals: physics: electricity ⎬ cycled
Metals: physics: electricity: conductivity ⎭ headings

It will be seen that the heading beginning 'Metals' will *not* file alongside the heading for the previous example, which represents a very similar subject; this means that there will be no kind of grouping at the term metals, and we shall have to scan all of the entries at that term to find out whether any of them deal with similar subjects. If this is true for one of the terms in the heading, it must clearly be true for all of them, and we have thus lost the grouping effect which is one of the major advantages of precoordination in ordered strings.

Cycling is widely used with UDC, and an example of its use is worked out in chapter 18. The fact that each element in the string forms an entry point does have an economic advantage, in that any semantic relationships need only be made to the single elements, and we do not need the cross-reference network arising out of the syntactic structure. In indexing a classified arrangement, this can save some work. To illustrate this symbolically, let us take a composite subject represented by the five notational symbols ABCDE, representing the five terms abcde. Chain procedure would give a single preferred class number with five cross-references—index entries in the entry vocabulary:

edcba	[see] ABCDE
dcba	[see] ABCD
cba	[see] ABC
ba	[see] AB
a	[see] A

Cycling involves five entries, and also five index entries, but this time the index entries are for the individual elements only, not for any composite subjects:

entries	index entries
ABCDE	a [see] A
BCDEA	b [see] B
CDEAB	c [see] C
DEABC	d [see] D
EABCD	e [see] E

This means that no matter what composite subjects may occur in the future, it will not be necessary to make any further index entries for these elements; using one-place entry and chain procedure, new composite subjects may involve extra chain index entries.

ROTATING

We saw that to construct a KWIC index, each significant element of the title had to be made the filing word in turn. If we consider our subject specification as a 'title' consisting of several elements, it becomes clear that we can construct the same kind of index, using these preferred terms instead of the words of the title. This method is known as *rotating*; in this, the combination order is retained, but entries are made under each element:

filing element
↓

*A*BCDE
A*B*CDE
AB*C*DE
ABC*D*E
ABCD*E*

Here the filing element is in each case the one in the same position as A in the first, but the relative position of each element with respect to the others remains unchanged. The method has been demonstrated with the London education classification by D J Foskett[6] It gives the same advantage as cycling, but without the problem of scattering: thus recall is as good but relevance is likely to be much higher. Both cycling and rotating may be used with alphabetical systems, but with the exception of KWIC indexes they are more commonly associated with classified files. It is important not to confuse these methods with permuting, an error into which a number of writers have fallen in the past. Permutation, as has been stressed, will normally involve an unacceptable number of entries, whereas cycling or rotating, though it will increase the number of entries we make, will not do so intolerably. We find, for example, that several thesauri contain what is referred to as a permuted index when in fact it is a rotated index of the KWIC type.

SHUNTING

All of the methods we have looked at so far have—with the exception of Farradane's relational indexing—been essentially *linear*: that is, they assume that any string of terms we devise will remain in a one-dimensional or single-line format. Even if the string is long enough to spill over on to a second line, which can happen with some very complex subjects, we still expect to read the string in the normal way, starting at the beginning and going on to the end. Austin saw that this restriction was the cause of the loss of syntactic relationships in such methods as cycling and, prompted by Farradane's venture into two-dimensional representations, he suggested a method of getting the best of both worlds: retaining the syntactical relationships, yet retaining the whole of the string while making separate entries for each significant word. This involves the use of a two-line structure: the first line contains the *lead* term (*ie* the access term) and the *qualifier*, while the second line contains the rest of the string in the *display*. Figure 9 shows this diagrammatically: we start with a string of terms A-B-C-D, with A in the lead position and B-C-D in the display. As B moves into the lead position, so A moves into the qualifier position, leaving C-D in the display. We thus retain the link between B and A which is lost by chain procedure and cycling. The method is used in PRECIS, and is further discussed with examples in chapter 14, but there is no reason why it should not be used with other systems, *eg* that of Coates.

MULTIPLE ENTRY

We have so far carried on the discussion on the basis that we would make one entry (*ie* heading *plus* document description) with cross-references to lead to that preferred heading from other forms. The economics of this have been briefly discussed, and it might be to the point to mention that most printed bibliographical tools, particularly those giving any considerable amount of document description, such as ab-

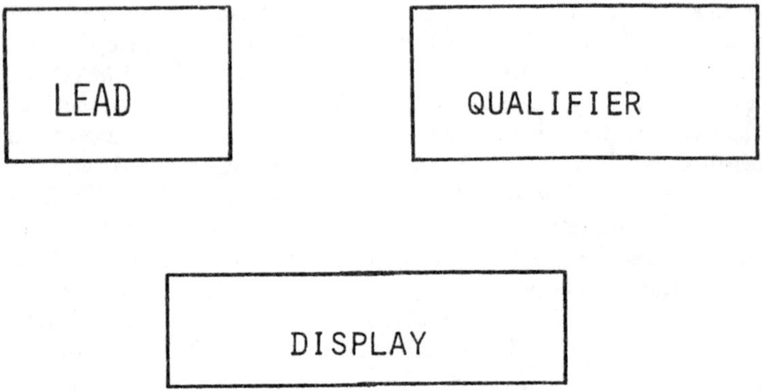

```
┌─────────────┐          ┌─────────────────┐
│             │          │                 │
│    LEAD     │          │   QUALIFIER     │
│             │          │                 │
└─────────────┘          └─────────────────┘
```

```
        ┌───────────────────────┐
        │                       │
        │       DISPLAY         │
        │                       │
        └───────────────────────┘
```

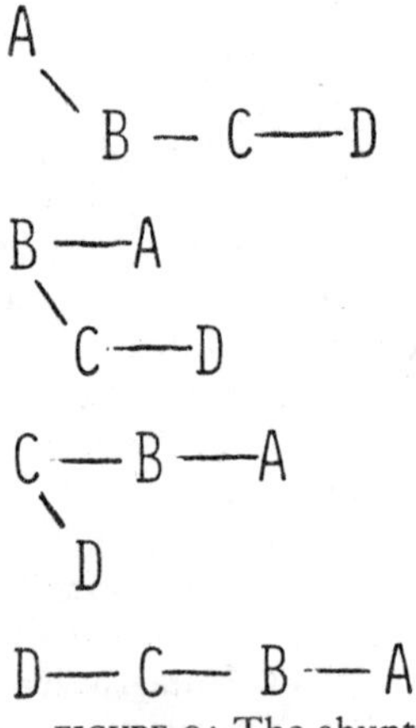

```
A
 \
  B ─ C──D

B──A
  \
   C──D

C ─ B──A
  \
   D

D── C── B ── A
```

FIGURE 9: The shunting technique devised by Austin.

stracting journals and national bibliographies, are of this kind. We have a single sequence of entries, which may be classified (*eg* BNB, ANB) or under broad alphabetical headings (*eg* CA) or in some other order (*eg* the chronological subarrangement in NSA): this is supported by indexes of various kinds leading users to the required single entry. However, with those methods of constructing variations on the entire string, *eg* cycling, rotating, shunting—but *not* chain procedure, there is nothing except economic considerations to prevent us from making

90

an entry at each access point: cycling, as we have already mentioned, is widely used with UDC, with unit catalogue cards all bearing the same information filed at each appropriate point. Unfortunately, the term 'multiple entry' is also used in a rather different sense in LCSH subject heading practice; this is discussed in chapter 7. We are here referring to the use of the whole subject description, as specified in a controlled string of terms from an indexing language, as the basis of the headings for a number of entries, as opposed to the use of one main entry supported by cross-references or indexes.

One final point that is worth stressing is that all of the methods described in this section, whether to obtain single or multiple entry, are essentially clerical, and can therefore be done by computer. Provided that the original string of terms is a meaningful one showing correct syntactical relationships, the results obtained will be satisfactory, as such examples as BNB and BTI show.

PHASE RELATIONSHIPS

So far, we have made the assumption that it is possible to construct a string of terms, using syntactic relationships either implicitly, or explicitly in the form of role indicators or relational operators, to produce a consistent representation of any given composite or simple subject (*ie* involving several concepts or just one), and then manipulate this string according to various straightforward methods to enable users to approach them not merely through the term denoting what we consider to be the most important concept, but through any of the other terms as well. Even when we have not explicitly indicated the role, or category, into which a particular term falls, we have again made an assumption that this would be evident from the context, and the examples that we have given so far do in fact justify these assumptions.

If we consider table 6, however, we can see that the kind of relationship demonstrated is one that we have not yet made provision for. We may use Ranganathan's term *phase relationships* to denote these, though the four kinds identified here do not entirely coincide with those in CC.[7] In the first group we see a subject treated with a particular audience in mind; it remains the same subject, but we will find that the examples used for discussion will come from the subject interest of the intended audience. Thus *multi-variate statistical analysis for biologists* is a book about a branch of statistics, using examples from biology; the essential point is that this work might well be of use to a nuclear physicist, (failing a work on multi-variate statistical analysis for nuclear physicists) but it is unlikely to be of any use to a taxonomic botanist. In these examples of *bias phase*, the subject is the subject treated, not the audience for whom it is intended.

In the second group, we see one subject influenced by another; in examples of *influence phase*, it is the subject influenced that is the core.

In the third, *exposition phase*, it is the subject expounded, not the 'tool' subject, which is the important one. The fourth group, showing *comparison*, presents a rather different problem; here we have no indication which is the primary phase, because both phases are equal.

A	1	The elements of astronomy for surveyors
	2	Fluid mechanics for civil engineers
	3	Multivariate statistical analysis for biologists
B	4	Classical influences in Renaissance literature
	5	The literary impact of the Authorized Version (*ie* its influence on English literature)
	6	The effect of PAS on the resistance to streptomycin of tubercle bacilli
C	7	A psychological study of Hamlet
	8	Literature through art: a new approach to French literature
	9	Typewriter behaviour: psychology applied to teaching and learning typewriting
D	10	Science and politics
	11	Church and state
	12	Religion and science

TABLE 6: *Phase relationships*

When we come to try to write strings to represent phase relationships, we find that we are obliged to make them explicit by using terms to denote the kind of relationship involved. For example, the heading

Aluminium: heat treatment

is of a kind which does not use prepositions, yet few users could misunderstand it. Even the much more complex heading

Cement, packaging, sacks, paper, kraft, multiwall, manufacture

takes very little effort to decipher, even if the user has not learnt the trick of reading the heading from back to front and mentally inserting the necessary prepositions to turn it into a natural language phrase. But if we omit the subsidiary words, the headings

Fluid mechanics: civil engineers

Anatomy: nurses (instead of anatomy *for* nurses)

Science: politics

French literature: art (instead of French literature: exposition though art either become meaningless or ambiguous. Furthermore, if we try to manipulate the headings by cycling, we may find ourselves with results that are again either ambiguous or incorrect. For example:

Female anatomy *for* nurses might become

Anatomy *for* nurses, female which suggests a different subject.

The Bible: *influence on* English literature might become

English literature: The Bible: *influence on* which is ambiguous. Phase relationships may be recognized by this characteristic: the need to make the kind of relationship explicit—in an alphabetical system by the use of words denoting ideas such as *influence, effect, audience* (for . . .), *tool* (psychology used as a tool to study Hamlet), *interaction* (and . . .), in a classified system by the use of notation. There is a further point about phase relationships which it is essential to grasp. They are necessarily *ad hoc* relationships: though we can tell in advance that books will be written in which one subject is treated in comparison with another, or to show how it has been influenced by another, or with a particular audience in mind, we cannot know which subjects will be so treated. Indeed, phase relationships are becoming more and more common now; bias phase may be the first indication of the growth of a new interdisciplinary subject, as may comparison, while influence and exposition clearly also may lead in this direction. Phase relationships cannot be foreseen; all that we can do in our system is to make adequate provision for them by recognizing the possibility of their occurrence.

In the first three kinds listed in table 6, we can identify one of the two separate concepts involved as the key concept. In bias phase, where a subject is treated for a particular audience, it is the subject treated which is the primary phase; in influence phase, it is the subject influenced; in exposition, it is the subject expounded. In these three cases, as we have seen, it is possible to construct a string of terms which will represent the subject unambiguously, and by providing for changes of prepositions or other words we can maintain the sense while providing the necessary cross-references. For example:

The Bible: *influence on* English literature   can become

English literature: *influenced by* The Bible

Hamlet: *expounded by* Psychology   can become

Psychology: *expounding* Hamlet

However, the only way to deal with the interaction relationship (which could be regarded as a two-way influence) is by treating both phases as being of equal importance:

Science *and* Politics

Politics *and* Science

The word 'and' can often be misleading. For example, if we have a volume entitled *Heat, light and sound*, we can be reasonably confident that this represents an economy move by the publisher by binding three separate works in one pair of covers: it is a physical, not an intellectual, association. Phase relationships are only concerned with intellectual associations. If we have a book on *The mining of silver and lead*, we have in fact *two* separate subjects, and should treat them as such: the 'mining of silver' and 'the mining of lead'. We must be sure that we are not misled by the title of a book into thinking that it deals with an interaction phase relationship in such cases, just because it contains the word 'and'. There are other situations where we must be cautious; for example, it is essential that we distinguish *science and politics*, ie the interaction between two normally distinct topics, and the *science of politics*, ie politics as a discipline. In the first case, we are studying the effect that political decisions may have on science (in determining, for example, which projects are to receive government funds, which may alter the whole direction of scientific progress) and conversely, the effect that scientific advances may have on politics (for example, by making it possible for politicians to reach an enormous audience, which may alter the whole direction of political progress). In the second case, we are studying the structure and mechanics of politics: how decisions are reached and implemented. Where two subjects are permanently related, *eg* when one forms an aspect of the other as does science of politics in the second case above, this should not be considered as a phase relationship.

In concluding this lengthy discussion of syntactic relationships, perhaps it is worth offering a word of warning. Syntax and semantics go together, and should be regarded as two different aspects of the same thing. A sentence may fill every requirement of syntax and be meaningless: Austin[8] cites Chomsky's example 'Colourless green ideas sleep furiously'. Equally, the same words with different syntax will have totally different meanings: a 'guide dog for the blind' is not the same as a 'blind guide dog'.

PARTITIONING AND INTERLINKING

As we saw in the previous section, a document may deal with more than one subject, and we should separate these subjects and treat them as separate *themes*. If we are indexing a document exhaustively, we may in fact have to deal with several themes, but in a general library it is usual to treat documents as units and make one entry covering the subject of the document as a whole. This process of division into themes is known as *partitioning*, and it is usually associated with the complementary process of *interlinking*; this involves linking the elements of each theme together so that they do not get confused. For example, if we have a document on 'the construction of houses using concrete walls and wood floors', we would not wish to retrieve this in answer to an enquiry for information about concrete floors. In precoordinate systems, this interlinking is done at the indexing stage, but in postcoordinate methods there is no built-in linking of this kind, and we have to use link indicators as well as role indicators if we want to show themes as units.

THE PURPOSE OF SYNTACTIC RELATIONSHIPS

We saw that the purpose of semantic relationships was to enable us to improve the recall performance of our system. By contrast, the purpose of syntactic relationships is to enable us to improve the relevance performance, by enabling us to specify subjects more precisely. We can do this through semantic relationships to some extent, by realizing that there is a more specific term than the one we first thought of, but the most powerful method of increasing specificity is by coordination. In fact, the specificity of an indexing language has to be measured not only in terms of its vocabulary, but also by the amount of coordination it permits; there are some parts of UDC which contain fewer terms than the corresponding schedules in DC, yet UDC is more specific because it permits a much greater use of coordination.

CLOSED AND OPEN SYSTEMS

If we are to be consistent in the use of an indexing language, we must record somewhere any decisions we take, for example on the choice of preferred synonyms or significance order. The record thus compiled becomes our *authority file*, and it may be our own entirely or it may be based to a greater or lesser degree on a published list. In the interests of standardization, it is usual for libraries to make use of published lists, and indeed Part III and Part V of the present work are given over to descriptions of such schemes. However, they may present a problem summed up in Ranganathan's phrase: *autonomy for the classifier*.

Knowledge, as we have stressed, is not static, and an indexing language needs continuous revision if it is to remain current. Furthermore, since general schemes may not relate to the literary warrant of any particular library, they may exclude some subjects which we find represented in our collections. What are we to do if we find that this is the case? Can we insert a new heading in the authority list ourselves, or must we wait until the compilers have produced a new edition or an amendment sheet? If the first of these is the case, the system is said to be *open*, while the second situation is a *closed* system. Dewey saw the problem at an early stage, and suggested that if a particular topic was not represented we should classify a document at the nearest inclusive heading, on the theory that new subjects usually grow from the splitting up, or 'fission', of already existing subjects. The central compilers would then make a specific place in a subsequent edition for the new topic, an optimistic hope which has not always been borne out by practice.

Since alphabetical order is self-evident, it is rather easier to insert a new heading in an alphabetical list than in one systematically arranged; all that we need to know is the form of a heading, *eg* whether we should use the singular or plural form of a noun. Alphabetical lists such as Sears and LCSH have rules for the insertion of headings for named individuals of a species, *eg* persons, flowers, places, animals. It is rather more difficult to establish in advance the correct piece of notation for a new topic in a classification scheme, since we are dealing with a wholly artificial language, and no satisfactory solution has been proposed. Ranganathan's *seminal mnemonics*, discussed on p 334 offer a temporary solution, but one in which the arrangement is dictated by the notation rather than the needs of the subject. It is for this reason that the method of revision adopted by a classification scheme is so important, and this point is discussed in relation to each of the schemes studied in Part III.

ENUMERATION AND SYNTHESIS
In a precoordinate indexing language we have to provide for both single concepts and composite subjects, and the problem of a closed system becomes that much more acute. Older systems set out to list, or *enumerate*, all the subjects which seemed appropriate, both single concepts and composite, leaving the individual classifier no autonomy to insert new subjects which might be found in his collection.

More recent systems have tended to be of the *synthetic* kind. These list only single concepts, but give the indexer rules for the construction of headings for composite subjects. The method is obviously a great deal more powerful than the purely enumerative, but does depend on the individual concepts being listed, or there being rules for construction of headings for them. A synthetic language is thus a great deal more open than an enumerative one, but may still not give the indexer complete autonomy if he is relying on a published list. It is for this reason that many special libraries have constructed their own indexing language; they have avoided being tied to a possibly out of date published list.

As we have pointed out, phase relationships are essentially *ad hoc*: it is therefore very difficult to deal with them in an enumerative scheme. Only those relationships which have already arisen can be enumerated; thus in DC we find 'Religion and science', because that was the subject of a number of books by the time Dewey compiled his classification in 1876, arising out of the publication, among other significant works, of Darwin's *Origin of species* in 1859—but we shall look in vain for 'Politics and science'. A synthetic scheme can make provision for phase relationships much more easily.

There is of course no hard and fast line between the two types of system; we may expect to find a complete range between the closed enumerative system where the indexer has no freedom at all, and the

96

open synthetic system which permits the indexer to specify any subject he wishes. Most systems fall somewhere between the two extremes, and it should perhaps be mentioned that although one of the advantages often claimed for post-coordinate systems is that they are much freer than pre-coordinate systems, this is not necessarily the case; a language such as that used in BTI can be almost unrestricted, while the ERIC *Thesaurus* [9] offered its users a very limited vocabulary indeed.

It is perhaps significant that the systems giving the extreme of complete freedom of input (the computer systems using natural language text mentioned in chapter 4) do require greater effort at the output stage than do those systems which have imposed a measure of organization at the input stage. On the other hand it may be argued that the greater the degree of organization we impose on our collection of information, the less likely we are to achieve that felicitous concatenation of hitherto unrelated subjects known as *serendipity*. Since many of the most important advances in science have been the result of serendipity rather than deliberate effort, we may perhaps be cautious of a system which excludes it altogether. However, it is doubtful whether we can in fact consider this factor in a system intended for the *organization* of knowledge—though subject analysis may itself reveal hitherto unsuspected relationships!

CRITICAL CLASSIFICATION

The indexer is serving as intermediary between authors and users; to what extent is he justified in interposing his own ideas and prejudices? The immediate answer is, not at all, but in practice this is found to be the case very rarely. An indexing language inevitably reflects to some extent the social and cultural background of its compiler, and while it serves users of a similar persuasion this is not necessarily a bad thing; it is when we try to impose one culture on users of another that problems are likely to arise, in a variety of ways. We may find examples of chauvinism:

   Women's periodicals, American *See* Women's periodicals (LCSH)
   Africa—discovery and exploration (Sears) [*ie* by Europeans]
   World War II: Germany's Conquest of Europe, Rescue by the United States (BC)
or genuine differences of approach:
   compare the schedules for *government* in, say, LC and CC
   or *education* in UDC (European continent) and DC (US)
or intellectual arrogance:
   821.9 Minor poets [*eg* John Donne!] (early editions of DC)
or euphemism:
   Vulgar fractions *use* Common fractions (ERIC Thesaurus)
   Voluntarily idle *use* Labor force non-participants (ERIC Thesaurus).
Whatever the reason, *critical classification*—the imposition of the

indexer's viewpoint on the user—is found rather more widely than we would like to admit. Even such schemes as UDC, which has a definite international policy, are not entirely free from bias. The indexer should be careful not to introduce bias needlessly, and the user has to be made aware of its possible existence, if our systems are to achieve their objective of making information available freely.[10]

RECAPITULATION

INDEXING LANGUAGES

A system for naming subjects in the way we have described is called an *indexing language*, and, like any other language, it will consist of two parts: *vocabulary* and *syntax*. If we use terms as they appear in documents without modification, we are using *natural language*. However, as has been seen, this can lead to many problems, such as those arising from the use by different authors of different words to denote the same idea—synonyms—which lead to a decrease in recall. Another problem is that we can often express the same idea in more than one way using the same or similar words but altering the kind of phrase: child psychology or psychology of children; adult education or education of adults. For these reasons, nearly all systems introduce a measure of control over the terms used; that is to say, we use a *controlled vocabulary*. We often find also that the flexible syntax of natural language is formalized to permit only certain constructions; instead of heat treatment of aluminium we use aluminium, heat treatment; instead of children's libraries and libraries for children we use libraries, children's. We are then using a *structured* language. A controlled vocabulary is part of an *artificial* indexing language, as is a formalized structure. The extreme example of an artificial language is the notation of a classification scheme; instead of the natural language terms heat treatment of aluminium, or the more formalized aluminium, heat treatment, we use 669.71.04.

The use of an artificial language enables us to use *concept indexing* rather than *term indexing*. In term indexing, we rely on the words used by each author to give us the subject descriptions we require, and hope that when we are trying to find information we can match the different terms used by different authors. In concept indexing, we try to establish a standard description for each concept and use that description each time it is appropriate, whether it has been used by the author himself or not. When we are searching our files, we again use the standardized descriptions, and should be able to match these much more consistently and reliably. Natural language is very flexible, particularly in a highly developed language such as English; this is a tremendous advantage for the author, who can vary his terminology to maintain the reader's interest, but is a handicap to the indexer, who is more concerned with the ideas conveyed than with the niceties of a graceful literary style.

If we use words for our subject descriptions, then the only way in which we can arrange them is alphabetically; if we try to arrange them any other way we shall not be able to find them when we want them, except by sequential scanning. But there are many occasions when an alphabetical order may not be particularly helpful to us; for example, if we want to follow the progress of a railway train, an alphabetical list of stops and the time the train arrives at each will be much less use than a list in chronological order. An artificial language such as the notation of a classification scheme can permit us to arrange concepts in any order we wish; in particular, it permits us to group similar concepts together to show a relationship between them. We can show that metals, ferrous metals, iron, aluminium, non-ferrous metals and similar terms denote concepts which are closely related, by actually bringing them together in our arrangement.

It is possible to take concept indexing a stage further than the simple standardization of subject descriptions. We can identify the same basic concept wherever it occurs, even though it may not have any common factor in the terms used for it. We might connect stream, current, flux, flow and evolution as being manifestations of motion; expurgation, disinfection, refining, Bowdlerization and whitewashing as being manifestations of cleaning. A list of terms showing their classification according to the ideas they represent is called a *thesaurus*, and the two examples quoted are taken from perhaps the most famous example, Roget's *Thesaurus of English words and phrases*. Such a list can only be compiled by concept indexing, and can form the first stage of development of a completely artificial indexing language. It should be noted that the term thesaurus has been somewhat abused by compilers of subject headings lists for post-coordinate indexing (*cf* p 386); the closest approach to a thesaurus in Roget's sense in a faceted classification scheme with its index rather than an alphabetical system.

PRE-COORDINATE AND POST-COORDINATE SYSTEMS

We have to be able to index both single concepts and composite subjects using our indexing language, but there are two ways of approaching this. The first is to treat composite subjects as units. To do this, we first analyse them into the single concepts, then select the 'correct' term from the vocabulary (this may be a piece of notation, or a preferred synonym) for each concept, and finally arrange these in a particular order dictated by the structure of the language. The resulting heading represents the subject as a whole, and we file an entry under it in the system with descriptions of any documents to which it applies. When we are searching, we formulate headings in the same way, and use these as a basis for matching what we can find in the system. However, this can lead to difficulties, particularly when the headings we use as a basis for searching differ slightly from those used already in the system; these difficulties arise from the structure that we have imposed, and are discussed later under the heading CITATION ORDER (p 132).

One solution is to abandon the use of structure altogether, and this is the second way of approaching composite subjects. The process of analysis is the same, and the selection of the correct term is the same, but we no longer combine these terms in a pre-determined order; instead, we file descriptions of the appropriate documents under each single concept. In searching, we have to have some method of combining concepts, or *coordinating* them, so that we can perform the required matching operation, and this second method is often known as *coordinate* indexing. It is however more useful to call it *post-coordinate*, to contrast it with the first method which we may call *pre-coordinate*. This emphasizes the fact that coordination takes place in both systems, but at a different stage of the proceedings. As a reflection of the history of the subject, pre-coordinate systems are dealt with first in this book, and the discussion of the problems which arise in their use leads logically to the section on post coordinate systems.

CONCLUSION

We have seen that there are various kinds of indexing language: pre-coordinate and post-coordinate, closed and open, enumerative and synthetic, with syntax and without, biased and highly biased. This variety should not blind us to the fact that the collection of documents we are indexing does not change if we change the method of indexing, nor do the demands made on it by the users. No matter what system we use, it must measure up to the same criteria.

BIBLIOGRAPHY

1 Farradane, J E L: 'Fundamental fallacies and new needs in library classification'. (Chapter 9 in the *Sayers memorial volume*.)

Farradane, J E L: 'Analysis and organization of knowledge for retreval'. *Aslib proceedings, 22*, (12) 1970, 607–616.

Farradane, J E L *and others: Report on research into information retrieval by relational indexing*. Part 1: methodology. London, City University, 1966. Though not as widely available as the other two references, this is probably the most detailed statement of the way in which Farradane intends his operators to be used.

2 Farradane, J E L: *Private communication*, based on work done at City University.

3 Willetts, M: 'Investigation of the nature of the relation between terms in thesauri'. *Journal of documentation, 31* (3) 1975, 158–184.

4 Neill, S D: 'Farradane's relations as perceptual discriminations'. *Journal of documentation, 31,* (3) 1975, 144–157.

5 Gardin, J C: *SYNTOL.* Rutgers, The State University School of Library Science, 1965. 106p. (Rutgers series on systems for the intellectual organization of information, ed Susan Artandi, Vol 4.)

6 Foskett, D J: 'Two notes on indexing techniques.' *Journal of documentation, 18* (4) December 1962, 188–192.

7 The phase relationships identified here are those used by BNB.

8 Chomsky, N, quoted by D Austin in the PRECIS Manual (chapter 16).

9 US Educational Resources Information Center: *Thesaurus of ERIC descriptors.* USGPO, 1967. The first edition has been superseded by regular new editions, which have introduced considerable improvements. The latest is described in Part V.

10 Foskett, A C: 'Misogynists all: a study in critical classification'. *Library resources and technical services,* 15 (4) 1971, 117–121.

Berman, S: *Prejudices and antipathies.* Metuchen, NJ, Scarecrow, 1971. This work is a savage attack on LCSH, arising out of the author's experiences in working as a cataloguer in African university libraries.

CHAPTER 7

Alphabetical subject headings: Cutter to Lynch

CUTTER: The first attempt to establish a generalized set of rules for alphabetical subject headings was Charles Ammi Cutter's *Rules for a dictionary catalogue*, published in 1876[1] (the year which also saw the first edition of Dewey's *Decimal classification*: truly an *annus mirabilis!*). Cutter laid down several rules which went some way towards solving the problems, but was handicapped by his acceptance of natural language as the only possible kind of terminology. For Cutter, subject names existed only insofar as they were generally accepted used by educated people. This reliance on what H E Bliss was later to name the 'scientific and educational consensus' meant that a new subject could not be named specifically until it was, in effect, no longer new. Accepted names were to be used very much as they stood; consistency was secondary to familiarity. However, when we come to look at Cutter's own examples, we find that there is room for doubt about what is meant by 'generally accepted'. For example, the heading

Circulation of the blood

is acceptable, but the very similar

Movement of fluids in plants

is not. Some odd phrases *may* be used 'if the name is accepted or likely to be accepted by usage', *eg*

Capture of property at sea

but the much more probable

Gothic architecture in Spain

is not. Evidently the cataloguer was expected to use a considerable measure of judgement as to what constituted accepted usage. This leads us to a consideration of another important rule introduced by Cutter. This was the idea of 'specific' entry: a subject was to be entered under its name, not that of an inclusive class. If we consider this carefully, we realize that what Cutter was referring to was *direct* entry, rather than specific. 'Cats' is the heading to be used, not 'Domestic animals—cats' or some similar *indirect* entry, ie entry under one or a series of containing classes.

We have used the word specific in this text in the sense of making a heading co-extensive with the subject it is intended to represent; Cutter, with his reliance on accepted names, recommends that when there is no name for the subject being dealt with, two or more entries should be made which together cover the subject. Thus 'Gothic architecture in Spain' must be entered under 'Gothic architecture' and 'Spain: *architecture*'. In effect, to find the documents having the specific subject we want we have to find the intersection of two or more classes; now we have seen that the act of coordinating at the time of searching is the characteristic of postcoordinate systems, which use physical forms which permit this. Cutter was thinking of the card catalogue or printed book form, which do *not* lend themselves to this approach. Yet Cutter's idea of double entry, or if necessary multiple entry, is still very widely accepted in order to retain as far as possible 'names in common usage' as headings, and avoid the use of complex but specific headings of the kind described in this book. For example, we are told that 'a phrase Mathematics in secondary schools . . . would need to be reduced . . . to the two code terms Mathematics and Secondary schools, *both of which are specific*' (italics added).[2] If we accept the meaning of the term *specific* used in this book, it is the coordination of the two terms which gives the specific subject in this instance; neither is specific on its own.

The question of where we draw the line also arises; 'Secondary schools' is acceptable, although it is actually a composite subject involving *institution* and *level*, so why not 'Secondary school mathematics', a composite subject involving *institution*, *level* and *curriculum subject*? It could be argued strongly that this is a 'name in common usage' to at least the same extent as some of the headings in LCSH, which follows Cutter's principles, *eg* 'Father-separated children' or the classic 'One-leg resting position', or 'Freight-cars on truck trailers'.

Cutter's acceptance of natural language names as the only source of headings brought him face to face with another problem that we have examined in chapter 6: the order of terms in a heading involving more than one word. Cutter saw that a strict adherence to natural language order would often lead to headings in which the first word would not be the most significant. His solution to the problem of significance order had the sublimity of innocence: put the more significant term first. Only if the second term in a heading was definitely more significant than the first was natural language order to be abandoned; a useful rule, but one which still leaves the definition of 'significant' to the individual indexer; this is almost an open invitation to inconsistency, and it has had the kind of consequence that we saw in the example from LCSH under the term 'geographical . . .'.

In some situations Cutter does give more definite rulings, as for instance when there is a clash between subject and place. Here we are instructed to enter under subject, qualified by place, in scientific and similar areas, but under place, qualified by subject, in areas such as history, government and commerce where the country might reasonably be taken to be the main focus of interest. For the humanities—literature, art—we are recommended to use the adjectival form of the country or language as the entry word: English drama, French painting.

To link related subjects, Cutter recommended a network of references giving a *syndetic* catalogue. He also recognized that to be able to compile such a network we need to have some sort of systematic approach to the subject; a purely alphabetical approach will not indicate genus-species relationships, though we can see syntatic links when two unrelated terms are used together in a heading. For example, the heading English drama itself shows the need to show a link with the related subject Drama, but does not show the relationship with the broader subject Literature; to reveal this, we need to study the whole subject area in a systematic way. However, Cutter restricted the links shown in practice to downward references, *ie* from broader to narrower subjects, and suggested that we should ignore on economic grounds both upward links (from narrower to broader subjects) and collateral (sideways) links from one term to another of equal rank. Thus Cutter would have cross-references such as

Literature *see also* drama

but not

Drama *see also* Literature

or

Drama *see also* Poetry.

Now it is certainly true that many users begin a search by specifying a much broader subject than they in fact want; needing information on the Moon they ask for information on Astronomy. A lead from Astronomy to Moon is therefore very valuable in helping users to clarify their specific needs. But suppose that after searching the system at a heading which is specific we still do not find what we need? We need to be able to broaden the search to include broader subjects, and we can only do this systematically if the system includes upward and collateral references as well as the usual downward ones. Like Cutter's advice to make double entry to overcome lack of specificity in the kind of headings he found acceptable, this practice tends to hamper the easy use and development of alphabetical indexes but is standard practice despite this. The cost of making the network of references complete would in most cases be prohibitive, and we therefore have to accept the fact that the alphabetical subject catalogue does not lend itself to the kind of search strategy which involves looking systematically for broader headings.

Cutter's *Rules* have been the basis of United States practice in subject cataloguing during this century, and are best exemplified in LCSH, Sears *List* and the H W Wilson indexes. Their use in the Library of Congress has meant that they have appeared on the printed cards used by most US libraries, while the fact that the Library adopted a dictionary catalogue has meant that this has been the norm. This influence has not been restricted to the US; the vast majority of Australian libraries, for example, follow the same practice, despite the efforts of such writers as Metcalfe to bring some degree of rationalization to Australian subject headings.

Cutter lived in a different age, less complex than ours. In referring to the problem of adjective-noun combinations, he wrote: 'But there are less than three hundred subject-names consisting of adjective and noun in a catalog which probably has over 50,000 names of persons'. Such a situation could hardly arise today, a reflection of the fact that, though the *Rules* may have been adequate to deal with nineteenth century literature, they are so no longer. Yet despite some dissatisfaction, there has been little progress in the US on the development of any kind of new theory, while the enormous size of the catalogues in the Library of Congress has itself been a weighty factor on the side of inertia. It should also be pointed out that the problems of size associated with a very large library catalogue are the cause of many of the defects found in LCSH, rather than any fundamental errors in the *Rules*.

We should not blame Cutter for not solving all our problems, or for not even being aware of some of them. The information we have to deal with is greater in quantity, and individually more complex, than anything Cutter envisaged his rules applying to. What he did do was bring order into a previously haphazard process, and in doing so point the way forward for later developments; his *Rules* can still be read with profit (and, more unusual in such works, pleasure) today.

KAISER

In 1911 J Kaiser published a work entitled *Systematic indexing*,[3] which took the practice of alphabetical subject indexing an important step forward. His ideas formalized the practices he had developed in trying to index information relating to business and industry, and to that extent are limited in their application; but they represent the first attempt to find a sound and consistent answer to the problem of significance order, and are still valid and useful in many cases. Kaiser pointed out that many composite subjects can be analysed into a combination of a *concrete* and a *process*, and stated the rule that in such a combination it is the concrete which is the more important and which should be cited first. This means that *Heat treatment of metals* and *Screw extrusion of plastics* are entered respectively:

METALS—Heat treatment
PLASTICS—Screw extrusion

If *place* is involved, Kaiser makes double entry, once under concrete and once under place; entry for localities is indirect, *ie* under country subdivided by more specific locality. Thus *Steel production in*

Sheffield would be entered:

    STEEL—Great Britain, Sheffield—Production

    GREAT BRITAIN, Sheffield—Steel—Production

Concretes are linked by a complete network of cross-references, to superordinate and coordinate as well as subordinate headings. An index constructed along these lines will contain a large number of cross-references, but this is not necessarily a bad thing; Cutter's objections were on economic grounds, not theoretical, and it is unfortunate that most libraries using the alphabetical approach do limit their references to the 'downward' kind. Concretes are often specified by more than one word, *eg aluminium windows*, and here Kaiser uses natural language order; however, many topics have now reached a degree of complexity when natural language is not necessarily much of a help, *eg Gas-cooled natural-uranium fuelled nuclear power reactors*, where natural language permits more than one arrangement.

Kaiser realized that many terms apparently denoting processes in fact could be analysed into the standard concrete-process formula; thus *cataloguing* could become *Catalogues—construction*. This kind of analysis can present problems, particularly those of inconsistency, in that it might well be possible to analyse the same subject in different ways on different occasions. In addition, the concrete revealed by this analysis might well be found in quite a different part of the alphabet from the original term, which would be the one normally sought by users: *welding* and *soldering* might both be found under *Metals* (Metals—welding, Metals—soldering), which would show their relationship but would not give direct entry.

This method of analysis is very much in line with the ideas put forward in chapters 5 and 6, and clearly is related to semantic factoring. By following the rule, we can arrive at a set of consistent headings, *eg*

    Books—Cataloguing

    Books—Classification

where LCSH has

    Cataloguing

    Classification—books

a difference of approach which defies any attempt at rationalization.

Another important point which Kaiser illustrated clearly in his examples is the effects of introducing systematic arrangement of subheadings as opposed to straightforward alphabetical filing. For any given concrete there may well be composites including place, as well as composites including both place and process; when one comes to arrange these, there are two possibilities—to use a strictly alphabetical sub-arrangement, or to group places together and processes together. The first approach gives:

    STEEL—Great Britain, Sheffield—Production

    STEEL—Smelting

STEEL—United States of America, Pittsburgh—Smelting
STEEL—Welding
while the second groups the processes *before* the places:
STEEL—Smelting
STEEL—Welding
STEEL—Great Britain, Sheffield—Production
STEEL—United States of America, Pittsburgh—Smelting

A further sequence may arise if we include bibliographical forms as subdivisions, *eg* Periodicals, Dictionaries, Indexes *etc*, as once again it may be helpful to avoid interfiling these with other kinds of subheading. The principle followed by Kaiser has been more fully investigated in the field of classification and will be considered later under the heading *Principle of inversion* (page 138). However, the idea of grouping subheadings is followed by most alphabetical subject catalogues, as is shown, for example, by the following headings from the Library of Congress *Subject headings:*

Sales	(Single term)
Sales—periodicals	(Bibliographical form)
Sales (Roman Law)	(Context)
Sales, conditional	(Qualification)
Sales accounting	(Two or more terms)

The problem with introducing systematic arrangement into an alphabetical catalogue is that the order is no longer self-evident, and in consequence a user following up a cross-reference may find himself lost.

COATES

Undoubtedly the most important contribution to the theory of alphabetical subject headings for many years is the work of E J Coates. In his book, *Subject catalogues*,[4] Coates has summarized succinctly the previous approaches, both theory and practice, and put forward his own theories as to the correct formulation of specific subject headings. He has also had the challenge of putting his ideas into practice on a large scale in the *British technology index*, of which he has been editor since its inception—an opportunity of a kind which rarely presents itself to the theorist.

He begins his study of order in composite headings by trying to establish the reason for Kaiser's selection of Concrete rather than Process as the entry point, and suggests that there is a sound psychological basis for this. If we try to visualize an action out of context, it is very difficult; we normally think of some 'thing' which is involved in the action. For example, we can visualize a piece of steel or aluminium undergoing heat treatment, possibly glowing, changing shape and so on; but it is much more difficult to visualize *heat treatment* on its own. We can therefore establish an order of *significance* reflecting this, and for this simple case it is of course the same as Kaiser's Con-

Type of compound	Subject Heading Order	Subject Heading agrees or reverses significance order	Subject Heading agrees or reverses amplified phrase order	Usual relationship words in amplified phrase
1 Action on Thing	THING, Action	Agrees	Reverses	of
2 Action on Material	MATERIAL, Action	Agrees	Reverses	of
3 Action A on Action B	Action B, Action A	—	Reverses	of, in
4 Material of Thing	THING, Material	Agrees	Reverses	of
5 Part of Thing	THING, Part	—	Reverses	of
6 Property of Thing, Material or Action	THING MATERIAL ACTION } Property	Agrees	Reverses	of
7 Partial viewpoint on Thing. Material or Action, or Property	THING MATERIAL ACTION PROPERTY } Viewpoint	—	Reverses	of
8 Thing *distinguished* by citation of Principle of Action	THING, Action	Agrees	Agrees	with based on
9 Thing *distinguished* by citation of Material	THING, Material	Agrees	Agrees	of
10 Thing *distinguished* by citation of Part	THING, Part	Agrees	Agrees	with
11 Thing *distinguished* by Material or Form of energy which it utilises	MATERIAL FORM OF ENERGY } Thing	Reverses	Reverses	operated by
12 Action A *distinguished* by citation of contributory or underlying Action B	ACTION A, Action B	—	Agrees	by
13 Thing A, *serving, supplying or aiming* at Thing B	THING B, Thing A	—	Reverses	for serving at
14 Thing A or Action A *distinguished* from a homonym by the fact that it *serves* Thing B or Action B	THING A, Thing B / THING A, Action B / ACTION A, Action B	— / Agrees / —	Agrees / Agrees / Agrees	for
15 Thing *serving or instrumental to* Action	ACTION, Thing	Reverses	Reverses	for
16 Thing A *caused* by Thing B	THING B, Thing A	–-	Reverses	caused by produced by devised by
17 Thing *caused* by Action	THING, Action	Agrees	Agrees	caused by produced by
18 Action *caused* by Thing	THING, Action	Agrees	Reverses	of caused by
19 Action A *caused* by Action B	ACTION A, Action B	—	Agrees	caused by
20 Thing or Action at a type of location	LOCATION, Thing / LOCATION, Action	— / Agrees	Reverses / Reverses	at, of / at, of

FIGURE 10: *Coates' 20 operators.*

crete-Process. Coates uses the terminology *Thing-Action*, but this is simply a new way of naming the same idea. However, Coates develops his ideas much further. If we think of a Thing and the Material of which it is made, it is once again the Thing which is more significant, because it conjures up a more definite mental image. So we can develop our significance order one stage further, to give us *Thing-Material-Action*; from here we can again move forward to incorporate *Parts*, which must depend on the *Things* to which they belong, thus giving us *Thing-Part-Material-Action*. Coates also shows how other variants can be built up by following the same principle.

If we had to try to establish the significance order every time we wished to establish a subject heading, it would take a great deal of intellectual effort, but Coates has pointed out a very valuable corollary of his ideas on significance order. When we translate the idea of a *Thing* being acted upon by an *Action* into natural language, we can very often do so by using a prepositional phrase, in the form *Action-Preposition-Thing*. To obtain a subject heading in accordance with the *Thing-Action* significance formula, all that we have to do is to reverse the phrase, omitting the preposition. Thus *Heat treatment of aluminium* becomes *Aluminium, Heat treatment*. These ideas enable us to establish a heading for very complex subjects, such as the following two examples taken from the *British technology index*:

1 Manufacture of multiwall kraft paper sacks for the packaging of cement.

2 Determination of the temperature of combustion of coal particles.

1 We can split this into two parts, Manufacture of multiwall kraft paper sacks, and, Packaging of cement. In the first part, the *Thing* is sacks, and the *Action* manufacture, giving us Sacks, manufacture. Paper is the *Material*, giving us Sacks, paper, manufacture, while kraft and multiwall are obviously type-specifying terms for paper, giving us for the whole of this part Sacks, paper, kraft, multiwall, manufacture. In the second part, we can easily derive the heading Cement, packaging. To link the two, we think of sacks for packaging, giving us Packaging, sacks; so for the whole heading we have:

Cement, packaging, sacks, paper, kraft, multiwall, manufacture.

2 Coal particles are clearly the *Thing* involved here, but is the entry term Coal or Particles? The phrase may be expressed as Particles of coal, leading us to Coal, particles; from here we have a series of similar prepositional phrases, which we reverse in order, giving:

Coal, particles, combustion, temperature, determination.

These headings are not natural use of language; they are lengthy and complex, and they are not obvious. (It is, however, fairly simple to learn to read the line from back to front with a little practice.) To set against these disadvantages we have the very real advantages of consistency and specificity, and—if Coates' ideas are correct—the first element of the heading is the one most likely to come into the mind of the enquirer seeking information on these topics. Coates distinguishes twenty different kinds of relationship, including Thing-Action, and tabulates these to show their relation to the corresponding prepositional phrase; there are a few exceptions to the reversal rule, for example Thing-Material, where the heading agrees with the amplified phrase order (sacks [made] of paper gives Sacks, paper, not Paper, sacks), but once these are known the rule is a very simple one to follow. As has already been mentioned, Coates has been able to put his ideas into practice in the *British technology index*, and some critics have complained that the kind of entry demonstrated here is no longer a direct entry to the specific subject. It is difficult to see how the entries could be made more direct; once we try to be specific, and name composite subjects, we must inevitably group to some extent under the first element in a heading. For example, as well as Cement, packaging, we may have Cement, manufacture, giving us a certain amount of grouping at the word cement—but this does not make either of the entries any the less direct. If we require specificity, we have at the same time to accept the concomitant complexity of headings and the occurrence of grouping. It must however be stressed that the grouping arises out of the need for a significance order, not from any attempt to bring together related subjects in a systematic way. The words at which grouping occurs are stated directly: Aluminium, heat treatment, *not* Metals, aluminium, heat treatment.

In addition to the problems of combination order of subject terms, Coates gave some thought to the question of Place in relation to subjects, and proposed the following ranking of subjects:

1 Geographical and biological phenomena (flora and fauna)
2 History and social phenomena
3 Language and literature
4 Fine arts
5 Philosophy and religion
6 Technology
7 Phenomena of the physical sciences.

The suggested ruling is that groups 1, 2 and 3 are entered under Place, except for individual species in biology. Works that are studies of these subjects, *eg* 'the teaching of sociology in Australia' go under subject, as do subject-place combinations falling into the other four categories. This is very much in line with Cutter's thinking, though in LCSH one may find such headings as United States—Intellectual life, and, United States—religion, both of which fall into group 5.

CROSS-REFERENCE STRUCTURE
A catalogue of this kind shows the problems of related subjects in an acute form. We not only have to establish a network of genus-species

relationships, but must also cater for those who approach a composite subject through a term other than the one we have used as entry word. The heading

ALUMINIUM, Heat treatment

involves us in both kinds of link. We must make cross-references

METALS *see also* NON-FERROUS METALS

NON-FERROUS METALS *see also* ALUMINIUM

and possibly also

FERROUS METALS *see also* NON-FERROUS METALS

MAGNESIUM *see also* ALUMINIUM

to express the permanent relationships within the field of metallurgy. These can only be established by a study of the subject in a systematic way, and BTI uses a number of classification schemes to suggest links of this kind. At a heading with a number of semantic links, these are tabulated, *eg:*

BUILDING

   RELATED HEADINGS

     AIR CONDITIONING

     BATHROOMS

     CEMENT——GLASS FIBRE: BUILDING MATERIALS

     CRANES, TOWER,, SELF-ERECTING: BUILDING PLANT

     DOORS

     PARTITIONS

     PLUMBING

     STRUCTURES

     VENTILATION

It should be noted that there is also a heading BUILDINGS, with a similar list of semantic links.

To cater for the hidden terms arising out of the syntactic structure Coates decided to use chain procedure, but found that strict reliance on this gave unsatisfactory results in some cases. As we saw in the example of chain procedure in chapter 6, the heading

Cement, packaging, sacks, paper, kraft, multiwall, manufacture

gives us a cross-reference

Sacks, packaging, cement *see* Cement, packaging, sacks

in which we have lost the word 'paper' which specifies the kind of sacks and thus gives the searcher useful information.

In some cases, notably Thing-Part, it is often difficult to tell which is the part of the heading most likely to be sought by users; in such cases Coates allows double entry under both forms, Thing-Part and Part-Thing. In order to take care of this situation and of the modifications to chain procedure, BTI introduced differential punctuation when computer processing was introduced in 1968; the above heading would now appear as

CEMENT: packaging: sacks; paper

in which the semi-colon indicates that the inversion reference will not be in strict accordance with chain procedure. The punctuation marks used are the colon, comma, double comma, double point and semi-colon, in accordance with the following schema:

Thing—Action, Property, Part or Auxiliary   :
eg MOTOR VEHICLES: Bodies
   PACKAGING: Labelling
   PLYWOOD: Building materials [*ie* Plywood as a building material]
Thing—Material   ;
eg BOTTLES; Polythene
Thing or Action—Kind   ,
eg MIXING, Batch
   ATOMISERS, Air blast
Thing—Material—Kind of material   ;   ,
eg BOTTLES; Polythene, Blow moulded
Thing—Kind—Material   ,   ;
eg PLATES, Clamped; Steel
Thing—Kind—Kind of kind   ,   ,
eg MOTOR CARS, Three wheeler, Types, Bond
Thing—Kind + Kind   ,   „
eg PLATES, Circular,, Anisotropic
Thing—Material—Kind of thing   ;   „
eg ELECTRODES; Glass,, Ion selective
Thing—Place   ..
eg MOTORWAYS.. Belfast

By replacing some of the syntax which is lost in headings of the earlier type, some ambiguities can be removed. For example, we can now distinguish

   STRUCTURES; Steel (meaning Steel structures)
from
   STRUCTURES: Steel (meaning Steel used in structures)
Some still remain; for example,
   METALS: Extrusion: Presses
can mean either the action 'Extrusion of metals using presses' or the thing 'Presses for the extrusion of metals'. However, as Coates points out, it is often very difficult to distinguish these in the reader's approach anyway; thing and action are so closely linked that it is hard to think of one without the other.

The effect of the punctuation on the network of cross-references is illustrated in the following examples, taken from BTI 1970. H indicates the heading, C the cross-references:

Straightforward
   I   H   NICKEL: Corrosion
       C   CORROSION: Nickel.   See NICKEL: Corrosion

2 H CATHODES; Nickel
   C NICKEL; Cathodes. See CATHODES; Nickel

Modified
3 H AIRCRAFT, Light
   C LIGHT AIRCRAFT. See AIRCRAFT, Light

4 H FILMS; Nitrogen, Solid,, Beta
   C SOLID NITROGEN; Films. See FILMS; Nitrogen, Solid
      NITROGEN, Solid; Films. See FILMS; Nitrogen, Solid

5 H (1) MOTORWAYS: Bridges; Concrete, Prestressed
      (2) BRIDGES (Motorways) Concrete, Prestressed
   C   CONCRETE, Prestressed; Bridges: Motorways. See
            MOTORWAYS: Bridges; Concrete, Prestressed
         PRESTRESSED CONCRETE; Bridges: Motorways. See
            MOTORWAYS: Bridges; Concrete, Prestressed

6 H PLATES, Clamped; Steel, Mild
   C STEEL, Mild; Clamped plates. See PLATES, Clamped; Steel,
         Mild
      MILD STEEL; Clamped plates. See PLATES, Clamped; Steel,
         Mild
      CLAMPED PLATES. See PLATES, Clamped

7 H LAMPS, Fluorescent, Indium amalgam
   C INDIUM AMALGAM FLUORESCENT LAMPS. See LAMPS,
         Fluorescent, Indium amalgam
      FLUORESCENT LAMPS. See LAMPS, Fluorescent

8 H AIRCRAFT, Military,, Vertical take-off
   C VERTICAL TAKE-OFF MILITARY AIRCRAFT. See AIRCRAFT,
         Military,, Vertical take-off

9 H FILMS; Aluminium,, Vacuum deposited
   C VACUUM DEPOSITED ALUMINIUM FILMS. See FILMS;
         Aluminium,, Vacuum deposited

10 H INDUSTRIAL HEALTH
    C HEALTH, Industrial. See INDUSTRIAL HEALTH

11 H EPOXY RESIN – GLASS FIBRE, Filament wound
    C FILAMENT WOUND EPOXY RESIN – GLASS FIBRE. See EPOXY
          RESIN – GLASS FIBRE, Filament wound
       GLASS FIBRE – EPOXY RESIN. See EPOXY RESIN – GLASS FIBRE

12   H   PRESSURE VESSELS; Steel – Chromium – Molybdenum
       C   CHROMIUM – MOLYBDENUM – STEEL; Pressure vessels.   See
           PRESSURE VESSELS; Steel – Chromium – Molybdenum
          MOLYBDENUM – STEEL – CHROMIUM; Pressure vessels.   See
           PRESSURE VESSELS; Steel – Chromium – Molybdenum
          STEEL – CHROMIUM – MOLYBDENUM; Pressure vessels.   See
           PRESSURE VESSELS; Steel – Chromium – Molybdenum
   N.B.   STEEL – files *after* the sequence including STEEL; STEEL,;
           STEEL:; STEEL;

13   H   NUCLEAR REACTORS: Neutron diffusion
       C   NEUTRONS: Diffusion: Nuclear reactors.   See NUCLEAR
           REACTORS: Neutron diffusion
          DIFFUSION: Neutron: Nuclear reactors.   See NUCLEAR
           REACTORS: Neutron diffusion

14   H   OLEFIN IODINE ISOCYANATE ADDITION COMPOUNDS
       C   ADDITIONS COMPOUNDS, Olefin iodine isocyanate.   See
           OLEFIN IODINE ISOCYANATE ADDITION COMPOUNDS
          IODINE ISOCYANATE OLEFIN ADDITION COMPOUNDS.   See
           OLEFIN IODINE ISOCYANATE ADDITION COMPOUNDS

15   H   SEWAGE: Determination of detergents, Anionic
       C   DETERGENTS, Anionic: Determination: Sewage.   See
           SEWAGE: Determination of detergents, Anionic
          ANIONIC DETERGENTS: Determination: Sewage.   See
           SEWAGE: Determination of detergents, Anionic

16   H   PARTICLES: Field emission: Effect of image force
       C   IMAGE FORCE: Effect on field emission: Particles.   See
           PARTICLES: Field emission: Effect of image force

Similar routines apply with such phrases as 'reaction with', 'correlation with' and 'conversion to'.

17   H   ELECTRICITY COUNCIL RESEARCH CENTRE.. CAPENHURST
       C   CAPENHURST.   See ELECTRICITY COUNCIL RESEARCH CENTRE..
           Capenhurst

18   H   MOTOR CARS, Types, Aston Martin DBS
       C   ASTON MARTIN DBS MOTOR CARS.   See MOTOR CARS, Types,
           Aston Martin DBS

There are various other modifications which are difficult to recognise in BTI because they involve the omission of certain words as entry terms; these may be terms which are otherwise treated in the usual way, or they may fall into a short list of 35 common words such as analysis, which do not give rise to inversion within the cross-references. The algorithm developed to take care of all these modifications has been described by Coates and Nicholson in a paper[5] which also lists the other advantages of computer processing. One point is perhaps worth stressing. At the outset of the computerization study, Coates had doubts as to how much of the process could in fact be mechanized, since he and his fellow indexers felt that what they were doing in modifying chain procedure was essentially an intellectual task. In the event it proved possible to mechanize all but the writing of the original string; much of what had been implicit turned out to be susceptible to explication when carefully analyzed. We must beware of attaching an intellectual mystique to subject indexing operations which may actually be no more than complex clerical procedures.

The punctuation is ignored in the arrangement, since its purpose is to operate the computer program for the generation of cross-references. However, though the network is now more satisfactory with a lower expenditure of effort than it was previously, there are still problems arising from the fact that many of the references are not specific. For example, suppose that a user wanting *Determination of neutron flux in a boiling water reactor* looks under the word REACTOR; all that he will find will be a reference

REACTORS, nuclear

see

NUCLEAR REACTORS

When he turns to this heading, say in the annual volume of BTI, he will find a very large number of entries, all beginning NUCLEAR REACTORS, and will have to work his way through these without being certain of the next term to look for. It might well be BOILING WATER, or perhaps WATER—but it might be that the only information on this subject in that particular year dealt with Boiling water reactors for power generation, in which case the next word after REACTORS might well be power. The price of economy here is loss of specificity, which leads to an increase in the amount of searching that has to be done when part only of the wanted heading is known.

There is no doubt that the ideas put forward by Coates and their implementation in BTI have been a solid step forward in the theory of alphabetical subject headings. So far, we have only seen these ideas in use in the field of science and technology. Indexing services in the social sciences and humanities are, in general, less well organized than those in science and technology, and this applies to their indexing just as it does to their other features. It will be interesting to see whether detailed application in these fields leads to any important additions or modifications to the significance formulae suggested by Coates. It should also be stressed that—as has already been mentioned—generalized rules for significance order are intended for the neutral situation; in a situation where it is possible to establish in advance the likely needs of the users, we may well need to use quite different rules.

METCALFE

One of the strongest supporters of the Cutter type of catalogue has been J W Metcalfe, who has written three major works[6] on the subject approach, yet has received little attention outside his adopted country, Australia—a prophet without honour save in his own country. Metcalfe argues very strongly for the alphabetic catalogue and against the classified; the latter arguments are not relevant at this point, but we should consider his case for the alphabetico-specific catalogue carefully.

He first defines the alphabetico-specific catalogue as consisting of known names in a known order; *ie* terms from natural language, arranged in self-evident alphabetical order. He lays stress on the importance of this to the reader, who is able to use the catalogue with the minimum of difficulty, though as we have seen in chapters 5 and 6, (and as Metcalfe admits) this may not always be quite as simple as it appears. Entry should be direct, in accordance with Cutter's rule; any departure from direct entry leads to alphabetico-classed arrangement, which is contrary to the specific approach. To clarify this point, Metcalfe introduced the important differentiation between *specification* and *qualification*; specification refers to division into species by adding a further term, while qualification refers to division by aspect, process or form. Thus 'prestressed concrete' is a species of concrete, and it would be wrong to enter it as 'concrete—prestressed', because this would be classed entry; but 'concrete—pouring' is correct, because pouring is a process applied to concrete, not a species of concrete.

The next question for discussion is what is meant by 'specific' entry. Metcalfe argues that the purpose of subject cataloguing is to indicate the subject classes into which a document falls, *not* to indicate necessarily the precise subject of the item itself. This view is of course directly contrary to the view advocated in this book, which is that the subject heading should be co-extensive with the subject of the document. Metcalfe recognises that many subjects that appear in documents involve the coordination of subject classes, and that the card and book catalogue do not lend themselves to this approach, but he points out that in many cases a reader faced with a non-specific heading will only have to look through a limited number of entries to find items on the specific subject he requires, and that this will be simpler than looking through the network of cross-references involved in the single entry, co-extensive type of heading used in BTI.

He suggests a modification of Cutter's rule:

Enter an item directly under the particular name, in alphabetical order, of one or more of the particular things it is about; for example, one on bleaching cotton with hydrogen peroxide, under Cotton, or Cotton-Bleaching, and under Hydrogen peroxide.

'This then has to be further developed, but what is the basic and minimum requirement that satisfies specific entry is entry in the example under Cotton not under Textiles. Item specification such as Cotton—Bleaching—Hydrogen peroxide as a rule, and entry under it and entry or indexing or cross reference under permutations, may be considered to be better and may supersede specific entry, but it is not specific entry.'

To illustrate his case, Metcalfe points to the entry of two items on this subject in the 1962 *Applied science and technology index* under both Bleaching—Cotton and Hydrogen peroxide; there are 18 entries all told under the latter heading, so the search is not particularly tedious. (In passing, we may note that Metcalfe's rule would make Cotton—bleaching the correct form, which is in line with Kaiser, whom Metcalfe admires, and Coates, whom he does not). By contrast, in the 1962 BTI 'three entry headings, with one entry under each, and seven cross reference headings, have to be combed through to find reference from HYDROGEN PEROXIDE, Bleaching, Cotton to its reverse'. Although single entry claims economy of space as one of its main justifications, Metcalfe argues from the above example that this claim is greatly exaggerated, and even a quick glance at BTI will show that the cross-reference structure does take up a lot of the space; we have already noted the other disadvantage pointed out by Metcalfe, *ie* that only one of the cross-references is in fact specific. Some of his criticisms have been overtaken by events; for example 'The economy of operation which is claimed is bound up with mechanical operation, metaphorical or actual, but so far only metaphorical'. As we have seen, the mechanical operation of BTI is not only actual but successful.

In an attempt to take the ideas of Cutter and Kaiser and bring them up to date, Metcalfe published a 'Tentative code of rules for alphabetico-specific entry' in 1959. In this, he suggests that the degree or extent of subject qualification by subheadings is entirely a matter of judgment according to number of entries and the specialization of literature under headings (Rule 2.41). This rule seems to assume that a library is static, and that the number of entries will remain the same; the alternative is to recatalogue documents on any subjects that grow too unwieldy. It would appear to be more efficient to use co-extensive headings in the first place, and avoid that particular problem altogether! Qualifications of qualifications by subsubheadings are permitted, *eg* Cattle—Diseases—Diagnosis; Motor cars—Painting,

Spray; Chairs—Upholstery, Leather, Natural—Preservation, Lanolin. At this point, we may begin to wonder how this differs from one of Coates' headings, which would be exactly the same except for the punctuation. Startlingly, we find also that Rule 2.44 would permit either Horses—Diseases *or* Horse—Diseases—Strangles for a document on strangles in horses (an infectious streptococcal fever); the first of these is blatantly class entry rather than specific, while the second is equally blatantly alphabetico-classed.

Even the cursory glance that we have been able to give them here will show that Metcalfe's rules do not go much further than Cutter's and certainly do not provide a solution to the problems of today's literature. Nevertheless, they do represent an attempt to provide a *modus operandi* for the multiple entry under known names approach. (By 'multiple entry' Metcalfe means the entry of a document under a number of headings, each of which may be less specific than the subject of the document, as opposed to the manipulation of a single co-extensive heading to give access under each significant term, which is the sense in which we have used it in chapter 6).

Unfortunately, much of Metcalfe's writing is marred by what appears to be a deep-rooted prejudice against the classified approach, particularly as exemplified by Ranganathan and the supporters of the analytico-synthetic method. When discussing the undoubted deficiencies of LCSH, the errors are claimed to be the result of human frailty in the application of a basically sound system; when discussing specific deficiencies in BNB or BTI, these are claimed to be the result of the correct application of a basically unsound system. A more moderate approach is found in the writings of R K Olding, who puts the case for multiple entry very concisely in a short pamphlet,[7] though this too seems to stop at a point where something like the theories of Coates would need to take over.

SPECIFICITY, COORDINATION, RECALL AND RELEVANCE
It is worth briefly recapitulating some of the points dealt with in earlier chapters in order to put the multiple entry/single entry controversy into perspective. We have seen that coordination is a device to improve relevance, whereas entry under class headings is a means of improving recall. Single entry systems attempt to provide specificity by means of precoordination; multiple entry systems attempt to provide the same degree of specificity without using coordination, since the kinds of bibliographic tool they are used in, *eg* the card catalogue, do not permit coordination of entries under two or more headings. Does the reader prefer to go to a specific heading, perhaps via one or more cross-references, in a form that is clearly not 'natural language', or does he prefer to scan a number of entries under a less specific heading which is much closer to natural language (though it must be stressed again that

any controlled list of headings cannot claim to be 'natural language')? If the latter, how many entries would he be willing to scan? In other words, what percentage relevance is the acceptable lower limit? We do not know the answer to these questions, and they may in fact depend on the individual reader. The results of the evaluation tests described in chapter 28 seem to indicate that coordination, preferably post-coordination, is the most powerful device available for achieving speci-ficity, and one may suspect that the popularity of postcoordinate mthods in the USA may be the result of disillusionment with the mul-tiple entry method divorced from the possibility of coordination by the limitations of the card catalogue. However, more research is needed before we can come to any definite conclusions; in the meantime, no doubt the debate will continue.

ARTICULATED SUBJECT INDEXES

A rather different approach from either of the two methods just dis-cussed has been made by M F Lynch.[8] Unlike Coates, who has deliber-ately set out to avoid using prepositions, Lynch bases his system on the prepositional phrase. The project, which was intended to devise a method of generating subject indexes by computer manipulation of a simple sentence-like statement, began with a study of the indexes to *Chemical abstracts*. Based on skills acquired over the years, these indexes set a very high standard, and the first step was to find out whether they were based on any implicit logical analysis which could form the basis of a computer program (which must necessarily be *explicit*). A method was found of transforming an index entry back to a 'title' which worked in a high proportion of cases, some 60 percent. Of the remainder, nearly half could be treated in the same way if a simple set of procedures was followed. The method is to treat prepositions as points at which the phrases can be pivoted; often a comma will appear in the final index entry in association with the preposition. A phrase beginning with a preposition is designated 0, one ending with a prepo-sition, 1. A type 0 phrase is now placed after the entry word, while type 1 phrases are placed before it, and the original 'title' (a descriptive statement, not necessarily the title of the work) can be regenerated. Take, for example, the index entry:

    Insects
       pollination by, of crops

'Pollination by' is a 1-phrase, while 'of crops' is a 0-phrase. By follow-ing the simple rule, we can derive the statement

    Pollination by insects of crops.

This very simple example shows how the method of regeneration works, but it is effective for much more complex index entries than this.

    The analysis of *Chemical abstracts* entries led to the development of methods for the generation of index entries from a title statement, based on the logic discovered in the reverse process. As might be expected, some modifications were found to be necessary to avoid the generation of 'awkward' entries, but it has proved possible to compile computer programs which will work very satifactorily, and articulated indexes are used in *Food technology abstracts* and the Safety in Mines Research Establishment abstract bulletin. The method avoids the necessity for the somewhat complicated process of subject analysis reqired for indexes of the Coates type, since all that the indexer has to do is to write a statement in the approved format, using merely a rather stylized form of English.

The method gives a complete subject statement at every entry point; a simple example from a demonstration index is as follows:

Character recognition by computer (title from *Documentation abstracts*)

Index entries:

Character recognition
    by computer
Computer(s)
    character recognition by

The programs can give very much more sophisticated results than this very simple example. Take, for instance, the title-like subject statement:

Complexometric determination of magnesium, calcium, strontium and barium <u>in</u> the presence <u>of</u> iron <u>and</u> chromium.

The computer is programmed to recognise the cues provided by the items underlined (these would *not* have to be underlined or otherwise signalled by the indexer) to give a complete set of entries:

Complexometric determination
    of barium, in the presence of iron and chromium
    of calcium, in the . . .
    of magnesium, in the . . .
    of strontium, in the . . .
Barium
    complexometric determination of, in the presence of chromium
    complexometric determination of, in the presence of iron
Calcium, Magnesium, Strontium——entries as for Barium
Chromium
    complexometric determination of barium in the presence of
Calcium, Magnesium, Strontium——entries as for Barium under Chromium
Iron——entries as for Chromium

The above entries would of course be interfiled with any others under the same headings, in alphabetic order of the first significant word, *eg*:

Thin-layer chromatography
    identification of hybrid white wines by
    on liquid anion exchangers
    of naturally occurring hydroxyanthones
    of synthetic food oils
    use of homogeneous mixtures in

The computer can decide which arrangement of the prepositional phrase subheadings is most advantageous from the point of view of collocating similar entries. Consider the following two titles:

    Cataloguing of non-book materials (Document no 641)

    Cataloguing of non-book materials in university libraries (Document no 732)

The first one must give rise to the entry

    Non-book materials
        cataloguing of   641

but the second offers a choice:

    Non-book materials
        in university libraries, cataloguing of   732

or

    Non-book materials
        cataloguing of, in university libraries   732

The computer will select the second, to give the collocation

    Non-book materials
        cataloguing of   641
            in university libraries   732

The method is clearly an appealing one, since it does not require any skill in recognising concept categories or combination orders, and it does give a full heading at every entry point. It remains to be seen whether it will prove as popular in the long run as methods involving more sophisticated analytical methods.

ALPHABETICO-CLASSED ARRANGEMENT

All of the systems described so far in this chapter have used what is called *direct* entry; that is to say, a topic is entered directly under the term or terms which most closely correspond to the subject. Another approach is to use *indirect* entry: a topic is entered under a broad heading which includes it, if necessary using a whole series of intermediate divisions of the broad subject. For example, instead of

    Aluminium

we might find

    Metals—non-ferrous—aluminium

Instead of

    Cans

we find

    Containers: tinplate: food: cans

The advantage to be gained from indirect entry is that related subjects are grouped together; in the above examples, everything on Metals will be together, as will everything on different kinds of container. However, there are certain difficulties associated with indirect entry which have led to its general rejection, though some examples are to be found, *eg* the Metal Box Company's card index to periodical articles closed some years ago but still used for older materials, and some published bibliographies. In the first place, how does one decide at what point to open the chain of division? And how many steps of division does one include? Should we have

Astronomy—solar system—sun

or

Science—astronomy—stars—sun

or perhaps

Science—physics—astronomy—stars—solar system—sun?

While we are still thinking of alphabetical arrangement rather than systematic grouping, such decisions are likely to be made on an *ad hoc* basis rather than in a consistent theoretical fashion. The second point is that this kind of indirect entry is only helpful if we arrange the resulting headings systematically. For example, alphabetical arrangement of a series of subheadings under Physics would give

Physics—electricity

Physics—heat

Physics—light

Physics—magnetism

The amount of grouping that can be achieved is too limited to be of any great value, and the objective is more satisfactorily attained by adopting systematic arrangement completely. However, both BTI and LCSH occasionally use headings of this kind, *eg*

MOTOR CARS, Types, Aston Martin DBS (BTI)

Shakespeare, William, 1564–1616—Characters—Falstaff (LCSH)

though one could argue strongly that these are out of place in direct entry methods, and they come in for trenchant criticism from Metcalfe.

Since the direct entry terms are hidden in indirect entry, it is necessary to build up a large network of cross-references in order to make sure that readers can find the topics they are looking for. This can be done by chain procedure, which is probably reasonably effective in this situation. On the other hand, we can cut down on the number of *see also* references we need to link related terms, since we do not need to link those which are brought together by the indirect mode of entry. For example, we need an entry

Cans: Food: Tinplate: Containers

see Containers: Tinplate: Food: cans

but we do not need a reference

Containers *see also* Cans;
Aluminium
   see Metals: Non-ferrous: Aluminium
Non-ferrous metals
   see Metals: Non-ferrous
are needed, but we do not need
   Metals *see also* Non-ferrous metals
or
   Non-ferrous metals *see also* Aluminium.

FILING ORDER

We have already seen that in any given entry in the telephone directory
we can find only the first word, the surname, but there are in fact additional problems if our subject names are more than one word long. In
order to separate them, we may need to introduce other symbols, for
example the comma; we may be in some doubt as to what to do with
insignificant words such as prepositions and conjunctions. Where do
we find *Smith's* in relation to *Smith, Smithers* and *Smithson*? Where
do we find *Galliher & Huguely* in relation to *Galliher Chas E*? These
are simple examples taken from a telephone directory, and the rules
governing their filing can soon be learnt—but we do have to have
rules. Similarly, we must have rules if the subject specifications we use
contain more than one word; the simplest arrangement is one where all
the entries contain one word only. Unfortunately, as we have seen, this
is very rarely the case; even in postcoordinate indexing we frequently
find multi-word headings in practice, while in precoordinate systems
they tend to be the norm. As headings in an alphabetical catalogue
become more complex, it becomes necessary to introduce quite complex rules to govern the overall arrangement. The first decision is
whether filing is to be *letter by letter* (all through) or *word by word*.
The index to the present work is word by word: thus 'index vocabulary' is found *before* 'indexing'; in a letter by letter arrangement the
converse would apply. A good example of a letter by letter index is that
to the *Encyclopaedia Britannica*. There are arguments on both sides,
and the case for each has been put forward in the *Indexer*.[9] A lot
depends on whether hyphens are taken as splitting or joining words;
for example, in the index to this work they are taken as joining words
into one whole, so that 'cross-references' follows 'Crossley', whereas
'cross references' without the hyphen would precede 'Crossley'. The
reverse convention is used by LCSH, where we find the sequence
   Pitch pine
   Pitch-pipe *see* Pitchpipe
   Pitching
   Pitchpipe
in which the hyphen is in effect deleted altogether.

The second decision is the one already mentioned in our consideration of Kaiser's rules: the problem of grouping. Again we have two possibilities; either we can use a strict alphabetical order, or we can group certain subheadings to give what may be a more helpful arrangement. The punctuation in headings consisting of more than one word can be highly significant, or it may be ignored, or there may be a difference between the filing position of two words separated by punctuation and two not separated. The following examples from Sears and BTI illustrate similar conventions, the difference being that BTI treats the dash and the space in the same way, whereas Sears treats the dash like other punctuation marks:

Sears:
Advertising
Advertising, Art in *see* Commercial art
Advertising—Libraries
Advertising, Television *see* Television advertising
Advertising as a profession

Ability
Ability—testing
Ability grouping in education

BTI:
GAS: Liquefaction
GAS, Natural
GAS, Town
GAS DISCHARGE
GAS-STEAM TURBINES
GAS TURBINES

Apart from this both BTI and Sears use strict alphabetical order, ignoring the punctuation, but this is not the case with LCSH; in that list a considerable amount of grouping takes place at some headings, and the punctuation used is given a filing value, as can be seen from the following examples and from the example Sales on p 107.
Shakespeare, William, 1564–1616
——Characters
——Welshmen
——Women
——Falstaff [Margaret of Anjou, etc]
——Chronology
Shakespeare, William, 1564–1616.
Paraphrases, tales, etc.
Shakespeare, William, 1564–1616, in
fiction, drama, poetry etc.

Women
  —Portraits
Women, British
Women, delinquent *see* Delinquent women
Women and socialism
Women and the sea
Women as statisticians
Women delinquents *see* Delinquent women
Women statisticians *see* Women as statisticians
Women's colleges

Pipe
Pipe—Welding
Pipe (Musical instrument)
Pipe, Aluminium
Pipe, Wooden
Pipe bending
Pipe-fitting
Pipe music
Piperonal
Pipes, Deposits in

(In the above examples, a selection of the headings is given to illustrate the filing order; there will be other headings in the lists at the points shown)

It is evident that LCSH is not alphabetically arranged, and one may question the purpose of the groupings illustrated.[10] The value of the direct alphabetical approach is that, given a working knowledge of the alphabet, one can find a heading for a specific subject very quickly; to gain this advantage one has to accept the consequential alphabetical scattering. If we want the advantages of grouping, we have to accept that access will become less direct unless we go over to systematic arrangement with its notation to guide us. Without a considerable knowledge of LCSH it is difficult to see how a user could find 'Falstaff' in the above arrangement, for example, while the deviation from strict alphabetization is highlighted by the need for the two references to 'Delinquent women' from 'Women, delinquent' *and* 'Women delinquents'.

The early part of this chapter was devoted to the construction of alphabetical headings, and means of devising rules for this. We also have to have rules for filing, otherwise we may not be able to find the headings we have constructed, but their existence suggests that even those who favour alphabetical headings may see some point in systematic arrangement!

BIBLIOGRAPHY

1 Cutter, C A: *Rules for a dictionary catalog*. Washington, Government Printing Office, fourth edition 1904 (reprinted by the Library Association).

2 Balnaves, F J: *A workbook in information retrieval*. Canberra College of Advanced Education, second edition 1975.

3 Kaiser, J: *Systematic indexing*. Pitman, 1911.

4 Coates, E J: *Subject catalogues*. LA, 1960. Now out of print, but for students who can obtain a copy the first six chapters are essential reading. Students should also look at Coates' methods in action in the monthly and annual issues of BTI, and contrast these with comparable issues of the H W Wilson *Applied science and technology index*.

5 Coates, E J and Nicholson, I: '*British technology index*—a study of the application of computer type-setting to index production.' (*In* Cox, N S M and Grose, M W: *Organization and handling of bibliographic records by computer*. Oriel Press, 1967, 167–178.)

6 Metcalfe, J: *Subject classifying and indexing of libraries and literature*. Angus & Robertson, 1959. Appendix H is the *Tentative code of rules for alphabetico-specific entry*.

Metcalfe, J: *Information indexing and subject cataloguing*. Metuchen, NJ, Scarecrow Press, 1957.

Metcalfe, J: *Alphabetical subject indication of information*. Rutgers, State University, Graduate School of Library Science, 1965. (Rutgers series on systems for the intellectual organization of information, *ed* Susan Artandi, vol 3.)

7 Olding, R K: *Wyndham Hulme's literary warrant and information indication*. University of California, Graduate School of Library Service, 1965.

8 Lynch, M F: 'Subject indexes and automatic document retrieval: the structure of entries in *Chemical abstracts* subject indexes'. *Journal of documentation*, 22 (3) 1966, 167–185.

Armitage, J E and Lynch, M F: 'Articulation in the generation of subject indexes by computer'. *Journal of chemical documentation*, 7 (3) 1967, 170–178.

Armitage, J E and Lynch, M F: 'Some structural characteristics of articulated subject indexes'. *Information storage and retrieval*, 4 1968, 101–111.

9 *The indexer, 3* 1962–3, 15, 21, 93–95, 158.

10 American Library Association: *ALA rules for filing catalog cards*. Chicago, ALA, second edition 1968. Opts for strict alphabetical order.

Horner, J L: *Cataloguing*. AAL, 1970. Chapter 24.

Section 3 of J L Horner's *Cataloguing* is valuable background reading for this chapter.

CHAPTER 8

Systematic arrangement

In chapter 5 we saw that one way of showing semantic relationships is by juxtaposition: by arranging related subjects together systematically. By grouping subjects in this way, we hope to present the user with a helpful order: one in which the subjects that he wants to find together are in fact in a group. In chapter 7 we saw that a systematic approach can also be helpful in constructing the network of cross-references needed in an alphabetical system. The most common use for systematic or classified arrangement is for the arrangement of books on open access shelves, but we may also find classified bibliographies and catalogues.

Classified arrangement is not self-evident; as we saw in chapter 5 a concept may be found in a variety of contexts. If we use this kind of arrangement we must have some authority to turn to to tell us what relationships we have decided to show: we do not want to have to keep making the same decisions over and over again. Such an authority is a *classification scheme*, and consists of four parts: the *schedules*, which are the index vocabulary, in which subjects are listed systematically, showing their relationships; the *notation*, which is the code vocabulary, having a self-evident order and thus enabling us to find our way around the arrangement; the *alphabetical index*, which is the entry vocabulary, linked to the index vocabulary by means of the notation; and an *organization* to maintain and revise it. In the next few chapters we shall be considering each of these in turn, but it is essential to remember that the key part of a classification scheme is the schedules—the index vocabulary. In particular, the notation is *not* the classification scheme, though to many people it appears to be.

SCHEDULES

Before we can start to arrange subjects systematically we have to establish what exactly are the subjects we wish to arrange; we have to carry out the same process of analysis as with alphabetical arrangement, but this time with the object of grouping the subjects rather than establishing which is the most significant element. Consider the titles enumerated in table 7. It quickly appears that they fall into two main groups, literature and metallurgy, and that these groups are homogeneous and distinct; such distinct, homogeneous subjects are called *basic classes*. If we want to arrange these titles systematically, then obviously the first move is to group them into the two basic classes. The next step is to consider each basic class separately, to see what prin-

1 The study of literature
2 Select methods of metallurgical analysis
3 The growth of the English novel
4 Elements of heat treatment of metals
5 Modern drama 1800–
6 A textbook of metallurgy
7 Playwriting
8 Methods for the analysis of aluminium
9 The poet's task
10 Iron and steel
11 The French drama of today
12 The metallurgy of beryllium
13 The literature of the Spanish people
14 The manufacture of iron and steel
15 A history of English drama 1600–1900
16 Equipment for the thermal treatment of non-ferrous metals
17 English literature of the twentieth century
18 Rare metals handbook
19 The background of modern English poetry, 1901–1915
20 Methods for the analysis of raw copper
21 Latin literature
22 Heat treatment of aluminium alloys
23 English literature and its readers
24 Heat treatment of steel
25 Some principles of fiction
26 Copper: the science and technology of the metal
27 A short history of German literature
28 Methods for the analysis of iron and steel
29 The temper of the seventeenth century in German literature
30 Twentieth century German verse
31 A few facts about aluminium
32 The decline of the Spanish novel, 1516–1600

TABLE 7: *Analysis into basic classes and facets*

ciples we can use to arrive at a useful order within them.

We therefore need to study the titles carefully to see whether any further groups suggest themselves. We find that in literature, such terms as German, French, English, Spanish and Latin occur and form a group of *languages*; drama, poetry, novels suggest a group characterized by *literary form*; while seventeenth century, 1901–1915, and 1800– are clearly periods of *time*. If we now go through the whole of the group, we will find that all the important concepts fall into one or other of these groups; no matter how many more similar titles we take, they will still repeat this pattern. In metallurgy, we find a number of terms denoting *metals*, either individual or families (*eg* non-ferrous), and others which indicate that some sort of *operation* is carried out, *eg* heat treatment.

In chapters 5 and 6 we saw that we can analyze concepts in such a way as to fit them into five basic categories, but that in practice it was useful to identify more specific categories within a particular subject. In classification theory it is usual to call these specific categories *facets*, because, as Ranganathan pointed out, they each represent a facet or aspect of a subject.[1]

If we consider a topic such as copper, we can place it in a number of different contexts; for example, there will be a metals facet in metallurgy, as we have already seen, but there will also be a materials facet in engineering, a substances facet in chemistry and so on. Copper as a topic taken out of context is an *isolate*, but if we place it in context in a facet in a particular basic class we can refer to it as a *focus* in that facet (plural *foci*). We can tell if we have carried out our analysis adequately by the fact that the foci within a facet should be mutually exclusive; that is, we cannot envisage a composite subject which consists of two foci from the same facet. We cannot have the seventeenth century 1800's, or German English, or copper aluminium, but we *can* have composite subjects consisting of combinations of foci from different facets: English novels, seventeenth century German literature, analysis of copper, heat treatment of aluminium.

We have to make two important decisions before we can start to write down our classification scheme. We have to decide on the order within a facet, and we have to decide on the order in which we cite the facets in a composite subject—the combination order, usually referred to as the *citation order*.

ORDER WITHIN FACETS

Whereabouts in the sequence does any given subject appear? We are trying to arrange subjects systematically, but it is important to remember *why* we are doing this; it is because we believe that by arranging related subjects together we will be helping our users. Our efforts to find a sound systematic arrangement must therefore be directed to finding a *helpful order*. There are a number of general principles which may be appropriate, particularly in the neutral situation where we cannot foresee the needs of the users.

Chronological: This is obvious where arrangement in periods may be envisaged, such as in literature, but it is also applicable where operations may be considered sequentially, *eg* Natural gas technology, where we find:

processing
storage
transportation
distribution
use.

Evolutionary: This is frequently similar to, or identical with, the previous arrangement. It suggests itself for the biological sciences, but may also be used elsewhere, and is also related to the next principle.

Increasing complexity: In many subjects we find a steady development from basic ideas to their most complex application, a good example being mathematics:

arithmetic
algebra
geometry
  Euclidean
  non-Euclidean
  trigonometry
  descriptive
  coordinate
calculus
  differential
  integral

Size: Many subjects lend themselves to a quasi-arithmetical arrangement, *eg* music:

solos
duets
trios *etc*

and government:

central/federal
regional/state/provincial
metropolitan/city
urban/town
rural/village

Spatial: This is the obvious choice for place, where we would try to arrange together countries which are contiguous, but it may also be used elsewhere, *eg* transport:

ground

    railway
    car *etc*
water
  inland
    rivers
    canals
  marine
air
  balloons
  aircraft
space
  rockets

Preferred category: We often find that our users are likely to be interested in one or a few of the foci within a facet far more than in the rest. The normal approach is to begin at the beginning of a sequence, and work through it from left to right (on the shelves), or forward (in a catalogue or bibliography). It will therefore be helpful if we arrange our sequence so that the most wanted items are at the beginning rather than in the middle or at the end. We may remove the *preferred category* from its normal place in the sequence and bring it to the beginning; for example, in Linguistics or Literature we may begin with English (or the mother tongue), even if this means that it will not fall into its logically correct place according to whatever principle we are using. It must be remembered that we are aiming at a *helpful* order, not necessarily a logical one (though in general of course a clear principle of arrangement logically followed *will* be helpful). An example of spatial arrangement with an exception made for preferred category may be found in astronomy:

Planets
  Earth (preferred)
  Mercury
  Venus
  Mars
  Jupiter   *etc*

Canonical: In some subjects we find a traditional order, named by Ranganathan *canonical order;* this will often in such cases form a useful basis for our arrangement, particularly as it will almost certainly be reflected in literary warrant. For example, in Physics we often find in textbooks the sequence Heat, Light, Sound, and unless we wish to use a different principle we can usefully follow this order in our arrangement. The archetypal canon is of course that of the books of the Bible, which are gathered together in a fixed and unchanging order. However, we must be prepared for the fact that where subjects are concerned, few groupings are likely to show this kind of permanence; new approaches call for different groupings from the traditional, and other arrangements are likely to prove more helpful.

Alphabetical: If we are arranging individual topics each of which has a distinct name which is likely to be used to identify it, there is a strong argument for using these names and arranging them in alphabetical order. The obvious examples are found in Biography, where the individual topics are people, and Literature, where we reach a point where we need to arrange by author's name but still need to sub-arrange each author's works systematically. Individual makes of car form another group where alphabetical arrangement may be helpful.

There will be occasions when it is difficult to see any helpful principle; for example, in what order should we arrange grain crops, root crops, legumes, *etc* in the crops facet in Agriculture? If after careful study we are unable to establish any principle to guide us in our choice of a helpful order, then it is equally unlikely that our users will expect any particular order; we should choose one of the general principles listed above and use that. In other cases, there will be an order which is unique to a particular subject, and is suggested by the structure of the subject itself. The careful study of the literature which is necessary before we start our analysis will reveal this.

CITATION ORDER

We have already seen that it is very important when using alphabetical headings to choose the most significant item in a composite heading as the entry word. We have exactly the same choice to make with systematic arrangement, but this time the effects are if anything even more important. The links in the chain forming a composite heading must come from different facets (foci from the same facet cannot be combined), so we are faced with the problem of deciding which facet is the most important, which is next most important, and so on down to the least important. This order of precedence—the order in which we cite the facets—is called the *citation order*. The effect of the citation order is to group material on topics which fall into the *primary facet*, but to scatter information on topics which fall into any of the other facets. Table 8 shows the effect of changing the citation order in Literature, using the titles from the list we have already studied in table 7.

The first section shows the groupings which result from citing Language first, then Literary Form, then Period, while the second shows the effect of citing Literary Form first, then Language, then Period. In the first case, the user interested in English literature, French literature, or the literature of any language group, will find all his material together; but the student of Poetry will have to look in several different places. In the second case, the user interested in a particular Literary Form, *eg* Poetry, will find all his material together, but the student of

Literature grouped by language, then by literary form:
    Playwriting
    Modern drama, 1800–
    The poet's task   (no language specified)
    Some principles of fiction

    English literature and its readers
    English literature of the twentieth century
    The growth of the English novel
    A history of English drama, 1660–1900
    English poetry, 1901–1915

    German literature, a short history
    The temper of the seventeenth century in German literature
    Twentieth century German verse

    The French drama of today

    The literature of the Spanish people
    The decline of the Spanish novel, 1516–1600

Literature grouped by literary form, then by language:
    English literature and its readers
    English literature of the twentieth century
    German literature, a short history   (no form specified)
    The temper of the seventeenth century in German literature
    The literature of the Spanish people

    Some principles of fiction
    The growth of the English novel
    The decline of the Spanish novel, 1516–1600

    Playwriting
    Modern drama 1800–
    A history of English drama 1660–1900
    The French drama of today

    The poet's task
    The background of modern English poetry, 1901–1915
    Twentieth century German verse

TABLE 8: *Effect of citation order on grouping*

English literature will have to look in several different places. Whichever citation order we choose, we have to accept the fact that we cannot please all of the people all of the time. Systematic arrangement brings related subjects together only if they fall into the primary facet. We accept the fact that secondary topics will be scattered because we consider that the groupings brought about by systematic arrangement will be helpful to an extent which will outweigh the disadvantages.

There is another point to having a definite citation order; this is, to provide one, and only one, unambiguous place for any given composite subject. Suppose that we have a document dealing with the Heat treatment of aluminium, and we do not have a fixed citation order; we do not know whether this item ought to go with other works on Heat treatment, or with those on Aluminium. Suppose again that we decide that this particular document ought to go with others on Heat treatment; next week, we may have another document on the same subject, but because of its different treatment of the subject we may decide to place it with other items on Aluminium. We now have two items on the same subject in two different places; the user trying to find information will find one, and assume that he has now found all that we have. The system has an inbuilt tendency to error which will cause us to miss items which we should find; the potential for recall will be greatly lowered. Placing the same composite subject in more than one group is known as *cross-classification*, and it cannot happen if we have a clearly defined citation order to which we adhere. If we are using an enumerative classification, we may have to make up our own rules if it does not cater for the composite subjects we have to deal with.

This is obviously another manifestation of the important factor of consistency and its corollary predictability which we referred to when discussing alphabetical systems. Not only can the classifier avoid cross-classification, by having one and only one possible place for any given composite subject, but the users can begin to recognize the pattern themselves. This can help in two ways; it can make using the arrangement easier, but it can also help in those situations where the users are not sure exactly what it is they want. In such cases the existence of a predictable pattern is an aid in the formulation of a satisfactory search strategy.

As with order within facets, there are some general principles which will help when we are trying to establish the correct citation order.

Subject before bibliographical form: In general, the subject of a work is more significant than the bibliographical form in which the information is presented, *ie* an encyclopedia of chemistry should be grouped with other works on chemistry, not with other encyclopedias; *New society* should be grouped with other works on the social sciences, not with other periodicals. However, there will be occasions when we will disregard this principle in favour of grouping by bibliographical form. We may have a periodicals room where we keep all periodicals, or perhaps only current issues; we may have an abstracts and indexes room where we keep all our tools for bibliographical searching, rather than scatter them by subject; if we have an active translations section associated with the library, as is the case in many special libraries, we may decide to keep all our technical dictionaries together; or we may decide to keep all 'quick reference' works together so that people using them do not disturb other users of the collections. All of these decisions relate to the locating of physical items within the library, but will be reflected in the catalogue; we can however make additional entries in the catalogue using the preferred citation order.

Purpose/product: Many basic classes represent subjects in which the objective is to construct some particular product, or achieve some particular purpose. In such cases, the primary facet will normally be the end product or purpose. For example, the purpose of agriculture is to produce crops; the crops facet will therefore be the primary one in the basic class Agriculture. This principle may be used throughout most of Technology.

Dependence: It is difficult to imagine such operations as Heat treatment without the materials they are applied to, as we have seen earlier when discussing Coates' ideas on significance order. These operations are in fact *dependent* upon the existence of the material; without the materials, there would be no operations. In such cases, the dependent facet should follow the one on which it depends.

Whole-Part: An extension of the idea of dependence is that of Parts being subsidiary to the Wholes to which they belong. Thus in the various branches of Engineering, Machines are more important than Parts, so the Machines facets should precede Parts facets in the citation order. In general, *kinds* of things are more important than *parts*. For example, in Packaging, kinds of container (cans, composites, paper boxes) is the primary facet, with parts (bodies, ends, lids) subsidiary to it.

Decreasing concreteness: Ranganathan has suggested that one, and only one, correct citation order for every basic class can be established, reflecting an order of decreasing concreteness. This order is usually known as PMEST, from the initial letters of Ranganathan's *fundamental categories*, Personality, Matter, Energy, Space, Time. These will be studied in more detail in the chapter on Colon classification; for the present, we should note that their generality frequently leads to doubt as to their precise mode of application, particularly in the case of Personality. In addition, a facet which is Matter in one basic class *eg* Materials in Library science, may become Personality in another basic class, in this case Bibliography; other similar changes are possible.

The above lines may be followed to give a generalized facet

order: Things—Kinds—Parts—Materials—Properties—Processes—Operations—Agents. However, it is by no means obvious how we can apply this to Literature, or some of the social sciences. We are faced with the same problem as in alphabetical order: what exactly is the most significant part of a subject? Once again we have to restate the purpose of systematic arrangement: to provide an order which will be helpful to the user. We must try to group together those foci which a user is likely to want to find grouped; if we can discover this, we have established at least the primary facet. As with significance order in alphabetical headings, it is when we have difficulty in establishing users' needs that we are obliged to rely on general principles, in the hope that these will prove valid for a good proportion of our users.

The idea of one place and one place only for any composite subject is central to the idea of shelf arrangement, or ordering of items in a bibliography. However, the essential corollary of the one place requirement, a fixed citation order, can lead to problems, and has been the source of most of the criticism of systematic arrangement and precoordinate systems. It assumes that we can satisfy our users by one fixed grouping, but as has been pointed out, we cannot please all of the people all of the time. Two examples may help to demonstrate this, one from Literature, the other from Engineering.

In a general library, the user's approach to Literature will usually be primarily through language, secondly through literary form. Our readers often take it for granted that all the English literature is together, and ask for novels, or plays, or whatever form is of interest to them. Period is usually less important, but has a role in that most readers are interested in *modern* literature. The situation in an academic library is rather different; here, students will usually be interested primarily in a particular language, as before, but within that language are likely to be studying a particular period rather than a particular form. Indeed, it can be argued that division by literary form is a hindrance to them, because it separates the works of an author who has written in more than one form. We have here two situations which differ in that the need of the users in one is for a different set of groupings from that required by users in the other. One citation order cannot cater for both, and it is interesting to note that the Dewey decimal classification (DC), which is directed mainly toward the general, public, library situation, has the language, form, period, citation order first outlined, whereas the Library of Congress classification (LC), intended to arrange a library for scholars, to a very large extent ignores form in its Literature schedules.

A fixed citation order implies that there is a 'standard' approach to a subject; but what of the situation in a library serving a research establishment? The essential characteristic of research is that it is intended to upset the accepted order of things, and we must therefore expect research workers to find an arrangement based on the old order something less than helpful. Such a situation arose in the Central Library of the English Electric Company, where a classified catalogue was in use, arranged by the library's own classification scheme for Engineering. This has a citation order Machines: Parts: Materials: Problems; thus a topic such as fatigue, which assumed a new importance in the 1950s as the unexpected cause of at least two major air disasters, is a Problem, and falls into the least important facet. For most of the users of the catalogue this is acceptable; the company produces machines, and most of its research is concerned with these—motors, generators, nuclear reactors, aircraft. However, this citation order does mean that fatigue is scattered at a very large number of places in the classified sequence, simply because it falls into the least important facet and is thus not used for grouping; in fact, more than 300 places. This is hardly likely to appeal to the groups of engineers who are working on this very problem; they cannot be expected to regard as helpful an arrangement which scatters their interests to over 300 different places. A similar difficulty was met in the Library of the Atomic Energy Research Establishment, Harwell, where it proved impossible to find a satisfactory citation order in some subject areas covered by the catalogues. Some methods of solving the problem by making multiple entry under various forms of the same heading have been described in chapter 6; D J Foskett uses rotation in conjunction with the *London education classification*, while cycling is very widely used in catalogues based on UDC. A detailed example is worked out in chapter 18. These solutions are mainly found in special libraries, and of course they can only apply to the catalogue, not to the arrangement of books on the shelves; we may assume for the time being that, for the general library at least, it *is* possible to find a citation order which will result in groupings helpful to the great majority of users, while remaining aware of the fact that in certain situations this is less likely to be the case.

FILING ORDER

We have now established the need for a careful study of the literature of a subject to determine the concepts likely to arise, and the facets into which we can group these concepts; the need for order within the facets; and the need for a citation order which will determine the order of precedence of facets in composite subjects. We now have to study the way in which we must write out the schedule which will show clearly whereabouts in the sequence any given subject—simple or composite—will be found.

It is a commonly accepted principle of systematic arrangement that general should precede special. This can apply both to subjects related as genus to species and to those in which the relationship is syntactic. For example, Metals should preceded Non-ferrous metals, which in its turn should precede Aluminium (though this does not indicate whether Aluminium should precede or follow Ferrous metals—aluminium does not lie in the same chain of subdivision). At the same time, Aluminium should precede Heat treatment of aluminium, as should Heat treatment, since both are more general than the composite subject of which they form part. But should Aluminium precede Heat treatment, or *vice versa*? We cannot say that Aluminium is more general than Heat treatment since we have no basis of comparison; we cannot determine a special/general relationship between foci from different facets, only between those within the same facet. We have determined the order of facets when more than one is represented in a composite subject, but we still have to determine the order in which the facets themselves should be written down so that we can arrange simple subjects in which only one facet is represented. The citation order, together with the general principle enunciated above, that general should precede special, will enable us to do this.

PRINCIPLE OF INVERSION

Consider the following seven titles, falling within the basic class Literature:

The English novel
Trends in twentieth century literature
The novel as a literary form
Twentieth century English literature
English literature
The English novel in this century
The modern novel, 1900-

Using the citation order Language—Literary form—Period, we can re-state these subjects in the formal manner:

English: novel	(1)
Twentieth century	(2)
Novel	(3)
English: twentieth century	(4)
English	(5)
English: novel: twentieth century	(6)
Novel: twentieth century	(7)

Having done this, we can group them according to the citation order into those in which a language is specified; those in which no language is specified but we have a literary form; and those in which neither language nor literary form is specified but we have a period.

Group A	English: novel	(1)
	English: twentieth century	(4)
	English	(5)
	English: novel: twentieth century	(6)

138

| Group B | Novel | (3) |
| | Novel: Twentieth century | (7) |

| Group C | Twentieth century | (2) |

Now, however we arrange them, we must keep the groups intact, because this is the purpose of having a citation order. Consider the three subjects (6), (7) and (2); if we are to arrange these so that general precedes special, it must be in the order (2), (7), (6).

Twentieth century	(2)	(Group C)
Novel: twentieth century	(7)	(Group B)
English: novel: Twentieth century	(6)	(Group A)

If we are to keep the groups intact, then equally *group* C must precede *group* B, which in turn must precede *group* A. Within *group* B, clearly (3) must precede (7). Within *group* A, (5) must come first, since it is more general than any of the others, and (6) must come last, as being more special than any. This leaves us with (1) and (4) to sort out, but (1) must be grouped with (6), since within the general group English literature they both deal with the novel, which is in the next facet to be considered. So we end up with the arrangement:

Group C	Twentieth century	(2)
Group B	Novel	(3)
	Novel: twentieth century	(7)
Group A	English	(5)
	English: twentieth century	(4)
	English: novel	(1)
	English: novel: twentieth century	(6)

We have now followed the two guidelines we established to begin with, the citation order Language, Literary form, Period, and the general-before-special principle. If we now study the result, we find that (perhaps contrary to expectation) it is the least important facet Period which comes first, with the most important, Language, coming last; that is to say, the filing order is the reverse of the citation order. This effect, which arises because we wish to preserve the idea of general before special for both semantic and syntactic relationships, is known as the *Principle of inversion*. If we do not follow this principle, then we shall find that general precedes special for semantic relationships, *ie* relationships between foci within the same facet, but that for some syntactic relationships general will follow special.

The principle of inversion is in conflict with the suggestion put forward under the heading *Preferred category* (page 131) that users like to find the material of most interest to them at the beginning of the sequence. In the example worked out above for Literature, before we come to any particular language (English will probably be the first), we shall have to scan through entries relating to the whole of Literature limited only by Period, and entries relating to particular literary forms—yet we have said that Language is the most important element. For this reason, some classification schemes have ignored the principle of inversion, for example the English Electric Company's scheme for *Engineering* previously mentioned, and the scheme for *Occupational safety and health* devised by D J Foskett. However, the introductions to editions of the English Electric scheme after the first have pointed out that in practice this has not worked satisfactorily, and if the scheme were to be started again from the beginning there is little doubt that the editors would decide to follow the principle of inversion.

A rather different way of showing the principle has been demonstrated by Palmer and Wells. If we indicate when a facet is present by a 1, and absent by a 0, we can write down a formula for each title in the form of a binary notation, using the citation order:

	L	F	P	
English: novel	1	1	0	(1)
Twentieth century	0	0	1	(2)
Novel	0	1	0	(3)
English: twentieth century	1	0	1	(4)
English	1	0	0	(5)
English: novel: twentieth century	1	1	1	(6)
Novel: twentieth century	0	1	1	(7)

If we now arrange the titles by the notation, we find that we get the order that we arrived at previously: (2) (3) (7) (5) (4) (1) (6). The notation has made the rearrangement simpler, but does not show quite so clearly *why* we get the result we do.

The principle of inversion is one that often causes students an unnecessary amount of difficulty. The easiest way to understand it is to arrange a set of examples using first a scheme following the principle, then a scheme ignoring it. The difference in the overall arrangement will then become clear. In the example used above to demonstrate the principle, we used the citation order Language: Literary form: Period. This gave us the groups A, B and C, since this is the function of the citation order; we chose that citation order because it would give us those groups, which represent the kind of grouping that we think our readers will find useful. If we ignore the principle of inversion, we will make our filing order also A B C, so let us consider the effect this will have on the overall filing order. In Group B, if general is to precede special, Novel must precede Novel: twentieth century. For the same reason, in the Group A (ignoring title 4 for the moment) we shall have the sequence

English
English: novel
English: novel: twentieth century

and since period now follows literary form we can add title 4 at the end of this sequence. The overall order will thus be

English
English : novel
English : novel: twentieth century
English : twentieth century
Novel
Novel : twentieth century
Twentieth century

It will be seen that the result here is not the orderly progression from general to special that we had before, but a progression which moves from general (English) to less general (English novel) to least general (English: novel: twentieth century), then back to more general (English: twentieth century) to more general (Novel) to less general (Novel: twentieth century) to more general (twentieth century). The same kind of result will occur whenever the principle is not followed. Later in this chapter a schedule is worked out for Library science, using a particular citation order; the way in which the principle of inversion works can be seen very clearly if the titles on p 147 are arranged first using the schedule with the citation order suggested, then using it with a different citation order but keeping the same filing order. (The exercise is easier if the schedule is given a notation, but can be carried out without this. The method is outlined within the next section, schedule construction.) The principle will be ignored if we keep the same citation order and alter the filing order, as we did just above, or keep the same filing order but alter the citation order, as is suggested for the exercise. In both cases the result is the same; instead of an orderly progression in which a general heading always precedes headings more specific, we shall find an order in which it is difficult to predict exactly whereabouts a particular degree of generality is to be found. We shall still be able to find subjects, and the order will still give us the groupings which we have decided are likely to be most helpful, but if we do not find what we want straight away, altering our search strategy is likely to be confusing.

SCHEDULE CONSTRUCTION

We have now established all the information that we need to enable us to construct a schedule, or table, in a given subject area. We have decided on the order of importance of the facets of the subject—the citation order; the order of foci within each facet; and, using the principle of inversion, we know that the order in which the facets should appear in the schedule is the reverse of the citation order. We now have to make a decision as to whether our schedules should be enumerative or synthetic; since the latter are very much easier to construct and use, let us consider them first.

In a synthetic schedule we need only list simple subjects; we do not try to list any composite subjects. All that we need to include in the schedule will be the foci within the various facets; the citation order tells us how to combine these whenever this is necessary. To write down the schedule, all that has to be done is to write down the facets, beginning with the least important and ending with the most important. Within each facet, the foci will of course be arranged according to whatever principle we have adopted.

To arrange composite subjects using such a schedule, we must first analyse them into individual foci, and rearrange these according to the citation order, so that the most important focus in each case is the first in the formal statement. Taking some of the titles from table 7 and using the citation order Language, Literary form, Period, we arrive at the following formal statements:

3 English: novel
5 Drama: 1800–
7 Drama: techniques
9 Poetry: criticism
11 French: drama: twentieth century
15 English: drama: 1600–1900
17 English: twentieth century
19 English: poetry: 1901–1915
25 Novel
29 German: seventeenth century
30 German: poetry: twentieth century
32 Spanish: novel: 1516–1600

(Note that in addition to putting these into our preferred citation order we have eliminated various synonyms, *eg* fiction, verse, plays). Using the schedule we have constructed, we can put the primary foci into order:

Novel   25
Drama   5, 7,
Poetry   9
English 3, 15, 17, 19
German   29, 30
French   11
Spanish 32

We have thus settled the order for some but not all of our examples. We still have to sort out those which have the same primary focus, once again using the schedule, but this time applying it *within* each group of items.

Drama: techniques   7
        1800–   5

(because techniques comes from a facet less important than period and thus precedes it), and

English: twentieth century   17
          novel   3

142

drama	15
poetry	19
German: seventeenth century	29
poetry	30

We now have arrived at the correct placings for each of the subjects in our list:

- 25 Novel
- 7 Drama : techniques
- 5 Drama : 1800–
- 9 Poetry : criticism
- 17 English : twentieth century
- 3 English : Novel
- 15 English : drama : 1600–1900
- 19 English : poetry : 1901–1915
- 29 German : seventeenth century
- 30 German : poetry : twentieth century
- 11 French : drama : twentieth century
- 32 Spanish: novel: 1516–1600

In this particular case we did not have to go beyond the second concept in any of the statements, but if we had been obliged to do so the procedure would have been exactly the same. Suppose for example that we had reached a stage where we had

English : drama : Restoration
English : drama : Jacobean
English : drama : techniques
English : drama : 1800–
English : drama
English : drama : 1840–1890

We should now have to arrange these according to the third concept in the formal statement, to give us

English : drama
English : drama : techniques
English : drama : Jacobean
English : drama : Restoration
English : drama : 1800–
English : drama : 1840–1890

and so on, until we had arrived at the most complete systematic arrangement possible. In a normal library situation, there will of course be more than one item at most points in our systematic arrangement, and these can then be arranged according to author's name, in chronological sequence, or by some similar characteristic additional to the subject specification.

The schedule is thus very simple, yet from it we are able to find an unambiguous place for any given composite subject (provided of course that the concepts involved in it are listed in our schedule).

Because we list only single concepts, with none of their possible combinations, the schedule can be very brief, yet be as powerful in arranging our collections as a much longer enumerative schedule.

If, however, we decide to compile an enumerative schedule, we have to follow a similar procedure, but this time for any and every composite subject. For each focus in the primary facet we have to envisage which foci from the second facet will be likely to co-occur in a composite subject, and list these; in addition, for each of these we have to consider which foci from the third facet are also likely to co-occur, and then list the composite subjects formed in this way. Then, when we come to classify by the scheme, we do not have to build up the composite subject represented in the item we are dealing with, but will instead find it, ready made, in the scheme.

An example will help to make the distinction clearer. If we are using the Universal Decimal Classification (UDC), we find that in the basic class Literature we have a completely synthetic schedule, which occupies about a page of the schedules; to classify a composite topic such as *The English novel of the 1840's* we have to find English, novel and 1840's, and combine these elements. If we are using an enumerative classification such as the Bibliographic Classification (BC), we turn to Literature, then find English literature, then find nineteenth century English literature, and finally the period 1837–1870, which is the closest we find to the precise one we require; then we find listed under that period: novelists (as well as the other literary forms). Problems of synthesis are mainly notational: can we combine the notation for the various elements to give us the correct composite notation? These are discussed in a later section. The problems of enumeration, on the other hand, are mainly those of quantity: can we enumerate all the composite subjects we are likely to need, or do we make a selection? LC is an enumerative scheme, and its schedules for language and literature occupy some 2,000 pages of print, as opposed to UDC's one; but even this is a selection of the possible combinations, because LC only includes subjects if there is literary warrant for them in the Library of Congress *and* it is thought that they need to be specified for the shelf arrangement. What usually happens in enumerative schemes is that a rather limited selection of composite subjects is listed and that others which are not listed have to be accommodated with their most important focus but without specifying other foci. In addition, enumerative schemes do not usually have a clear facet structure, so that one is often left in doubt as to which is the most important focus.

Consider the subject *Gothic mural painting in Bohemia and Moravia*; there are three foci here, *Gothic*, from the Time facet, *mural*, from the Form facet, and *Bohemia and Moravia* from the Place facet, all three facets within the basic class *Painting*. If we turn to DC18 to classify this, we find that we can classify any of the foci singly, but have no means of combining them, nor is there any clear indication of which is to be considered the most important. We find an instruction at 751 Processes and forms 'Class processes and forms of individual painters in 759.1–759.9', but no instruction relating to schools and styles. At 751.7 Specific forms we find the instruction 'Class subjects in specific forms in 753–758, techniques, apparatus, equipment, materials employed in specific forms in 751.2–751.6; mural painting is found at 751.73, a subdivision of specific forms, as expected. If we turn to 759, we find that 759.01–759.06 are Specific periods of development, including 759.02 500–1450, including Gothic, but there is an instruction at the heading 759.01–759.06 'Class here schools and styles not limited by country or locality.' So at 751 we have an instruction relating to individual painters, but no reference to schools and styles, while at 759.01–759.06 we have an instruction concerning schools and styles but no reference to individual painters. By digging around in the schedules for other instructions, we may come to the conclusion that the correct place is in 759.1–759.9 (the Principle of inversion would lead us to the same conclusion), but it would really be more satisfactory to have a clear and definite instruction telling us which facet is to be considered the primary facet. (In passing, we may note that the publication of this particular book led to the addition of a heading to LCSH; the 7th edition, like DC, cannot give a specific heading, but one is included in the Supplements and in the 8th edition. Such is the power of literary warrant!) This is only one example, but it is typical of the kind of criticism that inevitably arises with this kind of scheme, from the impossibility in practice of listing all the composite subjects that have occurred or may occur in the future.

Another problem that is often found in practice in enumerative schemes, despite the fact that theoretically it cannot occur, is that concepts of different kinds are found to be mixed up, so that cross-classification becomes not so much a danger, more a way of life. Consider the following excerpt from the abridged UDC schedules:

628	PUBLIC HEALTH ENGINEERING
628.3	Sewage, rain-, foul-water. Purification, etc.
628.33	Physical and mechanical treatment
.334	Screening. Grit and grease removal
.335	Flocculation: tanks, etc.
.336	Sludge: handling, disposal
.337	Electrical treatment of sewage
.34	Chemical treatment processes *etc*

It will be seen that in the middle of a series of methods of treatment (Actions, Operations, Processes) we find a material 'sludge' which is the result of a process of settling, not mentioned in the schedule. In another example we find:

361   SOCIAL RELIEF IN GENERAL

.9	Relief or aid in emergencies, disasters
.91	Earthquakes, storms, hurricanes
.92	Floods
.93	War, civil war
.94	Epidemics
.95	Famine
.96	Fires, conflagrations
.98	Technical (volunteer) relief services

Either technical (volunteer) relief services are to be regarded as disasters in themselves, or we are faced with considerable problems in finding the correct place for technical (volunteer) services for earthquake relief. We shall be in the same position as we found in the last paragraph, uncertain of the correct place to choose for a composite subject not specifically listed in the schedules.

As has already been indicated in chapter 6, all systems enumerate to some extent; a synthetic classification scheme has to list the foci in each facet, and if it fails to list the particular focus we are searching for on some occasion we shall again be faced with the problem of lack of specificity. For example, the subject *Design and construction of transistor superhets* implies a specification

    Communications engineering-radio-apparatus-receivers-
      superheterodyne-using transistors.

If we are using the Colon Classification (CC), which is as completely synthetic a scheme as possible, we find that this can only be classified with radio engineering; the scheme simply does not enumerate anything more detailed in this subject area. Even with UDC we find (using the abridged edition) that we can only specify receivers, not superhets, and are thus unable to be specific.

It should be remembered that we have been thinking so far of the classifier trying to find a place in the overall arrangement for each new subject as it arises. From the point of view of the user, who only sees the results of the classifier's work, there is no difference between a synthetic scheme and an enumerative, except in those instances where the enumerative scheme has failed to foresee a composite subject. If we were to write out all the possible combinations of concepts arising from the use of a synthetic scheme, we should have an enumerative scheme. The real problem for the classificationist, ie the compiler of a classification scheme, is that the number of possible combinations is enormous. Mathematically speaking, if we have a schedule containing four facets, with four foci in each facet, the number of possible subjects we can specify is 624! And this from a ridiculously simple schedule containing only sixteen concepts! It is small wonder that an enumerative scheme usually only lists a selection—but provided that it lists the *right* selection, it will prove just as effective as a synthetic scheme, and the user will have no means of telling the difference. The real problem lies in the fact that enumerative schemes are usually *closed*; if we do have to deal with a subject not enumerated, we have to wait for the compiler to tell us where we can put it in the schedule, rather than insert it ourselves as we can in a synthetic scheme.

CONSTRUCTION OF A CLASSIFICATION SCHEDULE
It may be helpful to demonstrate how we may set about constructing a classification schedule in a limited subject area, in this case Library science. By studying the following list of titles carefully, we can establish certain facets; we can then decide on a citation order and helpful order within each facet. Finally we can write down the schedule and use it to arrange the items (titles taken from *Library science abstracts*).

1 Progress of the Universal Decimal Classification in the USSR
2 Baltimore County Public Library initiates book catalog
3 An art reference library for children
4 Automation in the Detroit Public Library
5 Cooperation in government libraries
6 Non-standard material at the National Lending Library for Science and Technology
7 The National Library of Canada
8 Libraries and librarianship in Saskatchewan
9 Book selection tools for agricultural documents
10 An information retrieval system for maps
11 Aspects of recent research in classification
12 La Roche College classification scheme for phonograph records
13 The economics of book catalog production
14 Classification of law books in the University of South Africa Library
15 Book selection and acquisition processes in university libraries
16 Administrative problems of university libraries
17 Revision of classification schemes for Nigerian needs
18 Acquisitions
19 School libraries
20 Federal assistance to special libraries
21 The hospital library service in Lincoln
22 A mechanized circulation system
23 Automation in university libraries
24 Newspapers in technical college libraries
25 Library services to the blind in New Zealand
26 Public libraries in the New York metropolitan area
27 Metropolitan areas growing and under stress: the situation of the Detroit Public Library.

If we try to group the concepts arising from the titles, we find that a first approximation gives us four groups:

Libraries	Materials	Operations	Common facets
special	non-standard	cooperation	
government	newspapers	administration	automation
university	books	selection	research
technical	phonorecords	acquisition	revision
college	(*ie* records)	cataloguing	economics
public	maps	catalogues	various places
municipal	agriculture	bookform	
county	law	classification	
national		schemes	
hospitals		UDC	
blind		circulation	
children		finance	
reference		Federal aid	
art			
science			

It is clear that there is a group of 'Libraries' but that these fall into more than one subfacet:

kind	people served	mode of use	subject coverage
special	hospitals	reference	art
government	blind		science and
academic	children		technology
university			
technical college			
school			
public			
municipal			
county			
national			

We can of course extend the above lists even without literary warrant, by the addition of *eg*, lending, under mode of use, or industrial, under kind, once we have identified the facets.

We can also subdivide the Materials facet into two groups:

subject
law
agriculture
form

books	maps	non-standard
newspapers	records	

Within the Operations facet we find some concepts which depend on others, *eg*

    classification—schemes
    cataloguing—catalogues

In each case further subdivision by kind can be made. It would be possible to separate these into another facet, but for the time being we may keep them with the operations to which they belong.

We find a group of topics which may appear in any basic class, called common foci; as we shall see in the next chapter, there are usually four of these groups, but in the present example only two are represented, place and common subjects.

Having identified the facets, we need to decide on a citation order. For the neutral situation, this might well be Libraries—Materials—Operations, though in the context of a library school a citation order which brings Operations to the most significant place might well be more useful. Within Libraries, we may decide that kind is most important, then population served, then mode of use and finally subject; Materials may be arranged primarily by subject, then by physical form. Of the two common facets, place is more important than common subjects. This gives us an overall order:

Libraries—kind—population served—mode of use—subject—Materials—subject—form—Operations—Place—Common subjects.

If we decide to follow the principle of inversion, we shall arrive at a schedule outline as follows:

Common subjects
Place
Operations
Materials
  by form
  by subject
Libraries
  by subject
  by mode of use
  by population served
  by kind

Within each facet we need to arrive at some helpful order. In the Common subjects none suggests itself; for Place, we may use the schedule from an existing scheme; those Operations which form a logical sequence in time may be arranged chronologically, with circulation perhaps moved to a place under administration rather than its chronological place following technical services; in Materials, books, as the preferred category, begin the sequence; in kind of library, a progression by size of population served is a possibility. We can thus build up a schedule as shown in Figure 11.

There are several points to note from this schedule. The first is that it is very incomplete in its listing of foci, but that despite this it probably covers most of the facets of library science. The more literature we study, the more foci we can insert, but additional facets will be few. Secondly, we can show some hierarchical (ie genus-species) relationships by the layout, though if we apply the schedule to shelf or

FIGURE 11: *Tentative schedule for library science*

Common subject subdivisions
 revision
 research
 automation
 economics
Common place subdivisions
 (no schedule needed)
Operations
 Administration
  selection
  acquisition
  circulation
 Technical services
  cataloguing
   catalogues
    book form
  classification
   schemes
    UDC
 Cooperation
 Finance
  government aid
Materials
 Books
 Serials
  periodicals
  newspapers
 non-standard (*ie* non-printed word)
  records
  maps
 by subject
  (no schedule needed)
Libraries
 by subject
  (no schedule needed)
 by mode of use
  reference
 by population served
  children
  hospitals
  handicapped
   blind

by kind
  special
    government
    academic
    school
    technical college
    university
  public
    municipal
    county
    national

catalogue arrangement it will not be possible to do this. Thirdly, we need to carry our analysis rather further than we have; for example, we could have blind children as the population served—but we have said that it is not possible to combine foci from the same facet! We may need to introduce subfacets here, to distinguish persons by age (and sex also, perhaps). Experience may also suggest modifications to the facet order suggested here. A scheme of the kind adumbrated here was compiled by the Classification Research Group, and is in use in the libraries of the Polytechnic of North London Library School and the Library Association. It is also used to arrange the entries in *Library and information science abstracts* (LISA); largely as a result of studies of user reactions to this, the citation order was changed from the original Library—Materials—Operations to Operations—Materials—Libraries at the beginning of 1971. A revised edition of the first draft has now been published.[2]

BIBLIOGRAPHY
  1 Several of the items mentioned in the bibliography for chapter 1 contain sections on facet analysis, *eg*
    Vickery, B C: *Classification and indexing in science and technology.*
    Foskett, D J: *Classification and indexing in the social sciences.*
    Mills, J: *A modern outline of library classification.*
  See also the following items:
    Ramsden, M J: *An introduction to index language construction.* Bingley, 1974. Elementary. (Programmed text.)
    Vickery, B C: *Faceted classification.* London, Aslib, 1960.
    Vickery, B C: *Faceted classification schemes.* Rutgers, State University, Graduate School of Library Science, 1966. (Rutgers series on systems for the intellectual organization of information, *ed* Susan Artandi, vol 6.)
    Mills, J: *Guide to the Universal Decimal Classification.* British Standards Institution, 1963. A valuable introduction to facet analysis, this work also shows how it may be applied successfully in a scheme which is basically one of the older enumerative kind.

2　Daniel, R and Mills, J: *A classification of library and information science*. LA, 1974.

Students should also look at examples of faceted schemes, *eg*

Foskett, D J: 'The London education classification'. *Education libraries bulletin*, Supplement 6, second edition, 1975.

English Electric Company Ltd: *Thesaurofacet*. 1970.

Classification Research Group: Bulletin no 7: *Four faceted schemes of classification. Journal of documentation, 18*, 1962, 65–88.

It is a useful exercise to construct a schedule by examining the literature of a subject, as found for example in an abstracting or indexing service, identifying the concepts present, grouping them into facets and deciding on a citation order, in the same way as we have demonstrated for library science.

CHAPTER 9

General classification schemes

So far we have been considering the problems that arise within a particular basic class. If we wish to include more than this, we have to face additional problems, in particular the one of overall order; in what sequence do we arrange a collection of basic classes? In the early years of library classification in the modern sense (*ie* from Dewey's introduction of his decimal classification in 1876) it was assumed that the order of main classes was the one important feature of a scheme, and such classification theorists as H E Bliss devoted much time and thought to this. When Ranganathan introduced the idea of consistent facet analysis applied to all basic classes in the first edition of CC, published in 1933, interest began to concentrate on the development of 'special' classifications, *ie* those applied to a particular, limited, subject field, usually a single basic class, and during the 1950's the Classification Research Group in Britain devoted most of its thought to this problem. Techniques of analysis and synthesis, and the notational devices required to permit them, were developed, and several notable schemes were produced. In the 1960's there has been a swing back towards the general scheme and its problems, with the objective of developing a new classification of the whole of recorded knowledge, and some practical work has been done with the aid of a grant from NATO. We have therefore to consider now the problems of arranging basic classes in a helpful order, and the additional features which we must provide in a general scheme if it is to function properly.

COMMON FACETS

If the titles listed in table 9 are studied carefully, it will appear that there are certain kinds of concept which keep recurring, and which may be found in any basic class. We find for example dictionary, periodical, illustration, encyclopedia: all kinds of bibliographical form. Statistics, law, societies, research: all kinds of subject which exist in their own right, yet may be found as features within other subjects as well. We also find that all subjects may be considered from the historical and geographical points of view, or to use the more common terms, time and place. There are in effect four groups of subjects which may occur within any basic class: four *common facets*. In providing a schedule for a basic class, we may decide that it is not appropriate to include these common subdivisions, but obviously in a general scheme they must appear.[1]

1 *Metal industry* handbook and directory
2 Glossary of terms relating to iron and steel
3 English poetry and prose: an anthology
4 Metallurgical dictionary
5 British miniature electronic components data annual 1967–68
6 Colliers encyclopedia
7 The Oxford English dictionary
8 *Life* magazine
9 XIX century fiction: a bibliographical record
10 Cassell's encyclopedia of literature
11 *Washington post*
12 Bibliography on steel converter practice
13 Instrumentation in the metallurgical industry
14 The *voice of youth*: the Poetry Society's junior quarterly
15 Aluminium Development Association: Directory of members
16 Winston Churchill: the early years
17 The Highlands of Scotland in pictures
18 The rules of the game of netball
19 Statistical assessment of the life characteristic: a bibliography
20 A year with horses: John Beard's sketch book
21 American scientists of the 19th century
22 Handbook of chemistry and physics
23 Education in Scotland
24 Scientific and learned societies of Great Britain
25 Annual abstract of statistics
26 International who's who

TABLE 9: *Identify the common factors*

The titles in table 9 indicate that in some cases the bibliographical forms and the common subjects may be applied to the whole of knowledge as a unit, not just to a limited area such as a single basic class. A general encyclopedia presents information on the whole of knowledge in a particular form; a general periodical may treat of any or every subject. In a general scheme we shall therefore find it necessary to make provision for this, in what is known as a generalia class. Some general schemes also include in this class topics which may be regarded as pervasive or tool subjects; DC includes Library science and Documentation, while Brown included a number of subjects such as Logic,

Mathematics, and Education in the Generalia class in his Subject Classification (SC) which are more helpfully arranged elsewhere.

In a general scheme, we have to continue our process of grouping by arranging related basic classes together in sequence and imposing some sort of overall plan. To start in this way with the elements and build them up into larger groups is the inductive approach; in the past, the deductive method of taking the whole of knowledge and dividing it up into smaller areas has been the one more often used. The results are similar, but we find in many cases that the number of areas discovered by the deductive approach bears a close relationship to the number of notational symbols available, the most striking example of this being DC, where Dewey freely admits that 'Theoreticly division of every subject into just 9 parts is absurd', but nevertheless goes ahead to do just that. By using induction we are more likely to avoid this kind of trap.

A major problem has always been to define the term main class, which is commonly used for these large areas or groups. We can see that heat, light, sound, electricity and magnetism can be grouped with various other basic classes to form a group of subjects which we call physics; but physics can itself be grouped with such subjects as chemistry and astronomy to form the group of physical sciences, while these can further be grouped with the biological sciences to form the natural sciences group. Finally, we can group this with a similar large assembly to form science and technology. We can carry out a similar series of groupings in other disciplines, ending up with three assemblies: science and technology, social sciences, and humanities. At what point do we stop? Or do we conclude that there are only three main classes? The question is evidently one of terminology, and in practice we find no agreement between the compilers of general classification schemes as to what constitutes a main class. Ranganathan defines main class: 'any class enumerated in the first order array of a scheme of classification of the universe of knowledge. This definition is valid only for the scheme concerned'.[2] Elsewhere he suggests that main classes are conventional, fairly homogeneous and mutually exclusive groups of basic classes, and also introduces the idea of 'partially comprehensive' main classes as a means of differentiating the 'super-groups' such as physical sciences. The idea that main classes are merely conventional groups may serve to free us from having to find any theoretical justification for our selection and ordering, and it emphasizes the fact that there is unlikely to be long term stability in any particular selection we may make. However, it is important to study the arguments which have been advanced to justify one order or another of main classes, and to see what effect this factor has on the overall arrangement given by a scheme.

Dewey credits his arrangement of main classes to 'the inverted Baconian arranjement of the St Louis library . . .', but also points out that 'everywhere filosofic theory and accuracy have yielded to practical usefulness'. Palmer[3] suggests that if literary warrant be taken as the criterion BNB has identified no less than fifty four main classes in DC, rather than Dewey's nine. In many ways, the order in DC is poor, separating language (400) from literature (800), and history (900) from the other social sciences (300). It also reflects the state of knowledge of the latter half of the nineteenth century, with, for example, psychology shown as a division of philosophy. It illustrates quite well the point that an order of main classes which may be justified at one point in time may well cease to be acceptable as time passes; despite its grounding in Bacon's theory, nobody would now claim that Dewey's order is particularly helpful or theoretically valid.

BROWN

The order of main classes in the *Subject classification*[4] fits into the overall pattern:

Matter and force
Life
Mind
Record

which may be said to have some logical validity. However, Brown did not worry unduly about this aspect, and indeed placed the graphic and plastic arts in his generalia class, because he had some spare notation there which was not available under the 'record' section. Brown is however interesting in that he introduced a principle which is still somewhat controversial but seems to be useful: the grouping of a science and its technology. Dewey had grouped all 'sciences' together and all 'technologies' together (with the exception of medicine, where both science and technology appear together). Brown instead placed each technology with the science upon which it depended, so that electrical engineering is found with electricity in physics, for example. This can be a helpful approach, particularly in such subjects as electronics, where the technology of solid state devices is hard to differentiate from their fundamental physics. However, Brown allowed himself to be carried away by this idea, linking music and acoustics, horseracing and zoology and so on in a way which is clearly unhelpful.

BLISS

Bliss devoted a great deal of time to establishing the correct order of main classes, and the introductions to the two volumes of his scheme contain much that is of value in this discussion, as does his other work.[5] He introduced several ideas which are still of value. Perhaps the most basic of these is the idea of the 'educational and scientific consensus'. Bliss thought it vital that a classification scheme for recorded knowledge should reflect the structure of knowledge as recognized and taught by scientists, philosophers and educators, and that the more knowledge we acquire, the more clearly we shall see this desired structure. Unfortunately, this is not the case: knowledge changes, the structure of knowledge changes, and any widely accepted pattern is likely to be out of date, for the purpose of research is indeed to change the structure of knowledge as well as to expand it. Bliss himself recognized that 'the old order changeth', and that any classification scheme will inevitably become gradually more and more divorced from helpful order; what he does not seem to have recognized is the speed with which this process can take place.

To establish the order of subjects within the educational and scientific consensus, Bliss used three main principles. The first of these is *collocation of related subjects*. For example, Bliss considers that Psychology is related to both Medicine and Education, so that the relevant part of his outline is as follows:

Anthropological sciences
  Medicine
  Psychology
  Education
  Social science

Here it will be seen that psychology is linked to both of these other topics. However, it may also be seen that Bliss did not follow his own second principle, *subordination of specific to general*, for in order to collocate it with psychology, education has to precede the more general heading social science. However, in general these two principles are sound and can give a helpful arrangement.

The third principle Bliss called *gradation in speciality*, and it relates to what is in effect a kind of progression of dependence. If we compare mathematics and physics, we can see that though we use the ideas of mathematics in physics, the converse is not true; we do not use the ideas of physics in mathematics, and to this extent therefore physics depends on and should follow mathematics. If we now compare physics and chemistry we find that on similar grounds chemistry should follow physics. We can arrive at an order within the sciences which can be justified in this way:

logic
mathematics
physics
chemistry
astronomy
geology
geography

It becomes rather more difficult to apply this idea to the biological sciences and social sciences, but within its limitations it is a valuable principle.

Apart from Bliss we find few efforts to produce a philosophically justifiable order of main classes. Ranganathan has argued the case for his own order in CC, but without conveying any great conviction; he clearly recognizes the fluid nature of such groupings, and is in any case more concerned with order within classes. LC does not claim any sort of theoretical basis—it reflects the holdings and use of that library and is thus justified for its own purposes. UDC is based on DC, but is trying to arrive at a more satisfactory order by a slow process of change; so far there has been one major relocation, placing language together with literature, and others are foreshadowed.

PHASE RELATIONS

Assuming that we use the synthetic principle and thus restrict our needs to those of listing simple subjects in our schedules, we can compile a classification scheme that will now serve most purposes. We can analyse basic classes into facets, list the foci in each facet and state the citation order; the basic classes themselves can be grouped into a helpful order, with a generalia class and common facets added. We have accounted for semantic relationships by showing related subjects together in the sequence, and we have allowed for syntactic relationships within the basic classes, by permitting the combination of foci from different facets.

There is, however, one further kind of subject that we have to make provision for: concepts linked by one of the *phase relationships* discussed in chapter 6 and illustrated in table 6. As we saw there, these relationships are necessarily *ad hoc*, since though we can tell that they are likely to occur, we cannot foresee in advance which concepts may be linked in this way. It is in fact here that we see the final distinction between the enumerative and the synthetic approach. In an enumerative scheme, all that we find will be provision for phase relations that existed before the scheme was compiled; *eg* in DC we find *science and religion* listed (the Darwinian controversy) but not *science and politics*. Phase relations can only be accommodated as they arise in a synthetic scheme; even here there is a need to recognize the different kinds, *eg* in UDC the colon, :, is used to link the notation for the two phases in this kind of relation, but it is used for all four kinds and is thus not very precise. CC is the only scheme to set out detailed provisions for phase relationships, though the four given in chapter 6 are in fact taken from BNB rather than CC.

The examples given of phase relationships in Table 6 all illustrate the linking of concepts from essentially different basic classes, but this is not necessarily the case. Phase relationships can occur between foci

DC and UDC	LC	BC	CC
Psychology	Ethics	Anthropology	Recreation
Ethics		Recreation	Humanities and
		Psychology	Social sciences
		Education	
Social sciences	Anthropology	Social sciences	
Sociology	Folklore	Sociology	Psychology
Statistics	Manners and customs		Social sciences
Politics	Recreation		Education
Economics	Social sciences	Social welfare	
Law	Statistics	Ethics	Politics
Government	Economics	Politics	Economics
Military science	Transport	Law	Transport
Social welfare	Commerce	Economics	Commerce
Education	Sociology	Business methods	Sociology
Commerce	Social groups		Anthropology
Transport	Welfare		Social work
Folklore and customs	Political science		Law
	Law		
Anthropology	Education		Statistics is a
			common focus
Business methods	Military science		
Recreation			

TABLE 10a: *Comparative classification: social sciences*

NB A line between two subjects indicates that they are separated by a subject from some other area. Two lines indicates a considerable gap.

159

DC	UDC	LC	BC	CC
Philosophy	Philosophy	Philosophy	Philosophy	Humanities and Social sciences
Philosophy—topics	History of Philosophy	Logic	Logic	Spiritual experience and Mysticism
	Philosophy—topics			Humanities
Logic	Logic	Religion	Religion	Fine arts
History of Philosophy	Religion			Literature and Language
Religion		Recreation		Literature
	Fine arts		Fine arts	Language
	Photography	Music	Literature and Language (together)	Religion
Language	Music	Fine arts		Philosophy
	Recreation	Literature and Language (sometimes together, sometimes not)		Logic
Fine arts	Literature and Language			
Photography	Language			
Music	Literature			
Recreation	(or together)			
Literature				

TABLE 10b: *Comparative classification: humanities*

NB Opinions differ as to whether a subject such as 'recreation' is in the humanities or the social sciences; it is included here if that appears to be the intention of the scheme. LC treats 'language' and 'literature' separately for the major Western languages; UDC permits either approach.

DC and UDC	LC	BC	CC
Science	Science	Science	Science
Mathematics	Mathematics	Mathematics	Mathematics
Astronomy	Astronomy	Physics (including	Astronomy
Physics	Physics	some applications)	Physics
Chemistry	Chemistry	Chemistry	Engineering
Crystallography	Geology	Chemical technology	Chemistry
Mineralogy	Natural history	Astronomy	[Chemical] Technology
Geology	Botany	Geology	Biology
Biology	Zoology	Geography	Geology
Botany	Anatomy	Biology	Mining
Zoology	Physiology	Botany	Botany
Technology	Medicine	Zoology	Agriculture
Medicine (including	Agriculture	Anthropology	Zoology
scientific aspects	Technology	Medicine	Animal husbandry
Engineering	Engineering		Medicine
Agriculture	Building	Useful arts	Useful arts
Domestic economy	Mechanical engineering	Agriculture	
Business methods	Electrical engineering	Engineering	
Chemical technology	Chemical engineering	Manufactures	
Manufactures	Manufactures	Domestic arts	
Building	Domestic economy	Building	

TABLE 10c: *Comparative classification: science and technology*

NB Two approaches are shown: 'science' as a whole followed by 'technology' as a whole, or each individual science followed by its related technology. DC in 'medicine' and BC in 'physics' depart from their normal practice of separating the two.

161

in the same facet, *eg*

> The influence of Goethe on Sir Walter Scott
>
> Town and gown.

We have pointed out that foci from the same facet cannot normally be combined, indeed this is the criterion by which we judge whether we have carried our analysis to the point where foci in one facet are mutually exclusive. Phase relationships are obviously one kind of relationship in which foci cannot be mutually exclusive. This also illustrates the point that phase relationships do not in general present serious problems in alphabetical systems, except that it may be necessary to use a phrase to specify them; it is in systematic arrangement that we have to make special provision for them.

We saw in chapter 6 that in the case of bias, influence and exposition phase relationships, there is a primary phase and a secondary phase, the primary phase being the key subject. Thus in the subject 'anatomy for nurses' it is anatomy which is the primary phase, and we shall therefore classify such a work with others on anatomy, *not* with those on nursing. Similarly, 'a psychological study of *Hamlet*' goes with other works on *Hamlet*, not with other works on psychology. But what of the comparison or interaction phase?

We saw that in this case both phases are equal: there is no primary phase. This presents a problem if we are thinking in terms of shelf classification, where we have to find one place at which to locate a given book. Most general classification schemes have a simple rule that in this situation, the primary phase is to be the one appearing first in the schedules. This is an arbitrary rule intended to save the trouble of making a decision on merit each time the occasion arises; it means that using DC, 'Science and politics' will be classified with politics, whereas using CC, it would belong with science. In each case it would be necessary to make provision for the secondary phase, for example by making an added entry in the catalogue.

Having seen the need to include them, we now have to decide whereabouts in the overall order we want to file them. CC files all phase relationships immediately after the subject treated generally. The *BNB Supplementary schedules,* used in BNB between 1960 and 1971, made provision for bias phase to be filed there, but the others to be filed after the common facets but before the first facet of the basic class. DC now makes provision for bias phase by a standard subdivision, but this places such items in the middle of 'miscellany', with 'the subject as a profession' on one side, and 'directories' on the other. Other kinds of phase are enumerated occasionally in DC, but no consistent provision is made for them.

RECENT TRENDS

Traditional classification schemes rely on main classes which represent the traditional disciplines. Modern developments in all areas of knowledge tend to cross the boundaries between disciplines; that is, new topics develop not merely by *fission*—the splitting up of established subjects—but also by *fusion*—the merging of previously distinct subjects. It is very difficult to accommodate interdisciplinary subjects in a conventional classification scheme, just as it is difficult to take account of changes in relationships between existing subjects. The Classification Research Group has been working for some years now on the problems of developing a new general classification scheme, but has not so far found any satisfactory solution to the problem of a logical order for single concepts. This work is discussed in chapter 13, together with that of UNISIST and its Broad system of ordering. Meanwhile, existing schemes are subjected to increasing criticism for their failure to keep pace with changes in knowledge. The pace of change is itself increasing:[6] tomorrow is already with us, according to some writers, yet we still tend to think in yesterday's patterns.

It can be seen that the problem of finding a satisfactory overall order that will last for anything more than a few years is one of the most difficult problems facing systematic arrangement. Traditional approaches do not serve as a helpful basis for placing new interdisciplinary subjects in relation to the disciplines from which they arise; novel methods may fail to accommodate the mass of published information that still falls into the conventional framework. As Mr Bennet observed, 'it seems an hopeless business'[7]. The solution may lie in the recognition of the fact that any user of a scheme can only be aware of a relatively small part of it at any time, even in a small library; the overall order will in practice not be visible. It seems likely that information will continue to be presented in conventional ways, even though the conventions may change from decade to decade; the problem lies perhaps more in the area of keeping up to date than in that of theoretical study.

BIBLIOGRAPHY
1 Grolier, E de: *A study of general categories applicable to classification and coding in documentation.* Paris, Unesco, 1962.
2 In the rules for main classes in CC.
3 Palmer, B I: *Itself an education.* 1971. Chapters 2 and 3.
4 Brown, J D: *Subject classification.* Third edition revised by J D Stewart. 1939. This edition was very similar to the first, 1906, and second, 1914, and retained all of Brown's novel features. However, though it survived in a few British libraries till recently, it became too outdated to be usable and has been replaced.
5 See chapter 19 for details of Bliss's writings.
6 Toffler, A: *Future shock.* Bodley Head, 1970.
7 Austen, J: *Pride and prejudice.* 1813. Chapter 20.

CHAPTER 10

Notation

Unlike alphabetical arrangement, systematic order is not self evident, and indeed there may be differing views as to the best order at any given point. It would be tedious in the extreme if we had to consult the schedules every time we wished to find a subject in the catalogue or on the shelves, and search for it by following through the overall order; even if the catalogue and shelves were guided to a very high standard, in a large library searches for specific subjects would be impossible if we had to rely on the systematic arrangement on its own. To make it a practical proposition we must add to the arrangement a set of symbols—a *notation*—which does have a self evident order; we can then use the notation to find out the position in the catalogue or on the shelves of the subjects we want[1].

There are two important points here. The first is that the notation is something *added* to the schedules; it is the schedules which give the systematic arrangement, and only when we have decided on the arrangement can we start to think about the notation. It is an unfortunate fact that notation is often assumed to *be* the systematic arrangement, and classification schemes have been criticised for poor arrangement when it has been the notation which has failed, not the schedules. The notation cannot turn a bad schedule into a good one, but a poor notation may so hamper a good schedule that it becomes a bad one. To quote H E Bliss, 'notation . . . does not make the classification, tho it may mar it'[2].

The second point is that the notation has to show the order: that is its function. The notation itself must therefore have a self evident order, otherwise it will not serve its purpose. If we adopt a notation which does not have a self evident order, we may well find that we are no better off than we were with no notation at all; taken to its logical extreme, this would mean giving each subject in the schedule a symbol and then allocating to these symbols an arbitrary order reflecting the order of the schedules, a procedure which would not really be very helpful. The Chinese system of ideographs is such a set of symbols; in order to produce quite simple messages on a typewriter it is necessary to remember the position of some 2,000 separate keys. This is obviously not a practical means of finding our way round the library.

There are two sets of symbols which have a widely recognized order:

arabic numerals, and the roman alphabet. (Roman numerals are not widely known, nor are they so easy to manipulate as arabic; and while the greek and slavonic alphabets do have a self-evident order, it is not nearly so well known as that of the roman.) Using letters, we have the choice of lower or upper case (small letters or capitals) which means in effect that we have the choice of three sets of symbols rather than just two. A notation which uses only one set of symbols is called a *pure* notation, while one which uses more than one kind is known as a *mixed* notation. It is clear that only a pure notation will give us the completely self evident order we have stated to be necessary, but other factors enter into the picture which indicate certain superiorities on the part of a mixed notation, which may make it worth while accepting the loss of consistency.

MEMORABILITY

We have to *use* notation; it is the means by which we move from a subject expressed in words in an alphabetical index to that same subject in its context in the systematic arrangement; it has to appear on catalogue entries, backs of books, entries in bibliographies, stock records, shelf guides—anywhere, in fact, where we may have to find our way through a systematic arrangement. We must therefore be able to carry it mentally with ease, write it and type it without error, inscribe it on book covers which may be relatively narrow. The notation must lend itself to these activities; to do so it must possess a number of qualities which between them add up to what we call *memorability*.

The first quality is *simplicity*, by which we mean that it must be easy to grasp mentally. Consider the following ten digit number:

7382159142.

This looks much too long, and most people would find it difficult to grasp as a unit, but if we split it up into three shorter sections:

738 2159 142

it at once becomes much simpler. We are all familiar with ten digit numbers split up in this way, for the vast majority of telephone dialling codes are of this length or even slightly longer. By splitting the number up, we have increased its length by two digits (counting each space as a digit) but this leads to an increase in the ease with which we can grasp it.

This leads us to a consideration of the effects of mixing different kinds of notation. The following pieces of notation are all the same length, but clearly some of them are much easier to grasp than others:

1   738215914237
2   738LIN914237
3   738/215/9142
4   738:215:9142
5   BD7382GS5738

6   7382(159)142
7   73k,BD24:Kaw
8   TipModHafDun
9   TrdMbhHloDfx

We find that on the whole devices which normally act as separators—
ie punctuation marks—are psychologically acceptable for this purpose
in notation; on the other hand, a notation using punctuation marks
solely as separators must be longer than one without separators; these
are *empty digits* which convey structure but not meaning. Mixed notation *may* be easier to grasp than a pure notation of the same length, but
only if we can grasp some sort of pattern to the mixing; and numbers
are for most people more acceptable as an ordering device than letters.
Example 8 (above) shows a recent move in notation towards the idea
of organizing letters into recognizable groups, in this case pronounceable syllables.[3] The object is to provide a notation which is
easily grasped, and in this it is obviously successful, though one has to
remember that combinations of letters have semantic content and it
may be preferable not to use some of the possibilities. Numbers do not
in general have any semantic content, though we may have to except
from this such notations as 007!

The second quality which is important is *brevity*. Other things being
equal, a brief notation is more easily grasped than a long one; as we
have seen, other things are not always equal, but there is no doubt that
brevity is important. For example, it becomes difficult to write a long
piece of notation on the spine of a book, unless we can split it up into
shorter units. Brevity depends mainly on two factors: the *base* of the
notation, and the *allocation*. The base is simply the number of symbols
available in the system; for numbers this is ten (0/9) or nine if we
ignore the zero, while for letters it is twenty six. If we mix the notation
by using numbers and letters we may have thirty-five (it is not possible
to use both O (capital letter o) and o (zero) without confusion), while
if we use both upper and lower case letters and numbers we will have
slightly less than sixty. (On many typewriters l (lower case L) is also
used for 1 (one) and there is the possibility of confusion between written b and 6, or i and l, or o and O.) If we use numbers, we shall have
longer symbols than if we use letters. For example, if we have about
2,000 items in our schedule and we want to show their order, we shall
have to use up to four digits if we use numbers only, but only three if
we use letters (base 26), while if we use numbers and upper and lower
case letters we shall only need two digits ($57^2 = 3,149$). The longer the
base, the larger the number of items that can be arranged by a given
length of symbol; mathematically, if the base contains x symbols, then
by using up to n digits we can construct

$$x^n + x^{n-1} + x^{n-2} + x^{n-3} + \ldots x^3 + x^2 + x$$

different notational symbols. The general preference for numbers has to be set against the fact that letters will in general give shorter symbols.

Another factor affecting brevity is the way the notation is allocated. Some subjects are static; they have not developed in recent years. For example, the schedule for Logic in Dewey's first edition is almost the same as that in his eighteenth edition, ninety five years later. Compare this with a dynamic subject such as Engineering; here the growth of the subject is increasing almost exponentially, and whereas Dewey's first edition gave this subject less than a page, his eighteenth takes up ninety four pages to cover it. When we allocate the notation for a classification scheme, we should try to make sure that it gives a large share to dynamic subjects, even if this means fairly long notation for some static subjects to start with; after a few years, the notation for static subjects will not be any longer, while that for dynamic subjects will inevitably have grown. Of course, we cannot tell in advance which particular subjects are likely to grow most in years to come, but we can at least make some sort of intelligent guess, bearing in mind that if we could indeed foretell the future the construction of classification schemes would probably not be our chosen profession.

In his first edition, Dewey gave the same spread of notation to Logic as he did to Engineering: ten three figure numbers. As a consequence, in the eighteenth edition, we still find three figure numbers in Logic (which has been static now for the best part of 2,000 years), but in Engineering, particularly those branches which have had to be inserted since the scheme was first drawn up, we find that six digits are common, and ten digit numbers are by no means uncommon. What makes the situation worse is that the great majority of libraries have a lot of items dealing with engineering but relatively few on logic—so the short pieces of notation are rarely used. It must be remembered that, although we can provide for the growth of subjects to a certain extent it is not possible to make sure that dynamic subjects will retain a brief notation indefinitely; as we have already seen, any systematic arrangement will need revision over the years to keep pace with the growth of knowledge, and it may well be that in some areas knowledge is growing so fast that we cannot hope to keep pace with it and still retain a convenient notation.

A further factor affecting brevity is *synthesis* of notation. We have seen the contrast between enumerative and synthetic classification schemes; in the latter, only simple subjects are listed, and the classifier has to select the appropriate ones for any subject he has in hand and combine them according to the specified citation order. This means that the notation for the individual elements must also be combined to specify a composite subject, and this will usually lead to longer notation than if the symbols had been evenly distributed over all the required subjects, simple or composite. For example, the Library of

Congress classification rarely uses more than two letters and four figures for any subject in its schedule—though it is only fair to point out that the schedules often lack specificity where composite subjects are concerned. UDC has often been criticized for the length of its notation for this reason; synthesis leads to very long numbers, but it must be pointed out that in many cases this is because the notation was not designed with synthesis in mind, and in consequence the results are often clumsy, repeating certain sections of the notation. For example, at one time the notation for the subject

Power supplies for the electromagnet of a proton sychrotron was 621.384.61:539.185:621.318.3:621.311.6. Nobody can claim that this is brief or memorable, and it repeats 621.3 (Electrical engineering) three times. It is however specific, and UDC is the only classification scheme which is detailed enough to specify this subject and others like it. If we want specificity, we have in general to accept long notations; if in addition we are using a scheme in which the allocation of notation is poor in relation to modern needs, we must expect this to have a further adverse effect on the length of the symbols we have to use. It is not possible to avoid this kind of conflict eventually, no matter how carefully the notation is allocated in the first place; all that we can do is to try to minimize the problems by accepting the necessity for fairly drastic revision from time to time, a topic which is discussed at more length under 'Organization' (chapter 12).

· It is often suggested that *mnemonics* in notation are an aid to memorability—as indeed they should be! Mnemonics may be of two kinds, systematic and literal. A systematic mnemonic is found when the same piece of notation denotes the same topic wherever it occurs; for example, in UDC Great Britain must always be denoted by (42), USA by (73). In DC there are several mnemonics which fall into this category, but in a limited way; for example, in Literature, within a particular language 'drama' is always denoted by 2:

English literature	820	English drama	822
French literature	840	French drama	842
German literature	830	German drama	832

However, 2 does not by any means always mean drama, even within Literature. Great Britain is often denoted by 0942, but it may be shown by 942, 42, 042, or even 2, and while 0942 does nearly always mean Great Britain, the other symbols usually do not. So we do not have the consistency which is necessary if a piece of notation is to be truly mnemonic.

Literal mnemonics are associated with letters, and the theory is that by using the initial letter of the name of a subject for its notation we shall aid the memory. Thus in the Bibliographic classification Chemistry is C (but Physics is B); in LC Music is M (but Fine arts is N). This kind of mnemonic is so haphazard that it has little value; it only works for a very limited number of subjects, and then only for one particular term. For example, BC has U for Useful arts, while LC has T for Technology—but Dewey in his schedule now calls Technology the class which used to be called Useful arts!

It is clear that literal mnemonics depend completely on language; a piece of notation which is mnemonic in English may not be so in, say, French, but it may also not be so in American, since usage on the two sides of the Atlantic frequently differs. What could one use as a literal mnemonic for Lifts/Elevators, or Films/Movies? However, provided that the striving for mnemonic value does not distort the schedules of the classification, there would appear to be no harm in them; unfortunately, one gets the impression that in some cases the mnemonic value has led to the use of alphabetical order where a systematic order might be more useful, for example in the Generalia class in LC.

The value of mnemonics is doubtful. The non librarian user will not come across them sufficiently often to become aware that they are 'helping his memory', while the classifier using a particular scheme will have little difficulty in remembering large amounts of its notation, whether they are 'mnemonic' or not. On no account should the schedules of a classification scheme be modified in order to gain some dubious advantage of this kind.

Seminal mnemonics form a third kind, rather different in their intention from the other two in that they are wholly classifier-oriented. Suppose that we have a schedule that needs expansion; we have the choice of attempting an expansion ourselves, with the attendant risk that we shall clash with a future expansion published by the compilers of the scheme, or of abandoning specificity for the time being, until such time as an approved expansion is available. If we could be sure of drawing up the same schedule as the compilers, and allotting it the same notation, the dilemma would be resolved, and seminal mnemonics are an attempt to permit us to do this. The numbers 1 to 8 are given a fundamental significance: 1, for example, means first, unitary, one-dimensional; 4 means malfunction, disease, *etc.* Ranganathan developed the theory of seminal mnemonics after a careful study of the way that he had used notation in the early editions of CC, and we owe the name to Palmer and Wells in their *Fundamentals of library classification*. However, although their use may give a measure of autonomy to the classifier, it would appear to be a very clear example of notation dictating order, and to be suspect for that reason. Seminal mnemonics can in practice only be studied in the context of CC, and they are discussed further in chapter 20.[4]

Memorability is important, and the factors contributing to it must be carefully weighed when a notation is selected for a classification scheme. There is no doubt that much of the success of DC is owed to its simple, easily understood and widely known notation, rather than to any theoretical excellence in its schedules. Despite this, it is important to reaffirm that notation is subsidiary to the needs of the schedules, and that it is possible to worry too much about the difficulties caused by long or complicated symbols. Far more important is the need for the notation to possess other qualities, of which the most important is hospitality.

HOSPITALITY

Notation shows the order of the schedules, but the schedules are merely a helpful way of listing subjects; since knowledge is not static, our schedules cannot be static—we must be prepared to add new subjects as they arise, in the correct place (as far as we can see it) in the overall order. The notation must therefore also be able to accommodate insertions, at any point where we find it necessary to make them. We will most often need to insert a new topic within a facet, but we may occasionally need to develop a new facet, and we may well have to find room for new basic classes. The notation must not prevent us from accommodating any new subject in the correct place: *ie* it must be hospitable.

If we are using arabic numbers, we may use them as integers (whole numbers) or we may use them as decimals. Integers give a clear order which is known to everybody; 12 comes later than 2 but earlier than 115, for example. But suppose we have a series of foci in a facet, and we give them the numbers 1 to 7; if we now require to insert a new topic between the third and fourth we cannot do so, for there is no whole number between three and four. One solution is to leave gaps when we are allocating the notation originally, but of course this is only postponing the time when we run out of places; there is also the temptation to insert new subjects in the schedules at points where we have left gaps in the notation, rather than in their correct, systematic, positions in the schedules. And since it is very difficult to foresee where new subjects are going to arise, we shall often leave gaps in the wrong places, but none where they are necessary.

If however we use numbers as decimals, we can insert new symbols at any point in the sequence. Between 3 and 4 we can insert 31, 32, 33 . . . 39; between 33 and 34 we can insert 331, 332, 333 and so on. Now there is no longer any need to worry about leaving gaps in the right places, or to waste notation by leaving gaps in the wrong places. The facility of decimal numbers to incorporate new symbols at any point was seen by Dewey, and proved to be one of the most vital parts of his scheme—indeed, it gave the scheme its name.

The term decimal applies to arabic numbers and relates to division by ten. The idea can of course be applied equally well to letters, where it will mean division by 26, so the term decimal is no longer correct, and instead we should speak of 'radix fraction'. As the term decimal is widely understood it will be considered to apply to letters as well as numbers in this text. In a letter notation used fractionally, between B and C we can insert BA, BB, BC . . . BZ; between BB and BC, we can insert BBA, BBB, BBC and so on.

If we wish to have complete hospitality at any point, we must never finish a piece of notation with the first symbol of the base, 0, A or a; unless we follow this simple rule we will find that we cannot insert new items at the beginning of a schedule. For example, if we use all twenty six letters A to Z, we cannot in the future file anything before the established sequence, but if we begin at B we shall be able to insert AB/AZ before B and still maintain hospitality at all points. Similarly, between 2 and 3 we can insert the ten numbers 20 to 29, but if we use 20 we shall not in the future be able to insert anything between 2 and 20; if we restrict ourselves to the nine numbers 21 to 29, we can now insert 201 to 209 between 2 and 21. The effect of this is to reduce the length of the base by one digit; numbers to 9, letters to 25. In practice this loss is not likely to be serious, provided we make provision for allocating the notation adequately, whereas lack of hospitality may lead to distortion of the schedules—notation dictating order—which we must avoid.

EXPRESSIVENESS

There is another quality which notation is often expected to have, *expressiveness*. This means that the notation reflects the structure of the scheme, and such a notation is known as a *structural* or *hierarchical* kind, as well as expressive. This quality is a valuable one because it helps the user to find his way about the systematic order. We have to remember that the order of items on the shelf or in a bibliography, or the arrangement of cards in a catalogue, is perforce a single linear sequence which cannot show any kind of structure, and though we can (and should) do as much as possible to make the structure clear by guiding, an expressive notation is an added help. Unfortunately, we find that expressiveness and hospitality are mutually exclusive; sooner or later one or the other breaks down. The reason for this becomes clear if we consider a practical example such as the schedule for Engineering in DC. In the first edition, Electrical engineering was omitted, but this was included in the second edition as a subdivision of mechanical engineering; while this may have been an acceptable subordination at the time, it would not now find general agreement. However, by 1900 the motorcar was beginning to develop its own peculiar form of engineering, and since then we have had aviation engineering, nuclear engineering and control engineering.

600	Technology
620	Engineering
621	Mechanical

621.3	Electrical
622	Mining
623	Naval
624	Civil
. . .	
628	Sanitary

Clearly, car engineering and aviation engineering are similar to mechanical engineering rather than civil or sanitary, while control engineering, as one of the more theoretical studies, surely belongs at the beginning of the schedule with the other theory subjects rather than with the more practical branches of engineering listed later. Equally clearly, if branches of engineering of equivalent status to those listed are to be shown as equivalent by the notation, we cannot insert any of these subjects unless we use 629, for this is the only three figure number left vacant. Dewey realized this, and left 629 open for 'Other' branches of engineering, so that is where we find car engineering, aviation engineering and control engineering, while nuclear engineering appears at 621.48, which may be approximately the correct place in the schedules, but certainly does not show the relative importance of this new discipline.

In recent editions DC has introduced the idea of 'centred headings' to help in its retention of an expressive notation, and has also introduced new terminology. For example, Christian religion is now 220–289, instead of being equated with Religion generally as it was in the early editions, and many other cases of a similar kind can be found. The 'inserted' heading is centred on the page, and the use of the notation is not recommended, since it includes a hyphen and is thus not in the completely pure tradition of DC. (UDC is able to achieve the same end by using the stroke /: thus Science and technology 5/6.) An example of updated terminology is the substitution of Applied physics for Mechanical engineering at 621. This removes the anomaly of describing Electrical engineering as a subdivision of Mechanical, but carries with it the implication that the rest of 620 (*eg* Control engineering in 629) is *not* Applied physics. It may thus be as difficult to justify the amendment as the original, but the intention is sound. It seems a pity that the notation of centred headings remains in disfavour.

The fact is that immediately we start to require our notation to be expressive, we limit ourselves to an integral use of the final digit; in the example above, Dewey had only the nine numbers 1, 2, . . . 9 to list all the branches of engineering and at the same time show their equal status. As we have already seen, an integral notation cannot be hospitable; for the same reason, an expressive notation cannot be hospitable. Hospitality is more important than expressiveness. In effect, hospitality is the quality which allows us to govern the notation according to the needs of the schedules, instead of having the notation dictate the order within the schedules. Sooner or later, all notations which set out to be expressive break down; DC and UDC, both originally expressive, do not show structure in their notation in a number of places in the schedules, while Ranganathan has introduced two devices to overcome the problem in CC without completely achieving his objective.

The first of these devices is the *sector device*. This was first known as the octave device, as it was applied only to the numbers 1 to 9, but its wider use with letters as well has led to the change of name. It consists of using the final digit of the base, 9 or z, solely as a repeater; the sequence of numbers now runs:

1, 2, 3, . . . 7, 8, 91, 92, 93, . . . 97, 98, 991, 992, 993 . . . (*ie* in octaves) while with letters the 'extended' alphabet is:

a, b, c, d, . . . y, za, zb, zc, . . . zy, zza, zzb, zzc . . . etc.

The repeater digit shows us the place in the sequence where we will find a given symbol, but when estimating the 'status' of the topic denoted by this symbol we are to ignore the repeater.

As in many other instances, it would seem that Ranganathan's theory makes explicit and formalizes what had already been the practice, though unrecognized, in other schemes. We have already noted the use by Dewey of 9 to denote 'other . . .' in Engineering, but in fact he used the device throughout his scheme. (In the early editions he tended to use the word 'minor' instead of 'other', as has been mentioned in chapter 6 under the heading Critical classification.) A related though not entirely similar use of the 9 was the development in DC13 and UDC of a new schedule for Psychology at 159.9, first published in 1931, before the first edition of CC had appeared.

The second of these devices is *group notation*, or in its application to UDC, *centesimal notation*. In this, instead of showing subordination by adding one digit to the base notation (62 leading to 621, 622, etc) we add *two* digits. By so doing, we give ourselves 100 numbers (00 to 99) or 676 letters (AA to ZZ) instead of 10 and 26 respectively, so that we can show a great many more topics as being of equivalent status. However, neither of these solutions can really be said to be satisfactory. Sector device enables us to add *at the end of the array*, but not in the middle; we can extrapolate the series indefinitely but we cannot insert an expressive piece of notation between 3 and 4, or anywhere else within the array. Group notation merely gives us a longer base to start with, but is liable to run out of hospitality eventually, just as is any other integral notation. We can add at the end of the sequence or in the middle, but only for as long as we have gaps in the appropriate places.

Another possibility which has been suggested, and indeed is used in CC, is the introduction of symbols from another series, for example, greek letters. Ranganathan uses Δ (capital delta) to denote Mysticism, which has the status of a main class in CC. Other main classes are

173

all given roman letters (1963 reprint of the sixth edition), and we thus have the very real problem of determining whereabouts in the sequence we are to find Mysticism. There is no external guidance which tells us whereabouts in the sequence A/Z we are to find Δ ; in fact, the scheme itself seems to be somewhat uncommitted. In the fifth edition we find

M   Useful arts
μ Humanities and social sciences together
Δ Mysticism
υ Humanities
N   Fine arts

In the sixth edition (1960 printing) we find

M   Useful arts
Δ Mysticism
μ Humanities and social sciences
υ Humanities
N   Fine arts

and in the sixth edition (1963 reprint) this has become

M   Useful arts
Δ Mysticism
MZ   Humanities and social sciences
MZA   Humanities
N   Fine arts

The filing value of Δ lies between MY and MZ, which can hardly be said to be self evident, nor is it clear from a study of the schedules that it is the correct place, since we are given to understand that Mysticism is to be considered among the humanities and should therefore follow the general heading, not precede it.

It is evident that no satisfactory solution to the problem of re-conciling hospitality and expressiveness is to be found. If we insist (as we should) on hospitality, sooner or later we shall have to abandon expressiveness; if we insist on expressiveness we are likely to find ourselves either abandoning hospitality altogether or else introducing devices which permit a degree of hospitality by maintaining a semblance of expressiveness only. We may take the argument further by considering whether we *ought* to seek expressiveness in the notation. As has already been mentioned, the order of items or entries cannot show any kind of structure: it is a linear sequence. The purpose of the notation is to show the order within the sequence; should we in addition expect it to show the relationships which the order does not show? The argument for expressiveness is that it helps users to find their way through the systematic arrangement, which is sometimes puzzling to them; the argument against expressiveness is that it conflicts with hospitality. We can help users to find their way around by guiding the library, the bibliography, the catalogue; we cannot help them by distorting the systematic arrangement to fit in with the needs of the notation.

If on the other hand we abandon expressiveness, we give ourselves a valuable degree of freedom which can be put to good use. It is the case that in a systematic arrangement the schedule has to include some steps of division which are logically necessary but are represented by little or no literature. If we use an expressive notation, these steps of division will inevitably be given a shorter notation than their heavily used subdivisions; we shall be 'wasting' short symbols by never using them. Consider the following schedule:

MUSIC
    Individual instruments and instrumental groups arranged according to their basic mode of performance
        Keyboard instruments
        Piano
        Organ
        String instruments
        Bowed
        Violin
        Viola
        Plucked

If we apply an expressive notation to this schedule, Violin and Viola will have the same length of notation, which will be three digits longer than the notation for the general heading at the beginning; Piano, Organ, Bowed and Plucked string instruments will all have a notation two digits longer than the heading; and Keyboard and String instruments will have notation one digit longer. Now this is already inconsistent, for it means that individual instruments do not all have the same length of notation, depending on the number of steps it takes to define them by a process of division. More seriously in practice, it means that the short symbols will hardly ever be used (how many items are we going to need to place at the general heading, which has the shortest notation?) while the vast majority of items—those dealing with specific instruments—will have to be given a long notation. This is obviously an inefficient use of notation.

If we abandon expressiveness as a requirement, we can allocate the notation far more satisfactorily:

MUSIC
PVV	Individual instruments and instrumental groups arranged according to their basic mode of performance
PW	Keyboard instrument
Q	Piano
R	Organ
RW	String instruments
RX	Bowed

S	Violin
SQ	Viola
T	Plucked

Now, although the notation bears no relation to the significance of the subject in terms of extension, it does show the order, and it does bear a close relationship to the significance of the subject in terms of literary warrant.

This example, taken from the *British catalogue of music classification*,[5] shows the gain in efficiency that can result from the abandonment of expressiveness. Most classification schemes which set out to have an expressive notation have at some stage had to give up the idea; even Dewey, who started with a completely structured notation, was forced to accept that in some places he would not be able to maintain this. For example, 439.7 *Swedish language* is a subdivision of 439.5 *Scandinavian languages*, while in *Metal manufacturers, Tin* 673.6, *Mercury* 673.71 and *Magnesium* 673.723 are all individual metals and are thus coordinate. In some of the schedules in the Natural sciences, *eg Botany* 582–589, changes in the accepted order of plant species have meant that the notation now bears no relation to the structure of the schedules.

Although it is true that this loss of expressiveness makes the overall arrangement that much harder to follow, we can overcome this problem by adequate guiding of catalogues, bookshelves and indeed whole libraries. It can be argued that every time we use a class number we should also produce a guide showing the 'translation' of that number into words. This would mean a much higher concentration of guide cards in a card catalogue than is customary—but perhaps users would not then complain so often that they do not understand the catalogue. The *British national bibliography*, with its 'feature headings' for each class number used, shows very well what can be done to make a systematic arrangement intelligible.

SYNTHESIS

We have briefly mentioned synthesis as one of the factors affecting brevity of notation, and it is worth re-examining this point in the light of the discussion on synthesis in chapter 6. We saw there that coordination of single concepts was an extremely important device for improving retrieval performance from the point of view of relevance, and analytico-synthetic classification schemes are one important method of achieving coordination in an ordered fashion, according to a pre-determined combination or citation order. By listing single concepts in the index vocabulary, and providing rules for their combination, we can give the classifier a much more powerful tool than the enumerative scheme, which attempts to provide in advance for composite subjects, but inevitably cannot foresee all that are likely to arise.

In particular, we have seen that phase relationships are a form of coordination which cannot be predetermined, and *must* therefore be provided for by synthesis at the time of classification. The implication of this is that each single concept must have its own individual piece of notation, and that it must be possible to combine these individual pieces of the notation—the code vocabulary—to specify any composite subject, including those involving phase relationships. We must therefore now consider in more detail the problems that arise if we try to synthesize notational symbols for composite subjects from the symbols used for their elements. If we take the schedule for Library science that we constructed and go through it giving the facets an expressive notation, we shall finish up with something like the result shown in figure 12. Here we see that *History* (the generalized Time facet) is 3 and *Academic libraries* is 75; so the notation for *History of academic libraries* ought to be 753. But we can see at once that this will not do; 753 is the notation for *Technical college libraries*. We are of course trying to divide the heading *Academic libraries* in two different ways using the same notation, and this cannot be done because it causes ambiguity: the same piece of notation might mean more than one subject. What we have to do to remove this is to label not only the foci within a facet, but also the facet itself; if we do this, we can combine elements of notation from different facets to denote composite subjects without any risk of ambiguity.

There are various ways in which we can do this. We may use different kinds of notation for different facets; for example, BC uses lower case letters only for *Place*, while CC uses them only for common facets of *bibliographical form* and *subject*. In both cases it is possible to add these symbols directly to another piece of notation without confusion.

BC	Cricket (sports)	HKL
	Australia	ua
	Cricket in Australia	HKLua
CC	Physics	c
	Encyclopedia	k
	Encyclopedia of physics	ck

This method is clearly limited by the fact that there are only three kinds of notation we can use.

A more practical method is shown by the fourth column in figure 12. In this, capital letters have been used to denote the facets, with lower case used to denote foci within the facets. We can now combine notational symbols for foci without any possibility of confusion. In column 5 the method has been used with some modifications to give pronounceable syllables, which again may be combined unambiguously.

History	Q	Fab
Academic libraries	Qh	Ped

History of academic libraries	QhC	Ped Fab
Technical college libraries	Qm	Peg

The same results could be achieved by using letters and numbers instead of two kinds of letters. Letters were used in this way by the English Electric Company's classification for engineering,[6] while pronounceable syllabic notation is used in the London Education Classification.[7]

As mentioned, notations 1 and 2 require facet indicators; we can use Ranganathan's , for the Libraries facet, ; for Materials and : for Operations. For the common facets we can use . for Place, ' for Time, - for subjects and " for bibliographical forms. We can use these also for 3, but the rest do not need facet indicators separate from the notation. Independent facet indicators do permit us to change the facet order and the filing order; notice also that once we have introduced the idea of facet indicators, we can use the whole of the notational base in each facet. This will usually allow us to reduce the notation by one digit, to make up for the extra digit (the indicator).

Samples from the list of titles:

3 An art reference library for children
12 La Roche College classification system for phonograph records

Notation	3	12
Column 1	731,721,71(Art)	757;632:522.4(LaR)
Column 2	RB,QB,P(Art)	SFJ;KJF:GFF.E(LaR)
Column 3	84,81,79(Art)	95;76:61.4(LaR)
Column 4	NbLbJ(Art)	QrFwEnD(LaR)
Column 5	NadMadL(Art)	PemJelHidG(LaR)
Column 6	68767766(Art)	789576473(LaR)
Column 7	TSSR(Art)	XPHE(LaR)

These examples show that allocation has an important effect on length of notation, and that length itself is not the only factor involved in memorability. Note also the use of the *word* Art in the first example, and the *identifier* LaR in the second.

We would normally not use the , to introduce the libraries facet, because the fact that we use no label is itself a label. We would have to use the comma if we wished to combine concepts falling within the libraries facet, *eg* Children's reference library on art 731,721,71. If we do introduce such a system of facet indicators, we must lay down a filing order for them, which will normally (following the principle of inversion) be the reverse of the citation order of the facets they introduce, and we shall have to accept the fact that this order will no longer be the self evident kind that we have previously stated to be desirable. However, UDC and CC both function satisfactorily using punctuation marks for facet indicators, and they do have the advantage of being expressive. BC also uses punctuation marks as indicators, but Bliss does not seem to have fully realized the implications of this for filing order.

FLEXIBILITY
The use of arbitrary symbols for facet indicators may in fact be of some value. We have seen that for any given situation, it is important to have a fixed citation order, so that there will be one, and only one, place for a composite subject, but that different situations may call for different citation orders, for example in Literature, where DC and LC differ because they are intended to serve different groups of users. If we use capital letters to introduce facets, we immediately determine the filing order for them, so that if we wish to follow the principle of inversion we are limited to one citation order—the reverse of the fixed filing order. (Note that it is the filing order which is fixed here; we can alter the citation order if we accept the loss of the general-special progression.) We are thus obliged in effect to accept the citation order laid down for us by the compiler of the scheme, but this may not serve our particular needs as well as might some other.

Now if we have used arbitrary symbols as facet indicators, their filing order has to be laid down as a special rule, for they have no accepted order among themselves. We can alter the filing order to suit our own needs, and can therefore also alter the citation order and still follow the principle of inversion; we have introduced the element of flexibility. To illustrate this we may take two examples from UDC, which has a very flexible notation. The first of these is the literature class, where we find language shown by direct subdivision, literary form introduced by the hyphen - and period shown by quotation marks " . . . ". We can accept that language is always the primary facet and therefore needs no indicator (though even this may be altered if necessary by using the facet indicator for language, the equals sign =). For the second facet we may have either form or period; we can ignore form altogether as does LC; we can use the same facet order as DC, language—form—period; in short, whatever arrangement will best suit our needs can be selected.

The second example is taken from Political science, where we find a subdivision Political parties. Within this basic class we find that there are three facets: place, party and party organisation. For most purposes the last of these will be the least important, and we can consider the others on their own. Direct division in the notation is used for the party facet, and this then would normally be the most important, with place second, shown by the use of curves (. . .). However, for perhaps the majority of libraries it would be more helpful to find place as the primary facet; readers are likely to be interested in the parties within a

FIGURE 12

The seven columns to the left show how various kinds of notation might be allocated to the schedule for Library Science. Since the schedule itself is tentative, so are the attempts at allocation of notation. Some kinds lend themselves more easily to leaving gaps than others, and letters give a longer base to start with.

Column 1 is a simple expressive notation. The facets need indicators
        2 is the same, using letters
        3 is a non-expressive notation which tends to assume that the schedule is now fixed. It is usually shorter than 1 and 2
        4 uses capitals for facets, l/c for foci. Non-expressive.
        5 is similar, but uses pronounceable syllables
        6 is a non-expressive retroactive notation, using numbers (see explanation on p182)
        7 is similar, using letters. No facet indicators needed.

1	B	1	A	B	1	B	Common bibliographical
2	C	2	B	D	15	C	Common subject
21	CB	21	Bb	Dad	16	CC	revision
22	CF	22	Bf	Dal	17	CF	research
23	CJ	23	Bj	Dat	178	CJ	standards
24	CN	24	Bm	Deb	18	CM	automation
25	CR	25	Br	Dib	19	CP	economics
3	D	3	C	F	2	D	Time
4	E	4	D	G	3	E	Place
5	G	51	E	H	4	EZZ	Operations
51	GB	52	Eb	Had	44	F	administration
511	GBB	53	Ec	Haf	444	FG	selection
512	GBF	54	Ed	Hag	446	FK	acquisition
513	GBJ	55	Ee	Haj	454	FM	circulation
52	GF	56	Eh	Heb	459	FZ	technical services
521	GFB	57	Ei	Heg	46	G	cataloguing
5211	GFBM	58	Ej	Hel	465	GG	catalogues
52111	GFBMB	59	Ejz	Hep	4659	GL	by physical form
521113	GFBMBJ	60	El	Het	467	GP	book
522	GFF	61	En	Hid	47	H	classification

5221	GFFM	62 Eo	Hif	475	HG	schemes
52215	GFFMJ	63 Er	Him	478	HP	UDC
53	GJ	64 Ew	Hod	48	J	cooperation
54	GN	65 Ex	Hom	49	K	finance
541	GNF	66 Ey	Hop	495	KG	funding
5413	GNFF	67 Ez	Hot	498	KJ	Federal
6	K	69 F	J	5	LZZ	Materials
61	KB	70 Fb	Jad	55	M	Books
62	KF	71 Ff	Jag	56	N	Serials
621	KFB	72 Fj	Jak	565	NN	periodicals
622	KFF	73 Fm	Jal	566	NP	newspapers
63	KJ	74 Fpz	Jed	57	NZZ	non-standard
631	KJB	75 Fr	Jeg	575	O	maps
632	KJF	76 Fw	Jel	576	P	records
69	L	77 G	K	58	Q	by subject
7	P	78 H	L	66	QZ	Libraries
71		79 J			R	by subject
72	Q	80 L	M	67	RZ	by mode of use
721	QB	81 Lb	Mad	677	SS	reference
73	R	83 N	N	68	SZ	by population served
731	RB	84 Nb	Nad	687	T	children
732	RF	85 Nc	Nag	688	TT	hospital
733	RJ	86 Nd	Ned	689	TU	handicapped
7331	RJB	87 Ne	Nep	6897	TV	blind
74	S	88 Q	P	7	TZZ	by kind
741	SB	89 Qb	Pad	77	U	special
7411	SBF	90 Qc	Pal	777	UU	government
7412	SBJ	91 Qe	Pam	778	V	industry
75	SF	92 Qh	Ped	78	W	academic
751	SFB	93 Qi	Pef	787	WU	school
753	SFF	94 Qm	Peg	788	WX	technical college
757	SFJ	95 Qr	Pem	789	X	university
76	SJ	96 Qu	Pib	8	Y	public
761	SJB	97 Qv	Pif	88	YY	municipal
762	SJF	98 Qw	Pil	89	YZ	county
77	SN	99 Qx	Pod	9	Z	national

particular country and will wish to find them grouped, rather than in particular parties regardless of country. The notation permits either approach; we can choose a citation order to give us the arrangement we want and still follow the principle of inversion, for although there is a suggested filing order for the facet indicators in UDC, it is not mandatory.

Flexibility is a valuable quality in notation, but few schemes possess it. Even CC, which uses arbitrary symbols, has fixed filing and citation orders, while enumerative or semi-enumerative schemes usually give no flexibility at all. Bliss recognized the need for different approaches in different libraries, and in BC there are some subjects where it is possible to select one of several facet orders; however, the scheme itself is not clearly enough structured to give a great deal of potential for alterations of this kind. The most detailed example is once again Literature, where Bliss gives the classifier the choice of four 'modes'.

It is essential to realise that even if a scheme allows us to decide which of several alternatives we are going to adopt, once we have made that decision we must remove all the other options from the scheme. It is not possible to use one citation order one week, and then a different one the next week. Flexibility in the notation of a scheme enables us to make a choice, but once made that choice becomes unalterable.

The term flexibility is used by some writers to denote the ability to accommodate new concepts, for which we have used the term hospitality, an interesting example of the problem of terminology which has already been mentioned in earlier chapters. With this term, as is unfortunately the case with many others, it is important to make sure of an author's meaning if misunderstandings are to be avoided.

RETROACTIVE NOTATION

Mixed notation has some advantages in its potential for giving memorable notation, for flexibility and for *synthesis*. However, it loses the great advantage of pure notation, which is its completely self evident order. Is it possible to devise a pure notation which will permit synthesis without introducing as facet indicators symbols of another kind? A hint of the answer to this question is found in the use in DC of a zero 0 to introduce the standard subdivisions; here we have synthesis with a pure notation, achieved by reserving the symbol 0 to act as a facet indicator.

If we have a subject with, say, three facets, we may use 1 to introduce the least important, which ought to file first. We can now use 2 to introduce the second, and combine notation from the two facets according to the citation order, *provided that we never use the figure 1 in the notation for the second facet*. Similarly, we can use 3 to introduce the primary facet and still achieve complete synthesis, provided that we do not use either 1 or 2 in the notation for this facet. The penalty that we have to pay for the ability to synthesize within a pure notation is a progressive diminution of the base available; in the second facet above, the base is no longer 1–9 but 2–9, while in the third it is 3–9. If we continue, in a subject with nine facets we could end up with the single digit 9 as the base in the primary facet, with the only possible subdivisions 9, 99, 999, 9999 etc. This is clearly unacceptable; in fact, if we wish to use this idea we must begin by allocating an adequate amount of the base to the primary facet, and work back to the least important. Also the method is likely to prove more successful if we use letters, where the base is much longer to start with, than if we use numbers. Provided that we observe this precaution, we can devise a pure notation that will permit us to combine elements from different facets to give notational symbols for composite subjects; this notation need not be expressive, so that composite subjects which occur frequently may be given reasonably short symbols; and we can retain the advantage of pure notation, a completely self evident order. Examples of such notation are found in the *British catalogue of music* classification and in the *British national bibliography* supplementary schedules. Because the elements must be combined in order, beginning at the end and working backwards, it is known as *retroactive* notation. The rigid combination order does not permit any degree of flexibility, but apart from this limitation retroactive notation measures up well to the requirements we have discussed. The last two columns of notation in the sample library science schedule indicate how both letters and numbers may be used in this way, with letters having more potential because of the longer base.

HOSPITALITY IN CHAIN AND IN ARRAY

In the foregoing discussion we have treated expressive as being synonymous with hierarchical, but it is in fact possible to differentiate between the two in a manner which recognizes the distinction between genus-species and syntactic relationships. A notation which reflects genus-species divisions may be denoted hierarchical, while one which reflects syntactic relationships is expressive or structured. For example, in DC17 the convention of using an asterisk to show points at which notational synthesis is possible was introduced. This is usually found to apply where there is a general heading with several subdivisions; because the notation for the general heading is extended *hierarchically* to show its subdivisions, it is not possible to extend it *expressively* to show synthesis. On the other hand, the notation for the subdivisions is *not* extended hierarchically, so it is possible to use syntactic extension by synthesis. An example will make this clearer: in Agriculture, we have the general headings

633   Field crops
633.4 Root crops

Both of these are extended by genus-species division, 633 obviously to include root crops and other kinds of crops at 633.1, 633.2 and so on, and 633.4 to specify particular types of root crop, *eg* 633.49 Tubers, which is itself extended to specify Potatoes at 633.491*. It is therefore not possible to extend any of these numbers for general headings to indicate the composite subject 'injuries to . . .' since this would lead to ambiguity. To synthesize a piece of notation for 'injuries to . . .' we are told to add a 9 to the notation for the crop, then add the appropriate number from 632 Plant injuries, diseases, pests and their control. Injuries to crops in general is 632.1, so to specify diseases of root crops we would take the base number 633.4, add 9, then add 1 (taken from 633.1; this would give us 633.491, which is the notation for Potatoes! Because the notation is divided hierarchically we cannot divide it syntactically. However, when we get to the end of the chain of division, at potatoes, we *can* synthesize a number for 'diseases of potatoes' because there are no hierarchical subdivisions; to 633.491 we add 9, then 4, to give us 633.49194 Diseases of potatoes. The asterisk is used to show that we can use synthesis at 633.491*.

The problem arises because of the lack of facet indicators in DC; there is no means of distinguishing genus-species division in the notation from synthetic division at the same point, and since genus-species division is considered to be more important, this takes precedence. Although we can add more crops if any should arise, we cannot devise specific numbers for many composite subjects. The scheme may be said to be hospitable *in array*, but not *in chain*. In order to be completely hospitable in chain, a scheme must have notational means to permit synthesis as well as genus-species division, and will thus have an expressive notation. On the other hand, as we have already seen, it is quite possible for a scheme to permit synthesis and yet have a completely non-hierarchical notation, for example the BCM classification. We end up with a tabulation as follows:

Hierarchical but not expressive
    permits genus-species but not syntactic division (*eg* DC in part)
Non-hierarchical and expressive
    permits genus-species division and syntactic, but does not display genus-species (*eg* BCM)
Hierarchical and expressive
    permits both kinds of division and displays both (either explicitly or implicitly) (*eg most of* CC)
Non-hierarchical and non-expressive
    permits genus-species division but not systematic synthesis, and displays neither (*eg* LC)

(A scheme in the last category, such as LC, does permit some syntactic division; a glance at the schedules will show composite subjects enumerated on nearly every page. However, it does not permit *systematic* synthesis; each and every composite subject has to be fitted into the schedules as it occurs.)

Because a synthetic scheme lists only single concepts, and has to provide means for notational synthesis of composite subjects, it makes the distinction between hierarchical and expressive notation in the above sense very obvious. The limitations on hospitality concomitant with the use of hierarchical notation have already been discussed, as have those relating to synthesis, but since we have already emphasized the importance of the distinction between genus-species relationships and syntactic it may be useful to carry this distinction over into the discussion on notation.

The distinction between hospitality in chain and in array has also been applied to a purely hierarchical notation, *ie* one applied within a single facet, but here it has no meaning. Logically, we obtain a species by adding a difference to a genus; in any chain of division, we shall have a number of steps between the *summum genus* and the *infima species*, each step representing a stage at which a species itself is regarded as a genus which can be further divided. That is to say, at each stage of division we generate an array of new species, each of which forms part of a chain of division from summum genus to infima species. We cannot distinguish between hospitality in chain and in array. A hierarchical notation must be hospitable in chain *and* array or in neither; in practice, it usually begins by having room to be both and ends up either by losing its hierarchical nature or by ceasing to be hospitable to new concepts at all.

SHELF NOTATION

Up to this point we have been working on the assumption that the arrangement of books on the shelves of a library would parallel exactly the arrangement of entries in a classified catalogue or bibliography. However, whereas there are no real limits to the length of notation we can use on a catalogue or bibliography entry, to put a long piece of notation on the back of a book may be difficult. For this reason there has been for many years now a divergence of opinion between those who believe that shelf arrangement should be as specific as possible and those whose believe that this is not necessary. The introduction to DC always includes a section on how to cut back class numbers from their full length without changing the meaning, and much of the controversy over the relative merit of DC and LC seems to arise from the idea that DC numbers have to be studied carefully with a view to cutting back whereas LC numbers do not.[8] On LC cards, and in the British and Australian national bibliographies, DC18 numbers are set out in up to three 'segments', so that libraries can use as long or short a notation as they think fit. UDC numbers tend to be very long, and some libraries using this scheme compile a parallel set of shelf marks which may conveniently be placed on the backs of books, while retaining the full notation for the catalogue.

It is certainly easier to scan a series of books on a shelf than a series of cards for the same books in the catalogue. Whether this is a sufficient reason for abandoning specificity is not so clear. Notation can often be split up in such a way that it can be placed on the spines of books without causing any problems; a full LC call number may be quite long, *eg* Z695.1.E5E5 1967, but if this is set out in groups it is not inconvenient:

Z
695
.1
.E5E5
1967.

The notation from other schemes may be similarly treated.

One scheme was compiled solely with brevity of notation in mind; this was Fremont Rider's *International classification for the arrangement of books on the shelves of general libraries*, published by the author in 1961. Rider set out to provide a scheme which could be used for shelf arrangement and would never require more than three digits in its notation; he chose letters rather than numbers because of the longer base, but avoided mixed notation (which would have given a longer base still) because he felt that it was confusing for the users. However, Rider's allocation of the notation was in some cases ill-judged, and in many places brevity was achieved simply by ignoring composite subjects. As has been seen, this can cause cross-classification if no citation order is stated, but Rider seems to have ignored this also. The scheme was published as a preliminary edition, and unfortunately Rider died before he could take note of any comments or prepare any revisions. The scheme remains outside the mainstream of library classification, interesting because it illustrates the logical conclusion of the demand for brevity in shelf notation.

Although we stated earlier that there were no real limits on the length of notation that could be used on a catalogue card or a bibliography, there may in practice be certain limitations of convenience. To discover what piece of notation it is we require we have to look in an index of some kind, and then go to the main sequence, and this may prove difficult if the piece of notation we have to remember is long and complicated. There is no real solution to this problem in the card catalogue, but on the printed page it may not be quite so acute if we concentrate on the first one or two elements and then rely on our ability to scan a page quickly. LISA[9] is using the CRG classification for library science to arrange its entries, and to solve the problem of lengthy numbers it prints the first section only of each class number in the index so that it can be easily remembered. The first element is not in itself sufficient to get us to the specific place we want, but the layout on the printed page permits us to scan quickly over the entries at the point where we enter the sequence and thus find what we are looking for. This demonstrates in a rather satisfactory way that the function of the notation is to mechanize the arrangement, and in expecting it to do this *and* to be convenient as well we may be asking too much of it.

In recent years, there has been some rethinking on the question of notational convenience, which has highlighted the dilemma facing the classificationist. There is now general acceptance of the superiority of the analytico-synthetic approach over the enumerative, in enabling the classifier to accommodate unforeseen composite subjects. However, there is much less agreement over the notational consequences. Because of the necessity to assemble perhaps several different pieces of notation, each possibly having a facet indicator, synthetic notation tends to become long, and may be quite complex in addition. Shelving of books is normally carried out by non-professional staff, who may find difficulties in following the correct order, particularly if the notation is mixed or if arbitrary symbols are used as facet indicators. Earlier in this chapter we saw that the use of arbitrary symbols can have advantages in allowing us to choose an appropriate citation order, but when we consider that this may also mean that these symbols have a different filing order at different points in the overall arrangement, we can see that this may cause chaos. The professional classifier should be able to handle this without difficulty, but we should not expect the same degree of skill and knowledge from the nonprofessional worker.

With the introduction of MARC in 1971, BNB decided to use DC18 notation, and to abandon its own version of DC and its alphabetical notation for expansions beyond the official schedules. This means that the arrangement in the classified section is no longer specific at every point, and that the burden of specificity is transferred to the entry vocabulary, for which PRECIS (discussed in detail in chapter 14) is used. There is no doubt that the simpler notation has been welcomed by the majority of, if not all, users despite the less precise arrangement that results from the change. It is a very clear indication of the fact emphasized at the beginning of this chapter: for many people, the notation *is* the classification. Since it appears that the writings of several generations of classificationographers (?) have been unsuccessful in eradicating this idea, mistaken though it be, perhaps we should admit defeat and pursue other solutions to the problems of specificity and relevance.

BIBLIOGRAPHY

 1 There are several useful accounts of notational problems, *eg*
   Coates, E J: 'Notation in classification'. (Chapter *in* International study conference on classification research, Dorking 1957. *Proceedings.*)

Vickery, B C: *Classification and indexing in science and technology*. Butterworths, third edition 1975. Chapter 4.

Foskett, D J: *Classification and indexing in the social sciences*. Butterworths, second edition 1974. Chapter 9.

2 Bliss H E: *The organization of knowledge in libraries*. H W Wilson, second edition 1939. Chapter 3.

3 Foskett, D J: 'Two notes on indexing techniques'. *Journal of documentation, 18* (4) December 1962, 188–192. Also 1 above.

4 Ranganathan, S R: *Prolegomena to library classification*. Asia Publishing House, third edition 1967. Parts H, J, K and L deal with notation; seminal mnemonics are explained in chapter KE.

5 Coates, E J: *The British catalogue of music classification*. Library Association, 1960.

6 English Electric Company Ltd: *Classification of engineering*, third edition 1961. The latest edition, *Thesaurofacet*, uses uppercase letters only, which suggests that the mixed notation of upper and lowercase letters did not prove satisfactory.

7 Foskett, D J: 'The London Education Classification'. *Education Libraries bulletin*, Supplement 6, 1963. Second edition, 1975. In the second edition, problems of hospitality have led to the introduction of four-letter symbols in a number of places, thus losing the benefits of pronounceability.

8 Gore, D: 'A neglected topic: the COST of classification'. *Library journal, 89* (11) 1964, 2287–2291. Many recent discussions on reclassification have illustrated the same point.

9 *Library and information science abstracts*, published bi-monthly by the Library Association, supersedes the earlier *Library science abstracts*, which was arranged under very broad alphabetical headings. The complexity of the notation has led to a certain amount of criticism from professional librarians. One may draw a variety of conclusions from this, all of them equally depressing.

CHAPTER 11

Alphabetical index

Systematic order is not self evident; we need notation to show whereabouts in the sequence we shall find a particular subject. However, we also need some means of finding the notation, and this must be through an alphabetical sequence, for we inevitably use words in our first approaches to the system. A classification scheme must therefore have an alphabetical index to serve as its entry vocabulary, leading us to the schedules which form the index vocabulary by means of the notation which forms the code vocabulary. The importance of the entry vocabulary has already been demonstrated in chapter 5, and in this chapter we will be considering some of the practical implications. To begin with, how do we construct the entry vocabulary?

The obvious place to find the required words is in the schedules, where we have listed all the terms we wish to arrange. As a first approximation, we can indeed take all the words in the schedules, together with their appropriate notation, and simply rearrange them in alphabetical order. This is however something of a simplification, as we have seen, since there are a number of problems to be solved before we can claim that we have provided a good index. The first of these is *synonyms*. In the schedules we shall normally use only one term for a particular focus, but there may well be others; both the preferred term and its synonyms must form part of the entry vocabulary. For example, in the index to UDC we find:

Sleep-walking	159.963.5
Somnambulism	159.963.5
Arachnida	595.4
Spiders	595.4

The second problem is that of *homographs*. With systematic arrangement we have to distinguish the same word used with different meanings, just as with alphabetical arrangement. An example of this kind, taken from UDC:

Waders (birds)	598.3
Waders (footwear)	685.315

The same term may also occur in a number of places in the schedules, denoting the same concept but in different contexts. As we saw in chapter 5, these occurrences represent generic and quasi-generic relationships. An example of this kind, taken from DC16:

Tobacco	
botany	583.79
field crops	
agriculture	633.71
economics	338.17371
hygiene	613.8
products	
manufactures	679.7
social customs	394.1
use ethics	178.7

Here we have an example of a word that occurs several times in the schedules of a general classification scheme; it is represented by several pieces of notation, but each of these represents it only in one particular context. In indexing such a word, it would be less than helpful to give merely the word and several pieces of notation—though this would certainly lead us to all the places in the schedules where the word may be found. To make the index more precise, we give the context in which a particular piece of notation denotes the word we are interested in. There is really no need to distinguish these two kinds of entry typographically in the index; the earlier example might equally well have been set out:

Waders	
birds	598.3
footwear	685.315

In both examples, the qualifying words show the context which links word and notation.

Related subjects are not normally a problem with systematic arrangement, for this is itself intended to arrange related subjects together; however, we can only display relationships in one way, by juxtaposition, so that if a subject has more than one link we cannot show the others. It is possible to overcome this in two ways; one is to make cross-references in the schedules, for example (DC16)

550   Earth sciences
            Study of all earth materials, forces, processes
            Including geology
                For astronomical geography, see 525; *geography* 910;
                mineralogy, 549; *paleontology,* 560.

(Most of these cross-references were dropped from DC17.) The other way is to make the cross-references in the index, as does UDC:

Geology   55   *Cf.* Palaeontology; Surveying.

We do not normally make *see* references within the index, because this means referring the user to a heading which is still not the one he wants, and which will in its turn refer him to a piece of notation. However, there are some occasions when this is permissible, as for example when a common word which can appear in a number of contexts has a synonym. The following illustration is from UDC:

Marriage(s), customs, forms, etc.   392.5
  hygiene (guidance, etc.)   613.89
  insurance   368.45
  law   347.3
  registers   929.3
  sacraments   265.5
  statistics   312.3

Weddings. *See* Marriage(s).

COMPOSITE SUBJECTS

If we are using a synthetic scheme, it will list only single foci, which are relatively easy to index, though we saw in chapter 5 that some concepts may be denoted by terms involving more than one word. An enumerative scheme will however contain a good proportion of composite subjects, and we have to make sure that all of the terms in a composite heading are present in the entry vocabulary as access terms. The most convenient way of doing this is by using chain procedure, as described in chapter 6. We make an index entry for each term in the chain, qualifying it by as many of the previous terms as necessary to show the context, and ignoring terms after it. The notation may help us here if it is expressive, but we can use the procedure whether it is or not; the important thing is to ensure that the chain of division is correctly written down in the first place.

Even if we use a synthetic scheme, we shall of course have composite topics in the catalogue which we shall have to index. We must draw a distinction between the index to the scheme and the index to a catalogue compiled by using it. Although the difference is most clearly seen with a synthetic scheme, where the catalogue will obviously include subjects not enumerated in the scheme, it is equally present when an enumerative scheme is used. Even with a completely enumerative scheme there will always be some individual topics which are not named in the scheme, but which we shall wish to index; on the other side, there will always be a number of topics listed in the scheme but not represented in our collection and therefore not in our catalogue. They will appear in the index to the scheme, but should not appear in the index to our catalogue. The practice found in some libraries of using the index to the scheme as an index to the catalogue is a makeshift expedient, by penury out of ignorance, and must be condemned.

We may find that chain procedure is not entirely an automatic process because of the nature of systematic arrangement. To refer back to an example used earlier to demonstrate a notational principle, *violins* are a subdivision of the broader heading *Individual instruments and instrumental groups arranged according to their basic mode of performance*. If we were to index this chain of division, we should have to make an entry for that heading, but it is most unlikely that anyone would try to find it through the heading. Although it is necessary to insert it in order to achieve a proper progression from general to specific, we do not need to index it: it is an *unsought link*. It is normal to omit also, as being unsought, such weak entry points as periods of time, and common terms of wide application but low significance such as Methods, Equipment, Production, Calculations, Research, and so on; in practice, to index in detail bibliographical forms would lead to a large increase in entries in the index without a corresponding increase in its value, and they too are treated as unsought.

It should be clear from this that the problem is not an easy one to solve. To exclude unsought links requires an intellectual effort, which negates one of the big advantages of chain procedure; it also involves a decision as to whether a particular link in a given chain is sought or not, and there will be many occasions when a term falls into the borderline area of 'possibly sought'. By excluding a term we may be reducing the potential for recall significantly; we normally leave unsought terms unindexed because they do *not* have a significant effect on recall, but we cannot always be certain that we are doing the right thing. On the other hand, to index all unsought links would add considerably to the bulk of the index, without a corresponding increase in effectiveness.

Another kind of problem, that of *false links*, may arise if we place too much reliance on the notation to indicate the chain that we have to index. Ranganathan considers facet indicators to be false links, though they may more usefully be regarded as unsought, and in any case will not even be considered if we refer to the chain of division rather than the notation. Another kind of false link arises from errors on the part of the compiler of the scheme, or changes in the structure of knowledge, so that subjects appear to be subdivisions of other subjects when in fact they are not. DC shows several examples of this in the notation of the sixteenth edition, but the majority of them are shown correctly by the schedules. If we rely on the notation, we may go wrong, but this cannot happen if we rely as we should on the systematic chain of division. The following example shows this clearly:

600	Technology
620	Engineering
621	Mechanical
621.3	Electrical

If we rely on the notation, we will index the false link mechanical as part of the chain from engineering to electrical engineering, but this cannot happen if we rely on the schedules. The converse effect may also be seen if we rely on the notation and it is not expressive:

400	Language
430	Germanic
439	Other Germanic
439.5	Scandinavian
439.7–439.8	East Scandinavian languages
439.7	Swedish

Though the last example is untypical of DC, in which the notation is made expressive as far as is possible, it is the norm in a scheme such as LC in which a largely integral notation is used. Once again, provided that we follow the chain of division carefully through the schedules, we can apply chain procedure, as the following examples show:

ND	Painting
ND1700–2399	Water-color painting
ND2290	Still life
ND2300	Flowers
ND2305	Reproductions. Facsimiles

which would give index entries

Reproductions: flowers: still life water-color painting ND2305
Flowers: still life water-color painting ND2300
Still life: water-color painting ND2290
Water-color painting ND1700–2399
Painting ND

NB	Sculpture
NB60–198	History
NB69–169	Ancient
NB135–159	Special materials
NB145	Terra-cottas
NB150	Figurines
NB155	Greek
NB157	Tanagra

which would give index entries

Tanagra figurines: ancient sculpture NB157
Greek figurines: ancient sculpture NB155
Figurines: ancient sculpture NB150
Terra-cottas: ancient sculpture NB145
[Special materials—unsought]
Ancient sculpture NB69–169 [possibly unsought]
History: sculpture NB60–198
[or History of a subject *see* the subject]
Sculpture NB

The problem in applying chain procedure to a scheme with a non-expressive notation is that it is sometimes difficult to follow all the steps of the division through the schedules, particularly if they are not clearly set out, as is the case with, for example, BC. It will also be clear from the above examples that although chain procedure can sometimes be completely mechanical, as it is with BTI, it is sometimes necessary to modify the method to take account of unsought links and redundant qualifiers, and this means intellectual effort in a procedure which should be at the clerical level.

DISTRIBUTED RELATIVES

We have already seen in chapter 8, particularly table 8, that systematic arrangement only brings together the topics which we have decided shall form our primary facet; all the rest are systematically scattered. It is therefore useful to make explicit a point which is implicit in the earlier part of this chapter, *ie* that foci which are scattered by the systematic arrangement are brought together in the alphabetical index. These *distributed relatives* (concepts which are related but scattered) are shown clearly in the index, as is demonstrated clearly in the 'tobacco' example from DC. The index to a classification scheme or classified catalogue thus has a dual role; not only does it enable us to find the notation for a particular topic and thus its place in the overall arrangement, it also shows all of the several places where a particular concept is to be found even though they are scattered throughout the arrangement.

The index is thus much more than a convenience; it is an essential, integral part of a classified arrangement. As is emphasized in chapter 17, Dewey realized the importance of the index to his classification scheme from the very beginning, but all too often compilers of classified catalogues appear to regard an index as an expensive luxury. Chain procedure is one method of compiling an index, but there are of course others; in addition to the 'pot luck' method which some indexers seem to favour, we now have the use of PRECIS to serve as the indexing method in BNB, and with it the use of specific index entries at each point rather than the less satisfactory general headings generated by chain procedure. Whichever method we adopt, it is vital that we should not underestimate the importance of the alphabetical index.

BIBLIOGRAPHY
 1 Coates, E J: *Subject catalogues*. Library Association, 1960. Chapters 8 and 9.
 Foskett, D J: *Classification and indexing in the social sciences*. Butterworths, second edition, 1974. Chapter 10.
 Mills, J: 'Chain indexing and the classified catalogue'. *Library association record*, 57 (4) 1955, 141–148.

Horner, J L: *Cataloguing*. Chapter 16 has some useful examples demonstrating the fallibility of completely mechanical use of chain procedure.

Wilson, T D: *An introduction to chain indexing*. Bingley, 1971.

CHAPTER 12

Organization

Knowledge does not stand still, and a classification scheme left unrevised will, sooner rather than later, become unusable. There are several implications here which we must consider, beginning with those for the compiler. In the first place, continuing revision implies some sort of organization, rather than an individual, to carry it through. Individuals are mortal, but an organization can continue indefinitely. We find that those schemes which have relied on the genius of their compilers, without the backing of an adequate organization, have gradually fallen into obsolescence, whereas those schemes which have adequate backing continue to progress. Examples of the first kind are SC and BC, both interesting and successful in their day; SC is now to all intents and purposes of historical interest only, and while renewed efforts are being made to keep BC up to date, it is doubtful whether these are sufficient. In the second category we find DC, LC and UDC, which have the backing of the Library of Congress and the FID; despite the fact that they have serious theoretical deficiencies, and may in some ways be compared to their detriment with BC, they are likely to remain important practical schemes, largely because of their successful organization.

It may appear somewhat out of place to discuss management problems in a work largely devoted to information retrieval theory, but in fact it may be the managerial organization of a scheme that determines whether it is successful or not: a sad but clear case of the practical tail wagging the theoretical dog. The present author has discussed the future of UDC in some detail,[1] and reached the conclusion that the scheme cannot survive indefinitely unless the present organization is drastically altered. In particular, the central secretariat needs to be greatly strengthened, and preferably linked to a very large library, as are LC and DC. Developments over the past few years have given no cause for changing this deeply pessimistic view. If this is true of a scheme as well-established as UDC, one can hardly take an optimistic view of the future of less widely used systems. Many special classifications are developed, but by no means all of them survive, and though there is no doubt that the new edition of BC is an excellent example of classification theory put into practice, one may still doubt whether it will be successful in terms of use in libraries.

There are various ways of keeping a scheme up to date. The most obvious is to publish a new edition from time to time, but this may not necessarily be the best way. In a large and detailed scheme, some sections may need revising fairly frequently, *eg* science and technology (and within these areas particular topics may present more problems than the areas as a whole), whereas other sections will need little or no revision. It may therefore be better to issue the scheme in parts, and revise each part on an *ad hoc* basis, in this way keeping the whole scheme current with the minimum of publishing effort. DC is an example of a scheme which appears in a new edition at regular intervals (the editorial policy is to publish a new edition every seven years), while LC exemplifies the policy of piecemeal publication. UDC is interesting in that it uses both methods: for the full editions, publication is in fascicules, while for the abridged editions, the whole text is published anew at intervals. CC is also intended to fit into this pattern, but the publication of the full edition ('depth schedules') appears to be on a rather more haphazard basis. A limited number of subjects having been covered so far in *Annals of library science* and *Library science with a slant to documentation.*

Whichever of these methods is adopted, with a well organized scheme revision will be continuous, and it is therefore useful to have some means of publishing current revisions at regular intervals, so that users do not have to wait until the new schedules are published formally. DC is kept up to date through *Decimal classification: additions, notes, decisions* (DC&); UDC through *Extensions and corrections to the UDC;* and LC through *LC Classification—additions and changes.* One point that is perhaps rather surprising is that so far the use of computers appears to have been largely ignored in the revision of classification schemes. An attempt was made to produce the eighteenth edition of DC by computer, but the problems involved proved insoluble at the time, and the edition was eventually produced by conventional methods. By contrast, alphabetical systems are now well established in the computer-produced world; the thesauri used by BTI and PRECIS are both computer maintained, though neither has been published for general use, while LCSH has now gone one very important stage further. The seventh edition was produced by computer controlled typesetting, with a view to incorporating amendments at regular intervals. However, this plan did not reach fruition until the eighth edition, which was published in both the normal printed version and also in Computer Output Microfiche form. (COM) The Library of Congress now provides a service whereby the subscriber receives the initial set of 45 fiche, and then receives an updated version each quarter incorporating amendments and corrections. The AIP project described in chapter 18 demonstrated ten years ago that UDC schedules could be successfully produced by computer: with the developments that have taken place since then, particularly COM, it is not encouraging to realize that no progress whatever has been made since then, largely through lack of funds, though experience in Britain with the abridged edition suggests that an up-to-date, full version of UDC could be self-supporting.

Revision must also be planned, and must bear a close relationship to the needs of users. Editions of DC up to the fourteenth showed very clearly the problems of haphazard revision; for example, in DC14 Medicine occupied some eighty pages of the schedules, while the equally important topic Chemical technology (including fuel, food, industrial oils, and metallurgy, among other things) was given so little detail that it occupied only two pages; the most detailed schedule in DC2 was for Sanitary engineering, because Dewey had a friend who worked out the expansion. Later editions have shown the editors' concern that detail should be appropriate to the needs of the literature. UDC's revision is based to a much greater extent on the expressed needs of users, but the fact that much of the work is done voluntarily has, in practice, led to the same kind of inconsistency, with the social sciences generally lacking in detail in comparison with science and technology.

From the point of view of the person trying to use the scheme to arrange a library or catalogue, revision presents several other problems. Once a scheme has been adopted, the library begins to build up a vested interest in the scheme as it stands; there will be ever increasing numbers of cards, books and other documents and records with pieces of notation on them. If the scheme is changed, the librarian has to consider whether he can afford the effort needed to alter all these records, and rearrange them, in accordance with the new schedules. Dewey recognized this very early, and in his second edition adopted the policy of 'integrity of numbers': a piece of notation will not be reused with a changed meaning, and topics will not be relocated in such a way as to require a change of notation, though there may be expansions involving longer notation. There is no doubt that this statement contributed to the success of the scheme; librarians, who are by nature conservative (for many years the main duty of librarians has been seen as the need to preserve documents), welcomed this concession to administrative convenience. However, there is equally no doubt that its effect over the years was to remove the structure of DC further and further from the present day approach to knowledge; indeed, we have seen quite substantial amounts of reordering in all the editions since the fifteenth, to bring the structure more into line with modern thought despite the principle of integrity, and these changes have in many cases been the subject of strong criticism by users.

One means of incorporating changes while avoiding clashes with past practice is the UDC policy of 'starvation'. If a new schedule is drawn up, the notation previously used for that topic is left vacant, and may be used again if required after not less than ten years. It is felt that after a period of ten years, any material in a library still classified by the old notation will be of historical interest only and may be ignored for current purposes. This is probably true in some areas of science and technology, though by no means all; it is very doubtful if it is the case in the social sciences, and it is certainly not the case in the humanities, which are essentially cumulative, ie new writings add to, but do not necessarily supplant, older work. However, since most libraries using UDC are science and technology oriented, in practice the method seems to work without too much difficulty. Take for example the subject 'particle accelerators'; the schedule for these used 621.384.61 and 621.384.62, so when a new schedule was drawn up these numbers were not used, the new schedule being based instead on 621.384.63–621.384.66. Should it prove necessary to revise the schedule once again in the 1970's, the first two numbers may be reused with new meanings. The method is rather wasteful of notation, but as UDC notation in science and technology tends to be very long anyway (owing to its original basis of Dewey's allocation), users do not seem to be unduly worried by this prodigality.

The problem of keeping pace with knowledge is not restricted to systematic arrangement, of course. Terminology changes, new terms have to be introduced, new relationships arise, and all of these changes must be taken into account in any system. The problem is more acute with systematic arrangement because of the inflexibility of notation, which tends to crystallize (fossilize!) the arrangement in a structure reflecting the approach to knowledge at one particular time, and to make more difficult the process of changing. One suggestion that has been made is that libraries should begin a new catalogue at regular intervals introducing changes that become necessary in each new sequence.[2] Each of the BNB major cumulations has differed from its predecessors, but as far as possible changes of practice are not made within cumulations. The United Kingdom Atomic Energy Authority started a new catalogue of technical report literature at the beginning of 1959, and took the opportunity of introducing a number of changes; by 1960, the previous catalogue was used only rarely, illustrating very well the rapid decay of interest in scientific and technical subjects. It would be much more difficult to introduce a similar method into a large general library, where users might find themselves obliged to look through several sequences, but of course this is exactly the method used by all abstracting and indexing services and similar bibliographies, which rarely cumulate beyond five yearly periods. Users do not find this intolerable, so it may be that we tend to exaggerate the hostility that would be aroused by a similar approach in library catalogues.

There is no easy solution to this problem, but a policy of starting a new catalogue at regular intervals would at least recognize the impossibility of reconciling tradition and the need for change.

One way of facilitating revision is to link it to the current indexing operations of a service such as BNB, and thus making it a continuous process. This is the method adopted by LC, but many users complain that keeping pace with all the alterations is very time consuming, and impractical in a busy library. (It should be remembered here that nearly all libraries in the USA use the dictionary catalogue; the task of changing class numbers in the catalogue and on the shelves is much easier when a classified catalogue is in use.) As with so many library problems, the root of the matter is economic; can the library afford the effort of keeping pace with changes, either continuous or at periodic intervals? Administrative procedures may hinder revision, for example if class numbers are used widely in administrative records as well as in the catalogue and on the shelves. Whatever methods we adopt, we cannot afford to ignore the fact that knowledge is changing all the time; if we do, we may end up by finding that people who need information are ignoring us.

RECLASSIFICATION

A library which uses any scheme which is kept up to date will need to change its classification practice from time to time or even continuously, depending on whether the scheme itself is revised at intervals, *eg* DC, or continuously, *eg* LC. However, for many libraries a quite different decision has to be faced at some point in time: should the library adopt an entirely new scheme and reclassify all its material? This position was reached by a number of libraries in this country some years ago, when it became clear that we could not expect a new edition of Brown's *Subject classification*, and the result was a gradual change to DC which is now complete. The reason for this change is fairly obvious; a scheme which must have had a curiously old fashioned look even in 1939, when the third edition was published, proved to be less and less useful for the arrangement of post-war literature. This is not a reflection on Brown's theoretical ideas, many of which have formed the basis of modern theory, but of the practical fact that a scheme must be kept up to date, especially in today's rapidly changing scene. In recent years, however, there has been a move to use LC rather than DC, particularly noticeable in the USA, and in academic rather than in public libraries. There are a variety of reasons for this which are worth examining; some of them appear to be less justifiable than others.

It is important to remember that DC and LC are very largely intended for different sets of users. DC, though it began as a scheme used in a small university library, has developed into one which is aimed almost entirely at the general reader: the non-specialist using the public library. (The specialist tends to get his specialist materials from other sources.) LC has been developed over the years since 1900 with one particular set of users in mind: the readers served by the Library of Congress. We have already seen the difference in approach between the two schemes where Literature is concerned, and this difference is found in many other subjects areas as well. Because LC is aimed at a largely academic audience, it is likely to be more satisfactory for academic libraries serving the same kind of audience than is DC with its bias towards the non-specialist reader. On these grounds, there may well be a good case for changing classification.

There is however another reason, which seems to be rather more suspect. The vast majority of libraries in the USA use Library of Congress printed catalogue cards, and while all of these carry an LC class number, not all have a DC number. Financial and other problems meant that for some years the proportion of cards with DC numbers was relatively low; in order to concentrate the effort where it was most useful, numbers were given as a first priority to those works likely to be found in the majority of public libraries, while more esoteric works were left unclassified. It is of course precisely these esoteric works which are most likely to find a home in academic libraries, which may well ignore more run-of-the-mill publications. In consequence, libraries found that they had to classify a substantial proportion of their intake if they were using DC, but very much less if they used LC. In the interests of work load reduction, they decided to change to LC; however, administrative expediency may not be a very satisfactory reason for changing the arrangement of books on our library shelves.

Another reason which has been advanced is that each new edition of DC introduces major changes; for example, DC16, DC17 and DC18 have introduced new schedules for Chemistry, Psychology, and Law and Mathematics respectively. Libraries using LC cards and the DC numbers on them are obliged to accept these changes, which can lead to a substantial amount of work. However, this reason ignores the fact that LC is changing all the time, and often the only indication of change is that a different class number appears on a card for a book on a subject already represented in the library. Keeping pace with these changes may well mean more work than the seven year hitch experienced by DC users. In any case, this is again a case of administrative convenience dictating order, which may be hard to justify on the grounds of service to users.

The only real ground for reclassification is that a different scheme will give a more satisfactory arrangement. If we reclassify on grounds that it will be easier for the librarian, we may be in some danger of forgetting that the person who is meant to benefit from the arrangement is the user. This said, we may well agree that LC is likely to be more satisfactory in the academic environment than DC, though whether it is so much better that it justifies the effort of reclassification is by no means so certain. The problems of reclassification have been discussed at some length at conferences and in the professional press; since many of them relate to the practical implementation rather than theoretical considerations, they will not be further discussed here[3] The principle which we should always bear in mind is that we use systematic arrangement for the benefit of our users; if a change is to their advantage we should make it, but not otherwise.

BIBLIOGRAPHY

1 Foskett, A C: *The Universal Decimal Classification: the history, present status and future prospects of a large general classification scheme.* Bingley, 1973. Chapters 3, 4, 5, 7 and 8.

2 Lund, J J and Taube, M: 'A nonexpansive classification system: an introduction to period classification.' *Library quarterly, 7* (3) 1937, 373-394.

3 Perreault, J M, ed: *Reclassification: rationale and problems. Proceedings of a conference on reclassification ... April 1968.* College Park, Md, School of Library and Information Services, 1968.

Samore, T, ed: *Problems in library classification: Dewey 17 and conversion.* University of Wisconsin, School of Library and Information Science, 1968.

CHAPTER 13

Some recent developments in classification

In this chapter, we shall examine three recent developments in classification which may be said to be representative of recent trends. The first is the work done by the Classification Research Group towards *CRG* the development of a new general classification suitable for use in computerized retrieval systems. The second is the Broad System of Ordering (BSO) being developed as part of UNISIST (United Nations *BSO* Information System In Science and Technology), which may be said to represent an attempt to produce a new general classification of fairly broad areas of knowledge on rather conventional lines. The third is the work done by Sparck Jones on the development of computer-generated *computer* classification schemes, which may point the way forward for the *generated* future. All three represent the results of a considerable amount of research which has gone on over the past twentyfive years, and is of course still continuing. Some of the work discussed in chapter 28 may seem to call into question the value of this research; perhaps in another twenty five years we shall have a clearer idea as to which of the two views is correct.

THE CRG CLASSIFICATION

For many years the little research that was carried out on classification and indexing was largely the work of individuals engaged in compiling schemes or teaching. In the first category we may place H E Bliss, in the second W C Berwick Sayers, whose 'Canons of classification' formed one of the earliest attempts to present students with a complete rationale. One of Sayers' brightest students was S R Ranganathan, who returned to India determined to devise a new kind of classification scheme, in which ideas present in existing schemes such as DC and UDC in embryo would be brought to fruition. For some years this work went largely unnoticed in the West, until after the second world war it was discovered by a new generation of librarians, notably through the efforts of B I Palmer, who had met Ranganathan in India during the war.

At the same time that Ranganathan's ideas were beginning to make an impression in Britain, another important event took place; this was the Royal Society's Scientific Information Conference, held in London in 1948. One of the topics discussed was classification, and a committee was set up, with Professor J D Bernal as secretary, to examine the situation and suggest ways in which improvements might be made in existing methods of subject organization. Little progress was made, and in 1951 B C Vickery was invited to form a group to take over the work of the committee. The result of this invitation was the formation of the Classification Research Group (CRG)[1] in 1952— probably the first opportunity that librarians and others interested in the organization of knowledge had had to get together and discuss problems as a team over an extended period of time. Since its formation the CRG has met regularly at monthly intervals, though in true British fashion it has always remained an amateur organization—amateur in the sense that it does not dispose of large funds, and its members are actuated by enthusiasm for the subject rather than by the hope of wealth. Over the years, the composition of the Group has changed, and few if any of the founder members are now actively involved. Nevertheless, the general trend of thought has been maintained consistently, which seems to suggest that it must have at least a reasonable measure of fundamental validity. As was shown in chapter 5, it also links up with research in other areas such as psychology and linguistics.

During the 1950's the CRG was mainly concerned with the application of the principles of facet analysis and synthesis to the development of classification schemes for special subjects. Probably the largest of these was the English Electric Company's classification for engineering, which has now reached its fourth edition, but many other schemes were produced. Among these may be mentioned the Kyle classification for the social sciences, J E L Farradane's scheme for diamond technology, D J Foskett's scheme for occupational safety and health, and the classification of aeronautics drawn up for the Cranfield Project by Vickery and Farradane. The most recent special classification has been the one for library science which was mentioned in chapter 8.

In recent years the CRG has devoted more of its efforts to the formulation of principles for class order in a general scheme. Special schemes have the advantage that subjects not forming part of the core, but still of interest to libraries concerned with the core (*fringe subjects*), can be treated in a fairly cavalier fashion, since their importance is likely to be far less than that of core material. In a general classification there are, of course, no fringe subjects: all are of equal weight, and must be given their due place in the overall order. In 1955 the CRG published a memorandum[2] on the need for a faceted classification as the basis of all methods of information retrieval, and this was followed up at the 'Dorking conference', at which speakers from a number of countries were able to meet to discuss, and agree upon, this basic point. In their sixth *Bulletin*, the CRG report on some of the problems that they had been discussing in relation to a new general scheme; following a grant from NATO to the Library Association, a conference was held in 1963 to discuss the problems at some length and to report on the progress that had been made.[3]

Following this conference, a research assistant was engaged to work on the project full-time in 1964, with the guidelines being set by the CRG. It soon became apparent that some of these were mutually incompatible. For example, the scheme was intended to be suitable for shelf arrangement, but also for use in computer-based systems.

We have seen in chapter 10 that for shelf classification notation should be as brief as possible, and also as straightforward as possible. However, in a mechanized system, it is essential that a concept should be denoted by the same piece of notation wherever it occurs, otherwise programming becomes impossible. For example, it *is* possible to program a computer to search for 'England' in a UDC file, because England is regularly given the notation (42); it is *not* possible to program the same search in a DC file, because England is denoted by a variety of pieces of notation, some of which have different meanings elsewhere. Computer programming is linked to the consistent repetition of regular procedures (algorithms), and does not lend itself to the economic handling of large numbers of *ad hoc* decisions. The consistent use of the same notation for the same concept is implicit in special facetted classification schemes, but even there it leads to lengthy notation in many cases; in a general scheme this problem would be compounded. However, the problem is not simply one of notation, but of the fundamental approach to the organization of concepts into meaningful groups and a satisfactory overall order.

In chapter 5 we discussed the possibility of allocating any and every concept into five fundamental categories: Entities, Activities, Abstracts, Properties and Heterogeneous. This analysis was seen to be of value in establishing the kinds of concepts with which we have to deal and in identifying their verbal forms as nouns, or adjectives in the case of some Properties. However, in devising a practical system, it is usually of value to identify particular groups within these categories, *eg* processes, agents, etc. In devising a classification scheme inductively, *ie* on the basis of the concepts present in the literature, we saw in chapter 8 that we can identify certain basic classes which we can usefully analyze into facets. These basic classes can themselves be grouped into main classes, which turn out to be the conventional *disciplines* corresponding to the educational and scientific consensus. In other words, general classification schemes are discipline-oriented if they are constructed along the lines indicated so far, and this is true whether we approach them inductively, by building up from individual concepts, or deductively, by an analysis of knowledge into its recognized subject areas. This kind of organization into disciplines is certainly in line with literary warrant, but once again we find it leads to problems in the handling of individual concepts.

We have seen that if we analyze the literature of a given basic class, we can group the concepts we find into facets consisting of concepts which all bear the same relationship to the basic class. In chapter 9 we saw that in addition to those which relate specifically to a given basic class there are others which are common to the whole of knowledge. The four common facets described are those which have been identified as the result of several years' experience in classifying for BNB, but we can also find others which apply to substantial parts of knowledge, though not perhaps to the whole of it. For example in UDC and DC we find a 'persons' facet, which is obviously of limited value in, say, the physical sciences; in UDC we find a 'parts' facet which may be used throughout engineering, but is likely to be irrelevant to the social sciences, at least until bionic man takes over. Because these quasi-common facets are still discipline-oriented, they do not cause any problems, but we also find that there are certain facets which can occur in more than one place but are not discipline-oriented. For example, 'lamb' is a concept falling into an 'animals' facet which may be found in both science (zoology) and technology (agriculture), but also in social sciences (animals in folklore), as well as in various other contexts.

The position becomes even more confused if we look at something like 'tobacco' in a conventional scheme such as DC. We find that it may be regarded as a plant, in Botany; or as a crop, in Agriculture; as a raw material, in Manufactures; as a drug source, in Medicine and in Ethics; as a habit, in Customs; and in other places according to the point of view we adopt to study it. We have at once a problem: which discipline is the correct one to select for this concept in a particular document? And how do we deal with the documents which deal with several aspects of 'tobacco'? DC solves this problem on an *ad hoc* basis; for each such topic we find a place in the schedules which has the tag 'comprehensive works'. This works for those topics specifically dealt with in this way, but it gives us no guidance for those which are not.

While we are still thinking of manual systems such problems are a nuisance, but we can overcome them by the expenditure of more effort. However, we have just noted that mechanized systems cannot tolerate anomalies, which require individual programming. Apart from the cost, any attempt to tackle the problem in this way can only lead to a closed, enumerative, system, which sooner or later will break down when faced with an unforeseen addition.

In a discipline-oriented scheme, it is concretes which are scattered; if we gave up disciplines as our primary basis of division we could compile a scheme in which there would be one place, and only one place, for each concrete; the disciplines would now be scattered, but on balance it is more useful to have things this way round. The idea of concrete as primary concept was used by Brown in his *Subject classification*, and we have already seen how it has been the normal approach in systems for alphabetical headings such as those of Kaiser, Coates and others. If we are to apply the idea to a general classification scheme, two problems have to be solved: how do we arrive at our sets of concretes and subsidiary concepts, and how do we arrange them in a helpful order?

FACET ANALYSIS

The Kyle classification for the social sciences[4] demonstrated that it was possible to analyse the whole of that area into two large facets, persons and activities. The logical development of this line of thought was the postulate that we can allot any concept to one of two categories: it must either be an *entity* or an *attribute*. These terms are necessarily rather vague, but have a very respectable ancestry (they go back to Aristotle); for practical purposes the CRG proposed the following schema, which is rather more precise. Entities fall into seven categories:

Physical entities
Chemical entities
Heterogeneous non-living entities
Artefacts
Biological entities
Man
Mentefacts

while attributes fall into three categories which may themselves be further organized:

Relative and positional terms
Properties
Activities.

It will be seen that this analysis, representing the stage reached towards the end of the NATO grant, is obviously the precursor of the analysis described in chapter 5. However, although it was of value in identifying a set of facets which could be applied to the whole of knowledge, this did not in itself lead to progress in the search for an overall helpful or logical order into which the facets themselves or the concepts within them might be fitted.

INTEGRATIVE LEVELS

The philosophical theory of integrative levels[5] suggests that there is a recognizable order in nature which consists of a progression from lesser to greater levels of organization. If we consider sub-atomic particles in their own right, we find that they have certain properties, but if we consider them as united to form an atom we find that the atom forms a new *level of integration* which has its own set of properties. A car is more than a collection of parts; they have an organization imposed on them which means that the whole is greater than the sum of its parts. We can therefore use this principle to arrange the entities in our list in order; as a beginning we arrive at the order outlined in the previous section, which may be expanded to give a more detailed schedule:

Physical entities
Level   I   Fundamental particles
       II   Atoms, isotopes
      III   Molecules
      IV   Molecular assemblages
Chemical entities
Level   I   Elements
       II   Compounds
      III   Complex compounds
Heterogeneous non-living entities
Level   I   Minerals
       II   Rocks
      III   Physiographic features
      IV   Astronomical entities   *etc*

When we come to look at terms for activities, we can use the principle of general to special to give us an order in which static conditions precede dynamic, on the assumption that they are more general, and the overall order is one in which activities of the dynamic kind are ranked according to whether they lead to *aggregation, ie a mixing* of entities, or *integration, with the forming of a new* whole. (We may see a direct analogy in chemistry in the distinction between a mixture and a compound.) This gives, in outline:

General activity concepts
General static and kinetic conditions   static
Equilibrium
General kinetic conditions   mixing
Contacts and disturbances
Motions and transfers   aggregation
Assembly and disassembly   integration

The theory of integrative levels takes us so far along the road to an overall order, but it begins to break down once we reach a certain point, for example when we start to move into the biological sciences beyond the individual cell stage. It is also of limited value in dealing with aggregates. Here the idea of chronological sequence may be used; for example, when considering the relative position in the overall order of 'birds' and 'nests', birds must come first. (The chicken and egg situation has yet to be resolved definitively.)

At this point, the research had yielded a method of constructing a schedule which would give a unique place for at least a large number of concepts. At the same time, work had been in progress on the equally important question of citation order: the way in which the individual concepts in a composite subject should be combined to give a single definitive representation of that subject. Five different fundamental relationships between concepts may be distinguished. The first of these is the semantic type—the permanent relationships which we can establish by a study of knowledge. In order to cover these relationships, we have to build up a network of *see also* references which may be based on literary warrant, or our own knowledge, or other external sources.

The second type of relationship is the attributive: the relationship between entity and attribute, or attribute and attribute. The rule here is that in the basic statement, an attribute always *follows* the entity to which it is linked. This is the same as Kaiser's rule, concrete-process, except that Kaiser did not permit processes to stand on their own; they had to be related to a concrete. An attribute which is of general application may stand alone, *eg* Advertising, but in practice this is found to happen relatively rarely.

In the third and fourth types of relationship, more than one entity is present, in the possessive (thing-part) and interactive (thing-thing) modes. To clarify our approach to these two relationships, it is useful to introduce some ideas from general systems theory. This states that when two systems interact, it is possible to identify one of the two as the key system; this key system should obviously come first in the citation order. Thus in the possessive example it is the possessing system which is the key system, while in the interactive case it is the passive system which is the key system. (It will be seen that this also gives us a theoretical basis for our assertion that in an influence phase relationship, it is the subject influenced which comes first in the citation order).

The fifth kind of relationship is that in which an entity is defined by one of its attributes; for example, in Lewis Carroll's poem,[17]

I'll tell thee everything I can:
There's little to relate.
I saw an aged, aged man,
A-sitting on a gate.

the man (entity) described by the White Knight is defined (twice!) by one of his attributes, age. We may refer to an aged man, but we can also discuss the concept 'age' in its own right. It will be seen that this is the kind of relationship that we discussed in chapter 5 when we were considering the two grammatical forms in which properties might be expressed.

These relationships and their various refinements were expressed in the form of a series of relational operators consisting of a number within parentheses. A complex subject would be analyzed into its component concepts, the notation for these found in the schedules, and the individual pieces of notation linked together according to the citation order by the relational operators. This could lead to an extremely complex piece of notation; Austin[6] quotes the example

$$C35(5)q24(59)x75(599)v6(54)B27(546)r2$$

representing the subject 'energy balance in the turbulent mixing layers of a gas'. This subject is in fact by no means as complex as many to be found in the literature of aeronautics, and the notation for it could be handled quite straightforwardly by a computer, but it does raise doubts concerning its suitability for shelf arrangement.

When the work had reached this point,[7] the NATO grant ran out, and Austin, who had been seconded from BNB to work on the project during 1968–69, returned to BNB, where he used the ideas that had arisen during the project as the basis of PRECIS, to be discussed in the next chapter. As PRECIS is an alphabetical system, problems of order do not arise, and it may well be that the final result of this particular piece of classification research will indeed be an alphabetical system.

It is worth noting at this point the fact that the CRG has always been concerned with practical results, and has based its theorising on practical problems. The special schemes that have been compiled are in daily use, and many of the members of the group have been connected with bibliographical tools such as BNB and BTI. It is in the development of such large-scale services that problems are seen most acutely, and the solutions proposed have to stand up to detailed scrutiny by users. Much of the impetus for the development of a new general scheme arose from the dissatisfaction of BNB subject cataloguers with DC, and it was the intention that the new scheme should be used to arrange the bibliography in a more satisfactory way; DC numbers would be provided, but would not be used for the arrangement. In the event, this plan was overtaken by events, in that with the introduction of MARC in 1971, BNB decided to use DC18 and abandon its own version of DC in the interests of international standardization, using PRECIS for the alphabetical index.

There is no doubt that the CRG has been the most potent influence in the development of classification theory over the past decade. Starting with the theories of analytico-synthetic classification developed by Ranganathan, the group has moved forward in a rather different direction from Ranganathan himself; for a variety of reasons, it seems probable that future developments are likely to be along the lines indicated by the CRG rather than those used in CC. The present work is largely concerned with the exposition of CRG ideas, while if imitation is the sincerest form of flattery, the formation of a similar group in the USA, the Classification Research Study Group, must have given the members of the CRG some pleasure. The work of the group is best studied through the series of bulletins published in the

Journal of documentation, while students should also try to examine as many of the special classifications compiled by members of the CRG as possible. The CRG is also interested in postcoordinate indexing, as is clearly shown by the publication of *Thesaurofacet.* The technique of facet analysis is of quite general application in the construction of index languages, and the work done by the CRG on the development of both special and general classification schemes has helped greatly in clarifying problems which beset indexing languages generally.

Whether we shall ever see a new classification scheme of the kind envisaged by the CRG in 1963 remains in doubt. The latest generation of computers is able to handle strings of terms with the facility that earlier computers could only use on numbers. This has meant that one reason for the development of a new classification—the need for a scheme that lent itself to computer manipulation—has disappeared. In PRECIS we have an indexing system which can be linked to any desired method of arrangement, while the increasing international acceptance of MARC implies that bibliographies such as BNB and ANB will continue to use DC because it is so widely used throughout the world. There are also certain theoretical difficulties in adopting the kind of approach found in the CRG scheme. The vast majority of documents do fit, even if a little uncomfortably, into a conventional framework; disciplines, ill-defined though they may be, do exist; there *is* an educational and scientific consensus. We cannot ignore these facts, and our classification schemes must take them into account. Nevertheless, the significance of the CRG work should not be underrated; it has brought us a great deal closer to an understanding of how concepts are interrelated, and continues to point the way forward.

UNISIST AND THE BSO

The Royal Society's Scientific Information conference in 1948 demonstrated the concern of the scientific community that existing methods of publishing and disseminating information were proving inadequate to cope with the ever increasing flood of scientific and technical publication—the information explosion. Several possible lines of action were pursued. The Royal Society published two bibliographies, one a guide to scientific journals reporting original work, the other a list of journals containing abstracts; both of these were indeed useful when they were published, but the society appears to have assumed that they would remain valid indefinitely, an assumption that is unfortunately illfounded. Professor J D Bernal suggested the replacement of the scientific journal by the publication of abstracts only instead of complete papers, which would be available as separates on demand, a suggestion which has recently been revived by Garfield.[8] It will be interesting to see whether the latter is as successful as the former. All in all, there was general agreement that serious problems existed, but few practical solutions could be found.

The 1958 Scientific Information Conference in Washington[9] was dominated by the computer, with its glittering prospects of good things to come. Unfortunately, many of the predictions have proved to be overoptimistic, and though the computer *is* now playing a significant role in information retrieval, in general, developments have tended to be along rather conventional lines, linked to the improvement of existing services and their exploitation, rather than any startling new directions. Even *Science citation index*, possibly the only completely novel publication to have appeared in this field since 1958, is based on a principle which had been recognized many years earlier.

During the 1960's, a new force began to make itself felt. Those countries which were already to the fore in science and technology certainly faced problems in the handling of information, but were on the whole managing to keep these problems under control; the situation for the Third World countries was very different. They felt that they were increasingly at a disadvantage in not having the same access to the free flow of scientific information as the industrialized world. In 1967, a joint central committee was set up by Unesco and ICSU to carry out a feasibility study of a world science information system, to be given the name UNISIST. The committee produced a detailed report[10] after some four years of deliberation, and this was largely approved at an international conference in October 1971, at which 111 countries and 62 international organizations were represented. One of the recommendations of the report was that:

> The attention of scientists, learned societies, and information science associations should be drawn to the need for joint efforts in developing better tools for the control and conversion of natural and indexing languages in science and technology.

In particular, a need was seen for a universally acceptable 'switching language' which could be applied to all publications to indicate the subject field they covered.

The concept of a switching language needs some examination here. The generally accepted meaning had been an indexing language into which one could translate any existing index language as an intermediate stage in converting it into any other indexing language; for example, one might use UDC in this way, at least in those areas where the schedules are up to date. A German librarian faced with the indexing term 'optical character recognition devices' (from the EJC Thesaurus) could look this up in the English edition of UDC and find the notation 681.327.5'12: he could turn to the German edition and find the equivalent of this piece of notation. Coates[11] has pointed out that in order to make this possible, the switching language must be at least as detailed as the most detailed language it is expected to switch, otherwise the specificity of the original subject will be degraded. However, this was not the kind of switching language that UNISIST had in mind; what was envisaged was a much broader classification, to be applied to whole blocks of information, *eg* an abstracting journal, rather than to individual documents. It could also be used to indicate the subject coverage of an institution; for example, the International Atomic Energy Agency would be given the appropriate notation for nuclear science and technology. Such coding would be of considerable help to librarians faced with publications in an unfamiliar language (and we have to accept that a large proportion of the earth's population has not yet recognized the enormous advantages that would accrue if only everybody spoke English), and would facilitate the flow of information.

Aslib was commissioned as part of the study to examine existing classification schemes to see whether any of them would fill the bill satisfactorily, and came to the conclusion that UDC was probably the best of those available, but that none of them was particularly good. UDC might have shown up better if the schedules had been available in full, but as is shown in chapter 18, this is not the case even now, and at the time of the comparison a substantial part of the English edition was either not available at all or was so out of date as to be in effect unavailable. UNISIST therefore came to the decision that a completely new scheme should be developed, to be known as the Standard Reference Code. An alternative name was also suggested, the Standard Roof Classification: this also abbreviates to SRC, and was intended to emphasize the purpose of the scheme in providing a 'roof' which would serve to cover the whole of scientific and technical information at the broad level required.

A sub-committee of FID was set up to develop the proposed new scheme, including G A Lloyd, Head of the Classification Secretariat of FID and thus the man directly responsible for the day to day running of UDC. In recent years, the work appears to have been delegated to a smaller committee including Lloyd, now retired from FID, and E J Coates, together with a third member from Czechoslovakia. An initial draft of the scheme, now retitled the Broad System of Ordering (BSO), has been circulated, and work is currently in progress on a larger revised draft, likely to contain up to 4,000 terms (cf approximately 12,000 in the abridged edition of UDC). The broad outline is as follows:[12]

General, Formal and Structural sciences
Physical sciences
Space and Earth sciences
Life sciences: biology, agriculture, medicine
Behavioural sciences

Social sciences, including economics
Technology
Humanities and arts

The complete scheme is expected to be published in 1978, but anyone who cares to turn to the outline of BC on p 336 must surely be struck by the remarkable resemblance between the two outlines. As we have already pointed out, Bliss paid great attention to the overall order of classes in drawing up his scheme, and it is very interesting to see how the BSO is following so very closely the same lines. The detail will no doubt differ, but this is to be expected in a scheme with a bias towards science and technology, as this particular bias was clearly not shared by Bliss.

One is forced to question the decision by UNISIST that no existing scheme could have served their purpose. In the discussions of the various schemes in Part III it will become clear that they are all far from perfect, and that one major criticism is that they do not reflect the modern structure of knowledge, as this has changed radically since the existing schemes were formulated. If we accept this criticism—and there is little doubt that it is valid—what guarantee do we have that the BSO will itself not become obsolescent? And if the proposed new scheme bears such a strong resemblance to one of the existing schemes, can the overall structure of knowledge have changed as substantially as has been argued? In chapter 12 we pointed out that a successful classification scheme must be backed by a strong, adequately funded organization. So far, the development of the BSO seems to have followed the same kind of 'amateur' lines as UDC, which does not augur well for its future. It could well be argued that better long-term results would have been obtained had the funds for the development of the BSO, limited though these have been, found their way into the depleted coffers of the UDC, so that that scheme could have had a better chance of being brought up to date. Is a new scheme likely to succeed where all the rest have apparently failed? Only time can provide the answer to that question; meanwhile, we can only await with interest its publication and implementation.

AUTOMATIC CLASSIFICATION

We have now considered two quite different intellectual approaches to the problems of devising a new classification, one attempting to establish fundamental theoretical principles in order to construct an analytico-synthetic classification of the whole of knowledge suitable for computer retrieval of the most specific detail, the other attempting to identify the subjects likely to be treated in the literature or in institutions as units, and to arrange them in a helpful order, with no thought of computer use (though of course this is not excluded). The question that we must now consider is whether there is any way in which we might make use of the computer in the production of classification schemes? In order to answer this question, we have to go back to first principles, and look again at the *purpose* of classification.

As we saw in chapter 5, classification is one way of showing semantic relationships, *ie* by arranging related subjects together (juxtaposition). We may do this for two reasons: we may wish to help the reader browsing at the shelves, or we may wish to help the reader looking for information on a particular topic. In the first case, we are concerned with providing an arrangement which will be helpful, but in the second case we are trying to do something rather more positive. We are trying to suggest possible *substitutes* if the reader's first approach was unsuccessful. For example, if we are looking for information on coated paper (DC 676.283) and find nothing, we may possibly find some information in a document classified at 676.235—papercoating, or at the more general heading 676.2—paper and paper products. Classification brings together these and other related terms to form a group so that if we are unsuccessful in a search using one of the terms we can reasonably easily substitute another. In other words, classification gives us groups of terms based on the assumption that documents indexed by one of the terms in the group will be more or less acceptable substitutes for documents indexed by any of the other terms in the group. Obviously the degree of acceptabilility will depend on the kind of relationship between the terms in the group and how closely they are related. At one extreme, we usually use only one of two synonyms because a document indexed by one would *always* be an acceptable substitute for a document indexed by the other, and it involves less work to use one. At the other extreme, a reader looking for the neutron cross-section of uranium-235 would probably find a work on nuclear physics generally a rather poor substitute (though it might contain the information he wanted), and a reader wanting information on electrical engineering would be unlikely to consider a work on mechanical engineering as any kind of acceptable substitute at all, though in both cases the subjects suggested as substitutes are certainly related, and do fall into the same groups. (in DC, neutron cross-sections 539.75, nuclear physics 539.7; electrical engineering 621.3, mechanical engineering 621).

In the context of information retrieval, then, the purpose of classification is to provide us with groups of terms, each of which may be substituted for one of the others if we need to alter our search strategy. (It is perhaps worth reiterating that if we choose the right search strategy to start with, we do not need classification, cross-references, coordination or any of the other devices that enable us to improve recall or relevance). Is there any way in which a computer might be used to form groups of terms which would function in this way? The work

215

done by Sparck Jones at the Cambridge Language Research Unit suggests that there may well be, and it is this work that we shall be considering.

KEYWORDS AND CLUMPS

The first approach was based on the CLRU collection of off-prints of articles on automatic language processing, including a reasonably wide range of topics within that heading.[13] The documents were indexed by selecting keywords intellectually from the text (including the title), and an attempt was then made to fit these terms into a series of lattice structures corresponding to conventional hierarchical groupings except that a term could belong to more than one hierarchy. A peek-a-boo system (chapter 24) was used, the card for each term being punched for any documents indexed by that term or any terms below it in the lattice. Higher terms were noted on the card also. In searching, the appropriate terms were selected and coordinated; any document indexed by all of the terms was shown immediately, and of course this would include any indexed by lower terms. If the first search was not successful, terms would be replaced by higher terms; this would include any coordinate terms as well, thus widening the search formulation. In the lattice shown here, A is a higher term to B and C; C is a higher term to G, and a lower term to F, which has additionally D and E as lower terms. (For example, A might be 'mammals', B 'man', C 'dogs', G 'poodles', F 'domestic animals', D 'cats', E 'horses',) Let us assume that C is one of our original search terms; we shall find any documents indexed by C, but also any indexed by G. If that search is unsuccessful, we can substitute A and/or F for C; by substituting A we shall find any documents indexed by A and also any indexed by B; by substituting F we shall find documents indexed by F, D or E; by substituting both we shall retrieve documents indexed by any of the terms.

The main problem turned out to be the construction of the lattices, which grew more and more time-consuming as more documents were indexed. It was therefore decided to try to form groups by using a computer, instead of by intellectual effort. The computer can of course only recognize co-occurrence—it cannot recognize semantic content; any computer system therefore had to be one based on the number of times keywords were used together in the indexing of particular documents. This statistical approach was used to generate 'clumps', the criterion for a clump being that the terms in it should be more strongly associated with each other than with the terms outside the clump. The clumps are based entirely on the terms chosen to index the documents, though those which had only been used once were omitted; thus although some of the results look rather like conventional classificatory groupings, they do not include any terms which are not found in the collection of documents.

For example:

> grammar, paradigm, parts of speech, adjective, preposition, phrase, phrase marker, tense, ending, stem, syntax, diacritic

looks very much like the sort of group one would construct intellectually except that it does not include terms such as 'noun', 'verb', 'clause' *etc* because they do not occur in the indexing of this particular set of documents. Some of the clumps however differ substantially from conventional groupings, for example:

> style, text, paragraph, chunking, interlingua, post-editor, source language, thesaurus head, Roget, Pask machine, Latin, technical language

again reflecting the indexing of this particular collection.

The results obtained using this technique were somewhat disappointing, and led to a reappraisal of the approach. The difficulty of finding a suitable way to identify a clump, and the need to find methods of grouping that were practical in terms of computing effort needed, led to a continuation of the work on a new basis.

STRINGS, STARS AND CLIQUES[14]

A new set of documents was obtained from those which had been used in the Cranfield II experiment (chapter 28). This consisted of 200 documents in the field of aerodynamics, which had been indexed as part of the project. A total of 1500 keywords had been used; on average, each document had been indexed by 35 keywords, and the average number of documents indexed by each keyword was five. ($1500 \times 5 \backsimeq 200 \times 35$). The documents had been exhaustively indexed, and each document might contain more than one theme, with the consequence that the same keyword might be used to index more than one theme in the same document. About 400 of the keywords had only been used once; these were eliminated on the grounds that including them in a group could only improve recall by that one document if the group were substituted for one of its members. At the other extreme, some of the keywords had been used very frequently, with 'flow' at the top of the list, having been used in the indexing of 144 of the 200 documents. A further reduction in the total number of keywords resulted from the merging of word forms, giving a final vocabulary of 712 terms, with an average of 32 terms per document. Associated with this section of the Cranfield II collection were 42 requests for which relevance judgements had already been made; *ie* a search for documents to answer one of the requests, which averaged seven terms each, should yield a predetermined subset of the 200 documents.

Four kinds of group were selected as being suitable for the experiment: strings, stars, cliques and clumps. A string is a set of terms, each of which is found to be most strongly associated with the next; in the event, most strings terminate fairly quickly by looping. Term A is most strongly associated with term B; term B with term C; term C with term D; term D with term E; term E with term A, thus closing the circle and terminating the string. The maximum length of string was set at 7 terms. Stars were based on one term and those other terms most strongly associated with it; three sizes of star were used, containing four, six or eight terms. Cliques consist of sets of terms each of which is connected to each of the others by a minimum number of co-occurrences; this threshold was set at three different levels, 13, 16 or 21 links. Clumps were defined as groups in which each term was strongly associated with one or more of the others, three different definitions of strength of association being used, with minor variations within each.

A problem was seen with terms which had been used frequently. To take a specific example, the word 'flow' was used to index 144 of the 200 documents, as mentioned earlier; to include this word in a group would mean that every time the group of terms was substituted for one of its members, the number of documents retrieved would automatically increase to at least the 144 documents indexed by the term 'flow'. It was thought that there might well be some special significance in terms which were used infrequently, in that these ought to be able to give a high level of precision. Tests were therefore carried out on four vocabularies: the full vocabulary, in which all terms were treated alike: a restricted vocabulary, in which frequent terms were treated as unit classes, *ie* groups in themselves; frequent terms only; and infrequent terms only.

Three measures were used to determine the strength of association of terms, where C_{ab} is the number of co-occurrences of terms and b, and O_a and O_b are the total number of occurences of each respectively. The first is the cosine correlation function used by Salton in the SMART project:

STRINGS

STARS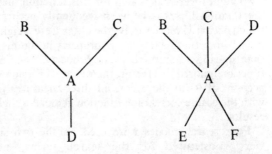

CLIQUES

CLUMPS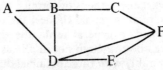

FIGURE 13: Strings, stars, cliques and clumps.

$$\text{strength of association} = \frac{\text{Cab}}{\sqrt{(\text{Oa}^2 \times \text{Ob}^2)}}$$

The second and third were based on the Tanimoto function:

$$\text{strength of association} = \frac{\text{Cab}}{(\text{Oa} + \text{Ob}) - \text{Cab}} \quad \left\{ ie \; \frac{\text{Oa} \cap \text{Ob}}{\text{Oa} \cup \text{Ob}} \right\}$$

Two values were calculated for this function, depending on whether the relationship was between frequently occurring terms or terms which occurred more rarely; the latter were weighted more heavily on the grounds that having a rare property in common is more significant than sharing a commonly found property. The unweighted Tanimoto function ignored this factor, the weighted version was modified to take account of it. In the event, all three measures performed similarly, with the cosine correlation function achieving slightly less satisfactory results.

Four search modes were used. In the two simple modes classes were substituted for the search terms, either by matching straight-forwardly on the classes or by taking into account the class frequency, given that a particular term may fall into several classes. In the mixed mode, again two approaches were taken: in the first, classes were substituted for any non-matching terms, while in the second, after finding the matching terms, matching was attempted on *any* classes not generated by those terms. In each case the performance was judged against that of matching the search terms as originally stated.

The results obtained were quite promising. Of the four vocabularies, the restricted one gave consistently better results. In this, the 96 terms in the vocabulary judged to be 'frequent' were treated as unit classes and the remaining 616 were grouped. The infrequent term vocabulary also performed quite well, both using the terms alone and in groups. However, in this connection it is worth remembering that we are thinking in terms of absolute frequency of occurrence here; as mentioned in chapter 4, a more significant measure is the frequency in relation to the expected frequency, but it would probably have been difficult to establish this in the circumstances.

Of the various methods of forming classes, those given by strings, small stars, high threshold cliques, and one form of clump were most successful, and in general terms the simple class matching search mode proved best, though not in all cases. Overall, the results compared favourably with those obtained during the Cranfield work and seem to indicate that computer-generated classification schemes can give better results than the use of simple terms alone. The results certainly suggest that this line of research is worth pursuing, though it must always be remembered that the test conditions were somewhat restricted and artificial.

One further point arose from this research, and it is one of fundamental importance. In chapter 5, we pointed out that the function of semantic relationships is to enable us to improve recall; Sparck Jones points out in her penetrating analysis of the whole project[15] that we may also be able to use classification as a precision device, in that it may enable us to achieve a match between document descriptions and search formulations at a higher level of coordination. An example will make this clearer. Let us assume that we are interested in the *cataloguing* of *periodicals* in *university libraries*: we will begin our search by looking for the combination of all four search terms (in italics above), but what do we do if we are unsuccessful? We may drop one of the terms; *university* might be the best one to drop first, on the grounds that we are really interested in the *cataloguing* of *periodicals*, and we may then obtain a match on the remaining three terms. In other words, we shall improve recall by lowering the level of coordination from four to three, but we shall almost certainly do this at the cost of a fairly low performance in terms of relevance. Now if instead of dropping *university* from our search formulation we substitute another term (or other terms) from a class containing university, *eg* 'academic' or 'college' we may well find that our search is successful, and that we have in fact maintained our level of coordination at four, instead of having to drop to three as we would have done without the benefit of our classification. This point is likely to become increasingly significant in the future, with the growth of large data bases indexed by systems which permit various levels of coordination but also have a network of semantic relationships built in. We shall be looking at this point again in our discussions of PRECIS and MEDLARS.

The work we have discussed is only one of several investigations into the use of computers to generate classifications.[16] Much of this work looks very promising, but it is perhaps worth sounding a note of caution in conclusion. Two points are worth noting. Nearly all of the work done has been carried out on small collections in the physical sciences, and there is no guarantee that their success would be repeated with a large collection in, say, political 'science'. The second is that in a classification tied completely to the collection of documents, each document added means the reprocessing of the total collection to establish the revised classification. In practice, it might prove necessary to think carefully about this on economic grounds, and perhaps carry out this process at intervals rather than continuously.

BIBLIOGRAPHY
1 For the history of the CRG, see
Foskett, D J: 'The Classification Research Group, 1952–1962'. *Libri*, *12*(2)1962, 127–138.

Crossley, C A: 'New schemes of classification: principles and practice'. *Library Association record*, 65 (2) 1963, 51–59.

The work of the CRG is reported in its bulletins. The first three of these were published as separates and are now out of print; since no. 4, the bulletins have appeared in the *Journal of documentation*, in the following issues:

12 (4) 1956, 227–230 (Bibliography of publications by members)
14 (3) 1958, 136–143 (Bulletin 4: BCM classification)
15 (1) 1959, 39–57 (Bulletin 5: Cranfield)
17 (3) 1961, 156–168 (Bulletin 6: new general classification)
17 (3) 1961, 169–172 (Bibliography of publications)
18 (2) 1962, 65–88 (Bulletin 7: special classifications)
20 (3) 1964, 146–165 (Bulletin 8: integrative levels)
20 (3) 1964, 166–169 (Bibliography of publications)
24 (4) 1968, 273–291 (Bulletin 9: new general classification)

The main topic in each bulletin is indicated, but many other matters are also discussed.

2 'The need for a faceted classification as the basis of all methods of information retrieval'. *Library Association record*, 57 (7) 1955, 262–268.

3 Library Association: *Some problems of a general classification scheme: report of a conference held in London, June, 1963*. Library Association, 1964.

Coates, E J: 'CRG proposals for a new general classification' (*in* Library Association: *Some problems of a general classification scheme*. 1964. 38–45).

4 Kyle, B: 'Towards a classification for social science literature.' *American documentation*, 9 (4) 1958, 168–183. This is also discussed by D J Foskett in *Classification and indexing in the social sciences*.

5 Foskett, D J: 'Classification and integrative levels.' (Chapter in the Sayers memorial volume, 1960.)

6 Austin, D: 'The development of PRECIS: a theoretical and technical history.' *Journal of documentation*, 30 (1) 1974, 47–102.

7 Foskett, D J: *Classification for a general index language*. This is the most general commentary on the CRG work available, and is intended for the student.

Austin, D W: 'Prospects for a new general classification'. *Journal of librarianship*, 1 (3) 1969, 149–169.

Classification Research Group: *Classification and information control*. LA, 1970 (LA Research pamphlet no 1). This sets out the reports produced during the development period of the new classification. It is very interesting to see how the ideas of the group clarified as the discussions proceeded. Unfortunately, it does not include one lengthy report by Austin in which he discusses the significance of general systems theory.

8 Garfield, E: 'Is there a future for the scientific journal?' *Sci-Tech news*, 29 (2) 1975, 42–44.

9 International conference on scientific information, Washington DC, 1958: *Proceedings*. Washington, National Academy of Sciences, 1959. 2v.

10 *UNISIST: Study report on the feasibility of a world science information system*. Paris, Unesco, 1971.

11 Coates, E J: 'Switching languages for indexing.' *Journal of documentation*, 26 (22) 1970, 102–110.

12 *FID/CR Newsletter 3* (2) 1975 contains a brief account of progress on the BSO.

13 Needham, R M and Sparck Jones, K: 'Keywords and clumps: recent work on information retrieval at the Cambridge Language Research Unit.' *Journal of documentation*, 20 (1) 1964, 5–15.

Sparck Jones, K and Needham, R M: 'Automatic term classifications and retrieval.' *Information storage and retrieval*, 4 (2) 1968, 91–100.

14 Sparck Jones, K and Jackson, D M: 'The use of automatically-obtained keyword classifications for information retrieval.' *Information storage and retrieval*, 5 1970, 175–201.

Sparck Jones, K: 'Automatic thesaurus construction and the relation of a thesaurus to indexing terms.' *Aslib proceedings 22* (5) 1970, 226–228.

15 Sparck Jones, K: *Automatic keyword classification for information retrieval*. Butterworths, 1971.

16 Moberg, Z: 'Automatic classification: directions of recent research.' *Drexel library quarterly*, 10 (4) 1974, 90–104. The whole of this issue is devoted to 'Classification: theory and practice'.

17 Carroll, Lewis: *Through the looking glass*. 1872.

CHAPTER 14

PRECIS

PRECIS (PREserved Context Indexing System) is an alphabetical system which falls to quite a large extent into the same kind of tradition as Coates. It would therefore have been possible to describe it in chapter 7, but it owes so much to the theory developed during the CRG work on a new general classification that it seems more helpful to deal with it after that work has been described.

BACKGROUND

PRECIS represents the merging of two separate but related streams of development. The first of these is the CRG work described in the previous chapter; it will be remembered that Derek Austin, who has been almost entirely responsible for the development of PRECIS, was seconded to that project in 1968–1969, though the original purpose of this was actually to develop a new classification scheme for the arrangement of BNB in place of DC. BNB was looking towards mechanization at the time, and wanted a scheme that would be better suited to this purpose than DC, as well as one that would give a more satisfactory arrangement than the unique version of DC then in use (chapter 17). This study led, as we have seen, to the recognition of the two fundamental categories of entities and attributes, and the development of a set of relational operators to express relationships between concepts. It had also given a theoretical basis for citation order in general systems theory, in addition to already existing theories (chapter 8); one of these, the idea of context dependence, was seen to be particularly important by Austin.

On his return to BNB, Austin became involved in the second stream of development: the involvement of BNB in the MARC project (chapter 15). This was a development of crucial importance. The MARC project is essentially an international one, which implies that all those taking part should use the same standards. In author/title and descriptive cataloguing, a large measure of agreement had been reached in the Anglo-American Cataloguing Rules published in 1967 (though even here there were a few minor differences between the British and North American versions, due to the reluctance of the Library of Congress to change a limited number of its long-established practices). If the same measure of agreement was to be reached on subject cataloguing, it was evident that BNB would have to abandon its own version of DC and adopt the standard version. As the 18th edition was due to be published in 1971, which coincided with the start of the BNB cumulation which was intended to be the first completely linked to MARC, it was decided that BNB would adopt DC18 at that time. However, this raised a problem, in that BNB's chain index was geared to their own version, and to attempt to use this procedure with DC18 would lead to serious problems. As has been said several times, computers cannot tolerate anomalies, and DC still contains too many departures from standard procedures for it to be possible to produce a chain index from feature headings geared to the schedules. While the compilation procedures had been manual ones, it had been possible to get round the anomalies, but this is not economically possible in a computer-based system. An additional complication was that the MARC format made provision for more than one subject description: not just DC, but LC, LCSH and perhaps UDC designations would be included. There was also a measure of dissatisfaction with chain procedure among users, arising from the defects discussed in chapter 6: only the first entry is specific, and there is a possibility that some of the less specific entries may be 'blind', *ie* they may lead to class numbers forming part of the hierarchy of the specific subject but having themselves no entries. Four requirements were therefore seen as necessary for an alphabetical access system to replace chain indexing:

1: The heading must be coextensive with the subject at all access points.

2: It must not be geared to any particular classification scheme.

3: Each entry should be meaningful to the user, preferably without the need for explanation.

4: The original indexing was to be intellectual, but *all* subsequent operations, including the generation of all entries and their filing, were to be done by computer.

While these discussions were going on, Austin had been experimenting with the CRG classification in working with sociological literature. This work led to certain crucial changes in approach. The idea of a citation order based on importance for grouping, or significance of first term, was abandoned in favour of reliance on the principle of context dependence. This decision was closely linked to the idea of multiple entry, with each important concept becoming the access point in turn, which in itself eliminates the need for any decision on significance. Certain key categories were identified as showing the subject structure, with other categories identified as subsidiary to the main categories, and possibly being repeated within each main category. Relational operators were dropped in favour of role operators; the major consequence of this decision was that the concept in the primary category was given a role operator, thus placing it on a par with all the other concepts, instead of standing at the beginning of the string without any kind of context definition. Finally, natural language forms were adopted as the basis of string organization, especially the passive declarative statement. For example, the active voice statement

Teachers	educate	children
(subject)	(action)	(object)

became the passive voice statement

Children	are educated	by teachers
(Subject)	(action)	(agent)

The notation of the CRG scheme was still in a rudimentary state, and the experimental work showed that it was in fact much easier to work with strings of terms. In addition, Farradane's work with two-dimensional structures had shown the possibilities of a two-line approach, and led to the development of the shunting technique described in chapter 6. The work on the classification had thus led, perhaps unexpectedly, to the development of exactly the kind of alphabetical system required by BNB for the MARC project to go ahead.[1]

The first version of PRECIS, including the modifications arising from research up to that point, was introduced into BNB in 1971, and proved successful. However, one or two minor points had still to be sorted out; for example, in some instances it became clear that the straightforward shunting technique gave results which were inconsistent in the generation of secondary statements from similar primary strings, depending on the particular sequence of operators. What happened was that primary statements which appeared to be similar gave rise to secondary strings which did not file together in every case, as in theory they should have done. In order to achieve a satisfactory transformation, to give secondary statements which did file together, it was necessary to take account of the operators used in building the original string. Until that time, the operators had been used to construct the string, but had then been discarded; the solution was to include them as part of the computer manipulation code, and program the computer to make the necessary changes in the shunting procedure when it found the appropriate operator in the code. Another point was that the operators had been used retroactively, as they would have been in the classification scheme, in order to comply with the principle of inversion; thus in any string, the most important concept—the one which set the context for the rest of the string—had the highest operator. For example, the subject 'remuneration of teachers in French universities' would be written down in a PRECIS string as:

(6) France (4) universities (p) teachers (3) remuneration

where (6), (4), and (3) represent major categories and (p) one of the minor categories. Since the question of arrangement no longer arose, there was no need to use the role operators retroactively, and they were reorganized to give the normal sequence ((0), (1), (2) . . . rather than (2), (1), (0)). The revised version was adopted in the BNB cumulation beginning in 1974, and a detailed *Manual* was published explaining the system and its practical implementation, and including both a full explanation of the theoretical background and various sets of test questions, to enable the reader to check whether he has comprehended the instructions (the answers are provided too!)[2] The account given here must obviously be very much curtailed, and students are warned that the *Manual* is essential reading for anyone who wishes to understand the system in all its intricacy. Fortunately, most of the difficulties only occur rarely, and it is hoped that enough detail is given here for most needs.

The procedure used in PRECIS indexing is relatively straightforward, and once the meanings of the various role operators have been grasped, strings can be written quite quickly; at least as quickly as searching through LCSH for the appropriate heading. The first step is to study the document and identify the overall subject to be indexed; the concepts involved are then put into the form of a title-like statement in natural language (by *concept* Austin means a topic which matches a PRECIS operator; as we shall see, this sometimes means a topic that we would consider to be a composite subject in the terminology used in this book). The subject is then written down as a string of terms, usually one to a line for clarity, each preceded by the appropriate operator, and with any necessary additional operators included within the term if it involves more than one word. Those terms to appear in the lead position, *ie* are required as access terms, are indicated, usually by placing a tick (check) over them, and any other conventional signals are added; for example, (LO) means that the term to which it is added is only to be printed when it appears through the shunting process in the lead position (Lead Only); (NU) means that the term is not printed when a term later in the string moves into the lead position, while (ND) means that a term is not printed when a term earlier in the string is in the lead position. Any necessary semantic structure is added, in the form of *see also* references to any of the terms in the string. The computer manipulation codes are then added, and the computer then does the rest. (The manipulation codes are not relevant to the study of the system, and would not be used in a manual system; they are therefore not considered in this discussion.)

The input is thus a string of terms with appropriate codings; the output is a set of entries, each one having a selected term as lead, the rest of the terms being moved into the qualifier or display positions. The lead term is printed in bold, the qualifier in roman (with rare exceptions); the terms in the display are printed in roman or italic depending on the role operator. One important point is that the terms in the output are always in natural language order; no inverted headings are used.

The BNB has of course built up a thesaurus of preferred terms over the years, and the indexer will check this to see whether any of the terms in the string have been used before; if they have, they are identified in the computer-based thesaurus by a number, the RIN (Reference Indicator Number), which shows their location in the computer storage, and will generate all the necessary semantic cross-references. It may be that the indexer will find that the complete string has been used before; each string is allotted a SIN (Subject Indicator Number), which in fact identifies a package, including not only the PRECIS string but also any other subject designations, eg DC, LCSH, LC. Experience at BNB has shown that after three years, about half of the throughput fell into this category, which means that it needed no further subject indexing than the inclusion of the SIN in the appropriate place on the cataloguing worksheet. The saving in time that this implies need hardly be stressed.

Before we proceed to look at the operators in detail, a couple of examples may help to make the layout clearer. The string

   (0) Dublin
   (2) architecture
   (6) illustrations

will give rise to the following two entries:

Dublin	**Lead**
Architecture—*Illustrations*	Display
Architecture. Dublin.	**Lead.** Qualifier
—*Illustrations*	Display

The string

   (1) carbon acids
   (2) ionisation

gives rise to two entries and a cross-reference:

Carbon acids	**Lead**
Ionisation	Display
Ionisation. Carbon acids	**Lead.** Qualifier
Acids *see also* Carbon acids	Cross-reference

In each case the layout, punctuation and typography of the entry are automatically provided by the computer program acting on the instructions conveyed by the operators, which are converted into the manipulation codings.

The operators are set out in table 11. One is omitted, j, signifying 'salient difference'. According to the *Manual*, this was intended to serve a particular purpose but has never actually been used in practice, and there seems to be little point in including it. The remainder fall into several distinct groups; Austin divides them into four, but some of these may be subdivided, and a slightly different approach is taken here to that in the *Manual*.

MAINLINE OPERATORS

The first group consists of the *mainline* operators (0), (1), (2) and (3). A string *must* begin with one of the three operators (0), (1) or (2), and all strings *must* contain either (1) or (2). (0) introduces location, and will be dealt with in conjunction with other means of introducing Place. (1) introduces the *key system*; this will be an entity (which may include abstract or heterogeneous concepts), and the normal rules for plural and singular form are followed—these are in effect identical with the EJC rules set out in chapter 5. (2) introduces *actions* and *phenomena*; the passive form of nouns signifying actions is preferred, *eg* classification rather than classifying (but cataloguing?). It may be possible to have more than one concept introduced by operators (1) and (2), as in the following examples:

Key system only
   (1) waves
   Entry
   Waves
Action or phenomenon only
   (2) diffusion
   Entry
   Diffusion
   (2) laughter
   Entry
   Laughter
Key system and action
   (1) primitive peoples
   (2) warfare
   Entries
   Primitive peoples
      Warfare
   Warfare.   Primitive peoples
Two key systems linked by reciprocal action
   (1) France
   (2) foreign trade $v with $w with
   (1) Great Britain
   Entries
   France
      Foreign trade with Great Britain
   Great Britain
      Foreign trade with France
Two actions
      (1) organic compounds

Main line operators

Environment	o	Location
Observed system	{ 1	Key system: *object of transitive action; agent of intransitive action*
(*core operators*)	2	Action/effect
	3	Agent of transitive action: aspects; factors

Data relating to observer	{ 4	Viewpoint-as-form
Selected instance	5	Sample population/Study region
Presentation of data	6	Target/Form

Interposed operators

Dependent elements	{ p	Part/Property
	q	Quasi-generic relationship
	r	Aggregate

Concept interlinks	{ s	Role definer
	t	Author-attributed association
Coordinate concepts	g	Coordinate concept

Differencing operators	{ h	Non-lead direct difference }
(*prefixed by* $)	i	Lead direct difference }
	k	Non-lead indirect difference }
	m	Lead indirect difference }
	n	Non-lead parenthetical difference }
	o	Lead parenthetical difference }
	d	Date

Connectives (*components of linking phrases; prefixed by* $)	{ v	Downward reading component
	w	Upward reading component

Theme interlinks	{ x	First elements in coordinate theme
	y	Subsequent elements
	z	Element of common theme

TABLE II: *PRECIS operators*

230

(2) synthesis $w of
(2) catalysis
Entries
Organic compounds
   Synthesis. Catalysis
Synthesis.   Organic compounds
   Catalysis
Catalysis.   Synthesis of organic compounds

The operator (3) denotes an *agent*, which may be an entity or an action causing the action introduced by (2) affecting the entity introduced by (1). This operator introduces a modification of the standard procedure in certain cases, known as the *predicate transformation*. An agent introduced by (3) may be an entity, which would normally be introduced by (1), or an action, which would normally be introduced by (2). In each case it would normally be the first or second lead term, and would have other parts of the entry in the display. However, if the normal shunting procedure took place, once the agent moved into the lead position any terms introduced by (1) or (2) would move into the qualifier position. We might thus have the anomaly of a term, followed by another term in the display in one case and in the qualifier in another. To resolve this situation, whenever a term introduced by (3) is preceded by an action introduced by (2), then the terms linked to the (2) which would normally have appeared in the qualifier are transferred to the display. As we mentioned earlier, PRECIS normally uses the passive voice, but if we think of an agent as the subject of a sentence in the active voice, it will be seen that the action (2) and the key system (1) together form the predicate; hence the name predicate transformation. An expansion of one of the examples already given will illustrate this point:
   (1) organic compounds
   (2) synthesis $w of
   (2) catalysis $w of
   (3) noble metals
Entries
Organic compounds
   Synthesis. Catalysis. Noble metals
Synthesis.   Organic compounds
   Catalysis. Noble metals
Catalysis.   Synthesis of organic compounds
   Noble metals
Noble metals
   Catalysis of synthesis of organic compounds
   Metals *see also* Noble metals
Normally the fourth entry would have been

Noble metals. Catalysis of synthesis of organic compounds but the predicate transformation came into play to give the entry shown.

If (3) is used to introduce *aspects* rather than an agent, it may be preferable to avoid the predicate transformation, and this can be done by inserting an 'empty' (2) into the string; the computer then 'transforms' this (2) and anything linked to it (*ie* nothing) into the display, leaving the rest of the entry as normal, *eg*

(2) aggression
(2)
(3) social aspects
Entries
Aggression
    Social aspects
Social aspects. Aggression

Since (3) may denote both agents and aspects, it is possible to have more than one (3) in the string, as in the following example:

(1) industries
(2) management
(2) control $v by $w of
(3) personnel
(3) economic aspects
Entries
Industries
    Management. Control by personnel. Economic aspects
Management. Industries
    Control by personnel. Economic aspects
Personnel. Industries   (predicate
    Control of management. Economic aspects   transformation)

The first group of operators are thus the key to the whole system; all strings must contain at least one of them, and they may be repeated if necessary. The terms introduced by them are always printed in roman, no matter in which of the three positions they appear, the only difference being that, in common with all others, they are printed in bold in the lead position.

The second group consists of the remaining three mainline operators (4), (5) and (6), which differ in two important respects from the previous group. The first is that once the string has incorporated one of this group, it is not possible to go back to one of the first group; the second is that they are printed in italic in the display, preceded by a dash, and similarly in italic in the qualifier if the occasion arises. In general, it may be said that although they are mainline operators, they represent less significant concepts than the first group.

(4) relates to the viewpoint of the author, and involves a similar transformation procedure to (3); this also applies to (5) and (6).

Two examples will demonstrate this, the first a very simple one, the second a development of the last example:

(2) religion
(4) sociological perspectives
Entries
Religion
   —*Sociological perspectives*
Sociological perspectives
   Religion

(1) industries
(2) management
(2) control $v by $w of
(3) personnel
(3) economic aspects
(4) socialist viewpoints
Entries
Industries
   Management. Control by personnel. Economic aspects—*Socialist viewpoints*
Management.   Industries
   Control by personnel. Economic aspects—*Socialist viewpoints*
Personnel.   Industries.
   Control of management. Economic aspects—*Socialist viewpoints*
Socialist viewpoints
   Industries. Management. Control by personnel. Economic aspects

It will be seen that when the inverted format is used, the terms in the display follow the order in which they appear in the original string, rather than the reverse order in which they would normally appear in the qualifier.

Every book is written from some point of view; (4) should only be used when the viewpoint has some significant effect on the presentation: common examples are those illustrated above, *ie* sociological and political, to which one could add religious (*eg* contraception from the Roman Catholic point of view). One other case is important: if the system is used to index a classified arrangement, as in BNB and ANB, the viewpoint may affect the discipline into which the topic should be correctly classified.

(6) is used to introduce both target and bibliographical form. It may thus be used twice, and the order can in some cases affect the meaning. By *target* is meant the audience for whom the work was produced: in other words, bias phase. *Bibliographical form* has its normal meaning of information presented in a particular physical or intellectual format, *eg* periodical, data book, encyclopedia etc.

(2) multivariate analysis

(6) business enterprise $h for
Entries
Multivariate analysis
    —*For business enterprise*
Business enterprise
    Multivariate analysis—*For business enterprise*
(1) stars
(6) tables
Entry
Stars
    —*Tables*
Normally target is cited before form, but this must always depend on the sense. To use a wellworn example, the string
    (2) physiotherapy
    (6) nurses $h for
    (6) bibliographies
obviously represents a different sense from the similar string
    (2) physiotherapy
    (6) bibliographies
    (6) nurses $h for
In the first example we have a bibliography on physiotherapy for nurses, whereas in the second we have a bibliography for nurses on the subject of physiotherapy. Strictly speaking, the term used should have been 'nursing'; the name of the activity is preferred to the name of the people involved in it, as in the following expansion of a previous example, again showing form preceding target:
    (1) stars
    (6) tables
    (6) land surveying $h for
        giving the entries
    Stars
        —*Tables—For land surveying*
Land surveying
    Stars—*Tables—For land surveying*
Note that in this instance, because the lead does *not* contain all of the terms introduced by (6), they are all repeated in the display, rather than the entry
    Land surveying
        Stars—*Tables*
which one might have expected.

PLACE
Discussion of (0) and (5) has been deferred to this point in order to present a reasonably comprehensive treatment of Place rather than a series of piecemeal explanations. Place may in fact be treated in several

different ways, depending on the sense.

If Place is the only focus, or the principal focus, use (1); this operator is also used if a concept consisting of a natural feature is defined by its location, or if an action implies the involvement of the whole community.

(1) Tibet
Entry
Tibet
(1) Australia
(6) encyclopedias
Entry
Australia
   —*Encyclopedias*
(1) Great Britain
(2) society
Entries
Great Britain
  Society
Society.   Great Britain

If Place is simply the environment for the main concepts, or if a man-made feature is defined by its location, use (0):

(0) Great Britain
(1) industries
Entries
Great Britain
  Industries
Industries.   Great Britain
(0) Dublin
(2) architecture
(6) illustrations
Entries
Dublin
  Architecture—*Illustrations*
Architecture.   Dublin
  —*Illustrations*

If Place is used in the sense of a particular example from which the author draws general conclusions, it is treated as a *study region*, introduced by (5) from the second group of mainline operators:

(1) man
(p) spina bifida
(3) social aspects
(5) study regions
(q) Scotland (LO)
(p) South-east Scotland

Scotland.   *Study regions*
    Man. Spina bifida. Social aspects—*Study regions: South-east Scotland*
Spina bifida.   Man
    Social aspects—*Study regions: South-east Scotland*
Social aspects.   Spina bifida. Man
    —*Study regions: South-east Scotland*
South-east Scotland.   *Study regions*
    Man. Spina bifida. Social aspects—*Study regions: South-east Scotland*

In this example, Scotland only appears in the lead position (LO); there is no (2), so no predicate transformation takes place when (3) social aspects moves into the lead position; when the sequence introduced by (5) moves into the lead, the place becomes the lead term and the rest of the entry moves into the display. Note also that the term *study regions* is followed by a colon which introduces the specific place.

Occasionally Place may be regarded as an agent, *eg* 'the role of Australia in the East Timor dispute', in which case (3) would be used, but this would be very rare. The usual operators for Place are (0), (1) and (5), with (0) probably the most commonly used.

INTERPOSED OPERATORS
We now come to the next group of operators, the *interposed operators*. These operators cannot be used on their own; they must be used with one of the mainline operators. The first three indicate elements which depend in some way on the operator to which they are subsumed. (p) indicates *parts* or *properties*, while (q) is used to denote the quasi-generic relationships discussed in chapter 5; we have already used these operators in some of the examples, but some further examples will illustrate their use:

   (1) organisms
   (p) cells
   (p) membranes
   (2) osmosis
   (6) reviews of research
   Entries
Organisms
   Cells. Membranes. Osmosis—*Reviews of research*
Cells.   Organisms
   Membranes. Osmosis—*Reviews of research*
Membranes.   Cells. Organisms
   Osmosis—*reviews of research*
Osmosis.   Membranes. Cells. Organisms
   —*Reviews of research*

(o) Great Britain
(1) higher education institutions
(p) curriculum subject
(q) mechanical engineering
(3) degree courses
Entries
Higher education institutions. Great Britain
    Curriculum subject: Mechanical engineering. Degree courses
Mechanical engineering. Curriculum subject. Higher education
        institutions. Great Britain
    Degree courses
Degree courses. Mechanical engineering. Curriculum subject.
        Higher education institutions. Great Britain

Two points should be noted about this example. The first is that (q) automatically causes the colon to be printed in the display after the containing term, in this case curriculum subject; the second is that if the qualifier overflows on to the next line, it is indented eight spaces, to distinguish it from the display, which is indented two spaces.

(r) is used to introduce terms representing aggregates, and is likely to be used on rare occasions. The examples used to illustrate the use of the operators are taken from BNB, with the strings reconstructed to give the results found, but the only illustration of the use of (r) comes from the *Manual*:

(1) wolves
(r) packs
sub 2 (1) wolf packs
(2) behaviour
Entries
Wolves
    Packs. Behaviour
Behaviour.   Wolf packs

This example also illustrates the use of the instruction *sub* (substitute). By using this, it is possible to replace a specified portion of the string preceding the instruction (in this case 2 lines) by a phrase which may read more easily.

(s) and (t) are denoted *concept interlinks*. (s) is used when an unusual role is involved, or an indirect agent, or an indirect action; this last is more familiar as *influence phase*.

(l) states
(p) size
sub 2 (1) size of state
(s) effects $v on $w of
(3) democracy
Entries

237

States
Size. Effects on democracy
Size. States
Effects on democracy
Democracy
Effects of size of state

(1) Great Britain
(p) society
sub 2 (1) society
(s) role $v of $w in
(3) British military forces
Entries
Society. Great Britain
Role of British military forces
British military forces
Role in society
In this example, it would be redundant to repeat Great Britain, since the word British occurs in the entry. If the subject had been the role of British military forces in, say, Northern Ireland society, the substitution would of course not have taken place.

(t) denotes author-attributed associations, specifically the phase relations exposition, comparison and relation to.
(1) society
(t) $v expounded by $w expounding
(2) literature
Entries
Society
expounded by literature
Literature
expounding society
The final operator in this group is (g), denoting coordinate concepts.

(1) sulphides
(g) selenides $v &
(g) tellurides
(p) thermodynamic properties
(6) technical data
Entries
Sulphides
Thermodynamic properties—*Technical data*
Selenides
Thermodynamic properties—*Technical data*
Tellurides
Thermodynamic properties—*Technical data*

238

Thermodynamic properties. Sulphides, selenides & tellurides—*Technical data*

A careful study will show that many of these procedures are in fact present in Coates' computer-based system, giving very similar results. However, the next group of operators, though they parallel Coates' use of 'Kind of thing' introduced by the comma or double comma, are treated rather differently in PRECIS, and reflect much more closely the CRG work.

DIFFERENCING OPERATORS

Instead of Thing, Kind, and Kind of kind, PRECIS treats the result of such qualifications as a single concept, consisting of a *focus* and one or more *differences*. There are four sets of differencing operators; the first three groups contain pairs of operators, the choice of which one to use depending on whether the term is to be a lead term or not, while the fourth 'group' consists of *date*. The first pair, h and i, are *direct* differences, *ie* they relate to the focus, just as Coates' single comma does. The second pair, k and m, are *indirect* differences, *ie* they relate to the preceding difference. Given more than one difference, Coates uses first the single comma, then the double comma for direct differences, *eg*

    Plates, circular,, anisotropic

and a series of commas to denote differences which apply to the preceding term, *eg*

    Lamps, fluorescent, indium amalgam

In PRECIS, these operators are introduced by the $ sign, and the above examples would become

    (1) plates $i circular $i anisotropic
    (1) lamps $i fluorescent $m indium amalgam

assuming that we wanted the differences to appear as lead terms, or

    (1) plates $h circular $h anisotropic
    (1) lamps $h fluorescent $k indium amalgam

if we did not want them in the lead position at all. We can of course mix the two pairs if we want one difference to appear as a lead term but not another. The results of using the two pairs are slightly different, as the following examples show:

    (1) compounds $i inorganic $i non-metallic
    Entries
Non-metallic compounds
    Non-metallic inorganic compounds
Inorganic compounds
    Non-metallic inorganic compounds
    (1) drugs
    (2) analysis $i chemical $m automatic
    Entries

Drugs
   Automatic chemical analysis
Chemical analysis.   Drugs
   Automatic chemical analysis
Automatic chemical analysis.   Drugs
Date is treated as a difference, introduced by $d, and is printed in italics, *eg*
   (1) Balkán peninsula $d c500—c1530
Entry
Balkan peninsula
   c500—c1530
The remaining pair, $n and $o, introduce *parenthetical differences*, and are used mainly in the social sciences, where we may need to distinguish between various methods of, say, measuring IQ. They are found only infrequently, and the following example is taken from the *Manual*:
   (1) infánts
   (p) intélligence $o Wechsler scale
Entries
Infants
   Intelligence (Wechsler scale)
Intelligence (Wechsler scale). Infants
Wechsler scale. Intelligence. Infants
If Wechsler scale had not been required as a lead term, the appropriate operator would have been $n instead of $o.

What happens if we have more than one difference acting on the same focus? In what order should they be written down to give a consistent and logical sequence? If the first difference related to the focus while the second relates to the first difference, there is no problem; for example, we refer to 'prestressed reinforced concrete' in that order because the 'prestressed' relates to the method of reinforcing, which in its turn relates to the concrete. But what of 'vertical take-off military aircraft', in which both the 'vertical take-off' and the 'military' refer to the 'aircraft'? Austin has worked out a table of precedence for such situations, based largely on the principle that those properties which least affect the entity to which they refer come first, and those most closely defining it come last. This does in fact reflect the order in which these terms are used in everyday language; we would speak of a 'very beautiful new blue coach-built Rolls-Royce', for example. This approach also solves the problem mentioned in chapter 7 of how to be consistent in stating such complex subjects as 'gas-cooled natural-uranium fuelled nuclear power reactors'. It is also nice to think that Chesterton anticipated PRECIS when he referred to 'a great big black teetotaller',[3] though he probably did not have any particular indexing system in mind at the time.

It should be noted that in order to achieve the correct result, *ie* to have the printed entry in natural language order, it is necessary to write down the focus first, followed by the differences in reverse order, using the appropriate operators to give the required lead terms, *eg*:

(1) cars $i Rolls-Royce $m coach-built $h blue $h new $h beautiful $h very would give entries under Cars, Rolls-Royce cars and Coach-built Rolls-Royce cars, but not under any of the other terms. In each case the full string would appear in the display, *eg*

Rolls-Royce cars
   Very beautiful new blue coach-built Rolls-Royce cars

The second example is perhaps more realistic:

(1) reactors $i power $i nuclear $i natural-uranium fuelled $i gas-cooled which would give the entries

Reactors
 Gas-cooled natural-uranium fuelled nuclear power reactors
Power reactors
 Gas-cooled natural-uranium fuelled nuclear power reactors
Nuclear reactors
 Gas-cooled natural-uranium fuelled nuclear power reactors
Natural-uranium fuelled reactors
 Gas-cooled natural-uranium fuelled nuclear power reactors
Gas-cooled reactors
 Gas-cooled natural-uranium fuelled nuclear power reactors

If these entries had to be generated manually (as for example by the present author) they could be regarded as repetitive and wasteful of effort, but since they are intended to be produced automatically by the computer program this is not an important consideration. In practice it has been found that the PRECIS index to BNB is relatively economic of space when compared with the previous chain index or with the (now separate) author/title index.

CONNECTIVES

The next group of operators are the *connectives* $v and $w; these have already appeared in a number of the examples, largely because they are frequently used. $v introduces a downward reading preposition or conjunction, $w an upward reading connecting term. They have an important property which may not have been completely obvious from the examples given and which is known as *gating*. What this means is that when these operators come into play, then the whole part of the string that they link is treated as a single unit. When the term to which they are attached is in the lead position, however, usually they do not function. The effect of this rule is seen in the following example:

(1) Great Britain
(2) political behaviour
(s) influence $v of $w on

241

(3) social class
Entries
Political behaviour.   Great Britain
   Influence of social class
Social class.   Great Britain
   Influence on political behaviour
and also by the earlier example on economic aspects of the control of management of industries by personnel.

The final group (x), (y) and (z) are used when there is more than one theme to index in the same document, and they have one or more concepts in common. In such cases, (z) is used to introduce common elements, (x) to introduce the first concept in a theme and (y) any subsequent concepts in that theme. On the whole, it is easier to index separate themes separately, and it is worth mentioning in this connection that the MARC cataloguing worksheets used by the National Library of Australia have z pre-printed!

The syntactic structure of PRECIS is obviously complex, but in fact it is a development of the ideas we have discussed previously, and many of the manipulations are available in the suite of programs used by BTI. The significant step forward is the provision of a complete and meaningful statement of the subject at each entry point, with the consequent avoidance of the necessity to establish a citation order to bring the most important term to the beginning. In fact, many strings begin with place as the environment, and in the BNB it is not thought necessary to have Great Britain as a lead term, even though it begins the string (as is shown by a number of the examples quoted here). Although the description given here is quite lengthy, many points are glossed over, and the *Manual* goes into these and a number of others at length.

SEMANTIC STRUCTURE

The semantic structure is built up quite separately, as indicated earlier, using such tools as Webster's dictionary, encyclopedias and other dictionaries. As it is built into the computer-held thesaurus, once the semantic structure for a particular term has been established, the appearance of that term as a lead term automatically calls up the necessary cross-references. There is however one refinement which is worth mentioning, since it illustrates very neatly the power of the computer to provide just what is wanted—given always that it has been properly programmed.

It is a generally accepted point that cross-references should *modulate*, that is to say, they should proceed from general to special by single steps. For example, we should not make a reference direct from Science to atoms, since the logical consequence of such a step would be to make similar cross-references from Science to every heading contained within it—an impractical proposition. By modulating the cross-reference structure we can keep the number of cross-references within bounds, yet still enable the user to get from the broad heading to the specific. In the example quoted above, we might have cross-references

Science *see also* Physical sciences
Physical sciences *see also* Physics
Physics *see also* Nuclear physics
Nuclear physics *see also* Atoms

Let us assume that in one of the weekly issues of BNB there is an entry under Kinetics. Using DC as a model for the chain of references that would lead to this, we should have:

Physics *see also* Mechanics
Mechanics *see also* Dynamics
Dynamics *see also* Kinetics

For the monthly cumulation the PRECIS index is generated, and would normally contain all of these references; but if during the month it should by chance have happened that there were no entries under any of the higher entries, the user who first looks under Physics will have a very tedious time going from one empty heading to the next by means of the cross-references until he eventually arrives at the heading Kinetics, where there *is* an entry. This is clearly undesirable, and is avoided by part of the computer program which checks whether a heading is empty. If so, the cross-reference structure skips that heading, and goes direct to the next, and so on until a heading is reached that does have an entry. In the particular example worked out here, the cross-references would become:

Physics *see also* Kinetics
Mechanics *see also* Kinetics
Dynamics *see also* Kinetics

In each case the user is directed to the heading within the subject field where an entry is to be found.

CUMULATION

As progressively larger cumulations are reached—four-monthly, annual, triennial—the number of empty headings obviously decreases, and the cross-reference structure necessarily becomes more complex and indirect; this is inevitable, and happens in any catalogue as it grows larger. However, there is by way of consolation the fact that the user who starts at a very broad heading is likely to find entries of interest to him as he follows through the chain of cross-references.

There is another feature of the PRECIS system which becomes more relevant as cumulations grow larger. The computer checks each lead term to see whether it occurs as lead term in more than one entry; if so, the entries are merged to form a set of subheadings under the one lead term, in a very similar way to that described for articulated indexing (chapter 7). This does actually result in two possible sequences under any given lead term: those entries in which it is *not* followed by a qualifier, and those in which it is. However, this again is comparable with the results found with other systems, as was shown in the discussion of filing order in chapter 7.

For storage within the computer, each term is given a code, the RIN, which identifies it and its associated cross-references. We have seen the problems that arise in applying notation (the code vocabulary) to a classification scheme, particularly in the imposition of a rigid structure which inevitably becomes obsolete. The codes allocated to terms in the PRECIS thesaurus are generated at random, and do not therefore impose any order of their own; the indexer has the power to include a term in as many hierarchical or associative structures as he wishes, and can change these at any time. The thesaurus is thus free of any of the structural rigidity associated with a classification scheme, despite its foundations in classification theory.

CONCLUSIONS

This discussion of PRECIS, lengthy though it has been, still does not cover all the refinements of the system; for these, it is essential to read the *Manual*, which is not only a very detailed explanation of the system, but also a mine of information on, and examples of, indexing problems. As we have seen, many of the features of PRECIS are to be found in other systems, but PRECIS is the only system to incorporate so many of the refinements that help to make life easier for the user as well as the indexer. It does not claim to be perfect, and it does have its critics, but it does appear to be one of the best, if not the best, systems that we have at present.[4] It is based on over twenty years of experience in the detailed indexing of large numbers of books for BNB, as well as on the theories developed by the CRG in the quest for a new classification. Some experimental work has also shown that, because it is based on linguistic principles, it can give good results when used with other languages than English. It now forms part of the MARC records generated in Australia as well as those in BNB, and has been used successfully in the indexing of non-book materials. It is certainly a major contribution to the theory and practice of alphabetical subject headings.

BIBLIOGRAPHY

1 Austin, D: 'The development of PRECIS: a theoretical and technical history.' *Journal of documentation*, 30 (1) 1974, 47–102.

2 Austin, D: *PRECIS: a manual of concept analysis and subject indexing*. Council of the British National Bibliography, 1974.

3 Chesterton, G K: *The flying inn*. 1914.

4 See correspondence from R Moss, D F Swift, C D Robinson and D Austin in *Journal of documentation*, 30 (4) 1974, 433; *31* (2) 1975, 116–120; *31* (4) 1975, 301–303; *32* (2) 1976, 147.

CHAPTER 15

Kinds of precoordinate index

We are now in a position to compare the ways in which precoordinate systems are used, and to point out the relative advantages and disadvantages of different methods. There are three basic areas to be considered:

1 Shelf arrangement of books
2 Library catalogues and bibliographies
3 Book indexes

All of these depend very largely on the fact that precoordinate indexes are 'one-place' indexes in that they can give us a single place which can be regarded as the primary statement of the subject, though they may well require also various secondary statements, *eg* in the form of supporting sequences in a different order.

SHELF CLASSIFICATION

We have seen in chapter 1 that there are a number of factors to be taken into account when considering the arrangement of documents in a library, and that we may finish up with several different sequences, some of which will be in an order dictated by their physical form, or mode of presentation, or identifying number. However, when all these things are taken into account, they still leave most libraries with a substantial collection of books which it is desirable to have on *open access*: that is to say, we permit the users to get at the books themselves and choose what they want, rather than have them come to us with the details of a book which we must then fetch from the book-stacks. (The idea of open access is now so widely accepted that it is salutary to remember that when J D Brown allowed the public of Islington to get at the books in the 1890's he was regarded by many of his colleagues as mad!) If we are to have open access, then presumably we should at least try to arrange the books in a way which will be helpful to the readers. There are various ways in which they might be arranged: size, author, title, alphabetically by subject, systematically by subject. Of these, it seems probable that the most helpful arrangement is one in which related subjects are brought together, *ie* systematic or classified arrangement.[1] Most of the major classification schemes have in fact

245

been devised with this objective in mind; Dewey intended his scheme to be used for this from the beginning, though he was also an advocate of its use in the catalogue, while LC is intended solely for this purpose and it is only outside the USA that one finds it used for catalogue arrangement.

We have already seen in previous chapters some of the problems that arise in shelf classification. If the scheme we are using is one that permits us to be specific, then its notation may well be long; if so, it may be inconvenient to inscribe it on the spine of a book, or—worse still—a pamphlet. Immediately we have put a piece of notation on the back of a book we have a vested interest in obsolescence: we do not want relationships between subjects to change because it may mean altering what we have done in the past. Unless we guide the shelves adequately, readers will find it difficult to follow the notation, especially if it is mixed.

Additional problems arise in a lending library. A good part of the stock will be on loan at any given time, the actual books involved changing of course from week to week. Under these circumstances it becomes difficult to maintain a classified sequence in good order, and there will be gaps and 'bulges' which will involve moving the overall sequence around on the shelves; this means that a reader accustomed to finding 'his' books on a particular shelf may well be aggrieved to find that they have been moved somewhere else. In a reference library, the main problem is that of an ever increasing stock, which can involve almost as many problems of location as in a lending library.

Despite the problems, there seems to be a general consensus that we should make the effort and provide our readers with an open access stock in classified order, though one gets the impression in some libraries that classification is merely a device to 'mark and park': a convenient piece of notation to stick on the back of a book so that we can locate it. If this is indeed all we require from shelf classification it would be a great deal cheaper to use some other method entirely —perhaps go back to fixed location and closed access!

We have already seen that with any kind of retrieval system it is not possible to please all of the people all of the time. A particular classified shelf arrangement may well suit a high proportion of our readers, but there will be some who will find it unhelpful. The shelf arrangement can usefully be backed up by a continuing series of displays bringing together subjects which are scattered by the classification. For example, DC scatters concretes such as Steel and Transport; these can form the topic of displays from time to time so that users of the library become aware of the fact that the primary arrangement on the shelves is not the only one possible. Many libraries do of course have a semi-permanent display of 'recent additions'; while this display is not subject-oriented, it is a very accurate reflection of the fact that for many readers novelty is more significant than subject matter. Since the whole object of our shelf arrangement is to help readers, we should not permit theoretical considerations to prevent our providing this useful service. When the novelty has worn off, the books can be returned to the normal sequence, as they can after any other kind of display.

LIBRARY CATALOGUES AND BIBLIOGRAPHIES

A library catalogue is intended to record the stock of that library; a bibliography, on the other hand, is not limited to the stock of any one library, but usually has some other kind of limitation, *eg* national, language, or subject. As far as the subject approach is concerned, both are very similar and can be considered together. For example, the theory of subject headings developed by Coates has been applied so far in BTI, a bibliography, but could also be applied in a library catalogue. Many libraries use UDC for their catalogue, and for their shelf arrangement (often in an abbreviated form), but UDC is also used by some bibliographies for their primary arrangement. LCSH is intended for use in library catalogues, but will be equally effective in a bibliography, and is in fact the basis of headings used in several indexing services. This point has been stressed by Vickery in his recent *Techniques of information retrieval*,[2] which goes a long way towards eliminating the gap which all too often exists between 'subject bibliography' and 'information retrieval'.

Bearing this point in mind, we can evaluate the different kinds of subject catalogue so far described, and point out the relative advantages and disadvantages. It must be stressed that if we start with systems having the same degree of specificity, and adopt the same policy with regard to exhaustivity, and build in the same system of relationships, there will be no difference in the information that can be found through the systems; what will differ is the ease with which the systems will give answers to particular types of enquiry. All systems are equal overall, but in any given situation, some are more equal than others.[3]

ALPHABETICAL SUBJECT CATALOGUE

The alphabetical subject catalogue contains subject entries and cross-references arranged alphabetically in one sequence. As we have seen in chapter 2, subject entries consist of a heading, from the index vocabulary, and a description which identifies the item being catalogued. Cross-references are of two kinds: *see* references, which lead from headings which appear only in the entry vocabulary (*ie* terms which users may think of but which are not part of the preferred index vocabulary) to headings in the index vocabulary; and *see also* references, which serve to link related headings within the preferred index vocabulary, either to show semantic relationships or to reveal 'hidden' terms in a composite heading, as discussed in the section on chain procedure in chapter 6.

Headings for the index vocabulary must be carefully chosen, to correspond as far as possible with the approach of the user. Where a heading contains more than one word, it is necessary to lay down a significance order, to bring to the front the word most likely to be sought. Entry should be direct, *eg* aluminium is entered as aluminium, not as metals—non-ferrous—aluminium. The order in which headings are arranged will have to be dictated by a set of filing rules unless all of our entries follow exactly the same pattern, which in practice is impossible. Two tools are almost essential: a source of headings—an index vocabulary—and an *authority file* showing our particular usage. The index vocabulary may be enumerative, *ie* may list composite headings as well as simple, and show a selection of ready made references from which we can choose the ones that are relevant at any given time; such lists as *Sears list of subject headings* and the more detailed *Subject headings used in the dictionary catalogs of the Library of Congress* are of this kind. It is possible to use the list itself as the authority file, by marking in it those headings and references we have used; *Sears list* is designed to make this easy, by having only one column of print to a page and thus leaving the right hand half of the page blank for annotations.

Alternatively we can compile an authority file separately on cards, on which we will note headings used, references made to them, and headings not used. It is possible to use the catalogue itself as the authority file; it certainly shows past practice, but it is rather more difficult to show references made to a heading clearly in the catalogue than in a separate file.

If we use a synthetic approach, then our index vocabulary will consist largely of rules as to the construction of headings, rather than the headings themselves. The compilation of an authority file is thus rather more important, for not only will we not find any composite subject headings in the index vocabulary—we may well not find many single terms either. We must however have a source for *see also* references to cater for semantic relationships; this may be a set of classification schemes, or a collection of dictionaries and encyclopedias. LCSH appears at times to rely on the cataloguer's flair, which may lead to useful cross-references, but may also lead to eventual confusion.

We may summarize the advantages and disadvantages of the alphabetical approach as follows.

Advantages: Self evident order (within limits—it is sometimes helpful to depart from strict alphabetical arrangement).

Hospitality—we can insert new topics at any time simply by filing the headings in the appropriate places, provided that the index vocabulary that we are using permits us to add terms.

Flexibility—we can show more than one genus-species relationship in exactly the same way, by making *see also* references; this freedom can be important when we are dealing with interdisciplinary subjects, though it can equally be misleading if we do not carry through an adequate analysis of the structure of the subjects we are dealing with.

Disadvantages: To set against the above advantages we have to consider the following points.

Alphabetical scatter—if we look under Zoology, we may be referred to Animals; having made our way to the other end of the catalogue we may find that really the heading we should have been looking for was Zebras. In other words, related subjects are not found together, but are scattered according to the accident of their names.

Conflict with natural language—if we are to be consistent in our selection of headings, we shall be forced to abandon natural language in favour of an artificial index vocabulary: artificial in the sense that the choice of terms will be strictly controlled, and headings will not conform to normal usage. The simplest example of this is the elimination of synonyms, but equally, or more, important are the problems that arise from the use of insignificant words. These form an essential part of natural language but are not always used consistently: a periodical may be 'Journal of . . .', or 'Journal for . . .' or 'Journal on . . .', for example. We therefore try to avoid their use in headings, and if we are obliged to use them there is always the problem of whether they are ignored in the filing or not. Conflict arises because our controlled vocabulary still consists of words taken from natural language. However, users are accustomed to finding artificial conventions in catalogues; how many authors put their names on the title pages of their books with the surname first? So perhaps we should not exaggerate the importance of this point.

Reports and papers in. . .
Reports from. . .
Reports in. . .
Reports in the. . .
Reports of. . .
Reports of the. . .
Reports on. . .
Reports on the. . .
Reports on (fmly of) the. . .

TABLE 12: *Entries beginning 'Reports' in a list of chemical journals*

Generic searching is tedious—if we wish to pursue a subject in depth, it can become quite difficult to follow up all the references that might be relevant; there is no question of finding the whole of a topic displayed at one point in the sequence.

Alphabetical arrangement works well in a situation where terminology is well defined, and where users are mainly concerned with requests for information on specific subjects having clearly defined and widely accepted names, for example 'retailing'. It does not lend itself so well to broad generic searching, in which the reader tries to follow up all the ramifications of a fairly comprehensive subject such as 'commerce', which might include not only 'retailing' but also 'wholesaling', 'accounting', 'consumer protection' and so on. It has however the advantage that the subject catalogue can be combined with the author/title catalogue to give a *dictionary catalogue* in one single sequence; this brings together works by and works about a given author, individual or corporate. However, this can also be achieved by keeping the subject catalogue separate, but making the author/title sequence a *name catalogue*. Many librarians have come to the conclusion that the advantages of the single sequence of the dictionary catalogue are outweighed by the associated filing problems, and keep the two sequences separate.

CLASSIFIED CATALOGUE[4]

Systematic arrangement brings related subjects together by using notation as its code vocabulary; there is therefore no question of combining the subject and author/title sequences in one. Entries consist of a heading, which in this case is a notational symbol, and a document description. References are necessary from the entry vocabulary to the code vocabulary, *ie* from the names of subjects in words to the correct notational symbol; we need an alphabetical subject index to the classified sequence. There are therefore essentially at least two parts to a classified catalogue: the systematically arranged sequence and the alphabetical index. In addition, we may have a third sequence of authors and titles, though BNB has shown that it is quite feasible to combine this with the subject index.[5]

Genus-species relationships and syntactic relationships are both shown by a combination of juxtaposition in the classified sequence and juxtaposition in the alphabetical index, but whereas in an alphabetical arrangement it is difficult to show *kinds* of relationship (the syntax of the indexing language), in a classified arrangement these are shown by the notation in many cases as well as by the arrangement, which groups together foci bearing the same relationship to the basic class containing them.

FEATURE HEADINGS

In a systematic arrangement, it is the notation which forms the code vocabulary, *ie* the headings by which subject entries are arranged, but this is merely a convenience, to make the act of finding a subject in the sequence easier. It does not help the user when he finds a piece of notation if he does not know what it stands for. Suppose that a user thinks of too broad a subject and finds the notation for this through the index; he now has to find his way through the systematic arrangement to the specific subject that he wants. The arrangement is intended to help him to do this, but if all he has to guide him are notational symbols this will not be of much help. This point was noted by Dewey, the first librarian to use a notation in the sense in which we now use the word, and he put forward the very simple solution of *feature headings*. A feature heading consists of a 'translation' of the notation back into words; it is not used for arranging purposes but simply to guide the user. A very good example of the use of feature headings is the *British national bibliography*, where in the classified section we find a liberal use of words to clarify the systematic arrangement. Feature headings are an obvious source for index terms, and were used for the purpose by BNB.

If we are using a published scheme, *ie* one where we have to rely on some external agency to publish expansions, we may find that the scheme is not specific enough for our needs. We can find notation for part, but not all, of our subject specification. Rather than lose specificity we may decide to use the feature heading to state the subject precisely, despite the fact that some of the terms we write down in the heading will not be represented by notation. These terms are *verbal extensions*; we can use them for indexing, but it is rather more difficult to use them in the arrangement, for this would mean that we had a systematic arrangement not shown by notation. Again, the best example of the use of verbal extensions is BNB; using DC14 to classify a very large collection of literature in detail quickly revealed deficiencies, which have been overcome to a large extent by this device. Its use is indicated by [1] and is demonstrated by the following examples:

630   AGRICULTURE
631—FARM EQUIPMENT & OPERATIONS
631.2—Buildings
631.2[1]—Lighting

400   LANGUAGES
420   ENGLISH
428—ENGLISH SCHOOL BOOKS
428.[1]—Comprehensive tests
428.[1]—Precis writing

330   ECONOMICS
333—NATURAL RESOURCES, LAND, REAL ESTATE
333.3—PRIVATE OWNERSHIP OF REAL ESTATE

333.33—REAL ESTATE TRANSACTIONS
333.33[1]—Surveying. *Reports*
333.33[1]—Houses. *Europe. Periodicals*
333.33[1]—Houses. *Great Britain*
333.33[1]—Houses. *Great Britain. Law*
333.33[1]—Investment in real estate

The third example shows the practice of arranging systematically despite the lack of notation; if there are a lot of specific subjects arranged in this way, as was the case in the first two five year cumulations of BNB, then even when the notation has been found through the index, the user has to search through perhaps several pages of entries, systematically arranged in an order which may be helpful but is unknown to the searcher. The advantages are those of helpful order and specificity; the searcher will find related topics together, and if there are two books on the same specific topic they will be found together. Without the use of verbal extensions these two advantages would have been lost; the user would still have had to look through as many entries, with no guarantee that if he found one on a subject he had found them all. With the introduction of MARC, BNB has adopted DC18 from the beginning of 1971, and the (1) is no longer used. Feature headings are still used, but they are now linked to the PRECIS string where the DC class number is not coextensive with the subject of the document.

Feature headings and verbal extensions, as well as being the major source of indexing terms, will indicate the terms which should be used for guiding, both in the catalogue and on the shelves. In general, libraries provide quite inadequate guides to their systematic arrangement, assuming that readers can find their way through the catalogue with a minimum of help. Readers do not make much use of library catalogues. It may be thought extreme to make a guide out for every feature heading, but this is what is done in BNB, and there is no doubt that it makes the systematic arrangement a great deal easier to use. Students should compare the careful guiding of BNB with, say, *American book publishing record*, in which the guiding is minimal; the superiority shows up very clearly in the cumulations. The use of verbal extensions to make up for the deficiencies of the classification scheme can be studied in the BNB cumulations for 1951–54 and 1955–59, at, for example, 656 or 791.4.

A practical problem can arise if we try to guide a card catalogue on the lines recommended above. Guide cards project above the body of the cards, and if there are a lot of them in a drawer they tend to obscure each other, and also to wear out—a point which does not diminish their theoretical efficiency but does affect the enthusiasm with which readers use the catalogue. On the printed page, as in BNB, guiding is far more satisfactory: a reflection of the superiority of the user-oriented printed catalogue over the indexer-oriented card form.

We may summarize the advantages and disadvantages of the classified catalogue as follows:

Advantages: Helpful order—the arrangement, though not self evident, is designed to bring related subjects together in a way that will help users.

Search strategy is simple—to broaden a search we need only look at the headings in the same part of the catalogue, while it is equally simple to do the same thing to find more specific subjects.

Disadvantages: Indirect access—because the order is not self evident, we have to have a secondary file in alphabetical order to gain access to the main sequence; any search, no matter how simple, thus involves two steps, whereas with an alphabetical catalogue the user who knows the correct terminology can go straight to the heading he requires.

Systematic scattering—in any basic class, only the foci in the primary facet will have all the relevant entries at one point; foci in the secondary facets will be scattered. Furthermore a subject which can appear in more than one discipline will be scattered by the normal classification scheme, in which the primary arrangement is by discipline rather than by concrete.

The classified catalogue works well in a situation where users are not sure of their approach and need help from the arrangement; it is best suited to searching for information on broad subjects, and to browsing, but may involve the user in an extra step in the situation where he knows the subject and the heading he requires. To set against this is the fact that if the shelf arrangement of books is systematic, the alphabetical index to the catalogue will also direct users to the correct place on the shelves; it is thus possible to bypass the catalogue if the user wishes to browse among the books on the shelf at the moment rather than scan the complete set of entries in the catalogue.

If a dictionary or other alphabetical catalogue is in use, the headings used in it will differ obviously from the notation used for shelf arrangement. If a classified catalogue is in use, this may still be the case, particularly if we use a shelf notation as described in chapter 10. However, future trends may tend to accentuate this division; it seems likely that a system which works well for shelf arrangement will be inadequate for information retrieval, while a scheme designed for information retrieval may not give a helpful shelf arrangement. We may have to accept the fact that two different objectives are involved, which cannot be attained by the use of only one system.

ALPHABETICO-CLASSED CATALOGUE

We may attempt to combine the self evident order of the alphabetical approach with the helpful groupings of the systematic approach by using an alphabetico-classed arrangement. In this, headings are indirect, in contrast with the direct headings we have been considering; aluminium is entered under Metals—non-ferrous—aluminium, not under Aluminium. Everything on metals will be grouped, just as with the systematic approach; equally, we need a system of references to serve as an entry vocabulary, to lead us from the specific terms to the broader heading under which they are subsumed. Within each heading, subheadings are arranged alphabetically, not systematically, so that subgroups may not be arranged in a helpful order.

In trying to get the best of both worlds, we may have finished up with the worst. We no longer have the direct entry of the alphabetical (or, more precisely, alphabetico-direct) sequence, nor have we the helpful order of the systematic. The alphabetico-classed catalogue has in practice few of its theoretical advantages and has found few advocates. In Britain and indeed Europe generally the classified catalogue is most popular, while in the USA it is the dictionary catalogue which is most commonly found.

MULTIPLE ENTRY SYSTEMS

In the discussion of citation order, we saw that there are likely to be situations where users are badly handicapped by insistence on one fixed citation order; the same is of course true of the alphabetical catalogue with a fixed significance order. The reason for having one, and only one, such order is to ensure that the same topic is not entered under more than one heading at different times, introducing an element of inconsistency which leads to lowered recall, and also to provide a definite place for the shelf arrangement. We can only put a document in one physical place, and there must be definite rules to make sure that we are consistent in choosing this one place; but there is no reason other than economics to stop us making additional entries in the catalogue. However, the economics of multiple entry are important; as has already been pointed out, permutation of all the elements in a composite subject may lead to a quite unacceptable number of entries. We have to find methods of increasing the number of entries to a level which is acceptable; these methods must be consistent, and simple to apply. Haphazard selection from the mass of potential permutations will not help the users; the penalty of inconsistency here, as everywhere, is sequential scanning of a much larger number of entries than is necessary if strict rules are followed.

We have seen in chapter 6 that there are various ways in which multiple entries may be produced. Cycling is almost exclusively associated with UDC, and a detailed example is worked out in chapter 18. Rotating is mainly associated with KWIC indexing, though it can be used with a facetted classification scheme, and has been used with the London Education Classification at the University of London Institute of Education. Shunting is used by PRECIS only, though it might be applied to other types of heading; it would be interesting to see what would happen if Coates' headings were treated in this way, and Farradane suggests that his analets can be manipulated in a number of ways and still retain their meaning.

One technique which is not dealt with here is SLIC—Selective Listing In Combination. This technique was devised by J Sharp,[6] and relies on *combinations* of terms in a fixed citation order, as opposed to *permutations*. Whereas there are 120 permutations of five terms, SLIC achieves the same objective with 16 entries. It suffers from the same drawback as chain procedure in that only one of the headings is specific, and has been superseded by other computer-based techniques; ICI now have a sophisticated suite of programs, ASSASSIN, for information retrieval purposes, and SLIC is now no more than of historical interest. *Sic transit* . . . A full description will be found in the first two editions of this book, or in the references quoted here.

PHYSICAL FORM OF INDEX
Although in theory the physical form of the indexing system should not affect its performance, in practice it does, to quite a large extent. There are two aspects to this: firstly, input problems; secondly, those to do with output.

In any system that is open ended, we need to be able to insert new items as necessary. If we have a fixed location serial file, *ie* one in which we give each item a permanent place, there is only one place that we can add new items: at the end. We cannot add in the middle, because that would disturb the items already filed. The only kind of arrangement that can be displayed is thus a chronological one, with the latest always at the end. Such a file is the accessions book in a library, or a file of data on magnetic tape, and to find entries by any but the chronological approach involves sequential scanning of the whole file; we do not have *random access, ie* the ability to go direct to any particular access point we may require.

The most popular form of catalogue in libraries is the card catalogue. This consists of a set of cards, usually of standard 12.5×7.5 cm size; the cards are arranged according to the indexing system headings. New cards can be added wherever they are needed, and we can go direct to any access point we want, provided that it is used as a heading. As has already been mentioned, we normally make a distinction between the headings, *ie* those points where we want to be able to find information, and the description, *ie* the information which identifies the document; we cannot find our way to any information in the description which is not used as a heading. For example, the date of publication forms part of the description, but it is not normally used as a heading; we cannot then find all the entries in the catalogue representing documents published in a given year, unless we are prepared to scan every entry. In a card catalogue, we need a drawer for every thousand cards; if we have 100,000 documents in our collection, and we decide to make an entry for each using the date of publication as the head, we shall require another 100,000 cards, or 100 drawers. There is a limit to the convenient height for a set of card catalogue drawers; the users have to be able to see what is in the top drawer. Equally, it is not usual to have drawers so near the ground that users have to kneel to be able to use them. If we allow users to remove the drawers from their place in the cabinet, we can use more vertical space, but there is still a limit at top and bottom; in consequence, when we increase the size of the catalogue, we have to think in terms of horizontal expansion. Space for 100 drawers might be five feet long; in depth it will have to be large enough for us to use with the drawers pulled out to their maximum depth, say three feet. This gives fifteen square feet as the requirement for the extra 100,000 cards, a not inconsiderable amount of floor space. Thus we may find that we are constrained in the number of entries we make in a card catalogue by the economic factor of space costs.

Filing entries in a card catalogue also costs money; although it is strictly speaking a clerical operation, it is usual for filing to be checked before the cards are finally inserted into the sequence. Furthermore, the larger the catalogue is, the more difficult it is to use; this is a significant example of the law of diminishing returns applied to librarianship. The card catalogue of the Library of Congress is now so large that the skilled librarian can find it difficult to use; to the uninitiated it must present a formidable barrier. The larger the catalogue, the greater the chances of misfiling, and the more likely it is that wear and tear will cause problems. The guide cards, which project above the main body of the cards in the catalogue, are liable to deteriorate fairly quickly, but over a period of time the same is true of the whole set of cards. For example, in 1965 it was estimated that the card catalogue of the New York Public Library contained eight million cards and was growing at the rate of two million cards a year—but that of the cards in the catalogue some 30 percent (nearly two and a half million!) were either worn out or illegible and ought to be replaced. Readers are reluctant to make use of a tool which is in poor physical condition, no matter how excellent its intellectual content.

If the catalogue is a classified one, then the larger it grows the less likely it is that readers will be able to appreciate the helpful arrangement, while in an alphabetical subject catalogue we may have to follow up a cross-reference which takes us from one point in the sequence to another some distance away through the accident of alphabetical scatter of related subjects. It is therefore clear that there are quite strong arguments in favour of keeping the number of entries in the catalogue

256

as low as possible, and that these are economic arguments rather than intellectual ones. In practice, the figure of (very approximately) one and a half subject entries per document has been suggested as being the average. This could mean that we make fewer entries than are justified for a particular document, but it is important to realise that this is an economic restriction, not an intellectual one; the card catalogue permits us to make as many entries as we like for any and every document, without any restriction other than the economic and practical ones outlined above.

On the output side, a drawback to the card catalogue is that it is only possible to see one entry at a time; to see a number of entries under one heading we must leaf through them singly. This can be a relatively slow process, even if we take a bundle of cards out of a drawer and turn them over one by one on a desk—a procedure which would normally be frowned upon, because of the danger of getting the cards out of order. It is possible to turn over two cards at once, particularly if the cards have been well thumbed in the past; in this way, important entries might be missed, and the searching process is necessarily slowed down by the attempt to avoid this.

To sum up, the card catalogue is very flexible; it permits us to arrange any number of entries in any way we wish, and to insert new entries as required. To set against this, it is relatively expensive, both in capital cost and in upkeep, it is not convenient to scan, and it is essentially a single copy device; it costs twice as much to maintain two copies as to maintain one.

The sheaf catalogue is akin to the card form in that entries consist of individual, independent, pieces of paper, but whereas in the card catalogue these are standard size pieces of thin card, in the sheaf catalogue thin paper is used, and there is no standard size; slips may vary from, say, $4\text{in} \times 2\frac{1}{2}\text{in}$ to $6\text{in} \times 4\text{in}$ of usable space. The slips are held in stout covers known as binders, working on the looseleaf principle, the binders being stored in racks. Once again we have complete flexibility; we can insert new entries at any point at any time, and of course remove them if necessary. However, slips are less convenient to handle than cards and for this reason filing is slightly slower—and therefore more costly. The binders are perhaps easier to consult than card drawers in that they are in the familiar book form, but the slips again are less convenient than cards to leaf through. Space requirements are less, and capital outlay is considerably less, though this is offset by the higher maintenance costs.

The question of producing multiple copies is important, for a variety of reasons. In the first place, we normally need more than one entry point to any given document and therefore need to be able to find the same description under a number of headings; so we need a number of entries in which the description will be the same but the headings will differ. In the second place, if we maintain only one copy of the catalogue, readers will have to come to that copy to be able to consult it; we shall be introducing one more hurdle for them to cross. It is therefore desirable to be able to maintain more than one copy; indeed, the ideal is to have as many copies available as there are individuals requiring them. If we look at the card catalogue from this point of view, it presents several disadvantages. If we want to produce more than one card we have either to type each one individually (and check to see that it is correct), or use some method of duplication. As has already been pointed out, to maintain two identical card catalogues involves twice as much work as maintaining one. Space is also a consideration. Sheaf slips are only marginally better; by using carbons, it is possible to produce up to six copies of an entry at one typing, but once we get beyond this limit the question of retyping arises. Space is still a consideration, though not so acutely as with cards, but filing is, if anything, more of a problem.

On the whole, the balance seems to be in favour of the card form, and this is strongly reinforced by the fact that cards are available from several central agencies, for example BNB and the Library of Congress. However, there seems to be little doubt that both forms are used with reluctance by the general public, and neither gives the user the opportunity to take the catalogue away and browse through it.

At one time, the printed catalogue in book form was the standard method used by public libraries, particularly those with closed access. The book form has several advantages: it is portable, it can be produced in multiple copies very easily, and it is convenient to use—the eye can scan a column of entries very easily instead of having to look at one at a time. It suffers however from one very important disadvantage: it is completely inflexible. The time taken to print it can mean that it is out of date when it is available, and though withdrawals can be shown by crossing out, additions cannot be shown at all. Supplements may be published, and from time to time a complete new edition, but this is not always a very satisfactory solution. The printed catalogue is then well suited to the situation where withdrawals are few, and additions are also a small proportion of the total stock. We find this situation in such large national libraries as the British Library (though even here it seems likely that the last complete catalogue has been prepared), and the special library concentrating on a particular subject, for example the Library Association. In both cases, the catalogue is of value to a much wider audience than can actually visit the library, and the production of multiple copies is of more importance than absolute currency (though of course the library producing such a catalogue will often maintain an up to date version in some other physical form for its own use).

There has thus been a conflict in the past between the convenience of the printed book-form catalogue and its inflexibility; this conflict can now be resolved by the use of the computer, which makes possible the regular production of up to date copies. During the 1960's a number of libraries started to use computers to produce their catalogues, in some cases as part of an overall computerization plan, in others to solve the problems mentioned above in relation to the card catalogue.[7] In London, a particular impetus was given to this by the local government reorganization in 1965; this left some librarians in the newly merged boroughs face to face with perhaps three separate catalogues to merge, using different versions of DC and AA1908 (the Anglo-American Code of cataloguing rules published in 1908, used in almost all British libraries prior to the introduction of AACR1967), and in some cases using different physical forms—different sizes of card, or card and sheaf! Book form catalogues produced from computer print-out became widely used, despite the disadvantages—inconvenient paper size, restriction to upper case letters, poor quality of print—and proved reasonably popular with library users. Some libraries used photoreduction combined with Xerox copying to give a more convenient size and better quality. However, the situation has been transformed by two developments which may be said to have introduced a new era in library cataloguing: Computer Output Microform (COM) and the MARC project.

COM[8]

The computer can now be used to produce output in the form of microfilm or microfiche. The process uses a matrix which may contain a large number of characters: upper case, lower case, and special symbols, depending on the price! It is considerably faster than the line printer, and the cost of the film is much less than the cost of the paper, because so much less is used; there are thus very considerable cost savings over line printer output, possibly of the order of eight to ten times.

A much more significant cost factor lies in the production of multiple copies. A line printer can only produce about four readable copies using carbon interleaved paper, so additional copies must either be produced by photocopying or by rerunning the computer, both of which are relatively costly. Multiple copies of microforms are by contrast cheap to produce once the master is available; the British Library Lending Division found several years ago that it was cheaper to make a copy of a report on microfiche to *give* to a borrower than to set up a loan record. It is thus possible for a library to make copies of its catalogue for distribution to all the locations where they may prove useful; this may be a catalogue of the holdings of the whole system, or of a branch library's holdings, depending on the decision of the librarian as to which will be most useful. Author, title and subject catalogues can be produced and updated at regular intervals; the old copies are simply discarded and replaced by the new cumulations. The capital cost of the readers must be set against these cost savings, of course, but these are becoming steadily cheaper, and modern models can be used in daylight, particularly with the white-on-blue microforms which are becoming standard for this purpose.

Despite some early scepticism on the part of many librarians, it is now clear that COM is to be the future medium of the library catalogue. Users who are accustomed to watching television no longer raise their eyebrows at having to use a microform reader, and this form of catalogue has won widespread acceptance among the public as well as among librarians.

MARC

In the early 1960's, a study was carried out of the feasibility of using computers to store and maintain the whole of the library's bibliographical records; the King report, as the final report on *Automation and the Library of Congress* came to be known, had a profound effect on thinking in libraries, even though many of its recommendations have yet to be put into effect.[9] One of the results of this study was the setting up of the MAchine Readable Cataloguing (MARC) project, which began in 1966 as a cooperative venture involving sixteen libraries other than the Library of Congress. Each library was sent computer tapes from which it could produce catalogue entries in a variety of formats, each entry containing similar information to that included on Library of Congress cards.[10]

The experiment, which lasted a year, proved reasonably successful, but revealed certain problems, of which the most serious was the limitations of fixed field working. This was discussed in chapter 3, but to recapitulate briefly, it involves allocating a certain fixed number of characters to each item in the catalogue entry, and though this is satisfactory for some parts, *eg* date of publication, it does not serve very effectively for the more important sections such as author and title. If the field allocated is long enough for the worst eventuality, then most of it will be wasted most of the time; if on the other hand it is made shorter, it makes cataloguing impossible for a proportion of the throughput—how great a proportion depends on how short the field is made.

One interesting and valuable finding of the project, which came to be known as MARC I, was that libraries could use the information on the tapes for a variety of purposes; although it was primarily intended as cataloguing copy, it was also used for acquisitions checking, SDI, and selection and ordering of materials. One library incorporated some of its own data in the same format. These results were all studied carefully, and in due course led to MARC II, a much more ambitious project with international implications.[11]

The MARC II project was seen as the basis of an international exchange of bibliographical data; any country that wished to cooperate would produce a full entry in the MARC format for all documents catalogued by its national bibliographical service, and this information would be made available on magnetic tape to any other country requesting it. This project implied a much more detailed description of each document than was usual; each individual item of information in the entry had to be identified and tagged, for two reasons. The first of these related to the use of variable fields rather than fixed fields, which had become possible with the introduction of third generation computers with their much larger programming capacity: the second was the necessity to be able to locate any particular piece of information so that the desired output could be obtained. One library might wish to use very full cataloguing, and would thus need to use most of the data; another might wish to use abbreviated cataloguing, and select only the author, title and date, and print these out in a format to suit their own purposes. Because it was intended primarily for the international exchange of bibliographical information, the format made provision for a variety of subject designations: not just DC and LC class numbers, but possibly also UDC, BC or any other classification scheme; not just LCSH but also PRECIS, or any other alphabetical system. The format is necessarily complex, but this is only to be expected in view of the demands that may be made on it.

After a year of experimentation, BNB went over to full MARC operation at the beginning of 1971.[12] The input to the computer is used to print the weekly issues and various cumulations by computer controlled typesetting; BNB cards can be produced in any required format: and the tapes are exchanged regularly with other national centres, so that each is building up a complete file of information. For example, the relevant entries from the BNB and Library of Congress tapes are used to produce *Books in English*. In Australia, the National Library has adopted the British MARC format, including PRECIS, so that the *Australian National Bibliography*, previously in dictionary form using LCSH, is now in the same form as BNB, a classified catalogue arranged by DC18 with author/title and PRECIS indexes. The MARC format has now been adopted by Canada, France, Germany and Denmark, although there are minor differences in the formats used, and work is in progress in an attempt to reach complete standardization.[13]

With the spread of the MARC format, libraries now have available a source of machine-readable cataloguing copy covering a substantial proportion of the world's book production. However, in some ways this is a two-edged sword; the Library of Congress format allows up to 2048 characters in each record, and is currently adding about 300,000 records a year; the Australian MARC record service (AMRS) has only been operational for a relatively short time, but it already contains nearly a million records gathered from various sources. Obviously, the sheer size of the available data base must present problems for the ordinary library, interested in only a small proportion of the total. This has led to the idea of centres which will process the records on behalf of subscribing libraries, and in effect produce their catalogues for them. In Britain, a pioneer in this field was Brighton Public Library, which carried out an experiment in collaboration with BNB; Brighton send BNB and ISBN for each title added to stock, and BNB use this information to select the appropriate records from the MARC file and produce an up-to-date catalogue in COM form monthly.[14] In Australia, the NLA is proposing to offer the same kind of service through its BIBDATA network,[15] while in the USA the Ohio College Library Centre is already providing a similar service to over a thousand participants, using the MARC data base and additional material in the same format.[16] OCLC would in fact appear to be a model of what will probably come to be the pattern for the future, with a central processing agency with very powerful computing facilities linked to any library that wishes to subscribe by on-line networks.

In a text restricted to the subject approach there is no space to go more deeply into the implications of the MARC project. BNB has already converted the whole of its files, going back to 1950, into MARC format, in connection with the LASER project,[17] while the Library of Congress has carried out a detailed study of the implications of retrospectively converting the whole of its very much larger catalogues in the same way.[18] Now that BNB is part of the British Library Bibliographical Services Division, it can surely be only a matter of time before we have the contents of both the Library of Congress and the British Library available in machine-readable form in this standard format. BNB now includes DC, LC, LCSH and PRECIS subject designations in its entries, using the PRECIS string as the basis, and also includes UDC numbers if these are available, as for example in UK Atomic Energy Authority reports. The prospects for the future are almost limitless, and many librarians have yet to grasp the full implications of this exciting new vista that is opening before us.

To conclude this discussion, we should remember that the physical form of the catalogue does not affect its content; what it does affect is the ease with which it may be used and produced, and its cost. The combination of COM and the MARC records can only serve to improve the standard of catalogue provision. Who knows? If we can do away with the card catalogue and replace it with something more acceptable to library users, they may even begin to use library catalogues!

BIBLIOGRAPHIES

Unlike library catalogues, bibliographies are normally printed and intended for wide distribution. Multiple entry is therefore almost unknown, because of its cost in a printed catalogue; instead we have a single main entry, which may range in detail from author, title and date to a full informative abstract, with various secondary indexes to give access through factors thought likely to be useful. We have exactly the same problems of arrangement and indexing as in library catalogues, but some other considerations also arise from the nature of bibliographies.

Bibliographies may be either current or retrospective. In the latter case, we select the entries to be included, and the list is then closed; we are thus in a position to be able to choose whatever method of primary arrangement we wish, and can opt for one which will reflect, as far as we can tell in advance, the needs of the potential users. Current bibliographies, on the other hand, are normally produced under some pressure to time; for example, one of the major reasons for the computerization of BTI and BNB has been to enable them to maintain a high degree of currency—in the case of BTI, published monthly, a maximum delay of seven weeks from the appearance of an article in print and its appearance in BTI. Under these circumstances, it may prove necessary to give up any pretence at helpful order in the main sequence, and use instead a chronological order of receipt. We find, for example, that in *US Government research and development reports* the main sequence is arranged by report number, *ie* order of receipt, while in other current bibliographies there is even less attempt to produce an order which is of some value in itself. (In the case of report literature, the report number is a significant identifying factor.) If the main order is an arbitrary one, the need for indexes becomes acute if we are to be able to conduct a search for a particular item or subject.

This need is related to the likely use to be made of a current bibliography. We have already pointed out in chapter 2 that there is a difference between bibliographies intended for current notification and those intended for retrospective searching; those intended for the later purpose will normally have more, and more detailed, secondary sequences than those meant for temporary use only. The contrast is exemplified by *Chemical titles* and *Chemical abstracts;* the first covers some 700 journals, and consists of a basic list showing the contents of each issue indexed plus a KWIC index based on the titles, while the second covers some 12,000 journals, giving a detailed abstract for each item, the abstracts being arranged under eighty rather broad alphabetical headings. Each issue has always had an author index, but to supplement this a subject index generated by machine manipulation of keywords taken from the abstracts is now included. For each volume there are cumulated author and subject indexes, the subject approach being catered for by very detailed indexes of the articulated type described in chapter 7; these have now been cumulated in ten or five year blocks since the beginning of CA in 1907. The extra effort involved in the compilation of the abstracts and their indexes means that the cost is very much greater—$2,900 compared with $60—but there is no doubt that the extra cost is justified if any considerable number of retrospective searches is carried out.

Many of the techniques described in earlier chapters have in fact been developed for use in abstracting and indexing services and other bibliographies. In particular, those techniques which lend themselves to computer manipulation are likely to be found in this kind of tool rather than in library catalogues, even though many of the latter are now being produced by computer printout, and with the coming of MARC many more are likely to be in the future. It is not always realized that the arrangement of, and indexes to, bibliographical tools are in essence exactly the same as comparable features in conventional catalogues, and should be subjected to the same kind of evaluation.

BOOK INDEXES

The indexing of individual books is usually also regarded as something quite separate from other kinds of indexing, but this is not the case. We can employ the same kinds of approach as we would with any other classified sequence, since the book itself presents topics in a systematic way; in particular, it is possible to use chain procedure to give a full and detailed index which is nevertheless within economic bounds, as examples taken from the index to the present work will demonstrate.[19]

If we consider a topic such as 'Dewey's use of notation' we might, taking into account the overall structure of the book, expect to find information on this in two major places: the first is the chapter on notation (chapter 10), the second the chapter on Dewey's classification scheme (chapter 17). If we turn to these headings in the index, we find under Notation (selecting the relevant headings):

Notation ch 10 164+
    applied to books by Dewey 278
   DC 18 287+

These three entries tell us that chapter 10, beginning on page 164, deals with notation in general, and may well be worth reading through, and that in addition there are two other pages we should turn to, the first for information on a particular innovation, the second on the notation of DC generally. If we now turn to the name Dewey in the index we find:

Dewey, M 277+
    notation: allocation 167
    integrity of numbers 198
    see also DC

If we follow the instruction *see also* and turn to DC, we find:

    DC ch 17 277 +
        notation
            distorting order 171
            in *Sears list* 376
            instructions for cutting 185
            mnemonic features 168
            not always expressive 172

By following up the various references we have found we can discover everything in the book relating to Dewey's use of notation, but some of the searching may be indirect. Under Notation we are referred to chapter 10, but are not told exactly where in that chapter we should look for information on Dewey, while if we follow up the references under Dewey and DC we may find ourselves reading through the whole chapter, or at least looking for section headings. The only entries under Notation which are specific are those leading us to places *not* in the general chapter; similarly, the entries under DC which are specific are those *not* leading to chapter 17. This is not entirely satisfactory, but the alternative soon begins to look impracticable if we consider that under Notation we should have to list all the significant contents of the whole chapter on notation, and under DC the whole contents of that chapter, in addition to all the other entries which are there already. In order to gain an economic advantage we sacrifice a degree of specificity, giving us a result which is consistent (even in its imperfection!) and is of reasonable size in relation to the book.

As in the classified catalogue, chain procedure forces us to rely to some extent on the use of headings within chapters, and on the systematic presentation generally. Since the index leads us to pages, not to cards, the scanning which may be necessary is not intolerable, and may in fact be useful in drawing our attention to, for example, other features of notation mentioned in chapter 10 but not necessarily associated with Dewey. The systematic collocation of distributed relatives which is one result of applying chain procedure does at least make sure that we can find everything on notation indexed under that heading, and on Dewey indexed under his name, even though the information we want may be scattered throughout the book.

In compiling indexes to individual books we are faced with a problem that we can sometimes avoid when indexing whole documents. We are obliged to formulate some kind of subject description; we cannot rely on a title provided by the author, because we are actually trying to pinpoint ideas *within* the text. To set against this there is the fact that, since we are only dealing with the work of one author, we can usually rely on the terminology of the book rather than have to worry about using a controlled vocabulary.

Book indexes are usually of the alphabetico-direct kind. Since we are indexing a systematic presentation—the text of the book—we will gain little from using a systematic index, which would itself need a further guide in the form of some kind of alphabetical sequence; we do however sometimes find examples of the alphabetico-indirect kind of index, which may be said to be open to exactly the same kind of objection. It is desirable to avoid *see* references within the index, for the same reason that they should be avoided in the index to a classified catalogue: they send us to a place from which we shall be sent on once again. In the present work, the problem of long lists of entries under synonyms, which is the reason for the existence of *see* references, has been avoided to some extent by indexing only the preferred synonym in full, but giving entries under non-preferred synonyms which lead to the preferred synonym but also to the main section in the text. For example:

Optical coincidence cards (peek-a-boo) 383 +

leads us to the main chapter, but also points out that the user may find more entries if he turns to the preferred synonym peek-a-boo:

Peek-a-boo 383 +
    compared with Uniterm 385
    use of punched cards

Once again we have an economy measure intended to keep down costs while nevertheless providing the user with complete access at the cost of a little more effort on his part. Since publishers are in general anxious to keep costs as low as possible, the author is obliged to use economical methods; like hanging, indexing a book concentrates the mind wonderfully.

SEARCH STRATEGY

So far we have looked at the theory and practice of the construction of pre-coordinate indexes, but we should also give some consideration to their use. How do we set about getting the best results from such an index? What procedure should we follow in conducting a search? We are faced with a question posed by a user, possibly not very well phrased, perhaps asking for something other than what is really wanted, but normally triggered off by some particular event or events. This question has to be resolved into an answer consisting primarily of a set of document descriptions identifying items which we think will provide the information wanted. The index or catalogue is the tool we use to perform this transformation, and, as in pantomime transformation scenes, the effectiveness with which it will do so depends on how well the machinery works and how carefully we have maintained it. (For some of our readers, no matter how we wave the magic wand of persuasion, the library catalogue remains obdurately a pumpkin.)

266

The first piece of advice may seem somewhat of a counsel of despair: it is that if we have some identifying factor, such as an author's name, it is easier to follow this up than to try to formulate a subject search. The whole success of such tools as *Science citation index* is linked to their avoidance of subject specification and their reliance on 'hard' information such as bibliographical references. Similarly, if during the course of a subject search it appears that a few authors are major figures in the subject field concerned, it is often worth following their names up in a largescale indexing or abstracting service such as *Chemical abstracts* or the French *Bulletin signalétique*, or even a biographical reference work, since this will frequently reveal items which it would have been very difficult or even impossible to find through the subject approach.

If we do not have any identifying factors to go on, we have to pursue our search through the subject. The first point is to establish as closely as possible the exact nature of the subject we are interested in, and this can be quite difficult. Users often find it difficult to express themselves, and in many cases they are not quite sure what it is they are looking for; they will however always have some kind of springboard or trigger which has led to their question, and we can work forwards from this. The *reference interview* is an important part of any information retrieval process,[20] and from recent research on the performance of the MEDLARS service it would appear that such an interview is best carried out without reference to any particular indexing language; *ie* the enquirer should be encouraged to express himself freely and if necessary at length, so that we have as complete a statement as he is able to give of what he wants, in his own words.[21] We can then think about translating these into the indexing language of our catalogues and bibliographies, or rather languages, since the likelihood of their all using the same indexing method is remote.

If the search is for a single concept, it will be relatively simple. We have to determine which terms have been used to denote that particular concept in our indexing language; in an alphabetical system this will probably be straightforward, but in a classified arrangement we may well have to determine the context in which a concept is required, since this will dictate the notation we shall have to look for. We can then turn to the sequence of subject entries and find what is filed under the appropriate heading. If we find nothing, then we have to consider which other headings to consult; in an alphabetical sequence we should look for *see also* references, in a classified sequence try searching round about the place we have found. In both cases we shall be looking for related headings, but whereas in an alphabetical sequence these will be scattered, in a classified sequence many of them should be juxtaposed. By moving back in a classified catalogue, *ie* in the direction of earlier class numbers, we can, if the scheme used is in accordance with the principle of inversion, come to a broader heading; by moving forward, in the direction of later class numbers, we may come to useful material at more specific headings. For example, if we are looking for information on potato blight in a catalogue arranged by UDC, the class number representing the subject will be 633.491–24. If we find nothing at this point, we can move forward to the more specific subject, treatment of potato blight, at 633.491–24–293.4; alternatively, we may move back to the more general heading potatoes at 633.491. If neither of these moves gives any useful information, we can move further back to even more general headings: control of plant diseases 632.93, fungus diseases of plants 632.4, diseases of plants, injuries etc 632. We may find material on fungus diseases of other plants, but it must be pointed out that, because this is a distributed relative, it will be scattered; we shall however be able to locate it positively through the index to the classified arrangement, though this is of course not making use of the arrangement itself to help us.

As we have pointed out earlier, it is not usual to make upward references in an alphabetical catalogue; this means that we shall not find any references telling us where to look for a more general heading. If we find nothing at Potatoes, blight (or Potato blight) we can obviously look under Potatoes or Blight, but there will be no further guidance as to headings more general than these. We shall have to turn back to the authority list (*eg* Sears) to find what more general headings might be worth trying, *eg* Plant diseases. If we are using a tool such as BTI, for which the authority list is not published, we may find some difficulty in selecting a broader heading, and it will often be useful to consult a classification scheme to establish what concepts we ought to look for.

At all times the needs of the user have to be kept in mind. If he is satisfied with one document, then we can stop our search directly we have found one relevant answer; we do not need to worry about whether there are other answers, or even whether one of them might not be better. If the enquirer is satisfied, we have achieved our objective. This does not mean that we should not advise him if we think that we can easily find something better; he may still be quite happy for us to stop searching. There will be other occasions when we shall have to discover as much information as we can, by making our search as complete as possible. This will normally involve some knowledge of the subject area, as well as skill in the use of catalogues and bibliographies, as is shown by some of the examples quoted by Vickery.[22]

Much of the research described in chapter 28 is concerned with the evaluation of indexing techniques, and an interesting outcome from this research has been the idea of ranking documents according to their likely relevance; instead of dividing the collection of documents into relevant sheep and irrelevant goats, we rank every document, from 'most relevant' to 'least relevant'. We can then cut off the search at any point to suit the enquirer, from (in theory at least) one document to the entire collection. It will be interesting to see how the results of this research can be applied to the practical library search situation.

SUMMARY

THE VALUE OF PRE-COORDINATE SYSTEMS

Pre-coordinate systems are basically one-place systems, but problems arise here from the necessity for a fixed citation or significance order. Multiple entry adaptations of the basic single entry solve many of these problems, while often giving rise to problems of their own, mainly through loss of specificity, which leads in turn to sequential scanning of large numbers of entries: low relevance. Post-coordinate systems avoid the need for the citation or significance order, and thus avoid the inherent problems; why then should we bother with pre-coordinate systems at all? The answer is twofold.

In the first place, there are situations where one-place systems are a practical necessity; we do not want to scatter copies of a document throughout the library to ensure that one is found at every possible entry point, and the single sequence of entries in a bibliography, dictated by economic considerations, is most helpfully arranged by a one-place pre-coordinate system. In a general library, it is often the case that we can find an order which suits the vast majority of users; in such cases, it is cheaper to spend more time on searching for the occasional difficult enquiry than to make multiple entries for everything 'in case'. Single entry helps to keep down the bulk of the catalogue and thus makes it simpler to use and less costly to maintain.

Secondly, pre-coordinate systems, whether single or multiple entry, present certain advantages at the search stage. It is possible for a number of searches to be conducted simultaneously; for example, with a card catalogue hold-ups only occur if two or more people need to use the same drawer at the same time. This is not the case with post-coordinate systems, where the number of searches that can be conducted at the same time is normally very limited. Pre-coordinate systems also lend themselves to changes in search strategy; we can follow up a narrower, broader or related subject without starting again from scratch, as would be the case with a post-coordinate system. The long term answer lies with the computer, which can accept single entry as its input, but give us the kind of access that is normally associated with multiple entry. Indeed, many factors in the catalogue description which are now not even considered as access points can be found through computer searching. Pre-coordinate systems, which have been severely criticised in recent years by advocates of post-coordinate methods, may yet be restored to their previous importance by the computer revolution.

BIBLIOGRAPHY

1 Foskett, A C: 'Shelf classification—*or else.' Library journal, 95* (15) September 1 1970, 2771–2773.

Hyman, R J: *Access to library collections.* Metuchen, NJ, Scarecrow Press, 1972.

2 Vickery, B C: *Techniques of information retrieval.* In this work Vickery goes much further towards integrating 'information retrieval' and conventional subject bibliography than any previous author. There are large numbers of excellent examples illustrating the problems.

3 Horner, J L: *Cataloguing.* Chapters 8–17 are essential reading.

Coates, E J: *Subject catalogues.* Chapters 7–13 are extremely useful, for those able to obtain a copy.

4 Shera, J H and Egan, M E: *The classified catalogue.* American Library Association, 1956.

Freeman, C B: 'Classified catalogue: a plea for its abolition in public libraries'. *Library Association record, 44* (10) 1942, 147–150.

Palmer, B I: 'Classified catalogue: a reply to Mr Freeman'. *Library Association record, 46* (4), 1946, 59–60.

Kennedy, R F: *Classified cataloguing.* Cape Town, Balkema, 1966.

5 With the introduction of PRECIS in 1971, BNB now has separate author/title and subject indexes.

6 Sharp, J R: *Some fundamentals of information retrieval.* Deutsch, 1965.

Foskett, A C: 'SLIC indexing' *The library world, 70* (817) July 1968, 17–19.

7 Maidment, W R: 'Computer catalogue in Camden.' *The library world, 67* (782) August 1965, 40.

Dolby, J L: *Computerized library catalogs: their growth, cost and utility.* Stechert-Hafner, 1969. A very useful summary of the advantages.

Hayes, R M and Shoffner, R M: *The economics of book catalog production*: a study prepared for Stanford University libraries and the Council on library resources, 1964. There have been a number of articles in periodicals in recent years on this subject, *eg* in *Library quarterly 34* January 1964; *Library trends*, July 1967; *Library resources and technical services, passim.*

Ganning, M K Daniels: 'The catalog: its nature and prospects.' *Journal of library automation, 9* (1) 1976, 48–66. (Report of a conference arranged by several American Library Association Groups.)

8 Spencer, J R: *An appraisal of computer output microfilm for library catalogues.* Hatfield, NRCd, 1974. (Reasonably enough, this is

available in microfiche form as well as hard copy!)

Stecher, E: *Catalogue provision in libraries of Colleges of Advanced Education*. Melbourne, Royal Melbourne Institute of Technology, 1975. Both this and the previous work contain useful bibliographies on this rapidly expanding subject.

9 Council on Library Resources: *Automation and the Library of Congress*, by D W King [and others]. Washington, USGPO, 1963.

10 Horner, J: *Cataloguing*. Chapter 32.

11 US Library of Congress, MARC Development Office: *Information on the MARC system*. Library of Congress, fourth edition 1974.

12 'British Library MARC services.' *Program*, 9 (2) 1975, 92–93.

13 US Library of Congress, MARC Development Office: *Books: a MARC format*. Washington, USGPO, fifth edition 1972.

MARC Task Force: *Canadian MARC* . . . Ottawa, National Library of Canada, 1972.

UK MARC manual: 1st standard edition. British Library Bibliographical Services Division, 1975.

National Library of Australia: *Australian MARC specification*. Canberra, NLA, second edition 1975.

14 Duchesne, R M and Butcher, R: 'BNB/Brighton Public Libraries catalogue project—"BRIMARC".' *Program*, 7 (4) 1973, 205–224.

15 National Library of Australia: *Bibdata network*. 1976.

16 Plotnik, A: 'OCLC for you—and ME?!' *American libraries*, 7 May 1976, 258–267 (includes a selected bibliography).

Hewitt, J A: 'The impact of OCLC.' *American libraries*, 7 May 1976, 268–275.

17 Bevan, A: 'The LASER retrospective catalogue conversion project.' *Catalogue and index*, (35) 1974, 1,4–5.

18 *RECON pilot project: final report* . . . by H D Avram. Library of Congress, 1972.

19 Langridge, D W: 'Classification and book indexing.' Chapter 15 in the *Sayers memorial volume*.

Langridge, D W: 'The use of classification in book indexing.' *The indexer*, 2 (3) Spring 1961, 95–98. *The indexer* is the journal of the Society of Indexers, formed in 1958 with the aim of improving standards of book indexing. The pages of this journal are essential reading for anyone wishing to undertake this particular form of indexing.

Collison, R L W: *Indexing books: a manual of basic principles*. Benn, 1962. One of the very few books on the subject.

British Standards Institution: *Recommendations for the preparation of indexes for books, periodicals and other publications*. BS 3700: 1964. A brief but useful manual.

20 Grogan, D J: *Case studies in reference work*. Bingley, 1967. Chapters 1 and 2 indicate some of the problems.

21 Lancaster, F W: 'Evaluating the performance of a large computerized information service.' *Journal of the American Medical Association*, 207 (1) 1969, 114–120.

22 Vickery, B C: *Techniques of information retrieval.* p 140–145.

CHAPTER 16

Introduction

So far we have studied the theoretical considerations which affect every system. In this section we shall be studying indexing languages that are widely used, to see how they measure up to the criteria we have established in parts I and II. The schemes will be discussed in the following order:

1) The decimal classification of Melvil Dewey (DC). This was the first library classification in the modern sense, and in it we see foreshadowed many of the ideas we have been discussing.

2) The Universal Decimal Classification (UDC). Originally based on the fifth edition of DC, this was the second major scheme to appear. It is possible to conjecture that this is the scheme most likely to succeed in the new computer age. Like DC, UDC is basically enumerative, but has many synthetic devices grafted on to its main core, which give it a great deal of flexibility. The full schedules of UDC are probably the most detailed of any classification scheme.

3) The Bibliographic Classification of H E Bliss (BC). This was perhaps the last of the great enumerative schemes, and though Bliss did include many synthetic tables he does not seen to have appreciated the importance of the principles of analysis and synthesis he himself used. The main class order of BC is probably the most satisfactory of the major schemes. Until recently, it has lacked a satisfactory financial structure, though the efforts of a committee of devotees have helped to keep the scheme alive. It now seems possible that a solution to this problem has been found, and the second edition is now in course of publication. This will mark a great advance on the first; in addition to the satisfactory main class order there is now a consistent use of facet analysis within main classes, and possibilities for synthesis will be found throughout the schedules. Despite this, one may still doubt whether libraries will feel sufficiently strongly attracted to the scheme to wish to change to it from one of the longer established schemes such as DC, though these may in theory be inferior.

4) The Colon Classification of S R Ranganathan (CC). This is the only completely synthetic general scheme and has many interesting and significant features, though from time to time one feels that the scheme is more of a testing ground for Ranganathan's theories than a practical means of arranging documents and catalogues.

5) The Library of Congress Classification (LC). This scheme is

unique in that it is intended for use in one library only, yet because of the significance of that library it is used in very many others. Here we have a scheme in which the compiler and the classifier are one and the same; the published version is almost completely enumerative, and the external classifier has to accept the scheme as it is or not at all. Another aspect is that it is intended for shelf arrangement, and to be complemented by an alphabetical subject catalogue (in practice, usually a dictionary catalogue) arranged according to

6) Subject headings used in the dictionary catalogs of the Library of Congress (LCSH). This is the most important general list of subject headings, and it is valuable to see how it fits in with the LC classification, and also how it measures up to our criteria.

7) Sears' list of subject headings is a much smaller work intended for the medium sized library. It is quite widely used in Britain in libraries using dictionary catalogues, whereas in the USA LCSH is far more popular.

In each case the object of the discussion will be to highlight what appear to be the significant aspects, particularly those concerning the background which affect the nature of the scheme. Little attempt will be made to go into the fine details of each scheme; it must be stressed that familiarity with these can only come as the result of a firsthand study. Similarly, facility in use will only come as the result of practice. However, it is hoped that the student who works through the following chapters will then at least be in a position to make good use of such firsthand examination, and will be able to estimate the overall importance of the individual schemes, both in isolation and in relation to each other. All of the schemes are here subjected to considerable criticism (though perhaps less considerable than that levelled by Bliss at all schemes other than his own!), but we have as yet nothing better to replace them; they are used in libraries all over the world, and librarians have to learn to live with them. We shall however be in a much better position to overcome their defects if we are aware of them and know what countermeasures to take.

It may be argued that it is not fair to judge the older schemes by criteria which did not exist when they were compiled. This is a plausible point of view, but it will not stand up to close examination. Classification schemes, like issue systems, are tools, devised to carry out particular tasks in the overall organization of libraries; we have to judge them in the light of how well they perform their set task today, not yesterday, and we must also bear in mind how well they are likely to stand up to tomorrow's demands.

Some features of the schemes, for example main class order, have been discussed in some detail already, and as far as possible this will not be repeated. Occasionally it may be necessary to reiterate a point already made in order to put it into a different context, but the discussion of the practical schemes should not be divorced from the discussion of the theoretical framework into which they fit.

The Subject Classification of J D Brown (SC) is not considered here, though a few references to it occur in the first part of this book. It is no longer a practical scheme, and many of its features do not stand up to any sort of examination. It is now of historical interest only, and is therefore excluded from this text.

It should perhaps be stressed that the length of each chapter should not be treated as being a reflection of the relative importance of the scheme discussed. DC, as is to be expected of a pioneer, introduced many new ideas, which are described in that chapter, though they now apply to most schemes; UDC, with its synthetic devices, requires more explanation and examples than does LC, which has, in effect, none. The main feature of CC, analysis into facets and notational synthesis, has become so much a part of modern theory that it is covered in detail in part II, and does not therefore appear in the description of CC, except insofar as that scheme has certain unique methods of applying it.

The two lists of subject headings do not involve problems of order (except in a very minor fashion); they have no notation, or index. There is therefore much less to describe when writing about them than there is in a classification scheme, but in practical terms the two Library of Congress publications, LCSH and LC, are of equal importance.

It does however appear that three of the classification schemes are more likely to survive than the other two. DC is very widely used in public libraries throughout the world. LC is growing in popularity, and during the 1960's a number of university libraries in the USA adopted it in preference to DC, all too often on grounds of administrative convenience; LC class numbers appear on all Library of Congress cards (and now on LC and BNB MARC tapes), whereas DC numbers only appear on a proportion of these records, and most university libraries acquire large numbers of books for which there is no 'ready-made' DC number. Another reason advanced was that there are fewer changes in LC than in DC, though this is in fact not true; there *seem* to be fewer because they are taking place all the time, whereas changes in DC come in chunks with each new edition. UDC is the scheme most widely used in special libraries in Britain and Europe. These schemes all have one feature in common: a powerful, adequately funded, central organization. It seems unlikely that any scheme which lacks this can survive, no matter how satisfactory it may be in theory.

BIBLIOGRAPHY
Readings for each scheme are given at the end of the text dealing with it. Students wishing to read further will find good accounts of the schemes in

Sayers, W C Berwick: *Manual of library classification*. Fifth edition edited by A Maltby. Deutsch, 1975. A brief account of each scheme will be found in

Needham, C D: *Organising knowledge in libraries*. Deutsch, 1971. An older work which contains trenchant criticisms of all of the schemes (except BC) is

Bliss, H E: *The organisation of knowledge in libraries*. H W Wilson, second edition, 1939.

CHAPTER 17

The Dewey decimal classification

Melvil Dewey was born in 1851, and at the age of five, we are told, he rearranged his mother's larder in a more systematic fashion; an early beginning for a career which was to transform librarianship! In 1872, at Amherst College, he obtained a post as a student library assistant, and in the following year put forward a plan for rearranging the library in a more systematic fashion. He was promoted in 1874 to Assistant College Librarian, and in 1876 published anonymously a work which was to have far-reaching effects: *A classification and subject index for cataloguing and arranging the books and pamphlets of a library*. When we consider that Dewey also became the first editor of the *Library journal* in 1876, was a founder member of the American Library Association in 1876 and became its first secretary, founded the first library school in the United States (Columbia University) in 1887, promoted the standard (12.5cm × 7.5cm) catalogue card, and in the course of a long life (he died in 1931) took an active interest, not only in all aspects of librarianship, but also in related topics such as spelling reform, we may realise the full stature of the man and respect him, even though the classification scheme which bears his name and is the best known of his contributions to librarianship may in some ways look inadequate for today's needs.

Dewey's first edition consisted of twelve pages of introduction, twelve of tables and eighteen of index, and its novelty lay in three main areas: the first of these was the assignment of decimal numbers to books rather than shelves: the second was the specification of relatively detailed subjects; the third, the provision of a relative index. It is possible to argue that these three principles were in fact a greater contribution to the progress of library classification than the scheme itself, despite its wide acceptance throughout the world.

RELATIVE LOCATION
Dewey did not introduce subject arrangement into libraries; many libraries had previously been arranged by subject. What he *did* do was to introduce the idea of relative as opposed to fixed location. It was the practice to allocate certain areas of the library to various subjects, arranging the books within each area by accession number and giving them a *shelf mark* which identified their exact position: room, bay,

tier, shelf, place on shelf. Once allocated, the shelf mark denoted the permanent home of a book in that library. New additions within any given subject area were invariably at the end of the sequence. Dewey introduced the idea of using notation for the subjects in his scheme, and *applying the notation to the books*, not the shelves. A new book on a given subject could be inserted into the middle of an existing sequence, in a position indicated by the notation; no longer was the end of the sequence the only place that new additions could be accommodated. The tool that enabled Dewey to do this was his decimal notation: the use of arabic numerals, arranged as decimals. As we have seen, there are certain problems arising out of the use of a pure notation, and Dewey did not foresee these; in places this inhibits synthesis in the scheme today, when subjects are far more complex than Dewey could possibly have envisaged a century ago. There is however no doubt that the simplicity of the notation has been an important factor in the widespread adoption of the scheme throughout the world.

DETAILED SPECIFICATION

Before Dewey introduced his idea of relative location, the number of subject groups into which the books in a library could be arranged was severely limited. It is not practical to leave large numbers of shelves empty so that books can be added at the end of a multiplicity of sequences. Once the idea of moving books at any particular point to accommodate additions is accepted, then it becomes far more feasible to specify more detailed subjects. Dewey listed nearly a thousand, and was criticized for giving unnecessary detail; the seventeenth edition, containing over 20,000 topics listed, was criticized for its lack of detail. Much of this change in attitude is due to Dewey himself, who made it practical for librarians to arrange their collections in a detailed fashion instead of in broad groups. The history of DC has, in general, been one of the provision of ever increasing amounts of detail to match the needs of documents which themselves treat of increasingly narrow areas of knowledge. By his adoption of the principle of detailed subject arrangement, Dewey made this progress possible.

RELATIVE INDEX

One of the objections raised to detailed subject specification was that it would be impossible to find any given subject in the complex systematic arrangement. Dewey overcame this problem by the provision of a detailed relative index, showing exactly whereabouts in the scheme any given topic was to be found, and listing synonyms also in some instances. Indeed, it seems that Dewey was if anything inclined to favour the index over the classification; in the second edition we find the statement 'an essential part of the Subject Index is the table of classification', and Dewey also wrote 'A clerk, if he only knows the subject of his book, by the use of the index can class just as the chief of the catalog department would class . . .'. While Dewey's enthusiasm for the index seems over-optimistic, there is no doubt that the detailed index was an important factor in the success of the scheme as a whole.

The three 'innovations' described here are now taken for granted in library classification, and it is important to remember that it was not always so. In his scheme Dewey foreshadowed many of today's developments, even if he did not always recognize them explicitly.

DECIMAL NOTATION

Dewey's plan was to divide the whole of knowledge into ten main classes, then to divide each of these into ten divisions, then each of the divisions into ten sections. In the first edition he suggested that in a catalogue it would be possible to continue the division to a fourth or fifth place, though he did not recommend this for shelf arrangement; for example, *geology of Mexico* might be given the number 5578. The point was used to introduce the book number: 513.1 was the first book on *geometry* 513. Another method of division after point was by size; 421.3.7 was the seventh book on the *philology of the English language* 421, filed in the third (*ie* oversize) sequence. Dewey recognized that decimal division might lead to some anomalies, but claimed that it worked in practice; his devotion to practice as opposed to theory led him in fact to distort the hierarchical structure of the notation in places, as is shown by the second edition of 1885, in which a number of changes led to the scheme which is very largely the basis of the latest editions.

In the second edition, Dewey claims: 'we have not sacrificed utility in order to force subjects on the decimal Procrustean bed'. However, when there are less than nine subdivisions of a subject, the 'spare' notation is used for further subdivision, while if there are more than nine, some—the 'minor' subdivisions—are all accommodated at one number. In this edition we find the three figure minimum notation, with a point following the third figure if further notation is used; we also find many of the synthetic devices which characterize the scheme. For example, whereas in the first edition the form divisions (common facets) were enumerated at the main class headings and could only be used there, in the second we find a table of form divisions which may be used anywhere. There are instructions to 'divide like' various other numbers; *eg* 016 Bibliographies of subjects, divide like the classification. Division by period under a country is possible, using a zero to introduce the notation. What is even more interesting is that we find in some places, notably Class 400 Philology, a very clear facet structure. Dewey does not appear to have seen the real significance of this, and it was left to Ranganathan some fifty years later to make explicit and generalized the principle which is implicit and restricted in this example; nevertheless, in this as in many other points, Dewey showed the way ahead at a very early stage.

INTEGRITY OF NUMBERS

Just as the notational pattern was set in the second edition for all succeeding editions, so also was the systematic arrangement crystalized. Dewey realized that a scheme which changed substantially from edition to edition would not succeed, because librarians would not accept it; change means reclassification, altering notation on catalogue entries and books, reshelving, refiling—a great deal of work. In the second edition Dewey announced that the structure of the scheme would henceforth not be changed; expansions would be introduced as necessary, but the basic outline would remain constant. This has certainly been an important factor in the success of the scheme, but has led to severe problems in keeping pace with the growth and development of knowledge. Dewey wrote: 'Even if the decisions reached were not the wisest possible, all practical purposes are served'; H E Bliss named this attitude the *subject index illusion*—the idea that the overall order is relatively unimportant, provided that each subject has its own little pigeonhole where it can be found.

It is in this edition that we first find Dewey's simplified spelling. Dewey, who was keenly interested in reforming the spelling of the English language, lost no opportunity of pursuing this particular hobby; christened Melville, he soon dropped the final le, and even went to the extreme of spelling his final name Dui for a time. The classification scheme reflects this interest from the second edition to the fourteenth, so that we find headings such as Filosofy and Jeolojy used throughout the text. Unfortunately, Dewey's simplified spelling did not take account of all the problems of expressing forty two sounds using only twenty six letters, and in consequence some of his improved spellings were ambiguous. This feature was dropped after the fourteenth edition.

THE FIFTEENTH (STANDARD) EDITION: A NEW APPROACH

Up to and including the fourteenth edition, progress was mainly in the direction of ever increasing detail, without much change in the basic structure of the scheme. There was one interesting innovation in the thirteenth edition, where a completely new schedule for Psychology was included at 159.9, in parallel with the earlier schedules developed in 130 and 150. Evidently this choice was not widely accepted by DC users, for it did not appear in the fourteenth edition, and the only sign of its existence to be found now is in UDC. Much of the detail in the fourteenth edition was unbalanced, and reflects a haphazard approach to revision, unhampered by any considerations of literary warrant; Medicine was developed in great detail in a schedule running to eighty pages, while Chemical Technology, including such topics as Food technology, Fuel technology and Metallurgy, was hardly changed from the second edition, with many important subdivisions completely undeveloped. It was decided to make a determined effort in the fifteenth edition to bring the scheme up to date, and to base the amount of detail in the various sections on a more realistic assessment of need; this edition, published in 1951, therefore introduced several novel features.

There are basically two ways to even out varying amounts of detail in different schedules; the first is to increase the amount of detail where it is lacking, so that all the schedules are detailed, while the second is to cut down the amount of detail that is given until all the schedules are equally brief. It was the second of these alternatives that was adopted; from the 31,000 subjects enumerated in the fourteenth edition, we find a slashing reduction to 4,700 in the fifteenth. Chemical technology was increased, relatively speaking, but this was achieved more by cutting down subjects such as Medicine than by increasing greatly the hitherto neglected subjects. The form divisions (Dewey's common facets) were reduced to nine, though this number was increased in the revised version. In History, 942 stood for England, including Great Britain, Thames River; apart from the period divisions, the only subdivisions here were 942.1 London, 942.34 Channel Islands, and 942.89 Isle of Man, though Scotland and Wales each had its own number and Ireland had two. The criterion stated was that sub-divisions were removed as being unjustified if no books were found to belong to them on the shelves of the Library of Congress, but evidently the reduction in the schedules went far beyond this. The objective seems to have been to have as few class numbers as possible longer than five digits; in view of Dewey's original allocation of notation, this decision was bound to bear hardest on the subjects such as Technology which had developed most since the original publication of the scheme.

In recognition of the changes that had occurred in the scientific and educational consensus since the second edition, many of the subjects found in the fifteenth edition were relocated from their place in the fourteenth edition schedules; in fact, of the 4,700 topics listed over 1,000 are in different relative positions. While the overall outline of the scheme remains the same, there are many changes in detail. In the tide of criticism which finally engulfed this edition, it was these relocations which were often blamed for its unpopularity, but one cannot help wondering if they would have caused so much dissension if they had not been associated with the overenthusiastic pruning mentioned above.

The index was also drastically pruned; so much so, in fact, that a revised index was published separately the following year, with one or two minor amendments to the scheme. The importance of the index to users of DC, shown by the need for this action, was evidently still not appreciated, for we find a similar state of affairs arising with the seventeenth edition, discussed at more length later.

On the debit side, then, lay several aspects of the fifteenth edition, but there were also some features on the credit side. The layout and typography was greatly improved, so that the structure of the schedules was clearly shown by a combination of indentation and typography; DC now compares favourably with any other general scheme in this respect. Dewey's spelling was dropped completely from both index and schedules, with the exception of the dozen words such as 'thru' which are now part of standard (American) usage. The terminology was revised to bring it too into line with modern usage, and the examples quoted were changed in many instances. Scope notes were a noteworthy feature; these were of two kinds, those defining the coverage of a given heading and those reminding the user of other related headings. To sum up, in presentation, the fifteenth edition was a tremendous success, but what it presented was not, and the sixteenth saw a reversion in some respects to the mainstream, while retaining those aspects of the fifteenth which had met with a favourable response.

As a matter of policy, the period of seven years was set as the publication cycle, and the sixteenth edition duly appeared in 1958. It went back to the detailed enumeration of the fourteenth edition, and re-relocated some topics back to their places in that sequence, but retained the improvements of the fifteenth edition, particularly those of presentation. Changes from the fourteenth and fifteenth editions were clearly indicated, so that librarians with materials classified by these previous editions could see at once where changes might have to be made. The index was published as a separate volume, and was relatively more detailed than that of the fourteenth edition; whereas that had 65,000 index entries for its 31,000 subjects, the sixteenth had 63,000 for its 18,000—more than twice as many.

The sixteenth edition also contained the first of the 'phoenix' schedules. It was recognized that certain schedules were so out of date that the only satisfactory way to revise them was to replace them with entirely new classifications, and in DC16 we find that 546 and 547, Inorganic and Organic chemistry, are completely new and bear no relationship to the previous editions. This means of course that anyone wishing to adopt the new edition has to reclassify their collections at those two points, whereas at many other headings it is possible to transfer with little or no change at all, and this has led to cries of anguish from librarians faced with extra work. However, it is one of the penalties we have to pay if we want to keep our arrangement in line with current thinking, and the task of reclassifying is made easier in that the old schedules are usually printed somewhere in the new edition together with tables of equivalents. In DC17 a new schedule for 150 and 130 General and special psychology appeared, while DC18 contains two, one for 340 Law, the other for 510 Mathematics. All of these revisions are valuable, with that for Law being perhaps the least useful in that it does not recognize division by country as being the primary facet and thus leaves us with one of the major disadvantages of the previous schedule unchanged.

The sixteenth edition did not satisfy some critics, notably those connected with the BNB,[1] but it was adopted by a great many libraries as being the first valid postwar edition. The appearance of the seventeenth edition[2] in 1965 was awaited with more than usual interest to see whether the trend towards modernization evident in the sixteenth edition would be continued. When it was published it was greeted with very mixed feelings; it showed a modern trend in that there were more facilities for synthesis than ever before, but on the other hand it dropped some of the good features of the sixteenth such as the cross-references between related subjects in different main classes.

This edition represents a considerable effort on the part of the editorial staff, particularly in two major directions. The first of these is the attempt to introduce, within the limits of the existing notation, a great deal more synthesis than was previously possible, and at the same time to remove some anomalies which had crept into previous editions, notably in the confusion to be found in some classes between subject and common subdivisions caused by the use of the single 0 (normally used to serve as a facet indicator for the common facets) to introduce some divisions of the subject for which there were no other places available. Two examples of this are to be found in the Social sciences, where Sociology, given the number 301, precedes the common subdivisions, and Engineering, where Engineering materials at 620.1 precedes these divisions also. The effect of this can be seen very clearly in the five year BNB cumulation 1955–1959, where such headings as Engineering—Periodicals at 620.5 can only be found with some difficulty after looking through several pages of entries relating to Engineering materials. Anyone not familiar with this peculiarity, or having only a slight knowledge of the scheme (enough to tell him, for example, that common subdivisions are to be found immediately following the main heading) would probably miss these entries for the common subdivisions of Engineering. In the seventeenth edition, the common facets, or standard subdivisions as they are now called (in previous editions the term 'form divisions' was always used), are always introduced by as many 0's as are necessary to distinguish them from subject subdivisions and to arrange them in their correct place, immediately following the heading to which they apply. In some cases this means as many as three o's (or even—very rarely—four), but it does achieve the objective, which is to return to the 'correct' placing of these subdivisions.

The second major effort was also in the direction of a return to 'correct' classification. Dewey adhered to the scientific and educational consensus (of Amherst College) for his main class order; that is, he classified primarily by discipline. Thus a work on the economics of the steel industry is classified with other works on economics in the social sciences, not with other works on steel in technology. A classifier who did not find a particular subject enumerated was instructed to place it with the nearest broader heading until such time as a specific place was provided; so a work on the sociology of the Jews would be treated as a general work on sociology, failing a specific means of denoting ethnic groups. However, though this method works well in theory—one can always use verbal extensions until the notation is developed—in practice there is a considerable temptation for the classifier to ignore the discipline and find instead a pigeonhole where what seems to be the important aspect of the subject can be brought out: in this example, there is of course a place for the Jews in Religion, so everything on the Jews tended to be classified there, ignoring the correct approach by discipline. Classification by attraction, as this is called, saves the classifier mental effort in that he does not have to place a subject in its right place without guidance from the schedules, but need only scan the index for a catchword to lead him to a convenient pigeonhole. To set against this is the fact that the purpose of systematic arrangement, to provide a consistent means of grouping related subjects, is completely defeated by this practice. In the seventeenth edition, a return has been made to Dewey's original principle of classification by discipline, though one can still find occasional departures from this, *eg* in 320 Politics, where 324 is Suffrage, 324.24 Voting including voting machines.

This problem arose because classifiers prefer to be specific, and will look for what appears to be a specific heading, even if it is strictly speaking incorrect, rather than choose the correct, but non-specific, heading. If the use of verbal extensions had been recommended to give the possibility of achieving specificity where it was lacking in the schedules, we may speculate that the problem of classification by attraction might never have reached significant proportions.

Other changes were made to bring the scheme into line with modern thinking. As has been mentioned, a completely new schedule for Psychology was included; Women as a social group were transferred to Sociology instead of Dewey's own placing in Customs and folklore (habits that have become traditional). Facilities for synthesis were greatly increased, though many of these were clumsy because of the basically enumerative structure of the scheme and its notation. The

Place facet was separated from the History schedules to give an 'area table' with the intention of making subdivision by this facet easier, and the common facets (Dewey's form divisions) were to some extent reorganized and retitled *standard subdivisions;* there was also a fairly detailed Time facet to replace the four divisions which seemed to have been included in earlier editions as an afterthought:

0901   Up to 500 AD
0902   500–1500
0903   1500–
0904   20th century.

A criticism which has been valid in the past is that DC is very much a Western-oriented scheme, with particular emphasis on the USA. Dewey seems to have assumed, as did Parson Thwackum, that Religion can only mean the Christian religion; other religions are, in past editions, largely neglected. In the sixteenth edition, about twice as many pages are devoted to the History of the United States as to the whole of Europe, including both world wars. In the seventeenth edition the editors have removed many of these examples of bias; non-Christian religions are developed in much more detail, and in many places it is possible for the user to treat his own country or religion as the preferred category and bring it to the beginning of the schedule.

THE EIGHTEENTH EDITION[3]

The publication of a new edition of DC is always an important event, and the eighteenth edition, published in 1971, is no exception. Perhaps the most significant point about it does not relate to the scheme itself, but to the use made of it; both BNB and LC have adopted it for their MARC records from the beginning of 1971, in the interests of international standardization. The scheme continues the developments seen in the sixteenth and seventeenth, with various changes intended to make the schedules easier to use. Instead of the 'divide like' device, we find instructions to 'add . . . to the base number . . .' followed by an example, *eg*

016   Bibliographies and catalogs of specific disciplines and subjects

Add 001–999 to base number 016, eg., bibliographies of astronomy **016.52**

The elimination of bias is carried a stage further by using a letter to permit the favoured category to be filed at the beginning of the sequence, *eg*

030   General encyclopedic works

.9   Historical and geographical treatment

Class encyclopedic works in specific languages in 031–039

▶ **031–039 In specific languages**
Class here specific encyclopedias
and works about them
Arrange by language in which
originally written as below; but if
it is desired to give local emphasis
and a shorter number to encyclopedias in a specific language, place
them first by use of a letter or other
symbol, e.g., Arabic-language
encyclopedias 03A (preceding
031)

The notation for Christianity 220–289 may be used for a different
'home' religion if preferred.

Perhaps the major development is the introduction of several more
tables of common subdivisions. From the single table of form divisions
in DC16, through the standard subdivisions and area table of DC17, we
progress to seven tables in DC18, not all of which are applicable everywhere throughout the main schedules.

Table 1   Standard subdivisions
Table 2   Areas
Table 3   Subdivisions of individual literatures to be added to base
          numbers in 810–890
Table 4   Subdivisions of individual languages 420–490*
Table 5   Racial, Ethnic, National groups
Table 6   Languages
Table 7   Persons

There are nearly 400 relocations, about half as many as in DC17; as
usual, these are all carefully indicated in the schedules. The new edition confirms the trend towards facet analysis and synthesis, though
the strain of fitting this into the existing framework results in some
problems and anomalies. On the whole, however, the editorial policy is
a satisfactory one, though whether the changes are keeping pace with
needs is a moot point. Certainly the scheme remains a very practical
one which will be used by a great many libraries.

THE SCHEME
The eighteenth edition is in three volumes, each of them substantial.
After a tribute to Melvil Dewey by his son, and a historical outline
forming the publisher's foreword, the first volume begins with the editor's introduction. This is an important part of the scheme, and must
be studied carefully by anyone wishing to use DC, for it is here that the
editor explains how the schedules and other features are to be used; it
also contains much sound advice on how to classify in general terms.
There follows a glossary, and an index to the preface, introduction and

glossary. After this comes the introduction written by Dewey himself for the twelfth edition; this again is worthy of careful study, for it sets out at some length Dewey's own views on classification in general, and his own classification in particular, though one may have a minor struggle with Dewey's simplified spelling.

The two introductions are followed by the seven auxiliary tables of common subdivisions. These begin with a page of brief notes explaining how they are to be used; then come the standard subdivisions, shown in summary form here:

-01 Philosophy and theory
-02 Miscellany
-03 Dictionaries, encyclopedias, concordances
-04 General special
-05 Serial publications
-06 Organizations
-07 Study and teaching
-08 Collections and anthologies
-09 Historical and geographical treatment.

There is some confusion here between bibliographical forms -02, -03, -05, -08, and common subjects -01, -06, -07, though some progress has been made in this edition towards tidying up these subdivisions. Some provision is made for phase relationships *eg* -024 Works for specific types of users, *ie* bias phase. There is a schedule for Time, rather more detailed than was provided in earlier editions but still rather inflexible.

In DC 17, -04 was left unused, its previous meaning of *essays* having been relocated in -08 (it had proved very difficult to distinguish between *essays* and *collections*). It has been reintroduced into DC18 to accommodate concepts which are common to a particular class but not to the whole of knowledge:

'This subdivision is reserved for special concepts that have general application thruout the regular subdivisions of certain specific disciplines and subjects; it is to be used only when specifically set forth in the schedules.'

An example can be found in Engineering:

620   Engineering and allied operations
  .001–.003   Standard subdivisions
  .004   General concepts
  .0045   Quality and reliability
  .005–.009   Other standard subdivisions

The object of this use of -04 is to avoid extra zeroes in the standard subdivisions. In DC17, if it was desirable to introduce a 'general special' facet, this could only be done by increasing the number of zeroes used to introduce the standard subdivisions; as has been seen, this could mean as many as four zeroes, *eg* Dictionary of public administration 350.0003. However, in avoiding this problem, the use of -04 introduces the problem of order; it means that these 'general special' facets will be filed in the middle of the standard subdivisions. In other words, notational convenience is dictating order, which can never be satisfactory, even if it does represent an attempt to minimize complaints by users distressed by long notation.

The standard subdivisions are followed by the Area Table. This was a new feature in the seventeenth edition, and the intention is to make synthesis clearer; previously it was necessary to manipulate the notation from the History schedules in order to specify Place, and because of the many subjects in the schedules with special provision for place division this became rather complicated. In addition to simplifying its application, the new schedule for Place includes many subfacets not found in earlier editions, eg -17 Socioeconomic regions and groups. Where no special instructions are given for its use at a particular point in the schedules, the Area Table notation is introduced by the standard subdivision 09. For both standard subdivisions and other tables the notation is shown as beginning with a dash. This dash is merely to indicate that none of these tables can be used on its own; the notation must always be added to the notation for the main subject, and the dash is not used as part of the final class mark.

The Area Table includes one interesting example of a relocation. In order to make room for extraterrestial worlds, Antarctica [formerly—99] has been transferred to —989, so that —99 can be used again, eg Venus —9922. Space in general is also included at —19.

Table 3 is for the subdivision of individual literatures. In DC17 the instructions in this class were difficult to follow, and the purpose of Table 3 is to make manipulation of the notation more simple and convenient. This table includes standard subdivisions in 01–07, collections in 08, and history, description and critical appraisal in 09, as well as specific forms in 1–8. However, for period divisions within any given literature it is necessary to turn back to the main schedules, where under English literature, for example, we find period subdivisions not just for English works from Great Britain but also for those written by authors in Asia, Australia, Ireland, New Zealand, South Africa (but not the American continent, which has a separate heading altogether). There is also in the main schedules a detailed table for Shakespeare at 822.33, which may be used to subdivide the works of any author, with appropriate modifications.

Table 4 is for the subdivision of those individual languages marked * in 420–490. Table 5 is for racial, ethnic and national groups, and Table 6 for languages. Table 7, Persons, is probably the most important of these new tables, and may be summarized:

01	Individual persons
02	Groups of persons
03	Persons by racial, ethnic, national background

04	Persons by sex and kinship characteristics
05	Persons by age
06	Persons by social and economic characteristics
08	Persons by mental and physical characteristics
1—9	Specialists

The latter heading is divided rather like the whole classification, *eg* persons occupied with psychology —15 corresponding to 150 Psychology.

There is a list of all numbers which have changed their meaning through relocations, those which have been discontinued, and the few three digit numbers which are not in use; in each case the classifier is given all the information he may require to adjust his own usage of the scheme.

The first volume concludes with the *Summaries*. The first summary lists the ten main classes:

000	**Generalities**
100	**Philosophy & related disciplines**
200	**Religion**
300	**The social sciences**
400	**Language**
500	**Pure sciences**
600	**Technology (Applied sciences)**
700	**The arts**
800	**Literature (Belles-lettres)**
900	**General geography & history**

The second summary lists the 100 divisions, *eg*

600	**Technology (Applied sciences)**
610	**Medical sciences**
620	**Engineering & allied operations**
630	**Agriculture & related**
640	**Domestic arts & sciences**
650	**Managerial services**
660	**Chemical and related technologies**
670	**Manufactures**
680	**Miscellaneous manufactures**
690	**Buildings**

The third summary lists the 1000 sections, *eg*

620	**Engineering & allied operations**
621	**Applied physics**
622	**Mining engineering & related**
623	**Military & nautical engineering**
624	**Civil engineering**
625	**Railroads, roads, highways**
626	

627	Hydraulic engineering etc
628	Sanitary & municipal engineering
629	Other branches of engineering

These summaries are a valuable aid to classification, and their use will often prevent classification by attraction, by ensuring that the classifier finds the correct discipline rather than a catchword in the index.

The second volume consists entirely of the schedules, preceded by a page containing brief notes on their use, and explaining certain conventions, *eg* the use of square brackets.

The schedules are carefully set out to show the various hierarchies and to define headings or illustrate their use. Examples are given to illustrate notational synthesis. Instructions given at a broad heading apply to more specific headings within that hierarchy, and it is therefore necessary to study the schedules carefully to establish exactly how to deal with composite subjects. At times, the classifier is referred to another heading to find out how to synthesize a particular piece of notation. For reasons which have been discussed in chapter 10, it is sometimes the case that synthesis is only possible at some headings within a particular class; in such cases, the asterisk * is used to indicate the headings where synthesis is possible.

The following examples will show some of the more important features of the schedules. Each of course represents an extract only from the schedules at that particular point, and is selected to illustrate a particular point. The numbers at the left hand edge are *not* part of the schedules, but refer to the notes following these excerpts.

1) **000**   **Generalities**
    001   **Knowledge and its extension**

SUMMARY

    001.2   Scholarship
    .3   Humanities
    .4   Methodology and research
    .5   Information and communication
    .6   Data processing
    .9   Controversial and spurious knowledge

    .4   Methodology and research
    .42   Methodology

2)   Derivation of basic principles, postulates, concepts

3)   Class surveys and appraisals [formerly 001.42] in 001.433

4)   Class methodology of a specific discipline or subject with the discipline or subject using "Standard Subdivisions" notation 018 from Table 1, e.g., methodology in linguistics 410.18; data processing and computerization in 001.6; mathematical methodology in 510

5)   .422   Statistical method [*formerly also* 311.2]

010   Bibliographies and catalogs
         Of books, other printed and written records, audio-visual records

6)   (It is optional to class here bibliographies and catalogs of reading for children and young adults; prefer 028.52)

7)   If preferred, class bibliographies and catalogs of motion picture films in 791.438

8) **350   Public administration   Executive branch**
Military art and science

9)   Use 350.0001–350.0009 for standard subdivisions of public administration, of executive branch

---

10) ▶   **350.001–350.009 The executive**
11)   Class comprehensive works in 350.003

▶   350.01–350.08 Specific executive departments and ministries of cabinet rank

---

▶   350.1–350.3 Government service [*formerly also* 350.4]

12)   [.4]   Government service
         Class in 350.1–350.3

  354   Other central governments
13)   .3–.9   National, state, provincial
14)   Add "Areas" notation 3–9 from Table 2 to base number 354, e.g., government of Canada 354.71;
15)   except for Germany add further as follows:
16)   0001–0009   Standard subdivisions
           001–009   Government service, specific administrative activities, governmental malfunctioning
                Add to 00 the numbers following 350 in 350.1–350.9, e.g., merit system 006
           01–05   Specific aspects of the executive
                Add to 0 the numbers following

350.00 in 350.001–350.005, e.g., cabinet 05

06   Specific executive departments and ministries

       Add to 06 the numbers following 350.0 in 350.01–350.08, e.g., ministry of foreign affairs 061

09   Special commissions, corporations, agencies, quasi-administrative bodies

       Add to 09 the numbers following 350.009 in 350.0091–350.0093, e.g., government corporations 092

17)   Unless other instructions are given, class complex subjects with aspects in two or more subdivisions of this table in the number corresponding to the one that comes last in 350.001–350.996

551   **Physical and dynamic geology**

18)   Lithosphere, hydrosphere, atmosphere

19)   Class here geophysics

20)   *For astronomical geography* see 525; *geodesy,* 526.1–526.7 *mineralogy,* 549; *petrology,* 552

.31   Glaciology

21)   Class here interdisciplinary works on ice

       Class a specific aspect of ice with the subject, e.g., ice manufacture 621.58

NOTES ON THE ABOVE EXCERPTS

1) A heading which is rather indefinite is often expanded by means of a summary giving an overall view which is difficult to get from the detailed schedules.

2) Where necessary, terms used in headings are defined.

3) Relocations are shown by means of the word *formerly* and the class number in square brackets, together with an instruction on the new practice to be followed. cf 12 below.

4) Instructions are given to class elsewhere if that is more appropriate.

5) Relocation from another number is shown by the words *formerly also* and the old class number in square brackets.

6) There are some alternatives in the scheme; the editor's preference is shown by the note in parentheses with instruction 'prefer'.

7) The converse of 6), showing a possible alternative for the classifier. The significance of the editor's preference is that it represents the number that will appear on Library of Congress cards, and in BNB.

8) The heading 350 includes in fact two quite separate classes,

Public administration and Military art and science. The scope of the heading is shown to reflect the hierarchy (350 includes 351–354 *and* 355–359)

9) Because of the number of facets and lack of facet indicators, the common facets are here introduced by four zeroes, in order to make sure that they file in the right place.

10) Centred headings are used where there is no single number which represents a single concept. In this particular case, the number which would include 350.001–350.009 is 350.00, which is not used by DC.

11) For this reason, a specific number has to be singled out to replace the missing inclusive number, in order to have a place for comprehensive works.

12) A class number which is not used in this edition because its content has been relocated is indicated by enclosing it in square brackets. cf 3 above.

13) Unsought heading showing a step in division.

14) Use of the Areas table.

15) Germany does not fit into the given pattern and is therefore enumerated separately, an example of the care taken not to force subjects into arrangements or subdivisions which do not fit them.

16) The various facets by which this topic may be subdivided are set out, with instructions on notational synthesis for each. Here again the lack of facet indicators makes synthesis somewhat complicated and the instructions, though clearer than those in previous editions, are still hard work until they become familiar.

17) It is not possible to synthesize notation for a multi-faceted subject, but we are given a table of precedence, *ie* citation order, which in general follows the principle of inversion.

18) Scope note.

19) Instruction to include a topic not obviously comprehended by the heading.

20) Cross-references lead to other parts of the schedules to assist the classifier in defining his subject.

21) Interdisciplinary is used here in a rather different sense from comprehensive, to take account of the increasing number of works which cross the artificial main class boundaries set up by any discipline-oriented classification scheme.

Because of Dewey's original allocation of the notation, this varies in length quite considerably. There is a three figure minimum, so that for the main classes and the 100 divisions the final 0's are retained, *eg* 600, 510. In a few classes this is not exceeded, *eg* 160 Logic, where the schedule bears a very close resemblance to the original of 1876; in others, *eg* 621 Applied physics, six figure numbers are common and many ten figure numbers can be found, for this section includes 'Mechanical, electrical, electronic, electromagnetic, heat, light, nuclear engineering'. These are all subjects which have developed since 1876, when Mechanical engineering sufficed as the heading. On the other hand, 626 is now unused, for the subject to which it was originally allocated, Canal engineering, has so decreased in importance that it no longer justifies a separate heading. The use of 9 for 'other' is well illustrated by 629 Other branches of engineering which includes:

> 629.1 Aerospace engineering
> .2 Motor land vehicles and cycles
> .3 Aircushion vehicles, Ground-effect machines, Hovercraft
> .4 Astronautics
> .8 Automatic control engineering.

While it has proved possible to accommodate all these subjects in 629, it cannot be argued that they are in the correct place in the schedules; they obviously are more closely related to Applied physics in 621 than to the subjects of Sanitary and municipal engineering in 628 with which they are in fact collocated.

In order to make the notation easier to use, a space is left after each three digits of a class number following the decimal point in both the schedules and index. This is purely for visual comfort, and is not an essential part of the class number; it is ignored in practice, *eg* by BNB, and has also been omitted from the examples given here.

INDEX

The final and not the least important part of the whole work is the *Relative index*. When the first and second editions of the scheme were published, Dewey stressed the importance of the index, as we have seen, and with the exception of the fifteenth edition, the indexes to the various editions have been well received. In the seventeenth edition an attempt was made to emphasize the importance of the schedules for correct classifying by restricting the number of index entries; many 'minor' subjects were not indexed directly but instead referred the user to a broader heading. This seems to have been the result of trying to graft an increased degree of synthesis on to a scheme which is basically enumerative; the editors were at great pains to point out that it was not possible to index all the composite subjects that might occur, and that it was therefore necessary to keep reminding users to consult the schedules. As we have seen, the index to a completely synthetic scheme makes no attempt to index any composite subjects; this is a reflection of the distinction between the index to the scheme and the index to the arrangement resulting from its application. In their efforts to stress this, the editors seem themselves to have missed the point at times. For example, Biophysics as an aspect of Biology had three index entries and a reminder:

Biophysics
  biology
    animals   591.191
    gen wks   574.191
    plants   581.191
    see also spec organisms.

These entries show that Biophysics is to be found in the Energy facet in Biology and its two main divisions Botany and Zoology, and that it may also form part of a composite subject with any individual animal or plant: *ie*, it is possible to combine the notation for foci from two facets. This is a useful reminder, but an adequate knowledge of the schedules and of the principles of synthesis make it superfluous. On the other hand, we have references such as

Hosea (O.T.) *see* Minor prophets

We turn to Minor in the index and find

Minor
    prophets (O.T.)
    gen wks   224.9

We turn to the schedules at 224.9, where we find

224.9   *Minor prophets
        For Hosea, see 224.6

Apart from the fact that this is apparently an example of special preceding general, there seems to be little point in making the user take this indirect route. The asterisk shows that some notational synthesis is possible, but this is shown also at the specific number for Hosea. Similarly, if we are interested in the biophysical effects of gamma radiation, when we turn to Gamma we find

Gamma
    rays
    biophysics *see* **Biophysics**

rather than a direct lead to the specific number. The bold face type tells us that Biophysics is further divided in the schedule (a very neat convention for indicating that a particular topic is not the final link in its chain of division) but a direct entry would have told us this too.

The index was very strongly criticized, and in consequence the editorial policy committee decided to produce a new index, based on the sixteenth edition, but taking into account any changes in the schedules or in the terminology. This revised index was distributed free of charge to all purchasers of the seventeenth edition, at the end of 1967, in the form of a new second volume.

The revised index was, as is to be expected, very similar to that of the sixteenth edition. It contains, very approximately, three entries for each place in the schedules, but avoids repeating information that can be gained by studying the systematic arrangement. The conventional use of boldface type has already been mentioned. Synonyms are reasonably well covered, though a comparison of the entries under Railroad and Railway(s) seems to show that more could be done in this direction. Foci from the standard subdivisions or area table are labelled by the use of abbreviations s.s.- and area-. The lack of punctuation, intended to improve the layout, occasionally leads to ambiguity, as for example

Depravity Christian
doctrine   233.2

where Christian is meant to qualify doctrine rather than depravity.

In the eighteenth edition, the editorial policy has been to combine the good features of both kinds of index as far as is possible. There are many cross-references to enable the classifier to find a topic even if it is not specifically mentioned in the schedules, that is, if a specific piece of notation can only be obtained by synthesis. As is pointed out in the editor's introduction, there has never been a time when every composite subject that could be specified by using the schedules has been indexed, a point that has been discussed earlier in chapter 11. Classifiers will still therefore find it necessary to use the schedules to ensure that they have the correct class number, and one that is as specific as the scheme will allow; in general, they will find that the index to the eighteenth edition enables them to find the right place to start looking in the schedules more easily than either edition of the index to the seventeenth edition.

The index volume concludes with the obsolescent schedules for Law and Mathematics, showing the concordance between old and new schedules, so that the classifier can see very easily how to bring his own usage up to date.

Taken as a whole, there is no doubt that the eighteenth edition has been a success. It represents a very real step forward in the transformation of a scheme that appeared at one time to be standing still. The two phoenix schedules have both been criticized, and seem to have pleased no-one. The schedule for Law still does not recognize jurisdiction as the primary facet, which is the method that would suit most law library users best, while the schedule for Mathematics appears to have been drawn up with the interests of the librarian, ignorant of mathematics but needing somewhere to place a book, in mind rather than those of the mathematicians likely to be making use of the arrangement.[4]

Many of the anomalies of classification by attraction have been removed, including the example of 'voting machines' quoted earlier in this chapter. A few oddities remain: for example, 'flying saucers' are classified at 001.94, as a subdivision of 'Spurious knowledge', which is a neat example of critical classification; although there is a perfectly good standard subdivision for 'illustrations', we find 'illustrations of dogs' and 'illustrations of cats' enumerated at 636.77 and 636.87 respectively, with an instruction not to use the standard subdivision, though no reason for this singularity is evident other than past practice; while the enumeration at 940.5316:

Children and other non-combatants
Pacifists
Enemy sympathizers

seems a little unkind, if nothing else.

The index is an improvement on that to the seventeenth edition, and the user can normally find what he is looking for without much difficulty. Here again though there are still some examples showing the bias built into the scheme by Dewey, for instance:

Sin
   religious doctrine
      Christianity   233.2
   Other religions see Man
     religious doctrines

By contrast, the entry
Laxatives
   pharmacodynamics   615.732

must surely be judged highly appropriate.

ABRIDGED EDITIONS

The aim of the full editions of DC has always been to provide as much detail as is likely to be necessary in the largest library, but for many years there has been a parallel series of abridged editions intended for small libraries not requiring this degree of specificity. The first abridged edition was published in 1894, and the latest, the tenth, was published in 1971, shortly after the full edition to which it is related. It is about one tenth of the size of the full edition—2,331 topics enumerated compared with 26,141—but has a very full index with some 20,000 entries. In general, the notation rarely exceeds five digits, with a few exceptions in such areas as Electrical engineering. The layout and typography correspond closely to the eighteenth edition, but the facilities for synthesis introduced into that edition are omitted in the interests of simplicity. This edition is quite widely used in school libraries, where its lack of specificity is not a handicap. In addition to this 'official' edition, there is also an *Introduction to Dewey decimal classification for British schools*, compiled by M Chambers and published by the School Library Association in 1961. A revision of this edition, which is now very much out of date, is being considered.

ORGANIZATION

Dewey was nothing if not practical, and he devoted some of his tremendous energy to setting up the Lake Placid Club, a 'self-help' real estate development which turned out to be highly successful. Profits from this went to the Lake Placid Club Education Foundation, which has provided the funds for the continuation of the scheme, which has itself been highly successful; some 30,000 copies of the sixteenth edition were printed, which makes it a bestseller by any standard. Over 20,000 copies of the eighteenth edition were sold within six months of publication, and its adoption as the standard for the MARC records has ensured its continuing success.

The Library of Congress started supplying catalogue cards to other libraries in 1901, and in the late 1920's discussions took place on the feasibility of including a DC number on these cards for the benefit of the many thousands of libraries using the scheme and buying the cards. In 1927 the Editorial Office was moved to the Library of Congress, and in 1930 a committee sponsored by the American Library Association started supplying DC numbers for LC cards. In 1933 the Library set up its own Decimal Classification Office to take over this function, and in 1953 was given the contract for the preparation of the sixteenth edition. In 1958 the Editorial Office and the Decimal Classification Office were merged, with the Editor given overall responsibility for both; the merged Office has now become the Decimal Classification Division in recognition of its increased status within the Library. With the backing of the Lake Placid Club and the Library of Congress, there is no danger that the scheme will collapse for lack of central organization.

At one time there was a considerable degree of hostility between the Editorial Policy Committee and the BNB, arising from the BNB's use of its own adaptation of the scheme. In recent years policy has changed somewhat, and there is a British Liaison Committee, with a representative on the Editorial Policy Committee. More recently an Australian Liaison Committee has been set up under the auspices of the Library Association of Australia. It is now possible for users in two of the major areas using DC outside the North American continent to comment on the existing schedules and on the proposals for the nineteenth edition. The Division is gradually increasing its coverage of the input to the Library of Congress; in fiscal 1970 about 75,000 titles were classified by DC, including all those in English published in North America and Australia, and this figure has now been increased to over 100,000. The fact that the editorial office and the classification office are now merged means that constant contact is kept with literary warrant, which is an essential part of the development of any valid scheme.

REVISION
The main method of revision is by the publication of new editions at regular intervals, at present seven years. In addition to this, users are

298

kept informed of new developments through *DC&: Decimal classification: additions, notes, and decisions,* now in its third volume. This originated in three series of *Notes and decisions on the application of the decimal classification* published by the Decimal classification office 1934–1955; the title was changed after the publication of the sixteenth edition, and the second volume began with the first issue, in Spring 1967, after publication of the seventeenth edition. The intention was to provide a regular service twice a year, but this was not adhered to in practice, and since the publication of the eighteenth edition issues have been infrequent. *DC&* provides a convenient method of publishing decisions likely to be controversial in advance of a new edition so that some sort of reaction can be obtained before they become irrevocable; for example, users were asked in the Spring 1967 issue to let the editors know if they had any views on the proposal to produce a completely new schedule for Law in the eighteenth edition.

One issue was devoted to the revised schedule for Great Britain arising from the local government reorganization in 1974; this schedule will officially be part of the nineteenth edition, but it is being used now to avoid the otherwise insuperable difficulties that BNB and other British users would face in classifying by the Area table.

AIDS FOR THE USER

The lack of guidance on citation order in early editions of DC and other classifications, together with the lack of suitable textbooks, led the American Library Association to publish in mimeographed form in 1914 a *Code for classifiers.* This code was revised by W S Merrill and published in 1928, with a second edition in 1939, and for many years formed an essential part of the classifier's equipment. While it is not tied to DC, and gives many examples from LC, it is arranged by and large in accordance with DC, and endeavours to answer such practical questions as: where should a work on geophysical methods of prospecting, especially for oil, be classed? The questions and answers are illustrated by examples of books quoted by the various libraries contributing to the collection. Merrill's *Code* was essentially a pragmatic work, which did not try to give fundamental principles but instead treated each case on its own. We may see here a parallel with the Anglo-American cataloguing rules, 1908 edition. A clearer understanding of the problems of citation order, together with more notes and instructions in the text, has made such a work less necessary nowadays, but to aid users of the sixteenth edition the Forest Press published in 1962 a *Guide to the use of the Dewey decimal classification; based on the practice of the Decimal classification office at the Library of Congress.* This work in effect gathered together all the scope notes, cross-references and instructions in the sixteenth edition, but did not add to them significantly; it therefore left unanswered many of the questions raised by that edition, and was for this reason a disappointment to many users.

The more frequent and detailed instructions on synthesis in the eighteenth edition are likely to make such a publication superfluous in the future, and there seems to be little point in merely extracting rules from the scheme and publishing them separately if they have to be used with the scheme.

An interesting development in recent years has been the publication of three programmed texts,[5] for DC16, DC17 and now the eighteenth edition. These enable the students to work through the schemes under supervision, and to gain sufficient firsthand knowledge to give them a reasonable appreciation of the structure and mode of use.

THE BRITISH NATIONAL BIBLIOGRAPHY AND ITS USE OF DC
Soon after the outbreak of war in 1939, the Library Association, looking ahead to the coming postwar days, commissioned L R McColvin to conduct a study of the British public library service. In his report[6]—one of the few really inspiring documents to have come out of librarianship—McColvin castigated the standards of cataloguing and classification he found, and emphasized the great need for a centralized service comparable with that offered by the Library of Congress. When discussions began on the practicality of this recommendation after the war, the difficulties soon became apparent; the obvious centre for such a service, the British Museum, did not use a classification scheme, and had its own code of cataloguing rules. The solution was to set up a new body, the Council of the British National Bibliography, which would have access to the books deposited at the BM, but would be a separate organization; it was to publish a weekly list, as being the most economic and useful way of disseminating the information needed, and DC was chosen as the classification scheme to be used to arrange the main part of the list, a classified catalogue. DC was the obvious choice in that it was used by the great majority of libraries in Britain; UDC was considered as being more suitable for a bibliography, but it was felt that UDC numbers, while valid for arranging the bibliography, would be of no use at all as part of a central cataloguing service.

The edition of DC then current was the fourteenth, already some years out of date, but it was adopted in the hope that it could be superseded by the fifteenth edition then in preparation. The BNB began publication in January 1950, giving a catalogue entry according to the AA code and a DC class number; no subject index was included, as it was assumed that libraries would make use of the index to the scheme. By the end of the year it had become clear that changes would have to be made if the BNB was not to fail for lack of support, and some important decisions were made. The first of these was that the scheme would be extended wherever this proved necessary by means of verbal extensions, which would form part of a complete set of feature headings; the second, that a detailed subject index would be included in each monthly or larger cumulation. The effects of these two decisions have been demonstrated and will not be repeated here (page 251). The fifteenth edition proved unacceptable, with the exception of a few of the relocations, and BNB continued to use the fourteenth edition while awaiting the sixteenth. When the latter was published in 1958, it was carefully examined, but the conclusion was reached that it did not offer enough advantages over the fourteenth to justify its adoption; it still had most of the faults of overall organization of the fourteenth edition, and had introduced some of its own. BNB decided to continue with the fourteenth, but to start using its own notation to replace the [1] in those places where it had developed a complete new extension to the official schedules; this plan was put into effect with the beginning of a new five year cumulation in January 1960, and the schedules were published in 1963.[7]

They fall into two main parts: the common facets, and extensions to subject schedules. The common facets are a complete revision of those in DC, separating the form divisions into the four facets we have seen to be necessary: bibliographical forms, common subjects, time, including history, and place. The place facet develops many of the subfacets which have now appeared in the Area Table in DC, but in addition brought Great Britain to the beginning of the political divisions as the favoured focus; a not unreasonable amendment in a national bibliography. BNB also makes provision for the four phase relationships: bias, which precedes the common facets, and influence, comparison and exposition, which follow them.

The subject schedules vary in size from a few minor amendments to existing schedules to complete new detailed schedules; a good example of the latter is that for nuclear science and engineering, in particular nuclear reactors; these do not appear at all in the fourteenth edition (the first nuclear reactor was built in great secrecy after DC14 was published) and are barely mentioned in the sixteenth.

In order not to conflict with official DC numbers and to avoid problems of copyright, BNB used lower case letters for their notation; this is used retroactively, so that composite subjects can be specified without the need for further facet indicators. For some time a conversion table was included in each issue to enable users to devise the standard DC number where this differed from BNB practice. The publication of the seventeenth edition did not make any fundamental difference to BNB practice, except for a few relocations, so that in effect BNB was using a mixture of DC15, DC16 and DC17 grafted on to the DC14 base; however, BNB did start to give a standard DC17 number in each entry as well as their own, which was used for the arrangement.

There has been a great deal of argument about the justification for BNB's usage of DC[8]. The editorial view has always been that DC on its own has proved to be inadequate for the arrangement of a national bibliography containing some 25,000 entries each year, and that all that BNB has done is to introduce detail and consistency, by applying the principles of analytico-synthetic classification. Critics claimed that DC was being distorted to satisfy the extreme views of an unrepresentative group, and that these distortions made BNB useless for one of its primary functions: the provision of centralized cataloguing copy. The editorial board of DC went so far as to advertise their dissociation from 'unauthorized' amendments, without actually saying where these were to be found. However, when we study the major changes introduced by the BNB's *Supplementary schedules* (more facilities for synthesis, revision of the common facets, provision of a more detailed place facet), we find an interesting parallel in the changes that were introduced in the seventeenth edition in 1965.

The introduction of the MARC project, with its emphasis on international standardization, has led BNB to abandon its own usage in favour of giving a straightforward DC18 class number, backed up by a detailed subject index using PRECIS, from the beginning of January 1971. The Library of Congress has also started to use DC18, and there is now constant communication between BNB and the Decimal Classification Division with a view to achieving transatlantic consistency.[9] In general, agreement is reached on a very high proportion of the class numbers used in BNB, though there are certain situations where the two teams agree to differ. One major factor here is the use by BNB of PRECIS, which is not discipline-oriented, to serve as the basis for, and alphabetical index to, DC class numbers, which *are* discipline-oriented. This has on occasion led to modifications in the DC schedules, for example the cancellation of one of two possible numbers for 'vibrations in physics', where the PRECIS string revealed the possibility of cross-classification. A second factor is the fact that BNB is a classified bibliography; this means that if a work deals with two subjects, there will be two entries in the classified file. In the USA, DC is used only for shelf arrangement, where a single place must be found for such a work, according to the rules set out in the Introduction to DC. A third factor is that BNB has built up a very considerable file based on its past practice, which is very carefully indexed; the Decimal Classification Division keep a shelflist file of usage, but do not have an alphabetical index to this. In some cases BNB decides to retain its past practice, where this is compatible with DC18, in the interests of consistency, even if this means some disagreement with the DCD practice. Because of the good relations which now exist between BNB and DCD, it has proved possible to continue in very close collaboration despite these divergencies.[10]

At one time it was thought that the nineteenth edition should be published in 1976, the centenary year. Practical considerations led to the abandonment of this idea—the preparation and publication of a new edition takes several years—and it will now be published in 1979 in accordance with the seven year practice. (Although BNB and LC started using DC18 at the beginning of 1971, it was not officially published until late in that year, having been brought forward from the normal publication year 1972. In fact, the use of DC18 by BNB before it was available to the library world at large caused a fair amount of critical comment!) The nineteenth edition[11] will continue in the same tradition as the seventeenth and eighteenth, but it is hoped to include phoenix schedules for sociology and the electoral process, the latter incorporating the present 324 and 329. Further phoenix schedules are in preparation for the life sciences, incorporating those sections of medicine which are sciences rather than technologies—anatomy and physiology; and for music, this latter being a facetted scheme prepared in Britain. However, at present it seems probable that these will not reach a state of general agreement in time for them to be included. The index will be on similar lines to that of the eighteenth edition, with continuing improvements to eliminate anomalies and to make it as easy as possible to use. One feature that is to be dropped is the use of boldface type to indicate topics that are further subdivided in the schedules; a survey in the USA revealed that very few librarians knew what it meant and fewer still made use of it. One may have one's doubts as to whether this is a reflection on the value of the device or on the teaching of classification in American library schools; however, it is not likely to cause any hardship, and it makes computer production of the schedules simpler.

Although the Editorial Policy Committee decided against the publication of the new edition to celebrate the centenary, they did mark the occasion by two other publications. The first of these is a facsimile reprint of the first edition, which will be extremely interesting in showing how the present structure, which seems in places to be completely out of touch with modern thought, has arisen from a structure which in its day reflected quite closely the then accepted structure of knowledge. The second is a history of the first eighteen editions by the present chairman of the Editorial Policy Committee, J P Comaromi, which gives a great deal of information on the personal factors which influenced the way in which the scheme developed.[12]

The nineteenth edition will be the last to be produced under the editorship of Ben Custer, who was appointed to the post in 1956. There is no doubt that the development of the scheme since that date, and in particular the healing of the breach between the DCD and BNB, has been directly due to his influence, and it was under his guidance that the scheme survived the flight to LC which was such a notable feature of the 1960's (a change which some librarians may now be regretting), and went on to its present secure position as the most widely used general classification scheme.

It is still possible to criticize the scheme, and faults have been pointed out in various places in this text. Nevertheless, no-one can doubt that Melvil Dewey and his Decimal Classification are assured of one of the more significant places in the history of library classification and the systematic approach.

BIBLIOGRAPHY

1 Coates, E J: 'The Dewey decimal classification, edition 16.' *Library Association record,* 61 (8) August 1959, 187–190.

Coates, E J: 'The decimal classification, edition 16: class 300.' *Library association record,* 62 (3) March 1960, 84–90.

2 Custer, B A: 'Dewey lives.' *Library resources and technical services,* 11 (1) Winter 1967, 51–60.

Metcalfe, J: *Dewey's decimal classification, seventeenth edition: an appraisal.* Bingley, 1965. 38p.

Several reviews of DC17 have appeared, *eg* Tait, J A: *Library review,* 20 Winter 1965, 220–224.

3 Matthews, W E: 'Dewey 18: a preview and report to the profession.' *Library Association Record, 73* (2) February 1971, 28–30. (Also in *Wilson library bulletin, 45* (6) February 1971.) Numerous reviews of DC18 appeared, in *Library resources and technical services, 16,* 1972, 383–93; Wilson library bulletin, *46,* 1972, 211–216; *Library Association record, 74,* 1972, 120–121; *Australian library journal, 21,* 1972, 117; and elsewhere.

4 Langker, R: 'Two phoenix, too ill-done: a critique of the eighteenth edition of the Dewey Decimal Classification.' (*In Outpost: Australian librarianship '73: proceedings of the 17th biennial conference held in Perth, August 1973.* LAA, 1974.)

5 Batty, C D *Introduction to the Dewey decimal classification.* Bingley, 1965.

Batty, C D: *Introduction to the seventeenth edition of the Dewey decimal classification.* Bingley, 1967.

Batty, C D: *Introduction to the eighteenth edition of the Dewey decimal classification.* Bingley, 1971.

6 McColvin, L R: *The public library service of Great Britain*: a report on its present condition with proposals for postwar reorganization. Library Association, 1942.

7 British National Bibliography: *Supplementary classification schedules* prepared to augment the Dewey Decimal Classification for use in the British National Bibliography and first introduced in January 1960. Council of the British National Bibliography, 1963.

8 Davison, K: *Classification practice in Britain: report on a survey of classification opinion and practice in Great Britain, with particular reference to the Dewey Decimal Classification.* Library Association, 1966. This report was sponsored by the Dewey Decimal Classification Sub-Committee of the Library Association's Research and Development Committee.

9 Bruin, J E: 'The practice of classification: a study towards standardization.' *Journal of librarianship, 3* (1) January 1971, 60–71.

10 Trotter, R: 'The use of Dewey in BNB.' *Catalogue and index,* (41) 1976, 3–6.

11 Custer, B: 'Dewey Decimal Classification: one hundred years after.' *Catalogue and index,* (39) 1975, 1, 3.

12 Comaromi, J P: *The eighteen editions of the Dewey Decimal Classification.* Albany, NY, Forest Press, 1976.

CHAPTER 18

The universal decimal classification

In 1894 two Belgians, Paul Otlet and Henri LaFontaine, conceived the idea of a 'universal index to recorded knowledge', to which people all over the world would contribute, and which would in its turn be available to all. An alphabetical arrangement was out of the question in so aggressively international an enterprise, and they turned their minds to systematic arrangement; what system could they use which would be acceptable on a worldwide basis?

Arabic numerals are used everywhere, and there existed a scheme already widely used in libraries in the USA which used arabic numerals as its only notation: the decimal classification of Melvil Dewey, then in its fifth edition. Otlet and LaFontaine wrote to Dewey and sought his permission to extend the detail in his scheme to make it suitable for arranging the kind of index they had in mind (although Dewey himself always stressed the importance of the classified catalogue, his scheme was then, as now, mainly used for shelf arrangement of books), and, having received this, settled down to classify several thousands of documents in time for the First International Conference on Bibliography, which they had arranged to be held in 1895. This conference welcomed the idea of an international index, and set up the Institut International de la Bibliographie (IIB) to act as the organization responsible. The development of the scheme went ahead, and in 1905 it was published as the *Manuel du répertoire universel bibliographique*, stressing its primary purpose. It already contained more detail than any edition of its parent scheme, and was adopted by many libraries and other organizations in Europe; indeed, it is still the most widely used classification on the Continent, where, in general, libraries have not seen the advantages of a common classification scheme and tend to use their own private schemes.

The Great War of 1914–1918 was a heavy blow for the Index, from which it never really recovered, and in the 1920's it gradually sank under its own weight, helped by a forced move from its previous quarters to make room for a trade fair. By this time, however, the scheme had become popular in special libraries all over the world, and a second edition was put in hand, with Otlet and LaFontaine to supervise the Humanities and Social sciences, and a newcomer, Frits Donker Duyvis, employed by the Dutch Patent Office, to supervise the Natural sciences. This second edition, published over the years 1927–1933, had the title *Classification décimale universelle*, an indication of the change of emphasis since the first edition. It was by far the most detailed classification scheme published up to that time, and its international nature was emphasized by the fact that the third edition, which started publication in 1934, was the German *Dezimal klassifikation*; this edition, interrupted by the war, was eventually completed in 1952, with an additional three volumes of index published 1951–1953.

Donker Duyvis became secretary of the IIB in 1929, and continued in that office until his enforced retirement (due to illhealth) in 1959; there is no doubt that UDC as we know it today owes a great deal to the tireless efforts of this one man (who incidentally continued to be paid by the Dutch Patent Office; either the Dutch are not very inventive, or their governments are more enlightened than most!). The IIB changed its name in 1931 to IID (Institut International de Documentation), and again in 1937 to FID (Fédération International de Documentation); neither of these changes altered its emphasis on the importance of the UDC (CDU or DK), but served rather to confirm and extend it. In Britain one of its most enthusiastic supporters was Dr S C Bradford, Librarian of the Science Museum Library; his book *Documentation*[1] is largely about UDC, he used it in the library, and he too started an index to recorded knowledge which eventually suffered the same fate as that of the IIB. (This is an interesting byway of British library history. Bradford built up a team of scientists to work on this index in a way that was unprecedented at the time, and the index quickly grew to considerable size; what it lacked was users. Too few people made their way to the library to make use of this invaluable resource; then, as now, information-seeking Mahomets want the mountain not merely to come to them but to be delivered to their desks packaged ready for use. By the time that the index had reached about two million cards it was no longer possible for the amount of effort spent on its compilation to be justified, and Bradford was obliged to abandon it. It is rumoured to be, at least in part, tucked away in one of the attics of the Science Library, a forgotten monument to a great but unsuccessful idea.) The first publication in English of any of the UDC was the work of Bradford, who published the abridged schedules used in the Science Museum Library with the title *Classification for works on pure and applied science in the Science Museum Library*, the third edition appearing in 1936.

In due course, the British Standards Institution became the official British editorial body, and publication of the full English edition, the fourth, began in 1943; unfortunately, like FID itself, BSI has always suffered from a lack of funds to prosecute this work, and despite the enthusiasm and hard work of the national committee, this edition has not yet been completed. The situation changed radically in 1967, when

OSTI made a grant to BSI to enable them to increase the scope and quantity of their documentation activities, including UDC; as a result of this, it now seems likely that the full edition will be available by the end of 1977 though some of the parts will by then be over thirty years old and badly in need of revision.

Other full editions in preparation include revisions of the German and French editions, and new ventures in Spanish and Japanese. The complete schedules are, of course, available on cards at the headquarters of the FID, but to publish them may mean translating into the desired language, and since most work is done voluntarily in the national committees, there is little access to the master copy. The lack of full schedules has, however, been overcome to some extent by the publication of abridged editions, now available in some sixteen languages. The first British abridged edition was published in 1948 and was based on the Science Museum schedules; the second edition, published in 1957, was more detailed, as well as being more up to date, and had a far better index, with 20,000 entries compared with the 2,000 in the 1948 edition. The latest abridgement is the third, published in 1961, and this is the edition most likely to be found in use. It was hoped to set up a regular revision schedule for the abridged English edition, but this has had to be postponed in favour of publication of the full edition.

An interesting venture was the publication in 1958 of the tri-lingual edition, BS1000B. The text in this is in three columns, German, English and French, and there are three separate indexes; the notation in the text is in a fourth column at the left, and applies of course to each of the three texts. A supplement to this has been published covering the years 1958 to 1968; this is in effect a supplement to all of the abridged editions, and can be used to update the English abridgement of 1961.

Two other methods of publication are used, the medium edition, of which the first to be published was the German;[2] as is evident from its name, this is intended to fall between the full and abridged editions, containing about 30% of the full tables, and to give enough detail for all but the largest collections. Work has now been in progress for some time on a 'Basic medium edition', to form the basis for all medium editions; this is now to be known as the International medium edition, and the German and English versions are expected to appear in 1977, with the French edition following shortly after.

The second of these other methods of publication is the special subject editions; these give detailed schedules for the area of specialization and abridged background schedules for related sections, and are now available in several subject areas, *eg* nuclear science, mining and metallurgy, and building. These editions are usually based on the practice of a large library system, *eg* the UKAEA or the Iron and Steel Institute, and are thus of considerable value in that they give the user

FIGURE 14: Comparison of Full, Medium and Abridged UDC editions.

Full English edition	Medium French edition	Abridged English edition
631.542	631.54	631.54
pruning and crown thinning	Soins aux plantes en cours de croissance	Tending and care of plants. Cf. 632
.1 Winter pruning	.542 Taille des arbres et des plantes	.542 Pruning. Thinning
.11 Theory of pruning	.1 Taille d'hiver	
.12 Methods of pruning	.2 Taille d'eté	
.13 Heading back	.3 Taille des plantes dans des buts spéciaux, par exemple pour donner une forme à celles-ci, pour influencer la croissance	
.14 Thinning		
.15 Notching		
.17 Time of pruning		
.2 Summer pruning		
.21 Pinching		
.22 Nipping off buds		
.23 Clipping		
.24 Notching and ring barking		
.25 Defoliation		
.26 Suppression of flowers		
.27 Fruit thinning		
.3 Cutting of plants for particular purposes		
.32 For shaping		
.33 For influencing branching		
.335 For promoting branching		
.34 For removal of infected parts or for combating parasites		
.35 For increasing blossom or leaf production		
.36 For promoting development of fruit, e.g. Cutting of palm leaves		
.4 Desiccation before harvesting		

309

some assistance which is not available from the ordinary schedules, in the form of scope notes, cross-references and instructions.[3]

ORGANIZATION
The way in which UDC and its revision processes are organized is so much a part of the scheme that it deserves special study. As has been mentioned, the FID is the body having the overall responsibility, which it exercises through its international committee on universal classification, on which all national member committees are entitled to be represented. Day to day control is vested in the central classification committee, FID/CCC; for many years this consisted of the editors of the full editions and the FID Secretary General, but in May 1965 the constitution was amended to extend the membership. Each member nation of FID may also have its own national committee, which will then have the responsibility for editions in that language; in Britain, the national committee is a subcommittee of the documentation standards committee of the British Standards Institution, and has editorial control of all English language editions of UDC.

In addition to these administrative committees, there are international and national subject committees; the international committees report to the FID/CCC, while the national subject committees report to the appropriate national committee. Work for these committees is voluntary, and it can be seen that the combination of voluntary effort and a complex structure of committees is not a particularly efficient way of getting things done: committees do not meet very frequently, business has to be transacted through correspondence, and most of the work of revision has to be undertaken as a sparetime activity by librarians who are usually fully occupied with their daily work. Only in recent years has there been more money available to finance the organization, and much of the revision of UDC has been undertaken within organizations, such as the UKAEA, which have been using the scheme and have been able to devote a proportion of their official library effort to its maintenance.

REVISION
Suggestions for revision normally come from users who find that the schedules in a particular subject are inadequate for their needs, either through lack of detail or through obsolescence. A request forwarded to the national committee, and through them to the CCC, may well result in the original requester's being asked to prepare a draft for comment! The draft is circulated to interested parties by the appropriate national subject committee, and when agreement has been reached it is forwarded to the international subject committee. If they approve, the draft is sent to the CCC, who study it carefully to see that it does not clash with any existing or proposed schedules; if it is satisfactory in

this respect, it is published as a *P-note*. These are provisional or proposed alterations, and lie on the table for four months, during which time any user of UDC may comment on them; if no substantive comment is received, the proposal is deemed accepted, and is entered into the master copy. Every year P-notes which have been accepted are cumulated into the *Extensions and corrections to the UDC;* this is itself progressively cumulated into series covering periods of three years. The first five series of *Extensions*, together with the German *Ergänzungen* (supplements used to bring those portions of the German edition published before 1939 up to date when publication was resumed), have been cumulated in six volumes. Series six to nine (part 1) have been cumulated into five volumes covering changes approved from 1965–1975. Because some of the schedules of the Full English edition are still to be revised from their original publication, and the latest Abridged edition is dated 1961, it is necessary to look in several different places to make sure that the most recent schedules are being used. To add to the confusion, P-notes may be issued in English, French or German, and it is the exception rather than the rule for these to be translated; so to use the *Extensions* or the *P-notes* it is useful to be trilingual.

As with any scheme, there is the conflict between keeping pace with knowledge and maintaining integrity of numbers, but since UDC is used by many scientific and technical libraries, and devotes much of its schedules to those areas, the conflict is if anything more acute than usual. One means of overcoming it is the 'starvation' policy. A piece of notation can be left unused for ten years, and at the end of this time can be reused with a different meaning; an example will show this. Prior to 1961 the schedule for Particle accelerators was found at 621.384.61 and 621.384.62; a new schedule was developed, using 621.384.63/.66 and leaving the previous numbers vacant. After ten years it will be possible to reuse 621.384.61 and .62, for example, to develop another new schedule for Particle accelerators. In science and technology the 'half life' of literature is only a few years, and after ten years any documents still classified at a vacated number can be reclassified or discarded; the same is not true, of course, of the humanities or social sciences, where the method is less likely to be successful.

The revision process in UDC is both a source of strength and a weakness. New schedules are drawn up by users who need them and are working with the literature of the subject; they are closely scrutinized by other experts, with the CCC to ensure that proposals are sound from the classification point of view. On the other hand, the procedure is slow and clumsy; it took some ten years for a proposal for a new schedule for Space science and astronautics to gain acceptance, and two years is almost the minimum. In fast developing subjects, a schedule may be out of date before it becomes official.

UDC was originally based on the fifth edition of DC, and though the two schemes tended to drift apart, there was for some time an attempt to bring them into line again, at least as far as the first three figures of the notation. In 1961, two studies of UDC commissioned by UNESCO[4] were published, which were highly critical of the scheme; much of the criticism arose from the unsatisfactory outline, still tied to a large extent to the outdated outline of DC. As a result of these studies, a decision was taken to try to carry out a large scale revision of the outline,[5] while still maintaining momentum on regular revisions of detail. The first move has been made: Language has been moved from its place between the Social sciences and the Natural sciences to Literature, where it occupies a place at the beginning of the schedule. This means that it will be possible to reuse the notation 4 in due course, and several suggestions have been made; the most useful of these seems to be to develop here those sciences, such as Communication, which may be described as bridges between the social and the natural sciences. This kind of large scale recasting will have to be done slowly if the scheme is not to lose its popularity with librarians who have large collections already classified, but it does offer an opportunity for the scheme to go forward rather than stagnate until it is completely overtaken by events. Unfortunately, it seems that this may indeed occur, as no schedules have yet been produced to fill the vacant notation, though a certain amount of work has been done, without as yet achieving the necessary international agreement.

THE SCHEME

In the absence of the whole of the full English edition, it is the abridged edition which is most widely used. The full edition is British Standard BS1000, while the abridged is BS1000A; BS1000B is the trilingual German-English-French edition published in 1958. The third abridged edition, BS1000A: 1961 is the one which will be considered here.

The scheme begins with a contents table which serves the dual purpose of indicating the contents and of showing the more important changes since the 1957 edition. After the foreword there is a brief note comparing DC and UDC; this is followed by the general introduction, which includes a brief historical outline and then describes the scheme as it is today. The 'auxiliaries', which will be described in detail, appear next, followed by an outline of the main divisions (corresponding to Dewey's second summary), and the schedules.

The overall outline of the schedules is similar to that of DC, but the notation is slightly different and the layout is rather less satisfactory. There is no three figure minimum in UDC, so Science is 5, Mathematics

51; in order to break up the notation, which tends to be rather long, a point is used every three digits, *eg* 621.039.532.5, if no other notational device is applicable. In general the notation is expressive and reflects the structure of the schedules, shown by choice of type face and indentation. The main outline is as follows:

0 GENERALITIES
1 PHILOSOPHY. METAPHYSICS. PSYCHOLOGY. LOGIC. ETHICS AND MORALS.
2 RELIGION. THEOLOGY
3 SOCIAL SCIENCES. ECONOMICS. LAW. GOVERNMENT. EDUCATION.
5 MATHEMATICS AND NATURAL SCIENCES.
6 APPLIED SCIENCES. MEDICINE. TECHNOLOGY
7 THE ARTS. RECREATION. SPORT, ETC.
8 LITERATURE. BELLES LETTRES. PHILOLOGY. LINGUISTICS. LANGUAGES
9 GEOGRAPHY. BIOGRAPHY. HISTORY

(NB This outline takes into account the transfer of Linguistics etc to 8, which took place *after* the publication of the 1961 edition.)

Because the final 0 is not used to give the three figure minimum, it can be used with some meaning, *eg*

8   Literature, etc
82   Western literature in general
820   English

Many of the schedules are short because they use synthesis for composite subjects; for example, the Literature schedule occupies less than a page. There are occasional cross-references, *eg*

523.78   Eclipses of the sun. *Cf* 521.8

and instructions, *eg*

632.4   Fungus and mould diseases. *By A/Z or as*
             582.28

Scope notes are rare, but are found in a few places. Terminology is good; the 1957 edition was thoroughly revised from this aspect and the terms used are up to date and represent correct usage.

However, if we had to judge UDC solely on its main schedules, we should have to admit that it compared unfavourably with DC; it is in the auxiliaries, which provide UDC with its means of synthesis, that the difference lies. There are several of these, which may be divided into two groups: the common auxiliaries, which may be used at any point in the main schedules, and the special auxiliaries, which have different meanings according to their context. The auxiliaries are, in fact, a set of common facets and facet indicators which enable us to synthesize freely where the more restricted notation of DC does not. Some of them are of fairly restricted application while others may be used frequently. They appear in the scheme in the following order:

313

a) Addition and consecutive extension signs + and /. The plus sign +
may be used to join the notation for two subjects which are commonly
associated but are separated by the scheme. Its use is not recommended, as it is difficult to index such combinations satisfactorily and
because they file before the first number on its own they may easily be
overlooked.

Example: 539.1 + 621.039 Nuclear science and technology.
In filing, the plus sign may be ignored if an entry is made under each of
the elements.

The stroke / (slash in USA) is used to join consecutive UDC numbers
to indicate a broader heading for which no single piece of notation
exists. As the basis for UDC left out some quite important steps of division, the / can be very useful; it too files before the first number on its
own.

Example: 22/28   The Christian Religion.
b) Relation signs : [] ::
The colon is the most widely used of the synthetic devices, but is an
imprecise weapon which may have several different meanings. It may
be used for phase relations:

Example: 635.965:697.38   Effect of hot-air central heating on
                           indoor plants
or it may be used to combine foci from different facets of the same basic
class:

Example: 635.965:632.38 Virus diseases of indoor plants
or it may be used to enumerate the foci within a facet by using the schedule from another class (as DC uses the divide like device):

Example: 635.965:582.675   Indoor anemones
The colon enables the classifier to make multiple entries very simply by
cycling, and is popular for that reason; however, it is so generally used
that it lacks precision, and it seems probable that if UDC is to be used in
mechanized systems, the colon will have to be replaced by a set of more
precise indicators.

In the introduction to the abridged English edition, square brackets
are suggested as a means of 'intercalating', ie changing the facet order
when the normal means of subdivision would be by means of the colon.
If we wanted to gather everything on particular plants together under
the general heading Horticulture, we might change the above example
to 635.9[582.675]65 to make the main facet the individual plant (in
this case anemones), with environment (indoor . . .) a secondary feature. This use of square brackets has never had the official seal of
approval of the FID, but this has now been given to another use, that is
as a form of algebraic grouping device. If we join two UDC numbers by
means of a + or :, and then follow this by, say, a form division, it may
be difficult to arrive at an unambiguous subject statement. By using
square brackets, the ambiguity can be eliminated:

Example: 01 + 655(05) Bibliography, and, Periodicals about printing
[01 + 655](05) Periodicals about Bibliography and Printing
22/28:294.3(540) Christianity in relation to (Buddhism
in India)
[22/28:294.3](540) (Christianity in relation to Buddhism)
in India
(Note that the stroke already performs a similar function; in the above
example, we read 22/28 as a unit before considering the relationship
implied by the colon).

As mentioned above, the colon is widely used as a 'pivoting' device
for generating additional entries by reversing or cycling. Once the
indexer has generated the original class number, cycling is a purely
mechanical task which can be done by a clerical worker or a machine.
There will, however, be occasions when we do not want to reverse because the second part of a class number is very clearly subsidiary. The
use of the double colon is now suggested as a means of indicating this
situation. If for example we did not think it necessary to make entries
in the Botany section for individual plants specified in Horticulture,
we could use the double colon thus:

Example: 635.965::582.675
This would *not* lead to an additional entry under 582.675.

c) Common auxiliaries of language =
The schedule for Linguistics may be used to give the notation for this
common facet, which applies rather as part of the description of a particular book than as part of the subject.

Example: 678(038)=82=20   Russian-English dictionary of rubbers and plastics.

d) Common auxiliaries of form (0. . .)
The bibliographical forms are listed in some detail in this facet, which
is generally satisfactory, though the use of (091) for Historical presentation may lead to a separation between general histories (091) and
works dealing with specific periods in which the dates are used without
the (091).

Example: 678(038)   Dictionary of rubbers and plastics.

e) Common auxiliaries of place (1/9)
This is well worked out, containing not only the usual political divisions but also several other subfacets of place. It may be used as a primary facet, though there is the possibility here of separating entries
which should be together if both the auxiliary numbers and the geography numbers are used. Relationships between countries may be
shown by the use of the colon within the brackets.

Example: 327(42:44)   International relations between Britain and
France.

622.33(73)   Coal mining in the USA.

Because the facet indicator shows the end of the notational element it may be intercalated, *ie* inserted into the middle of an existing piece of notation to change the facet order.

Example: 329.14   Socialist parties
329(42)14   The Labour party.

f) Common auxiliaries of race and nationality (=. . .)

These are based on the common auxiliaries of language and may be developed from the main linguistics schedule in the same way. This facet is obviously of rather more limited application than the others.

Example: 301.185(=924) The sociological importance of kinship among the Jews.

g) Common auxiliaries of time ". . ."

Dates may be specified in detail, and in addition many other aspects of time are listed, though their use will be rare. The complete flexibility of the time facet in UDC is very useful, and is superior to any other scheme.

Examples: "1969.12.25" Christmas day 1969.
820"19"   Twentieth century English literature
05"53"   Weekly periodicals.

h) Alphabetical and (non-decimal) numerical subdivision

There are occasions when it is useful to be able to name individuals, or to list items denoted by a number. This can be done, though care must be taken to distinguish such numbers from the ordinary subdivisions.

Example: 025.45 DC17   Seventeenth edition of Dewey

Names of individuals can be inserted in the middle of a piece of notation if this is appropriate; this is convenient in such subjects as Literature, where it permits the systematic arrangement of the works of an author.

Example : 820–2"15" Shakespeare 7 Hamlet 03 = 30 of which a complete restatement is: literature-English-drama-16th century-Shakespeare-individual works-Hamlet-translations-into German

Names may be abbreviated if this is preferred, *eg* Shakespeare might be denoted by his full name, or by Shak, or SHA.

i) Common auxiliaries of point of view .oo. . .

These may be used straightforwardly by adding them to the main number.

Example : 621.039.577.003.3 Nuclear reactors for power production, from the accountancy point of view.

A more sophisticated use is described in the introduction; this is to add precision to the colon by using the point of view numbers with it to give, in effect, an extended facet indicator. By this means the 'blunderbuss' effect of the use of the colon for a wide variety of purposes can be countered, and a more satisfactory arrangement results. The three different uses of the colon exemplified earlier might be expanded thus:

635.965:697.38 ⟶ 635.965.004:697.38
635.965:632.38 ⟶ 635.965.004.6:632.38
635.965:582.675 ⟶ 635.965.002.3:582.675

This device can introduce an element of order into what could become an unhelpful arrangement if the colon is used indiscriminately to introduce a large number of different kinds of subdivision.

A recent addition to the point of view numbers, not included in the 1961 abridged edition, is the use of .000.0/.9 to indicate the author's point of view. This is a rather different kind of approach, but one which could be useful.

Example: 162.6.000.335.5 Dialectics from the Marxist point of view

k) Another recent addition to the common auxiliaries is the use of -0, of which the only example so far is -05 Persons. In the 1961 abridgement, this facet was enumerated under 3 Social sciences, and instructions were given in a few other places permitting its use; since then, it has been transferred to the common auxiliaries, and may thus be used at any point where it is appropriate.

Example: 02–055.1 Male librarians.

A similar common facet for materials has also been adopted, but is so far only available in the *Extensions*.

The common auxiliaries may be added to any main number, and always have the same meaning; there are in addition three other facet indicators which form the Special (auxiliary) subdivisions, and which have different meanings depending on their context. These are the hyphen -, the .0. . ., and the apostrophe '. The - and .0 are used to introduce facets peculiar to a given basic class; in Engineering the - is the indicator for the parts facet, in Literature it introduces the Literary form facet, while the .0 is used in Electrical Engineering to introduce various facets, and in Chemical Engineering to introduce the Operations facet.

Examples: 62–31   Reciprocating valve gear parts
820–31   English novels
621.3.066   Electrical switch mechanisms
66.066   Clarification etc: chemical engineering

These indicators can only be used within the class in which they are enumerated. The apostrophe is at present used with a rather different meaning, in Chemistry and similar subjects, where it is used to indicate synthesis of material elements as well as notational.

Example: 546.33   Sodium (chemistry)
546.13   Chlorine
546.33'13   Sodium chloride (*ie* common salt)

However, the apostrophe is a useful symbol, and its use may be extended in the future. All of the symbols used to introduce the auxiliaries are available on a standard typewriter keyboard, but there are not many left now, and those that are available will need to be exploited as fully as possible.

NOTATIONAL PROBLEMS

It should be clear from the examples given and from a study of the schedules that the notation of UDC tends to be clumsy. The scheme is most detailed in science and technology, to which Dewey allocated insufficient notation in his original outline; in the third edition (the full edition in German, which is the latest to be published *in toto*), science accounts for 20%, technology for 52%, of the schedules, but of course they only have 20% of the notational base. In consequence the notation in these subjects is frequently long, even without the addition of any of the auxiliaries. Another source of undue length is the need to repeat the notation for the basic class when using the colon to combine foci within it, *eg*

621.384.6:621.318.3:621.311.6 Power supplies for the electro-
magnets of particle accelerators

in which 621.3 is repeated twice. This seems to be inevitable when synthesis is used with an enumerative base. For private purposes, *eg* within a library, base numbers can be replaced by a letter; the UKAEA use N instead of 621.039, for example. Since such devices do not have universally accepted meanings, they cannot be used outside the organization, but must be replaced by the full official notation. The complete revision of the outline which is under consideration might lead to a reduction in the length of the notation, as would a more consistent approach to synthesis within basic classes; however, UDC is intended to give detailed specification of detailed subjects, and it is not possible to do this without long notation.

CYCLING

Cycling is frequently used with UDC, where numbers may be combined by using the colon; when only two numbers are concerned the cycled entry is simply the reverse of the primary entry, and the technique is often known as *reversing*. An example will show the effects of the technique in terms of indexing and number of entries.

Let us suppose that documents are received on the following topics

Steel pipes for fluid distribution	669.4 : 621.643.2
Copper pipes	669.3 : 621.643.2
Aluminium pipes	669.71 : 621.643.2
Steel saucepans	669.14 : 643.352.3
Copper saucepans	669.3 : 643.352.3

Aluminium saucepans	669.71	: 643.352.3
Steel conductors (Electrical)	669.14	: 621.315.5
Copper conductors	669.3	: 621.315.5
Aluminium conductors	669.71	: 621.315.5
Welding of steel	669.14	: 621.791
Welding of copper	669.3	: 621.791
Welding of aluminium	669.71	: 621.791
Annealing of steel	669.14	: 621.785
Annealing of copper	669.3	: 621.785
Annealing of aluminium	669.71	: 621.785

Assuming that we have one document on each topic, and that we reverse colon combinations, there will be fifteen pairs of entries in the classified catalogue, thirty in all, and eight entries in the alphabetical index (ignoring for simplicity the entries for superordinate terms in the chain for each term, *eg* Metals):

Aluminium	669.71
Annealing	621.785
Conductors : electrical engineering	621.315.5
Copper	669.3
Pipes : fluid distribution	621.643.2
Saucepans	643.352.3
Steel	669.14
Welding	621.791

If we now add documents on brass pipes and brass conductors:

669.35.5 : 621.643.2 and reversed 621.643.2 : 669.35.5
669.35.5 : 621.315.5   621.315.5 : 669.35.5.

Another four entries for the classified file, but only one for the index:

Brass   669.35.5

Seventeen documents have now given rise to thirty four entries in the classified file, nine in the alphabetical index. But if instead of one we have thirty documents on each of these subjects, there will be the same nine entries in the index, but 1,020 entries in the classified sequence—a drawer full of cards. If we add another document on the annealing of copper pipes, this will give rise to three cycled entries in the classified sequence:

621.643.2 : 669.3 : 621.785
669.3 : 621.785 : 621.643.2
621.785 : 621.643.2 : 669.3

but will give no further index entries. There are thus two advantages to cycling: it makes the indexing simpler, and it means that any user can find all his information at one point in the sequence.

If we have the same fifteen subjects, but decide that instead of reversing we will have a fixed citation order and detailed indexing, the results will be rather different. Assuming that we adopt the citation order Product: Material: Process we shall have entries at the following points (note that these are in every case *one* of the entries we make in reversing):

621.643.2 : 669.14
621.643.2 : 669.3
621.643.2 : 669.71
643.352.3 : 669.14
643.352.3 : 669.3
643.352.3 : 669.71
621.315.5 : 669.14
621.315.5 : 669.3
621.315.5 : 669.71
669.14 : 621.791
669.3 : 621.791
669.71 : 621.791
669.14 : 621.785
669.3 : 621.785
669.71 : 621.785

Fifteen entries to be inserted in the classified sequence, but more than this for the alphabetical index:

Aluminium	669.71
Aluminium : conductors	621.315.5 : 669.71
Aluminium : pipes	621.643.2 : 669.71
Aluminium : saucepans	643.352.3 : 669.71
Annealing : aluminium	669.71 : 621.785
Annealing : copper	669.3 : 621.785
Annealing : steel	669.14 : 621.785
Conductors : electrical engineering	621.315.5
Copper	669.3
Copper : conductors	621.315.5 : 669.3
Copper : pipes	621.643.2 : 669.3
Copper : saucepans	643.352.3 : 669.3
Pipes : fluid distribution	621.643.2
Saucepans	643.352.3
Steel	669.14
Steel : conductors	621.315.5 : 669.14
Steel : pipes	621.643.2 : 669.14
Steel : saucepans	643.352.3 : 669.14
Welding : aluminium	669.71 : 621.791
Welding : copper	669.3 : 521.791
Welding : steel	669.14 : 621.791

Twenty one entries in the alphabetical sequence, compared with eight, but only fifteen in the classified sequence compared with thirty. If we now add documents as before, on brass pipes and brass conduc-

tors, we shall have the following entries:
classified sequence

  621.643.2 : 669.35.5
  621.315.5 : 669.35.5

alphabetical sequence

  Brass : pipes   621.643.2 : 669.35.5
  Brass : conductors   621.315.5 : 669.35.5

This will raise the number of entries in the alphabetical index to twenty three, with seventeen entries in the classified file. If however we have thirty documents on each of these subjects, we shall still have twenty three index entries, but only 510 in the classified file instead of 1,020. We have economized to the extent of half a drawer of entries; the penalty we pay for this is that we can no longer tell our readers that everything on their topic will be found in one place, unless it happens to be a Product. Furthermore, if we add a document on annealing of copper pipes, this will mean only one new entry in the classified sequence, but also one in the alphabetical index:

  Annealing:copper:pipes   621.643.2:669.3:621.785

Every new composite subject will give rise to additional index entries, even if the elements of which it is composed are already indexed.

Cycling is thus a partial solution to the problem of systematic scatter, but it tends to increase the bulk of the classified file; it also may have other shortcomings. To consider again our symbolic example ABCDE, let us assume that we add another document, this time on ABCD. The cycled entries for this will be as follows:

  ABCD
  BCDA
  CDAB
  DABC

If we interfile these with the cycled entries arising from ABCDE, we find that only at the primary entry are they certain to be found in the same place; at D, for example, the first will be under the heading DEABC, while the second will be under DABC, and these two entries could well be separated by a number of other entries at D. While it is true that cycling brings together at one place all the information to be found on any given topic, it does so at the cost of making us search the whole body of entries at that heading instead of being able to go to the specific ones we want. In this example, we shall have to scan every entry at D to make sure that we have found something on DA; to quote the detailed example worked out earlier, if we want to find everything on copper pipes, we shall have to search every entry under copper, because although there is a heading for *copper pipes*, it is not the same as the heading for *annealing of copper pipes*:

  669.3:621.643.2
  669.3:621.785:621.643.2

INDEX

The index to the abridged edition is, in general, very satisfactory; various examples have been quoted from it already, and will not be repeated. The terminology is good, synonyms are covered, there are cross-references; there are about 20,000 entries all told, for about 12,000 estimated topics in the schedules. Occasionally, however, the index can be confusing; in some cases it gives a number more detailed than can be found in the schedules (*eg* Ku-Klux-Klan is 363.2(73) in the index, 363 in the schedules), while in other cases the reverse is true. These are minor problems which will no doubt be removed in the next edition.

AIDS FOR THE USER

A very useful *Guide to the Universal Decimal Classification (UDC)* has been published by the BSI as BS 1000C: 1963; compiled by J Mills, this is not merely a practical tool for users of UDC, but contains also much on classification that is of quite general interest. Similar works exist in other languages, and further works are planned in English. There is also a programmed text,[6] similar to those for DC.

An additional help is that UDC is used by many bodies which publish, such as the UKAEA; these bodies often include a UDC number in their publications which can be of considerable assistance in libraries where the subject matter is covered is unfamiliar.

The main problem from the user's point of view, the lack of rules within the scheme, is only reduced to some extent by these aids. This flexibility has been cited as an advantage, in that the user can select for himself the way in which he will use the scheme in any given basic class (page 179), but there is no doubt that it is at the same time a source of danger. No classification scheme can work without rules; if these are not included in the scheme, they must be added by the classifier, otherwise inconsistency will be the result. This is also possible because of inconsistencies in the scheme itself; for example, fractional distillation appears in the operations facet in Chemical engineering as .048.3, so that fractional distillation of petroleum can be denoted 665.5.048.3— but it is also enumerated as 665.52. The classifier has to build up a set of rules for himself to avoid this kind of difficulty. The 'Code of practice' drawn up by the UKAEA for its own purposes later became the basis for the special subject edition in nuclear science and engineering; these editions often give the user more help than the standard abridged or full editions.

THE FUTURE

At one time it looked as though the future held little for UDC, but recent developments have changed the picture considerably. The editorial decision to try to revise the outline to bring it up to date over the next few years was a big step forward, though we have still to see the implementation of this beyond the transfer of Linguistics. However, of possibly greater significance is the research programme which was carried out in the USA under the auspices of the American Institute of Physics[7] to examine the feasibility of using UDC in computer-based information retrieval systems. The first problem faced was the lack of schedules for anything fuller than the abridged edition in English. The text of the German medium edition was made available, and much of this was translated; the results were fed into a computer, together with the text of the abridged edition and those parts of the full edition that were available, and from these a printout was obtained. It was shown that the computer provides a practical means of updating and printing out UDC schedules; it even proved possible to introduce typographical distinctions based on the length of the UDC number (though this has to be treated with caution, as the rather haphazard development of UDC has meant that the relative importance of subjects is not reflected by the notation). It also proved possible to produce alphabetical indexes to the schedules, though these could not always be used exactly as they stood.

Once a usable set of schedules was available, it was possible to get to the main point of the project, ie to see whether they could be manipulated in a computer file. It was found that in general the schedules could be fitted without much expenditure of time or money into an already existing system, the Combined File Search System, a set of programs developed by IBM and used by a number of information centres in the USA. The system was intended for use with a thesaurus of alphabetical headings, but this did not prove to be an obstacle. One problem was that UDC notation is in some ways not suitable for computer processing. The basic decimal notation presents no difficulties, but the arbitrary symbols used for the auxiliaries are a different matter. The colon is too ambiguous to be used conveniently (as has been pointed out earlier), and some of the other symbols have different meanings in different situations. For example, the equals sign = means one thing on its own, something rather different when enclosed by a parenthesis (= . . .); the point . is normally used for visual convenience only, without any significance, but when it is followed by 0 or 00 this is not the case. A new set of indicators was worked out using letters to overcome this problem.

Experiments were carried out using both batch processing and on-line operation. In both cases UDC performed quite adequately, and demonstrated that it could be used in such systems. The overall conclusions reached were on the whole favourable. Because it was not designed with computer manipulation in mind, it is probably not as satisfactory as a scheme devised specifically with this objective could be; on the other hand, there are some situations where UDC would have particular advantages, for example in a library with large amounts of material already classified by the scheme, or in a situation where documents were being processed for international use. The fundamental problem is the one which bears no particular relationship to computer processing, *ie* the difficulty of obtaining the complete schedules in up to date form. This is basically a problem of finance; if UDC were linked to a large library, and backed by adequate funding, as are both DC and LC, then it might be possible to be more optimistic about its future. There have now been three international seminars[8] on the possibility of using UDC in computer-based systems, and at each of these papers have been presented showing that this is a practical proposition, yet because of the weakness of the central organization nothing of any real consequence has resulted.

UDC could have served as the international switching language required by UNISIST; a user faced with a technical term in a language unknown to him could look it up in the appropriate edition of UDC, find the class number, then look this up in the edition in his own language. The tri-lingual edition has shown this to be possible for English, French and German, yet UDC was rejected by UNISIST largely because the Aslib team investigating the feasibility of using an existing scheme for the UNISIST switching language felt that in the case of UDC both the classificatory structure (based on Dewey's original outline) and the management of the scheme were inadequate for the purpose. Following that decision, the FID set up a small committee to develop the SRC described in chapter 13, and Geoffrey Lloyd, who had taken the place of Donker Duyvis as head of the Classification Secretariat, began working on the project, with the consequent loss of his services to UDC. Lloyd retired in 1976, after striving to keep the UDC afloat almost single-handed for some fifteen years at FID, having tried to do the same for the English edition at BSI for several years before moving to the FID. (The continued use of the abridged edition published in 1961 is itself a tribute to his efforts in producing it.) The FID Classification Secretariat has now reverted to a single man (Hugo Verschoor) with some secretarial assistance, and the funding remains totally inadequate for any kind of realistic maintenance.

The present author has written a detailed study of the scheme, concentrating on ways in which it might be brought up to date and made more effective.[9] Unfortunately, one can only be pessimistic about the future of the scheme if it continues along its present path. Proposals have been made to reduce the size of the CCC in order to make it a more practical body, but there is already an Executive Group CCC/EG, consisting of the editors of the Full editions, so it is difficult to see how making the full Committee smaller will help. What is needed is more money and—in this author's opinion—a transfer of responsibility from FID to a large and active library. There has probably been more discussion of UDC than of any other scheme (Lloyd described the revision system as 'hyperdemocratic'), but it remains discussion; without the means to translate words into actions, no progress will be made, despite the good intentions of those involved, and despite the fact that it has been amply demonstrated that UDC does indeed have the potential to remain the most important bibliographical (as opposed to shelf arrangement) classification available.

BIBLIOGRAPHY

1 Bradford, S C: *Documentation*. Second edition edited by J H Shera. Crosby Lockwood, 1953.

2 Dezimalklassifikation DK-Handausgabe: *Internationale mittlere ausgabe der Universellen Dezimalklassifikation* (FID 396). Band 1, Systematische Tafeln. Deutscher Normenauschuss (DNA) 1967. This edition has served as the basis for several other medium editions in, *eg*, French and Portuguese. It has also served as the starting point for the International medium edition, though it has of course required considerable revision and updating.

3 For an indication of the wide range of editions available, and the various associated publications, *see* 'Keep up to date with your UDC'. FID *News bulletin, 17* (12) December 1967, 137–138. Unfortunately this listing is not nearly as out of date as it ought to be, but a complete list can be found each year in the annual *FID publications*.

4 Kyle, B: 'The Universal Decimal Classification: a study of the present position and future developments with particular reference to those schedules which deal with the humanities, arts and social sciences'. UNESCO *Bulletin, 15* (2) 1961, 53–69.

Vickery, B C: 'The UDC and technical information indexing'. UNESCO *Bulletin, 15* (3) 1961, 126–138, 147.

5 See the articles by G A Lloyd (science and technology) and R Dubuc (Human sciences) in *Revue internationale de la documentation, 30* (4) 1963, 131–140.

6 Perreault, J: *Introduction to the UDC*. Bingley, 1969. Not everybody found Perreault's programmed text to their liking and an alternative is available.

Wellisch, H: *The Universal Decimal Classification: a programmed instruction course*. University of Maryland, School of Library and Information Services, 1970.

A useful account of the scheme is to be found in Mills, J: *The Universal Decimal Classification*. Rutgers, the State University School of Library Science, 1964. 132 pp. (Rutgers series on systems for the intellectual organisation of information, edited by Susan Artandi. Vol 1.)

7 Freeman, R R: 'Computers and classification systems'. *Journal of*

documentation, 20 (3) 1964, 137–145.

Freeman, R R: 'The management of a classification scheme: modern approaches exemplified by the UDC project of the American Institute of Physics'. *Journal of documentation,* 23 (4) December, 1967, 304–320. For other similar research see

Rigby, M: 'Experiments in mechanised control of meterological and geoastrophysical literature and the UDC schedules in those fields'. *Revue internationale de la documentation, 31* (3) 1964, 103–106.

Cayless, C and Ayres, F: 'The use of punched cards for the production of multiple copies of an alphabetical subject index in the UDC'. *Library Association record,* 66 (10) 1964, 439–442.

Ayres, F H *and others*: 'Some applications of mechanization in a large special library'. *Journal of documentation,* 23 (1) 1967, 34–44.

8 Seminar on UDC in a mechanized retrieval system: conducted by R R Freeman and Pauline Atherton, Copenhagen, 2–6 September 1968. *Proceedings.* Danish Centre for Documentation, 1969. (FID/CR report no 9.)

Seminar on UDC and mechanized information systems; conducted by Robert R Freeman, Frankfurt, 1–5 June 1970. *Proceedings.* Danish Centre for Documentation, 1971. (FID/CR report no 11.)

International symposium: UDC in relation to other index languages. held in Herceg Novi, Yugoslavia, 28 June-1 July 1971. *Proceedings.* Yugoslav Center for technical and scientific documentation, 1972.

Rigby, M: *Computers and the UDC: a decade of progress 1963–1973.* FID, 1974. Describes over 60 experimental or operational systems, and includes an extensive bibliography.

9 Foskett, A C: *The Universal Decimal Classification.* 1973.

CHAPTER 19

The bibliographic classification

Henry Evelyn Bliss devoted his life's work to the study of classification, and BC is the results of his efforts, tested over a number of years in the library of the College of the City of New York, where he was librarian. In addition to a number of articles in periodicals, he published two major works on classification: *The organisation of knowledge and the system of the sciences*, 1929, and *The organisation of knowledge in libraries*, second edition 1939. Yet despite his great erudition and powerful writings, his scheme has had little success in establishing itself as a major competitor to such schemes as DC, UDC and LC, which Bliss himself held in some contempt; in the fifteen years after it was finally published, BC was adopted by about eighty libraries, some of which have since changed to other schemes, and in many ways it is no longer adequate for today's literature.

This situation may change with the coming of the new edition edited by Jack Mills. However, at the time of writing (late 1976) none of the new schedules is available. The following discussion therefore relates to the existing edition prepared by Bliss; the new edition will be discussed in the section dealing with the future of the scheme.

Bliss considered that the most important part of a classification scheme was its order of basic classes, and BC demonstrates this emphasis very clearly. The three major principles on which Bliss based his order of classes: collocation of related subjects, subordination of special to general, and gradation by speciality, together forming the scientific and educational consensus: have already been discussed in part II. While in theory these ideas are sound, and are in accordance with the philosophical systems of such writers as Comte, in practice their application is not so simple, and in BC sometimes leads to unsatisfactory results, for example the separation of science (including some technology) from useful arts (the rest of technology) by the whole of the social sciences.

Although he recognized the need for some forms of synthesis (composite specification), Bliss was hostile to the idea of complete analysis and synthesis put forward by Ranganathan; his scheme may thus be regarded as the last of the great enumerative classifications, despite its provision of systematic schedules.

The scheme was first tried in outline before 1908, and first published in this form in *Library journal* in 1910. In 1935, in *A system of bibliographic classification*, Bliss published the scheme in much more detail; the reception of this venture led him to begin publication of the full schedules, which took him the rest of his life. Volume I, containing the common facets and classes A to G, appeared in 1940, volume II containing classes H to K, in 1946; these two volumes were revised and published in one in a second edition, 1951. Volume III, containing the remainder of the schedules (classes L to Z), appeared in 1953, as did the index, volume IV. Bliss died not long afterwards, leaving the scheme as his memorial.

THE SCHEME

Volume I–II begins with a long (188 page) introduction, falling in effect, into two parts; the first is a general introduction to problems of bibliographic classification, including such matters as 'the dictionary catalogue versus the classified', while in the second Bliss discusses the problems arising in the Natural sciences, which form the area covered by this volume. (NB The introduction is divided in the contents list into two parts, corresponding to the separate volumes rather than the theory/practice separation given here.) These discussions are valuable contributions to classification thought, and may be read with profit by any potential classifier, not merely those intending to use BC. The schedules section begins with two synopses, one concise, the other general; in these, Bliss sets out as a two dimensional matrix the 'order of sciences and studies'. It is the conversion of this synopsis into linear order that gives Bliss his order of classes, which is the next table; this is followed by tables of systematic and auxiliary schedules, alternatives, and literal mnemonics.

The systematic schedules are an important feature of the scheme. Bliss recognized that composite specification was necessary, and that there were two kinds; the first is the provision of common facets which may be applied anywhere, the second is the provision of facets appropriate to particular subjects. Schedule 1 includes bibliographical forms, some common subjects, *eg* Biography and History (separated here from period subdivisions, as in UDC), and one division for 'antiquated or superseded books'. Schedule 2 is for place division; there are two versions, one condensed, the other detailed. Schedule 3 is for division by language or nationality, while schedule 4 is for division by period. Other schedules numbered 4a, 4b and 4c, are found in the History schedules; 4a is for division of any country, 4b for division of any state, county or smaller unit, and 4c for division of wars, but there does not seem to be any good reason for not allocating them a separate set of numbers as they bear little or no resemblance to the common facet.

The other systematic schedules, 38 in number, relate to particular classes or persons, *eg* 13 for subclassification under any disease or disorder, 7 for special subjects relative to any personage. However, despite this provision Bliss found it necessary to enumerate many composite subjects which could have been adequately designated by synthesis, and in some cases allocated notation which was not in accordance with the systematic schedule. For example, we find in Religion P a systematic schedule, 16, 'for specification under any religion, sect, church or religious community' in which C is used to indicate Founder; but Buddha and Mohammed are enumerated, as PJC and PKC respectively, while Christ is also enumerated, but at PNB. This kind of redundancy is found in nearly every case where a systematic schedule is given; Bliss does not seem to have been convinced of the efficacy of his own devices.

Alternatives are of two kinds, alternative locations and alternative treatments. Though Bliss laid such stress on the educational and scientific consensus, on the grounds that it provided a universally acceptable order, he realized that for some situations it would be more helpful to give some other arrangement. For example, aviation and aeronautics can be treated as branches of science in Physics, or as branches of useful arts in Engineering and shipbuilding; international law may be placed in Law or in Political science following international relations; Religion in P and Sociology in K may be interchanged. Within a given class, it may be necessary to suit the arrangement to the users, and Bliss gives a number of alternative treatments; for example, biography of individuals may be scattered by subject, or gathered in one place; law may be similarly treated; the fine arts may be treated in a variety of ways; literature may be arranged in any one of four modes. This flexibility is valuable, though as usual once a decision has been made as to which method is to be adopted, the others must be deleted from the scheme; this is not as simple as it sounds, for in literature, for example, the different modes are largely enumerated as well, and it is not just a question of making a decision on synthesis. In some cases, for example the systematic schedule 1, there are so many possibilities that the classifier may feel that he has the task of constructing the scheme from scratch!

Following systematic schedules 1 to 4 we find the anterior numeral classes; these correspond to some extent with the common subdivisions in schedule 1, *eg* 6 is Periodicals in both. The intention is to provide for those books which for some reason or other are not primarily classified by subject, *eg* reading room collections, segregated books and historic books. Many classification schemes do not allocate any of their notation for this purpose, and using DC, for example, it is necessary to introduce some symbol to indicate that a book is in the stack rather than in the main sequence.

The schedules themselves are variable, both in their validity and in the amount of detail given. The biological sciences have been found acceptable, though they do not include any of the recent startling developments in those fields, but the librarian of a College of Art[1] found it necessary practically to rewrite the schedules to produce an arrangement acceptable to his readers. In physical science and technology, some of the schedules have an old-fashioned air; under illumination, we find incandescent mantles—a term long since disused—but we will look in vain for any trace of nuclear engineering (though atomic bombs find a place). Radio communication has a halfpage schedule (including a mention of television, which existed as a public service[2] some years before the publication of the first edition of these schedules), but when we find that this includes geiger counters as radio receiving apparatus, we may begin to lose confidence.

Classes M to O cover both history and geography of the various nations; there is not the separation that we find in DC between these two aspects of a country. The social sciences in general are probably the best worked out in the scheme, though the schedules for language and literature are also quite detailed. Bibliography and Library science reflect the changes that have taken place in recent years; almost as an afterthought we find a mention of mechanical devices for sorting and resorting index cards.

There are some cross-references, *eg* under Libraries—relations to the public—special services, we find a note: see also Adult education. Some scope notes are given, *eg* under Documentation we find: for the definition of documentation and discussion of the distinction between documentation and bibliography see the introduction . . ., while in some cases extended headings serve this purpose, *eg* under Industrial insurance we find: Casualty, accidents, health, illness, death; compensation; pensions; social security. Instructions for the use of the systematic schedules are given with each of these, but in addition special instructions appear at some headings, *eg* at United States—history—Civil war, we find: Schedule 4c is adaptable in part, but the numeral subdivisions should not repeat those for the period . . .

NOTATION

Bliss had strong views on notation, and criticized schemes such as UDC and CC for the complexity of theirs. He believed that brevity was an important quality, and set out to allocate his notation in such a way that most items would not need more than three digits. For the main schedules he chose capital letters, giving him a base of 26; to this he added the numbers 1 to 9 for the anterior numeral classes. Numerals are also used for the common subdivisions of schedule 1, while place subdivisions are shown by lower case letters. Thus although the main enumeration uses a pure letter notation, if synthesis is used the notation becomes rather mixed; furthermore, Bliss uses the comma, as an indicator to introduce the language and period divisions, both of which use capital letters, and mentions the possibility of using the hyphen - to show phase relationships (though only in a footnote). Some of the examples of composite notation provided are far from simple, *eg* TSQ,BbsvU; JTNbd,o6,L; admittedly, Bliss seems to have chosen some peculiar topics to demonstrate notational synthesis, but this kind of symbol can arise if the systematic schedules are used in almost any class.

Bliss does not seem to have appreciated some of the problems arising from synthesis. As we have just seen, the comma is used to introduce both language and period divisions, both of which have the same notation and are thus indistinguishable. As an afterthought, Bliss does suggest using 4 from schedule 1 to introduce the language divisions, and 3 to introduce period divisions, but this does not give a very satisfactory order.

The notation is not always expressive, and Bliss makes good use of this to achieve short notation for topics with considerable literary warrant, *eg* in the Place facet:

d	Europe, Eurasia, Eastern hemisphere
dw	western Europe
e	British Isles

and another example:

AK	Science in general
AZ	Physical science in general
AZD	Physics and Chemistry
B	Physics
C	Chemistry

However, we sometimes find examples where Bliss has allowed his wish for short notation for an important subject to outweigh considerations of correct order:

YE	Elizabethan, Jacobean and Caroline periods of English literature
YEN	Drama—Shakespeare's contemporaries
YEW	Caroline period
YF	Shakespeare

Here, in order to obtain a two letter base notation for the subject likely to have most literature, Shakespeare, Bliss has distorted the order. General works on the history of the Caroline period (1625–1649) will be separated from individual authors of the period, who will be found in YEI (Poets), YEP (Dramatists); between Shakespeare and his contemporaries there is a great gulf fixed; and altogether the schedule does not give any sort of logical order.

Though Bliss stressed that literal mnemonics are not important, he thought them significant enough to justify tabulation in the preliminary pages. Examples given above include dw for western Europe, YE Elizabethan literature; in the preliminary table we find NA North America, NB British America. These mnemonics are not so helpful as the consistent use of the same piece of notation which is found in UDC and to a lesser extent in DC

Some phase relationships are enumerated; for others, Bliss recommends the use of Y (special subjects) or the comma. The first of these transfers these relationships to a place after the subject subdivisions instead of before them, while the second leads to even more confusion. The use of the hyphen, suggested in the introduction as a possible substitute for the comma, is recommended by Mills to avoid at least some of the problems.[3]

Bliss occasionally used other symbols such as &, *eg* MN& Finland; he also uses lower case letters for some subdivisions in Chemistry, *eg* CIg Hydrogen peroxide. We also find the apostrophe in places, *eg* v' Africa, R'5 1905. Altogether, the notation can be quite complex; more serious is the fact that no guidance is given on the filing order of all these different symbols. For example, CIg is evidently (from the schedule) meant to file immediately after CIG and before CIH, but if the lower case letter denoted the place subdivision, as it usually does, this would not be true; for example, HYe Dentistry in England files before HYA, not between HYE and HYF. We are not told where HYe files in relation to HY,E Dentistry in the sixteenth century. In the article referred to already, Mills has suggested the filing order:
1/9; a/z; - ; , ; A/Z
with the use of 3 and 4 to distinguish time and language.

To sum up, the notation of BC is good, provided that only the basic symbols shown for enumerated subjects are used (though even here one has to enter the proviso that brevity is often simply a reflection of lack of detail). However, when any of the synthetic devices are used, the notation tends to become less satisfactory and the mixture of different kinds of notation is unhelpful. It is also clear that the allocation was poor to begin with; far too much of the base is given to History, far too little to Science and Technology. If the scheme is developed, before very long notation in the latter areas will certainly exceed Bliss's economic limit of three to four digits by a considerable margin.

OUTLINE OF THE SCHEME

1	Reading-room collections
2	Alternative for Z (NB similarity of symbol)
3	Select or special collection, or segregated books
4	Departmental or special collections
5	Documents or archives of governments, institutions, etc
6	Periodicals

7	Miscellanea
8	Collection of local, historic or institutional interest
9	Antiquated books, or historic collection

A	Philosophy and general science
AK	Natural science in general
AM/AY	Mathematics
AZ	Physical sciences in general
B	Physics (including some technologies)
C	Chemistry (including chemical technology)
D	Astronomy
DG	Geology
DQ	Geography
DU	Natural history
E	Biology
F	Botany
G	Zoology
H/HL	Anthropology (including human body, hygiene, physical education)
HM/HZ	Medicine
I	Psychology
J	Education
K	Sociology, Social science
L	Historiology, Ancillary studies, General history, Ancient history (including L9 Collective biography)
LY	Modern history (general)
M/O	Modern history (particular places) (including travel, etc)
P	Religion
Q	Social welfare, Amelioration, Women, Socialism and Internationalism
R	Political science
S	Jurisprudence and law
T	Economics
U	Arts in general, and useful and industrial arts
V	Aesthetic arts
W	General and comparative philology, Linguistics, and Languages not Indo-European
X	Indo-European languages and literatures, except English
YA	English language
YB/YN	History of English literature
YO/YT	English literature, collections
YU/YY	Literature in General and Comparative literature
Z	Bibliology, Bibliography, Documentation, and Libraries.

Bliss did not prepare all the schedules himself. In some cases he acknowledges assistance, for example in U, 'compiled with the assistance of J Albani' and T, revised by F W Weiler and J Mills; while in others it appears to have been Bliss who did the revising, for example P, where the schedule is based on one submitted to Bliss by J Ormerod.

Y, which is devoted by Bliss to English literature, may be used in other countries for the 'home' literature by changing round the basic notation and redeveloping the schedule. This would still leave Literature in general at the end of the sequence, of course. Q Social welfare is separated by the whole of History and Religion from Sociology in K; hardly the collocation of related subjects, though Bliss does permit us to interchange K and P to bring the two together.

INDEX

Some 45,000 entries appear in the index to BC; Bliss's own estimate was that only 5,000 of these represented synonyms, and that there were therefore some 40,000 topics enumerated in the schedules. However, we have seen from DC that thorough indexing can give as many as three times the number of index entries as topics enumerated. The index to BC must also be criticized on the grounds that it is not a 'correct' relative index; in many entries it repeats, in alphabetical order, some of the subdivisions found in the systematic arrangement, a practice which is both wasteful and misleading. For example, under the term Chemistry we find first a useful reference to see terms such as Agriculture for Agricultural Chemistry; useful, because we do not find an index entry for Chemistry, Agricultural. We then have an entry for Chemistry itself, leading us to C-CA in the schedules, and immediately followed by a reference, see also Biochemistry, which simply repeats the reference already given. We then have some ninety entries, of which only one does not direct us to a subdivision of C; we find an entry Chemistry—calculations in—Electrochemistry, but we do not find a similar entry Chemistry—Experiments in—Electrochemistry, though the two are side by side in the schedule, and there *is* an index entry for Chemistry—Experiments.

There are some odd omissions; for example, we search in vain for Sermons, but have to turn instead to Preachers, Preaching, which leads us to PXP, where we find sermons. There are also some errors, as for example the entry *Pearl, The*, Middle English poem, XBV, which should be YBV (XBV is Czech literature). These would almost certainly have been corrected for a second edition. However, to be an adequate tool the index would probably have to be completely revised and recast; at present it is too erratic to be reliable.

ORGANIZATION

As has already been indicated, BC was very much the work of one man, and this has had a number of effects. The first of these is the fact that Bliss himself typed out the whole of the schedules, which are reproduced from his typescript. The layout and typography leave a lot to be desired, particularly if it is compared with a scheme such as DC; Bliss had a very limited range of type faces and sizes available to him, and on some pages we find a slightly larger than usual type used for main headings, normal size for intermediate and slightly smaller than normal for subordinate divisions, together with italic for scope notes and reverse italic for cross-references. Some use is made of indentation to show subordination, but this too is limited. The overall effect is unpleasant to look at and difficult to use; this is accentuated by the fact that the schedules are not paginated (a convenient means of showing serial order which DC ignored till its fifteenth edition!), and the systematic schedules are only located by their relative place in the schedules, *eg* schedule 4a follows MC in volume III. The practising classifier is almost obliged to thumb index the volumes to make their use less time-consuming.

The large number of alternatives has also to be considered. Though these give the scheme a good deal of flexibility, they are usually set out rather clumsily from the point of view of the classifier wishing to select one, and only one, method, and the schedules often need considerable annotation to eliminate all the unwanted possibilities; such annotation, added to the already confusing typography, makes the scheme unwieldy to use. While none of these points affects the validity of the systematic arrangement, it must be remembered that classification schemes have to be used, and poor presentation and layout can actively hinder this.

ABRIDGED EDITION

Because of its close adherence to the educational and scientific consensus, BC has found most favour with educational establishment libraries, and for some years an edition for schools was mooted. This project finally came to fruition in 1967, when the School Library Association published the *Abridged Bliss classification*. Schools are less likely to be affected by the need for revision in science and technology, and more likely to find the overall order suited to their needs, than are most other institutions, and this edition could well be a success, though here again the need for revision will eventually arise.

THE FUTURE

The scheme was published by the H W Wilson Company, as were

Bliss's other books, and they continued for some years to publish the Bliss Classification Bulletin as a service to the profession. However, at the end of 1966 they decided to withdraw and to hand over the rights to the British committee, which was then reconstituted as the official supporting organization. Enough funds were gathered together to make it possible to appoint a research assistant at the Polytechnic of North London School of Librarianship to revise the scheme under the editorial direction of Mills, and work began in the middle of 1969. Before the change, some progress had already been made. We have already noted Mills's rationalization of filing order in BC; in September 1964[4], he proposed a method of keeping at least some of the schedules up to date, which was to use the *BNB supplementary schedules* wherever appropriate, by simply changing the lowercase notation to uppercase. This has provided several new schedules for the revised edition, and substantial progress has been made in working out others along the same lines.[5]

At one time it was hoped that the new edition would be published in two volumes in 1973, but this proved impossible, and it began to seem that the publication would begin to parallel the publication of the Full English edition of UDC, with its ever-postponed completion date. However, in 1975 the Bliss Classification Association (BCA), the committee of British supporters referred to above, decided to publish the scheme in parts, beginning in 1976 with the Introductory volume and classes J (Education), P (Religion) and V (Fine art), and completing the programme within three years.[6] The twenty parts show the same order of main classes as the original scheme, with the exception of Z (Bibliography and library science), reflecting the great care with which Bliss chose his overall order. We have already pointed out the startling resemblance between this and the published outline of the 'new' BSO being prepared for UNISIST, and the work done by the CRG on the order of entities for their new scheme also gave very similar results. It is evident that in this part of his scheme at least Bliss prepared a foundation which has yet to be bettered.

The twenty parts are listed as follows:

1) Introductory volume, with full instructions on use, a full outline of the whole scheme, and the common facets for Place, Time etc

2) Classes 1/9 Generalia, including Communication and Library and information science. (In the original scheme 2 was an alternative to Z for the latter, a sensible move in the days when class numbers were lettered on to the backs of books by hand)

3) Class A Philosophy, Logic, Mathematics, Statistics

4) Class B Physics and Applied physics

5) Class C Chemistry, Materials technology

6) Class D Astronomy and space science, Earth sciences including Geography

7) Classes E/G Biology, Botany, Zoology
8) Classes H/I Health sciences, Psychology (E/I in effect are the Biological sciences, B/D the Physical sciences)
9) Class J Education
10) Class K Sociology, Customs, Folklore, Ethnography
11) Classes L/O History
12) Class P Religion (alternatively, if Religion is thought to be more akin to the Humanities than the Social sciences, it may be classed at Z)
13) Classes Q/S Social studies, including Social welfare, Politics and Law
14) Class T Economics, Management
15) Classes UA/UD Agriculture
16) Classes UE/UN Civil engineering
17) Classes UO/UW Industrial, Production and Mechanical engineering (alternatively, *all* technology, including Applied Physics and Materials engineering, may be classed in U)
18) Class V Fine art, including Music
19) Class W/Y Literature and Language
20) Alphabetical index

TABLE 13: *Proposed publication patterns for the revised BC*

Each class is worked out on strict analytico-synthetic principles, and will have its own index; both these and the final complete index will be compiled on chain indexing principles, so that each significant term will be an access point. They will be indexes for the classifier, not the user, and it will be necessary for each classifier to compile an index to his own usage, as no composite subjects will be indexed—none will be present in the scheme.

The scheme remains discipline-oriented, as Bliss designed it, but in order to accommodate works about Entities, Processes or Attributes from all aspects (the situations where DC is obliged to give an instruction 'class comprehensive works here'), classes are provided for these in the Generalia section, with the option of placing them in the main schedules in their place of 'unique definition'—in other words within their permanent generic hierarchy rather than any of the quasi-generic locations in which they might be found.

Each class has been rigorously analysed into facets and a definite citation order established; in general, the principle of dependence has been followed, with, for example, Product as the primary facet, but in some classes, *eg* Medicine, Process (Pathology) or Operations (Clinical medicine) may take precedence. In accordance with the principle of inversion, the schedule order is the reverse of the citation order.

The notation has been simplified, and now uses only upper case letters and numerals; the latter are used to introduce the common facets and phase relationships. To give complete freedom of synthesis without the need for facet indicators, the notation is used retroactively; as we saw in chapter 10, retroactive notation can be neat, but does present some problems. One of these is that the classifier is tied completely to the citation order decided by the compiler, which may not always be the most suitable for the classifier's purpose; in this situation, the classifier may use the hyphen as a linking device to enable him to use a different citation order. Since the schedule order is fixed, any variation of the citation order will necessarily mean abandoning the principle of inversion, with the result that general will not always precede special, as explained in chapter 8. Since the vast majority of users will probably be satisfied with the citation order given, this is not likely to be a serious problem in the manual systems for which the new scheme is likely to be used; however, the use of retroactive notation may lead to a different kind of problem in computer-based systems.

In the article describing the new scheme, Mills gives the following example of the way in which the notation will work. JM is the notation for Primary schools, JKO for Foreign languages as a curriculum subject and JIE for Audio-visual aids. The notation for Audio-visual aids in the teaching of foreign languages in primary schools thus becomes JM KO IE (Mills splits this up JMK OIE, but this is immaterial; it is merely a question of how best to break up the notation into manageable blocks). Now in a manual system this is quite acceptable, since we can look up, say, Audio-visual aids in the index to the arrangement (NB *not* the index to the scheme) and find this particular composite subject and any others of interest in that way. But suppose that we want to be able to program a computer to carry out our searching? We cannot program the machine to search just for JIE, since it will obviously not retrieve the above document; we have to write a program that will identify the J at the beginning of the class mark, and *then* search for IE, and this will require much more complex programming than would be necessary if facet indicators were used.

MAINTENANCE

The launching of what is in effect a new scheme must raise questions of whether it can be adequately maintained without the support of some large central organization, and whether it will be used in libraries. Because the scheme is completely analytico-synthetic, Mills claims that the amount of revision involved will be very much less than is the case with schemes which include composite subjects; the vast majority of new subjects arise from the combination of already existing concepts rather than from the emergence of totally new concepts. If new concepts do arise, they can be accommodated without too much difficulty, as the notation is not expressive (though we must note this as another

338

problem in computer searching), and publication in classes means that individual classes can be revised and republished without necessitating the revision of the whole scheme—though it will mean a revision of the *index* to the whole scheme. The British Library has signified its willingness in principle to include BC class marks in its MARC records, and there is no technical difficulty in this; however, economic considerations are another matter, and at the moment there seems to be little chance of any additional subject designations being included in the British MARC records; the Library of Congress has already indicated that it is unlikely to include any beyond LC, DC and LCSH. To set against this is the fact that because the new scheme is built on many of the principles underlying PRECIS, it should be relatively easy to generate BC class numbers from the PRECIS string—certainly a great deal easier than for any of the existing schemes.

The BCA has been successful in raising enough funds to prepare and publish the new edition, and Mills believes that sales will be sufficient to make the venture self-supporting; he also believes that in the long term, more and more librarians will come to use it as its superiority over other schemes becomes apparent. There is no doubt that the scheme *deserves* to succeed, but we live in a harsh world, where success tends to go to the successful rather than to the deserving, and one can only reserve judgement for the next few years. One thing does seem fairly certain; a good many library schools will use it to demonstrate what a good general classification scheme ought to look like!

BIBLIOGRAPHY

1 Many of the comments on BC in this chapter reflect the views of the staff of the Library of Loughborough Colleges of Art and Further Education, where the scheme had been in use for some fifteen years.

2 The first public TV service was provided by the British Broadcasting Corporation in 1936; by the time the second edition appeared in 1951, television and its equipment were well established, but this is not reflected in the schedules.

3 Mills, J: 'Number building and filing order in BC.' *Bliss classification bulletin, II* (1) March, 1957.

4 *Bliss classification bulletin, III* (1) September, 1964.

5 The *Bulletin* contains information about the revision in general in the 1969 and 1970 issues, the latter including also a detailed discussion of the problems that have been resolved in the revision of the schedules for Class Q, Social welfare.

6 Mills, J: 'The new Bliss classification.' *Catalogue and index,* (40) Spring 1976, 1, 3–6.

CHAPTER 20

The colon classification

Shiyali Ramamrita Ranganathan, the 'onlie begetter' of CC, began his academic career as a mathematician, until in 1924 he was appointed Librarian of the University of Madras. One of the conditions of his appointment was that he should spend some time in England studying library science, and it was while attending a series of lectures by W C Berwick Sayers[1] on classification at the University College School of Librarianship that he began to formulate his own ideas on the subject, spurred by his dissatisfaction with DC and UDC.

Undeterred by the warnings of Sayers as to the task he was setting himself, Ranganathan determined to compile his own classification scheme; the basic essentials were in fact worked out during his passage home to India. After some years of experimentation in the Madras university library, he published the first edition in 1933; subsequent editions appeared in 1939, 1950, 1952, 1957 and 1960. The latest edition, the sixth, was reprinted in 1963 with some important amendments, and the seventh is in preparation. This is a rate of publication which has only been equalled by DC, but, unlike Dewey, Ranganathan has never accepted the idea of integrity of numbers, and has in fact from time to time introduced major changes. Few libraries have adopted the scheme (a not unexpected result of its continual state of flux), yet it has been one of the most influential classifications ever published, and the ideas incorporated in it have affected the whole of classification theory. As we have seen, Dewey included some synthetic elements in his scheme, but only in certain places; Ranganathan developed the theory of facet analysis, demonstrating that analysis and synthesis apply in every basic class and could be systematized. He also developed his own terminology in a correct scientific fashion; much of this is now widely used (for example in the present work), though some of it has excited the contempt of unsympathetic critics unwilling to accept the often flowery metaphors of the East.

As stated above, there have from time to time been major changes in the scheme. One such change was the decision after the fifth edition to develop two parallel editions, the basic classification (Stage 1) and the depth classification of microthought (Stage 2); in effect, an abridged and a full edition comparable with UDC. A further similarity to UDC lies in the fact that the abridged edition is published as a whole, whereas the full schedules (which are still being developed) are to be published in parts; some have appeared in *Annals of library science, Revue internationale de la documentation,* and *Library science with a slant to documentation,* while another important vehicle is the *Proceedings of the DRTC Annual Seminars.* Because of these changes, the following remarks are to be understood as applying only to the 1963 reprint of the sixth edition, unless otherwise stated.

In the first edition we find each basic class analysed into its facets, but with only one notational device for synthesis, the colon; in the beginning, the use of this symbol was so much a part of the scheme that it gave it its name, just as Dewey's notation did to his scheme. However, we have seen the problems that may arise in notational synthesis if the devices used are inadequate, and his struggles with these problems led Ranganathan to develop one of his most important theories: the citation order of decreasing concreteness, PMEST. This new idea was first introduced in the fourth edition, and led to a complete reconstruction of the scheme.

PMEST

In the first three editions Ranganathan had used the kind of *ad hoc* analysis described in the earlier chapters of this work, but in this, as in all aspects of library science, he was continually seeking the underlying principles which had led him to select one method rather than another. By studying carefully the kind of facet to be found in different basic classes, he was able to establish that despite their apparent surface differences they could be accommodated in five large groups. Time and place, as we have seen, can apply to any topic: they are common facets, but important nevertheless, and Ranganathan included them as Time [T] and Space [S] in his *fundamental categories*. He isolated the concept of Energy [E] as being the common factor appearing in such apparently disparate topics as Exports in Economics, Curriculum in Education, Grammar in Linguistics, and Physiology in Biology. Matter [M] is straightforward; we find such examples as Gold as a material of Money (Economics), various instruments in Music, Ivory in Painting, and Periodicals in Library Science; however, though we have earlier referred to Metals in Metallurgy as the materials facet, they do not appear as [M] in CC but rather as the final, somewhat elusive, category of Personality. Personality [P] is hard to define, but easier to understand; it corresponds to what we have called the primary facet, and usually includes Things, Kinds of things or Kinds of action. We find as examples Persons in Sociology and Psychology, Christianity in Religion, Electronics in Engineering, and Periodicals in Bibliography. The last of these examples indicates that the same isolate (in this case Periodicals) does not always fall into the same fundamental category; we find other examples of this, *eg* in Fine arts, where Personality is a combination of Space and Time.

The same fundamental category may occur more than once in the same basic class; it would in fact restrict us to not more than three major facets if this were not the case. For example, in an Energy facet we normally list kinds of operation or problem; this listing is thus a combined Energy plus Personality (kinds of thing) facet, denoted by Ranganathan [E] [2P]. This second *round* of Personality may itself be followed by another round of [M] and [E]; for example, in Medicine we find the first round of [P] is the organs of the body; there is no [M], the first round of [E] including problems such as Physiology and Disease; for Disease there is a second round of [P], kinds of disease; again no [M] in the second round, but [E] is represented by Treatment, with a third round of [P] to indicate kinds of treatment; for Injections, we may have a manifestation of [M] to show the substance injected. The citation order (facet formula in CC) is thus [P]: [E] [2P] : [2E] [3P]; [3M].

There may be more than one occurrence of a fundamental category, particularly [P], within the same round; these are then denoted by the term _levels_. We have already seen that the Personality facet in Fine arts is a combination of [S] and [T], these two form the first two levels, but there are in addition others; *eg* in Architecture we find the third level [P3] is Kinds of building, and the fourth level [P4] is Parts of buildings. In Literature there are four facets: Language, Literary form, Author and Work; these are respectively first, second, third and fourth level [P]. (Authors are arranged chronologically; the arrangement is in fact the same as in DC.)

There are now no _ad hoc_ facets in CC; every basic class is given a facet formula in terms of [P] [M] and [E]. ([S] and [T] are not normally quoted because they may be used anywhere that they apply.) Analysis into Ranganathan's fundamental categories is often useful in establishing the correct citation order for subjects in other schemes, but we must be cautious about accepting them uncritically. For example, as we have seen, Periodicals fall into the Matter facet in Library science, but are in the Personality facet in Bibliography; when we ask why they are [P] in the second case, the answer seems to be that in Bibliography, materials are the primary facet, and the primary facet is Personality. If we ask why all the four facets of Literature are Personality (it could be argued that Literary form is Energy), the answer seems to be that that is the way Ranganathan decided. In fact, PMEST does not solve the problems of citation order; it simply removes them to a different stage of the process of analysis, though it does give us a framework which may help in guiding our decisions. However, the fact that it is possible to disagree with the use of PMEST does *not* mean that the citation orders found in CC are incorrect; in the vast majority of cases they are both clear and helpful, and this is the only scheme in which we find this situation. One disadvantage is the lack of flexibility; we cannot select a facet order which suits our particular group of users if this conflicts with PMEST. However, to get over this rigidity Ranganathan has introduced the idea of 'Special Collection', in which the user can adapt the schedules to his own needs.

Ranganathan's fundamental categories have been subjected to a great deal of criticism, much of which can only be described charitably as ill-informed. Ranganathan himself was careful to stress the point that the existence of the five categories PMEST is *postulated* to provide a helpful aid in the formulation of citation order. Those who did not wish to use them were not under any obligation to do so, and no philosophical basis was ever claimed to justify their selection. PMEST is in fact a pragmatic solution to the problem of finding a generally acceptable citation order, and it is often useful to bear it in mind when faced with this problem, even if we give our facets *ad hoc* names. The idea of rounds is also useful, and we have seen some examples in the chapter on PRECIS, where operators (2) and (3) in particular may be used more than once. Again, the concept of levels is useful in the analysis of a complex facet such as Persons, though we have preferred the term subfacet; in one student exercise in the construction of a classification scheme, some fifteen subfacets were identified in the Persons facet, and no doubt this list could be extended. Though Western thought has developed along rather different lines from those laid down by Ranganathan, there is no doubt that progress would have been very much slower without his basic ideas, of which PMEST is only one, though it is the one which has attracted most attention.

SELF PERPETUATING CLASSIFICATION

One of the other basic ideas behind CC is that of 'autonomy for the classifier'. We have seen that in an enumerative scheme we have to wait for the decision of the compiler before we know where to classify a composite subject that is not already listed, and in an analytico-synthetic scheme we may find ourselves in the same position if the foci we require are missing—though we can cater for composite subjects if the individual foci are enumerated. Ranganathan has tried to go one stage further: to give the individual classifier the means to construct class numbers for new foci which will be in accordance with those that the central organization will allot, by means of a set of devices or rules of universal applicability. In this way, the need for a strong central organization is reduced, though it still exists. In CC there are a number of such devices, which may apply to the formation of modified basic classes or to the enumeration of new isolates.

SYSTEMS AND SPECIALS

An existing basic class may be modified in two ways. The first of these is the situation when there is more than one mode of approach to the whole basic class; for example, in Physics, relativity theory and quantum theory have led to a new approach to the whole of the subject. These new approaches are called *Systems*; the favoured system is the one into which the majority of the literature falls—in this example, classical physics—while the other systems have to be catered for separately. The second way in which a basic class may be modified occurs when part of it can be considered in a special context; for example, in Medicine, Space medicine is a *Special* of this kind.

DEVICES FOR THE ENUMERATION OF NEW FOCI

Within a basic class we may from time to time have to make provision for new foci, and cc gives five ways in which this may be done. The first of these is the Chronological device; we specify a new focus by means of its date of origin. cc uses this device in Literature, where authors are specified by their date of birth (though Ranganathan has a rather tetchy note about the difficulty of establishing this in some cases). This device is often used to specify systems also. The second is the Geographical device, which simply means the use of the place facet other than in its normal way. We have already seen the use of a combination of Time and Space, *ie* (CD) and (GD), to form the first two levels of [P] in the Fine arts.

The third is the Subject device. This is the use of a schedule from elsewhere in the overall order, *eg* in Education, where any subject may form part of the curriculum; in DC, this used to be called the 'divide like' device, but with the increase in the amount of synthesis possible in recent editions this has been replaced by the 'add to base number . . .' instruction, which does not mirror the use of subject device in cc to anything like the same extent. The fifth is Alphabetical device, which is simply the use of names as a method of arrangement; this is not recommended unless no other device gives a more helpful order.

The fourth is rather more interesting, though, as with PMEST, we may view it with caution. Ranganathan's study of the schedules that he drew up in the early editions led him to believe that he had unconsciously followed certain principles in allocating the notation; these principles, extracted from practice, form the Mnemonic device, or, to use the term coined by Palmer and Wells[2], 'seminal mnemonics'. For example, the digit 1 is used for unity, one dimension, solid state, the first, etc; 2 is used for two dimensions, second, constitution, etc. So far, the device does not seem to stretch probability too far; but when we come to 5, which is intended to represent 'instability', we may begin to wonder when we find energy, water, emotion, controlled plan, women, sex, crime, all lumped together. The real objection to seminal mnemonics appears to be that this is a case of notation dictating order, but Ranganathan himself sounds a note of caution when he warns that, because the use of this device requires an uncommon degree of 'spiritual insight', any notation suggested by it should be discussed widely before being finalized.

A sixth device, the Superimposition device, is used to specify composite topics arising from the combination of foci which fall into the same facet. For example, in the Libraries (*ie* [P]) facet of Library science, we can consider libraries from several points of view, giving us several subfacets or *arrays* within the same facet; we may need to combine foci from these subfacets, and the superimposition device permits us to do this. Note that if we treat these subfacets as facets in their own right we shall have to devise a notation that will permit us to combine them anyway; the need for the superimposition device arises from the rationalization of *ad hoc* facets into the PMEST frame work

THE SCHEME

The sixth edition of CC consists of three parts: part 1, the rules; part 2, the schedules of classification; part 3, schedules of classics and sacred books with special names. In previous editions, part 3 consisted of some 4,000 examples of CC class numbers, but it is now felt that there are enough textbooks and bibliographies demonstrating the use of the scheme for these to be superfluous.

Parts 1 and 2 have to be considered together, as it is not possible to use the schedules without the rules. A more satisfactory arrangement would in fact be to merge the two parts so that the rules for a particular class were found with the schedules to which they apply. As an example, let us consider Literature, Class O. The complete schedule for this is as follows:

CHAPTER O

LITERATURE

O [P], [P2], [P3], [P4]

Foci in [P]

as the Language divisions in Chapter 5

Foci in [P2]

1	Poetry
2	Drama
3	Fiction, including short stories
4	Letters (literature written in the form of letters)
5	Oration
6	Other forms of prose
7	Campu

Foci in [P3]

1	To be got by (CD)
2	For authors born later than 1800, if year of birth cannot be found out at all, (CD) to be worked only to one digit. Thereafter, (AD) may be used.

Foci in [P4]

See Rules in Chapter O of Part 1.

On the other hand, we find that the rules for this basic class occupy some six pages of close type in part 1. In contrast, there are rather more than five pages of schedules for Engineering, but only one page of rules. Reference from one part to the other is faciliated by the use of parallel chapter numbering (each chapter of the rules has the same notation as the class to which it refers), but even so the arrangement is not convenient.

Ranganathan distinguishes between the class number, denoting the subject of a work, and the book number, which identifies a particular document once the subject has been determined; the two together form the call number, which shows the exact place on the shelves or in the catalogue that the item is to be found. Book number includes Language, Form of exposition (not specified for prose), Year, Accession number, Copy number, etc, *ie* those factors which do not affect the subject matter. The first four chapters of the rules cover the construction of the call number, including the Collection number, *eg* reference, junior, etc. Chapter 05 is a useful exposition of the essentials of analytico-synthetic classification theory as it appears in cc; this is followed by various minor sections, *eg* a list of contractions.

Chapter 1 of both rules and schedules is concerned with Main classes, including the partially comprehensive groups. In the 1960 printing several greek letters are used, but these have been dropped from the 1963 reprint with the exception of Mysticism *Δ* . The problems created by the use of greek letters have been discussed, and it is perhaps surprising that Ranganathan introduced them at all. The table of main classes is followed by the common facets, which are of two kinds, anteriorizing and posteriorizing. Anteriorizing common isolates include the bibliographical form divisions, and are so named because they precede the subject on its own; thus a Dictionary of physics ck files before a general work on Physics c. Posteriorizing common isolates include many of the common subject subdivisions, and file after the subject number; thus a learned society in the field of physics c,g files after c.

OUTLINE OF THE SCHEME

z	Generalia
1	Universe of knowledge*
2	Library Science
3	Book Science†
4	Journalism†
A	Natural sciences*
AZ	Mathematical sciences*
B	Mathematics (including Astronomy)
BZ	Physical sciences*
C	Physics
D	Engineering

E	Chemistry
F	Technology (*ie* Chemical technology)
G	Biology
H	Geology
HX	Mining (printed as Hz in the schedules)
I	Botany
J	Agriculture
K	Zoology
KX	Animal husbandry (printed as KZ in the schedules)
L	Medicine
LX	Pharmacognosy (printed as KZ in the schedules)
M	Useful Arts
Δ	Spiritual experience and Mysticism
MZ	Humanities and Social Sciences★
MZA	Humanities★
N	Fine Arts
NZ	Literature and Language
O	Literature
P	Linguistics
Q	Religion
R	Philosophy
S	Psychology
Σ	Social Sciences★
T	Education
U	Geography
V	History
W	Political Science
X	Economics
Y	Sociology
YX	Social Work†
Z	Law

There are certain peculiarities about the outline which are worth noting. The Generalia class consists of the common isolates (shown by lowercase letters) applied to the whole of knowledge, and though it is shown by z in the outline, in fact the z is dropped in use, so that the generalia class is shown by the whole lowercase alphabet used for common isolates. z itself is used for generalia materials on a specific area, *eg* z7 Americana; of a specific person not assigned to a particular subject, *eg* zG Ghandiana.

There are no schedules for the partially comprehensive main classes (marked ★ in the above list); the reason for this is that the main subdivisions are the main classes, *eg* the divisions of A are B to M, and therefore the only pieces of notation to be added are those for the common facets. This was set out explicitly in earlier editions under A, but in the current edition A only appears in the Outline; this is an example of Ranganathan's 'canon of parsimony'—there is no need to repeat something explicitly if it is clearly implicit—but it is somewhat puzzling at first.

There are also no schedules for some of the basic classes (those marked † in the above list); the reason for this would appear to be that the schedules have not as yet been developed. In the 1963 reprint most of the greek letters have been removed and replaced by the use of the 'empty' digit z to signify partially comprehensive classes.

For each main class, the rules show the facets, what they represent and how the foci are obtained; for example under NR Music we find

Facet	Term	(IN) by
[P], [P2]	Style	(GD) and (CD)
[P3]	Music	Enumeration
[M]	Instrument	Enumeration
[E], [2P]	Technique	(To be worked out)

In addition, there are comments on the kinds of classification problem likely to be met, and on the subject where it is thought necessary; in some cases useful reference books are noted, *eg* in Literature. The rules for each class conclude with a set of examples showing how the notation for specific examples is worked out. The parallel chapter in the schedules begins with the facet formula, then enumerates the foci in the various facets as appropriate (*cf* the outline for Literature previously given). Rules and schedules must be used together; the rules are of no use without the schedules, and the schedules are not usually selfsufficient enough to be used without the rules.

Most of the general schemes have been criticised for their Western bias; it is probably true to say that CC reveals an Eastern bias. While the schedules for such topics as Hindu sacred books are worked out in detail, major classes such as Engineering are not; the lack of detail here is one of the more important factors militating against the widespread adoption of the scheme.

NOTATION

It will have become clear already that the notation of CC is very mixed. The main classes are denoted by capital letters or, in a few cases, arabic numerals. Division within a facet is usually by arabic numerals, but in some cases capitals are introduced to increase the base available; lower case letters are used for the common bibliographical forms and subject divisions, numerals for the place facet and capitals for time. In addition to these symbols denoting classes or the foci within them, there are several connecting symbols (facet indicators): [P] is introduced by a comma, (not needed for first level personality); [M] by the semicolon ;; [E] by the colon :; [S] by a point .; and [T] by an apostrophe. Notation obtained by the use of the subject device is enclosed in curves (). The zero o (not to be confused with the capital O) is used to show phase relations, which in CC are well worked out. The filing order of these connecting symbols is the reverse of the citation order PMEST, so that the principle of inversion is followed. Unless this filing order is borne in mind, some confusion may arise, for in the schedules it is the Personality facet which is listed first, though it files last.

The notation of CC has been criticised on the grounds of its length and complexity. Ranganathan has always endeavoured to make his notation an 'artificial language of ordinal numbers' into which the subject of a document can be completely translated; specificity and synthesis combined are bound to give lengthy notation for complex subjects. However, the schemes with which CC is contrasted frequently avoid long notation by avoiding specificity; for simple subjects CC frequently gives notation which is comparable in length with, or shorter than, such schemes as DC and LC, though it cannot be denied that many class numbers are confusing because of the variety of symbols used.

INDEX

It is not strictly correct to write of the index to CC, for there are in fact four; in addition to the general index there are indexes to the place facet and to the natural groups in Botany I and Zoology K. Like the separation of rules and schedules, this is perhaps a good idea in theory, but not in practice. The general index is of the kind we should expect in an analytico-synthetic scheme; it does not list any composite subjects, but shows the places in the schedules where a particular isolate is to be found, as does any relative index. Until the method is understood, the index entries may well be puzzling, especially to someone accustomed to the straightforward nature of the index entries in, say, DC. For example, if we turn to Fire in the index we find the following:

Fire   E[E], 2131.J,KZ,L, [E], 4 [2P], 91.Y [E], 4351,831

_____   clay H2 [P], 3311

_____   damp HZ [E], 41

_____   insurance X [P], 8191

_____   place NA [P3], 2 to 9 [P4[, 94

These somewhat cryptic entries can be deciphered quite easily once the method is learnt, but it would obviously be unwise to attempt to classify from this index without referring to the schedules! The interpretation of the above entries is as follows:

Fire appears in the Energy facet of Chemistry with the notation 2131; this turns out to be part of Physical chemistry, and the correct class number is E: 2131.

It appears as a cause of disease in Agriculture, Animal husbandry and Medicine, where it is found in the second round personality facet following disease; the correct notation is: in Medicine L : 491, in Agriculture J : 491, in Animal husbandry KZ: 491.

In sociology, fire appears twice in the energy facet; Y : 4351 denotes fire as a cause of destitution, while Y : 831 denotes fire as an item of social equipment, used for cooking, etc.

Fire clay appears in the Personality facet of Petrology as a form of rock; notation, H23311.

Fire damp is a hazard in the Energy facet in Mining; notation, HZ : 41.

Fire insurance is a branch of Insurance in Economics; notation, X8191.

Fireplace is a part, appearing in the fourth level of Personality in Architecture, where it may be subordinate to any of the kinds of Building enumerated in the third level, *eg* fireplaces in domestic dwellings NA,3,94 (NB the first comma is necessary because we have not specified either of the first two levels).

The index is set out in this way to emphasize the synthetic qualities of the scheme, but there does not seem to be any very good reason for not casting it in a more conventional form. This would certainly make it easier to use, without any loss of its special qualities.

CLASSICS AND SACRED BOOKS

The third part of CC is a long and detailed list of Indian classics, with a few exceptions such as the *Bible*. There is a separate index, but in any case the Western classifier will have only rare occasion to turn to this section, which does not form an essential part of the scheme as a whole.

ORGANIZATION

CC began as the work of one man, and most of the work on the early editions was carried out by Ranganathan himself. In recent years a band of disciples (the word hardly seems too strong) has grown up in India, and has contributed to the revision and expansion of the schedules. An organization now exists, endowed by Ranganathan, and charged with the maintenance of the scheme now that he himself has died. Whether this will prove strong enough to perpetuate the scheme indefinitely has still to be seen.

REVISION

New editions of the scheme are published at intervals, but in the past each new edition has differed in some quite important features from its predecessors. In some cases the changes have been discussed in print in advance, for example the change in the facet indicator for Time from a point to an apostrophe, which was first published in *Annals of library science*[3]. Development of the scheme is still grossly inadequate in some sectors.

AIDS FOR THE USER

The scheme itself gives the user rather more help than do most, by including the detailed rules for each class. It has been the subject of one of the Rutgers seminars on systems for the intellectual organization of information[4], and a programmed text exists to help students to gain familiarity with it[5]. Ranganathan wrote several text-books setting out his ideas on classification, notably the *Elements of library classification* and the more advanced *Prolegomena to library classification*; an understanding of these is a considerable help in using the scheme, particularly in respect of some of the terminology[6].

It must however be pointed out that as a practical tool for the working librarian, CC has many defects of production. It is poorly printed; mistakes abound, and while the 1963 reprint corrected some of these, it introduced others of its own. In many cases, revision from one edition to the next has been inadequate; some of the examples are incorrect according to the present schedules, but are found to have been correct at some point in the past. Some topics have disappeared between editions; for example, a search in the schedule of common isolates or the index for Instruments is fruitless, but one may come across a schedule in Electrical engineering which shows that the correct notation is e, and reference back to the second edition confirms this. In the index, Mustard appears between Multiphase and Multiple. It is possible to feel that if a new edition were produced which measured up to the high standards of DC, it would create a rather better impression of the scheme than can be obtained from the present format.

THE SEVENTH EDITION

Work began on the seventh edition in the early 1960's, and even after his retirement Ranganathan continued to make significant contributions to the development of the scheme, though most of the detailed work has been carried out at the Documentation Research and Training Centre (DRTC); Ranganathan lived an ascetic life, and devoted all the profits from his many books to the setting up of the Sarada Ranganathan endowment for library science, and this body has provided much of the necessary finance—again an interesting parallel with Dewey and the Lake Placid Club Education Foundation. In 1969 Ranganathan published an article setting out the outline of the proposed new edition, with a detailed explanation of the changes that were to be made, and giving 1971 as the likely publication date.[7] He also expressed the hope that the changes to be made would enable the scheme to last for a considerable time into the future. In this article changes were apparent in definitions of terms, in the schedules, in the notation and in the index, some of these being quite startling.

The scheme was said to be a 'freely faceted' classification, the term facet being defined:

a generic term used to denote any component—be it a basic subject or an isolate—of a compound subject.

A basic subject (single concept) on its own cannot have facets; they are essentially a reflection of the structure of composite subjects. This appears to be a tightening up of the definition rather than a new approach, but some of the examples would appear to be more than this; for example, 'bones' and 'leg' are said to be subfacets in the compound isolate facet 'bones of the leg'. Another statement may give rise to some surprise:

A facet formula is in a sense meaningless; it is indeed an anachronism.

However, for the benefit of the weaker brethren the scheme will continue to give facet formulae for the main classes. The objective of the whole exercise seems to be to make it possible to combine concepts quite freely, without any restrictions imposed by a pre-conceived pattern; for depth classification, *ie* the close classification of periodical articles and similar documents, any predetermined rules are likely to prove more of a hindrance than a help.

In the schedules, there are several new ideas as well as some rearrangement. From the forty six main classes of the sixth edition we find no less than one hundred and five: eighty two main classes and twenty three partially comprehensive classes. Among the former we find a new group of 'distilled' classes, including Cybernetics, Management and Research methodology; among the latter another new group of 'fused' main classes, arising from the fusion of previously distinct subject areas, for example Chemical engineering and Biophysics. Although these topics were represented in the sixth edition it is only in the seventh that they are recognized as main classes. Another kind of main class for which provision is being made, particularly in the natural sciences, is the 'subject bundle', for example Space sciences. These may be described perhaps as *agglomerations* of subjects for which there is literary warrant; indeed, they formed a part of Wyndham Hulme's argument for literary warrant. To some extent they may be regarded as the first signs of a new fused subject in the making, though Ranganathan suggests (as did Wyndham Hulme) that they are the result of the way books are produced rather than intrinsic to subjects.

Another major change has been the recognition of properties as a manifestation of matter rather than energy. In the original PMEST analysis in the fourth edition, (E) was taken to include (correctly) isolates representing actions, but also (incorrectly) any other isolates listed in energy schedules. Sceptics might adduce this as another example of the unreliability of PMEST as a basis of analysis, along with the elusive personality.[8] Be that as it may, in CC7 we find that (M) is divided into two categories, (M-M) Matter-Material and (M-P) Matter-Property, with many concepts previously treated as (E) being transferred to the latter (including incidentally Curriculum, Grammar and Physiology, quoted earlier in this chapter as typical manifestations of

(E)!) This rather large stone in the pond casts quite widespread ripples, as not only do many (E) and (E) cum (2P) facets become (M-P), but this means that many (2E) and (2E) cum (3P) facets become (E). The effect of the change is to alter the facet indicator form : to ; for the Property isolates, and to alter the facet formulae for a number of classes, eg Medicine, in which L [P] : [E] [2P] : [2E] [3P] becomes L, [P] ; [M-P] : [E], [2P].

Systems and Specials are now regarded as forming part of compound basic subjects, as are such concepts as Style in Fine Arts, so that the facet formula for, eg, Architecture changes from NA [P], [2P] [3P], [4P] : [E] to NA, [P], [2P] ; [M-P], with the primary division of NA not forming part of the facet formula.

In the past, there have been common fundamental category isolates (ie common facets in the terminology we have used earlier) for [S] and [T]; in CC7 there are additional tables for [P], [M-P] and [E]; these correspond to some extent with the BNB table of common subject subdivisions.

In the notational plane, there are some changes in addition to those already mentioned. In previous editions lower case roman letters were used for common subdivisions, with anteriorizing value; in order that they should be generally available, their anteriorizing value has disappeared, and the symbol ↑ is used to denote this instead, so that a Dictionary of physics now becomes c↑k. Instead of being introduced by a zero o, phase relations are now shown by the ampersand &, releasing o for its normal purpose in the sequence of arabic numerals. The upper-case letters T to Z are used as empty digits, with z frequently used for partially comprehensive main classes, thus eliminating greek letters altogether, with the exception of Δ. All levels of [P] are now introduced by the comma, where previously first level personality was taken not to require a facet indicator; in addition, second level personality on its own is introduced by a zero, to ensure that it files in the right place.

With Ranganathan's death in 1972, responsibility for the development of the scheme passed completely to DRTC under the direction of Professor A Neelameghan, who in 1973 published another outline of the scheme differing in some important respects from that published four years earlier by Ranganathan.[9] The notation appears to be somewhat simpler, in that only five different kinds of symbol are used. These are: lower case roman letters (except i, l and o, which are likely to be confused with other symbols in writing or typing); the numerals o to 9; upper case roman letters A to Z: parentheses (); and the indicator digits - and *. The latter plays an important role in that it is used as an anteriorizing symbol to give the notation for agglomerates, which in effect correspond to the 'partially comprehensive main classes' of previous editions. We thus find the sequence:

B*Z   Mathematical and physical sciences

B*ZZ   Mathematical sciences
B   Mathematics

in that order; with the 'empty' digits T, V, X and Z, this device is intended to provide infinite hospitality for the insertion of new subjects, but there is no doubt that the filing order will cause some headaches for the uninitiated. Also, the fact that there appear to be several quite important relocations since Ranganathan's 1969 article is hardly calculated to inspire confidence that we have now seen the definitive outline of the seventh edition. Table 13 gives a selection of the major classes from Neelameghan's outline.

z	Generalia
I	Universe of subjects: structure and development
2	Library science
3	Book science
4	Journalism
5	Exhibition technique†
6	Museology†
7	Systemology† (7T in R69)
8	Management science ((x) in CC6)
9b	Career†
9c	Metrology†
9d	Standardisation†
9f	Research methodology†
9g	Evaluation technique (energy common isolate in CC6)
9p	Conference technique (common isolate in CC6)
9P	Communication ((P) in CC6)
9Q	Symbolism†
9S	Computer science† (N73)
A*Z	Sciences natural and social (9ZZ in R69)
A	Natural sciences
B*Z	Mathematical and physical sciences† (N73)
B*ZZ	Mathematical sciences (AZ in R69)
B	Mathematics
BT	Statistical calculus (Statistical analysis B28 in CC6)
BV	Cybernetics† (7X in R69)
BX*Z	Astronomy and astrophysics (BUZ in R69)
BX	Astronomy (B9 in CC6; BV in R69)
BZ	Astrophysics (B9:6 in CC6; BX in R69)
C*Z	Physical sciences (BZ in R69)
C	Physics
CV	Space physics†
D*Z	Engineering and technology† (CZ in R69)
D	Engineering
DT	Draughtsmanship† (DV in R69)

E*z	Chemical sciences† (DZ in R69)
E	Chemistry
F	Chemical technology (Chemical engineering EYD in R69; D9E in CC6; Technology F in CC6)
G*z	Biological sciences† (FZ in R69)
G	Biology
GV	Microbiology (GT in R69; G9I in CC6)
GWA	Molecular biology† (GUA in R69)
GWB	Biomechanics (GUB in R69; G:(B7) in CC6)
GWB	Biophysics (GUC in R69; G:(C) in CC6)
GX	Biochemistry (GUE in R69; E9G in CC6)
H*z	Earth sciences† (Geological sciences GZ in R69)
H	Geology
HUB	Geodesy (B9182 in CC6)
HV	Geophysics (H:(C) in CC6)
HWT	Geochemistry (HVT in R69; H:(E) in CC6)
HX	Mining
I*z	Plant sciences† (HZ in R69)
I	Botany
J*z	Agriculture and forestry (Agriculture and animal husbandry IZ in R69)
J	Agriculture
JX	Forestry (JB in CC6)
K*z	Animal sciences† (JZ in R69)
K	Zoology
KX	Animal husbandry
L*z	Medical sciences† (KZ in R69)
L	Medicine
LT	Physical exercise and sports (Medical technology in R69)
LU5	Public health (L:5 in CC6)
LU6*z	Hospital and sanitorium (LU5Z in R69)
LU6	Hospital (L:14 in CC6)
LU7	Sanitorium (L:15 in CC6)
LUD	Medical technology (LT in R69)
LX	Pharmacognosy (LV in R69; LZ in CC6)
LYX	Medical jurisprudence (LYZ in R69; L:(Z) in CC6)
M	Useful arts
MZ*z	Humanities and social sciences (MZ in R69)
MZ*ZZ	Humanities (MZZ in R69)
MZ	Mysticism and spiritual experience (Δ in CC6)
N*z	Fine arts and literature† (N73)
N	Fine arts
O*z	Language and literature (NZ in R69)
O	Literature
P	Linguistics

Q*z	Religion and philosophy† (PZ in R69)
Q*zz	Religion and ethics† (PZZ in R69)
Q	Religion
R*z	Philosophy and psychology† (QZ in R69)
R	Philosophy
s*z	Behavioural sciences† (N73)
s*zz	Psychology and education† (RZ in R69)
s	Psychology
T*z	Social sciences (SZ in R69; Σ in CC6)
T	Education
U*z	Geography and history† (TZ in R69)
U	Geography
v*z	History and political science† (N73)
v*zz	History and economics† (UZ in R69)
v	History
vx	Historical source (as a pure discipline)† (VT in R69)
w	Political science
wx	Geopolitics (WUU in R69; WOgU in CC6)
x	Economics
xx	Economics in theory of business enterprise (XB(A) in CC6)
y	Sociology
z	Law

TABLE 14 : *Outline of CC7 (extracts from N73)*

Additions to CC6 are shown by † (*eg* BV Cybernetics†).
R69 refers to Ranganathan's outline of CC7 (ref 7).
N73 refers to Neelameghan's outline (ref 9).
Relocations are shown from CC6 or R69 (*eg* WX Geopolitics (WUU in R69; WOgU in CC6).

It will be clear from this outline that there have been a number of changes, not only from the outline of CC6 but also from that produced by Ranganathan as his own final version. Many of the latter reflect the use of the *, *eg* v*zz instead of UZ, and do *not* imply any change in the filing order; some however do imply fairly major changes, *eg* Cybernetics, added in R69 at 7X, moved to BV in H73. Most of the notational changes have been introduced to make possible the combination of notational elements for any desired combination of concepts, or the insertion of new classes at any point in the schedules. Since both of these requirements were stated many years ago by Ranganathan, and it is largely to him that we owe their explicit recognition (and incorporation in, for example, the new BC), it is perhaps a little surprising to find that his own original notation did not possess this hospitality to new subjects.

There will be only one index in cc7. The idea of having several indexes, tried out as an experiment in cc6, has not proved to be a success and has been dropped, with the four indexes merged into one for the new edition. The index is still compiled along the same lines, but again it must be stressed that this is an index for the classifier, not for the user of the catalogue; the latter will have a detailed index to all the topics in the catalogue, as should be the case with any classified catalogue.

THE FUTURE

The DRTC is now well established, giving cc the institutional backing which we have stressed as being essential to the success of any classification scheme. Following a dispute over the editorship of *Annals of library science*, the Centre started its own journal in 1964, *Library science with a slant to documentation*, and sections of the full schedules (depth classification) for cc7 are regularly published in this; these are being compiled with computer retrieval specifically in mind, and some of the sample class marks which have been published, for example in the field of automotive engineering, can perhaps best be described as awe-inspiring (though critics might be more inclined to describe them as unrealistic!)

Ranganathan's ideas formed the basis of much of the progress made in classification theory in England during the 1950's, though in recent years the two streams of thought seem to have diverged more and more, particularly in the development of ideas on notation. It is to cc that we owe the consistent development of such ideas as facet analysis and phase relationships, which certainly appeared in such schemes as DC, but haphazardly and without any underlying plan. No matter what becomes of the scheme, Ranganathan's contributions to librarianship must rank in breadth and significance with those of Dewey, and we certainly cannot afford to ignore them.

BIBLIOGRAPHY

1 Ranganathan has given an interesting account of this in his chapter 'Library classification on the march' in the *Sayers memorial volume*.

2 Palmer, B I and Wells, A J: *The fundamentals of library classification*. Allen & Unwin, 1951. Although this text is now rather out of date, it does give a very clear introduction to many of Ranganathan's ideas.

3 Ranganathan, S R: 'Connecting symbols for time and space in cc.' *Annals of library science, 8* (1), 1961, 1–11.
Ranganathan, S R: 'Connecting symbols for space and time in cc.' *Annals of library science, 8* (3) 1961, 69–79.

4 Ranganathan, S R: *The colon classification*. Rutgers, the State

University, Graduate School of Library Science, 1965. 298pp. (Rutgers series on systems for the intellectual organization of information, edited by Susan Artandi, vol. 4.)

5 Batty, C D: *Introduction to colon classification*. Bingley, 1966.

6 Ranganathan's own writings are of course an important source of information about CC. In particular, the *Elements of library classification*, second edition 1959 or third edition, 1962, and the *Prolegomena to library classification*, third edition 1967 (both published by Asia Publishing House) may be consulted; the former is a good elementary textbook, while the latter is rather more advanced.

7 Ranganathan, S R: 'Colon classification edition 7 (1971): a preview'. *Library science with a slant to documentation*, 6 (3) September 1969, 193–242.

8 Moss, R: 'Categories and relations: origins of two classification theories'. *American documentation*, *15* (4) 1964, 296–301.

Roberts, N: 'An examination of the personality concept and its relevance to the Colon classification scheme. *Journal of librarianship*, *1* (3) July 1969, 131–148.

9 Neelameghan, A *and others*: 'Edition 7 schedule of basic subjects.' *Library science with a slant to documentation*, *10* 1973, 222–260.

CHAPTER 21

The Library of
Congress classification

In 1814, the Capitol of the United States, together with its library of 3,000 books, was burned to the ground by British soldiers. Thomas Jefferson, third President of the US, offered his own library to Congress to replace the books lost, and with this library of 6,000 books came a classification scheme, devised by Jefferson himself, which was to be the basis of the library's arrangement until the end of the century. The range of Jefferson's library was also wider than that of the previous Library of Congress, and formed the basis of an increasing breadth of coverage, which was greatly accelerated when Ainsworth Spofford became Librarian in 1864. Spofford set out to make the library, in fact if not in name, the national library of the United States, and to this end increased the rate and scope of accessions to such an extent that towards the end of his tenure of thirty three years as Librarian a new building had to be provided. When the move took place in 1897, shortly after Spofford's retirement, it was found that some threequarters of a million books needed reclassification or recataloguing, and that there was a backlog of some thirty years of uncatalogued and unbound material.[1]

Jefferson's classification, though it had been modified and extended, was no longer adequate for a library of the size to which this had grown, and the decision was made to reclassify the whole collection—but by what scheme? Three possibilities were considered carefully: Dewey's *Decimal classification*, the *Expansive classification* of C A Cutter,[2] and the Halle *Schema*, used in the library of the German University of Halle. None of these commended itself for the particular situation of the library, and in 1900 Herbert Putnam, Librarian from 1899 to 1939, decided that the staff should proceed to devise a new scheme, intended to fit the library's collections and services as precisely as possible, without reference to outside needs or influences. The classification which has resulted, LC, reflects this situation very clearly, and some of its special features can only be understood in this context.

The first part of the new scheme to be developed took shape before the decision had been made to develop a new scheme at all. The urgent need to be able to make use of the uncatalogued material led logically to the recognition of the bibliographical collections as the key to this,

359

and the first outline of class z Bibliography was drawn up in 1898, drawing on Cutter's unpublished seventh expansion. Since then, the various classes have been drawn up over the years and published separately, with no apparent overall plan. American history was the first of the new schedules to be published, in 1901, and Russian language and literature the last, in 1948, but many of the schedules have now been revised several times, *eg* Q Science, now in its sixth edition.

One surprising gap remains: the schedules for class κ Law have not all appeared. Though the decision to allot κ to this subject was taken when the outline of the scheme was first drawn up, and some progress seems to have been made in the first few years of the century, works dealing with the law of a subject were arranged with the subject, and no progress was made on a schedule for Law as a whole. However, in 1949 it was decided to end the classification of law as a common subject subdivision and to concentrate all legal works, and not merely those dealing with law in the strict sense of the term, in the Law library, bringing together well over a million volumes. Work on the schedules began and that for law of the United States, κF, was completed in 1967, and the schedules were published in 1969. The final draft for κD, British law, is now published, and a draft outline for the whole class was published in 1970.

THE SCHEME
The outline of the classification most closely resembles that of Cutter's Expansive Classification, but is dictated by the organization of the library, rather than by theoretical considerations. Because the scheme is primarily an internal one, in which the schedules are matched to the needs of the collections—*ie* compiler and classifier are one and the same—there is no need for synthetic devices, and the scheme is very largely enumerative. In some classes there are tables, *eg* for division of the works of individual authors in Literature, but these are not synthetic in the usual sense, and there are no common facets such as we have found in other schemes. In consequence, the schedules are very bulky; in all, the twenty one classes occupy some 6,000 pages, with Literature and Language accounting for about a third of this.

The notation is mixed, but the different symbols used fall into a clear pattern, so that no problems arise. Main classes are denoted by a capital letter, and in most of them a second capital is used to denote the major sections, *eg* Q Science, QD Chemistry. Arabic numerals are then used to denote the divisions; they are used integrally, from 1 to 9999 if necessary, with gaps left liberally to accommodate new topics as they arise. However, there is no question of notation dictating order; if a new topic has to be inserted where no gap exists, a decimal point is used for further subdivision. Further arrangement is often alphabetical, using Cutter numbers after a point; these consist of a capital followed by one or two figures, to give a shorter arranging symbol than the name of the topic. Alphabetical arrangement is in fact used very frequently, even in places where its use would seem to be unhelpful, *eg* in Science. In some cases, no facet analysis has been carried out, which gives the possibility of cross-classification; for example, at TK6565, Other radio apparatus, we find arranged alphabetically

.A55 Amplifiers (circuit)
.C65 Condensers (part) (NB outdated terminology)
.R4 Recording apparatus.

Condensers (capacitors) may be used in amplifiers, and amplifiers may be used in recording apparatus, but we are given no guidance as to which of these is the primary facet. In other cases, straightforward alphabetical arrangement scatters topics within the same facet which could be arranged more helpfully; *eg* in Psychology we find

BF575   Special forms of emotion
     eg .A5   Anger
         .A9   Awe
         .B3   Bashfulness
         .F2   Fear
         .H3   Hate
         .L8   Love
         .S4   Selfconsciousness

(among others) where some grouping would have been more useful. At some points an indication of facet order is given; for example, at the above number BF575 there is an instruction: Prefer BF723 for emotions of children. Such instructions are the exception rather than the rule, and the external user finds little help in the scheme from this point of view; within the library, of course, procedure is well established, and the answers to questions of facet order are found by reference to previous practice.

    Gaps are left in the notation to accommodate the tables referred to above, which are inserted rather than added; for example, in Literature, we find within English literature, 19th century, individual authors:

PR5400–5448   Shelley, Percy Bysshe (II)

This shows that the numbers allocated to this author are to be defined by using Table II from the set at the end of the schedules; turning to this, we find that 3 or 53 is the number for Selections, 24 or 74 the number for Parodies. Inserting these numbers in the gap, we have

PR5403   Selections from Shelley
PR5424   Parodies of Shelley.

Had we instead been looking at Wordsworth, PR5850–5898, we should have used the second set, thus:

PR5853	Selections from Wordsworth
PR5874	Parodies of Wordsworth.

There are thirteen such tables in Literature; the one to use depends on the importance of the writer, and is shown in the schedules. Class H Social sciences also includes a number of tables, particularly for division by place.

ORGANIZATION

The way in which the schedules are compiled is again unique to LC among the general schemes. Literary warrant is very important; there are no provisions for subjects not represented in the library. The original technique of compilation was to arrange the books in what seemed to be a helpful order; this order was written down and studied carefully to remove anomalies, and the arrangement of the books was revised to take account of any changes. There was thus a constant interaction between the collections and the scheme, with the latter matched as closely as possible to the needs of the former. In the case of Law, this technique has had to be slightly modified—it is not practical to experiment with the arrangement of over a million volumes—but there is still the very close interaction.

REVISION

Each main class is revised on its own, without reference to the publication schedule for other classes, though cross-references are included where they will be useful, eg

HM Sociology

HM (31) relation to Religion, see BL60

HM (32) relation to Education, see LC189–191

The class numbers in parentheses are not used by LC but are included in case any other libraries prefer the alternative. The process is continuous; as new books are received, new places are made to accommodate them in the schedules if this is necessary. When it seems appropriate, a new edition of the class is published; in recent years, the normal method has been to reprint the previous edition, but to insert a supplementary table and index listing additions and changes. This means of course that the user has always to look in two places to make sure that he has the latest schedule. All the changes are published as soon as they occur in *LC Classification—additions and changes*, quarterly; in addition, the publication of revised editions of main classes is noted in the Library of Congress *Information bulletin*, published weekly. The number of new class numbers generated in a year can exceed three thousand, a point which is not always realized by those advocating a change from DC on account of the reclassification involved with each edition.

LC class numbers are of course included in LC cards, which are a major source of cataloguing copy in the USA; libraries using the cards have therefore to check carefully to see that class numbers have not been changed, and to decide whether to take account of changes as they occur or to retain their past practice. The MARC record is now the other major source of cataloguing copy in the USA, and both Library of Congress and British MARC records contain LC class numbers. If anything, this makes it somewhat more difficult to keep track of changes because of the change of physical format.

Each class has its own index, with the exception of A and some parts of P, but there is no overall index to the scheme.[3] The lack of schedules for law has in the past been considered an insuperable barrier to the production of such an index, but consideration is now being given to the use of data processing techniques to produce an index to all the rest of the schedules, with of course the intention of incorporating K as it is completed. Users must therefore select the correct main class before they can consult the index, though in some cases the index to one main class does contain cross-references to another; for example, if we look in Religion for Freemasons, the index will direct us to HS397 in Social sciences. To some extent the Subject headings list acts as a general index, as it gives LC numbers for many of the headings listed[4]; there is also the *Outline* of the scheme, which is available free and which shows the overall arrangement, though not in much detail.

The indexes to the individual classes are reasonably full, but somewhat wasteful, in that they tend to repeat much of the detail of the schedules; for example, in Religion there is an index entry Bible: BS, which is followed by two columns of entries, of which only 25 (out of nearly a hundred) lead to other parts of the schedules; on the other hand, many of the topics within BS are *not* indexed in this way, *eg* Astronomy, for which one has to turn to Astronomy in the index. The haphazard approach to indexing illustrated here renders the indexes less reliable than they should be.

THE FUTURE
LC would appear to be very well established, but there are two factors which may influence it in the long run.[5] The first of these is the transfer of the library's bibliographical records to computer operation, which will render the shelf arrangement far less important; in the system envisaged, consoles would replace the conventional catalogues, and would provide the facility for browsing now afforded by the open stacks (though it must be remembered that a catalogue entry, whether automated or not, is not a substitute for the book it represents!). The second factor is the need to economize on space in order to accommodate new accessions over the years; one way in which it has been suggested that this might be done is to abandon

classified arrangement in the stacks in favour of a more economical method, involving primary arrangement by size. Here again the need for the classification as a means of shelf arrangement disappears.

To set against these two factors are two on the other side. In the first place, even if the stacks are closed, there will still be an open access browsing collection, substantial in relation to most libraries, and this will need to be systematically arranged. Secondly, progress towards total automation is slow within the Library, because of the enormous task of converting the existing records into compatible machine-readable MARC format records; programs have been designed to speed up this process by automatic format recognition,[6] but it is sure to take some time, just as it will in the British Library, or any other large library. Similarly, although a great many other libraries currently using LC are converting their catalogues to machine-readable form, there remains the need to arrange the books on the shelves, which is the basic purpose of the scheme. There is thus likely to be a continuing demand for the schedules to be maintained, and the Library seems to be willing to accept this responsibility.

That a degree of confidence in the future of the scheme exists is shown by the number of libraries that adopted it during the 1960's.[7] In 1964 it was estimated that 800 to 1,000 libraries had adopted it, and that this number might double in eight years; however, the flight from DC appears to have slowed down rather more quickly than was anticipated, and we no longer read of large numbers of libraries making the change, which in any case was confined very largely to academic libraries in the USA. The fact that Library of Congress cards give a ready-made call number certainly appeals to librarians hard pressed for staff, but the Decimal Classification Division now covers a very high proportion of books bought by public libraries in the USA, so pressure from this direction is now almost non-existent.

On looking at the recent additions to the schedules, one is sometimes tempted to believe that all attempts at classification in the sense of helpful, systematic, arrangement have been abandoned, and all that is now sought is a place to 'mark and park'.[8] The use of alphabetical arrangement (as in the examples from Radio apparatus and Psychology quoted earlier) appears to be almost universal in any new expansions, whether it is appropriate or not; we may indeed raise an eyebrow we find in Botany and Zoology, the classificatory sciences *par excellence,* the note (in several places) 'Further systematic subdivisions, *alphabetically arranged*' (italics added)! Unless the arrangement is to be helpful and systematic, there is little point in having classified shelf arrangement at all, as has been pointed out in chapter 15. It will be interesting to see what effect the increasing use of computer-based catalogues will have on the use of the classification in those libraries which have adopted it, particularly academic libraries.

OUTLINE. 2nd ed 1970. This revised edition gives more detail than the first, particularly for Science and Technology.

A   GENERALIA. 1911. 4th ed 1973. Some literal mnemonics, *eg* AE. Encyclopedias. AZ is now used for History of the sciences in general, Scholarship, Learning.

B-BJ   PHILOSOPHY. 1910. 2nd ed 1950 (1968s). Includes Psychology, Ethics, Etiquette.

BL-BX   RELIGION. 1927. 2nd ed 1962.

C   AUXILIARY SCIENCES OF HISTORY. 1915 (except Epigraphy, 1942). 3rd ed 1975. Includes Archeology CC and Numismatics CJ. Collective biography CT, but normally biography is classified with the subject.

D   HISTORY: GENERAL AND OLD WORLD. 1916. 2nd ed 1959 (1966s). DA is Great Britain (Favoured category); other European countries in approximately alphabetical order, with DE Greco-Roman world between Germany and Greece. DX Gypsies.

E-F   HISTORY: AMERICA. 1901. 3rd ed 1958 (1965s). The first of the main schedules to be published, this does not use a second letter in its notation. There are special tables for Jefferson and Washington.

G   GEOGRAPHY. 1910. 4th ed 1976. Includes maps and atlases. Most branches of Geography are in this schedule, also related topics such as Anthropology GN, Folklore GR, Recreation GV.

H   SOCIAL SCIENCES. 1910 (except Social groups, 1915). 3rd ed 1950 (1965s). Economics occupies HB-HJ, but Socialism, Communism, Marxism in HX follow Criminology in HV.

J   POLITICAL SCIENCE. 1910. 2nd ed 1924 (1966s). Place is the primary facet in many of the basic classes in this group, *eg* Local government JS, where the schedule under United States consists largely of a long list of individual towns etc arranged alphabetically. JX International law.

K   LAW. The schedules for American law KF were published in 1969. British law KD was published in 1973. An outline of the whole schedule was published in 1970. The classification for Law compiled by E Moys[9] has been suggested as an alternative.

L   EDUCATION. 1911. 3rd ed 1950 (1966s). Curriculum is subordinate to grade of school. Much of the schedule is simply a listing of educational establishments under country.

M   MUSIC. 1904. 2nd ed 1917 (1968s). M used for scores, ML History and criticism, MT Instruction. Ballet music appears to be a form of vocal music (M1520).

N   FINE ARTS. 1910. 4th ed 1970. The latest edition has been completely revised, and in addition introduces a publishing innovation; it is printed on one side of the paper only, to facilitate looseleaf filing and consequent updating.

P   LANGUAGE AND LITERATURE. 1909–1948 in parts, each of which is revised as a unit, *eg* PB-PH Modern European languages, 1933 (1966s). For 'minor' languages, literature and language are treated together; for major languages, the two are treated quite separately. The very detailed enumeration includes provision for particular editions of the more important works, but twentieth century literature is poorly treated in comparison with earlier periods. Literary form is usually ignored (an exception is the Elizabethan period of English literature, where drama is an important factor). Fiction and Juvenile literature go in PZ, which has led to problems of cross-classification with juvenile non-fiction and novels which may claim to be 'literature'.

Q   SCIENCE. 1905. 6th ed 1973. There is no synthesis in this class at all, and though science might be expected to lend itself to systematic arrangement, the schedules are notable for their use of alphabetical order.

R   MEDICINE. 1910. 3rd ed 1952 (1966s). Primary division is by medical discipline, *eg* RD Surgery.

S   AGRICULTURE. 1911. 3rd ed 1948 (1965s). Crop subordinate to pest at SB608. SB975 ends with SB987 General Works; there is no provision for the treatment of a particular pest by a particular method.

T   TECHNOLOGY. 1910. 5th ed 1971. This edition incorporates all the amendments found necessary since the 4th edition, 1948, but retains the same structure, which differs little from that of the 3rd edition published in 1937.

U   MILITARY SCIENCE. 1910. 4th ed 1974.

V   NAVAL SCIENCE. 1910. 3rd ed 1974.

Z   BIBLIOGRAPHY. 1902 (but prepared earlier). 4th ed 1959 (1965s). Includes Book industry and trade, Library science. Copyright has not been developed since 1949, as it will in due course be transferred to a new schedule in K. Basic arrangement of bibliographies is by subject, arranged alphabetically; a parallel arrangement to the whole classification would now be considered more useful, but the schedule was the first to be prepared and a decision had to be made quickly and on the basis of very little experience.

All the schedules were in print in mid-1976, and since the process of revision is a continuous one some of the dates given here as the latest printing will have been superseded. (The dates given in curves with an s indicate that the latest *edition* was reprinted at that date with supplementary pages.)

BIBLIOGRAPHY

1 By far the best account of the development of the scheme is to be found in

LaMontagne, L E: *American library classification, with special reference to the Library of Congress.* Shoe String Press, 1961. Although this began as a work specifically on LC, it is in fact much broader in scope, and presents a valuable outline of the history of library classification.

2 Cutter, C A: *Expansive classification.* The idea of this scheme was to enable librarians to select a classification detailed enough for their needs, but not too detailed; it was intended to have seven expansions, the first having only seven classes, the seventh being large and detailed enough for the largest collection. The seventh expansion was never completed, but the first six were published together by Cutter in 1891–1893.

3 Although the Library itself has not produced an official index, one does now exist:

Elrod, J M *and others: Index to the Library of Congress classification . . . : preliminary edition.* Canadian Library Association, 1974.

4 The LC class numbers given in LCSH have served as the basis of: Williams, J G *and others: Classified LCSH.* Dekker, 1972. 2v.

5 Angell, R: 'On the future of the Library of Congress classification.' (*In* International study conference on classification research, 2nd, Elsinore, 1964. *Proceedings* p 101–112). See also the annual report of the Librarian of Congress for current progress.

6 Butler, B: 'Automatic format recognition of MARC bibliographic elements: a review and a projection.' *Journal of library automation*, 7 (1) 1974, 27–42.

7 American Library Association: *The use of the Library of Congress classification*: report of a seminar held in New York, July 1966. ALA, 1968. Edited by R H Schimmelpflug and C D Cook.

Immroth, J P: *A guide to the Library of Congress classification.* Rochester, NY, Libraries Unlimited, second edition, 1971.

8 Immroth, J P: *Analysis of vocabulary control in Library of Congress classification, indexes and subject headings, and formulation of rules for chain indexing of Library of Congress classification.* Rochester, NY, Libraries Unlimited, 1971.

9 Moys, E: *A classification scheme for law books.* Butterworths, 1968.

Piper, P L and Kwan, C H: *Manual on KF, the Library of Congress classification schedule for law of the United States.* Rothman, for American Association of Law Librarians, 1972.

CHAPTER 22

Subject headings used in the dictionary catalogs of the Library of Congress [1-3]

When the Library of Congress moved to its new building in 1897, two problems had to be faced: the selection of a more satisfactory classification scheme, and the choice of the kind of catalogue to be compiled. In the nineteenth century several classified catalogues of the library's holdings had been published, but the practice was discontinued by Spofford, who was not in favour of classification. However, it was decided to conform to the majority practice in US libraries at the turn of the century, and a dictionary catalogue was chosen to be the main information retrieval tool. Work began on the compilation of a list of subject headings in 1897, and the first edition was published in two volumes, 1910–1914. Since then the list has grown enormously, and the latest edition, the eighth, is in two substantial volumes weighing several pounds each. (Even this is slightly more convenient than the seventh edition, which was in one massive volume.) Published in 1975, the list contains headings used by the Library from 1897 to December 1973, and is kept up-to-date by quarterly supplements, which cumulate progressively into an annual volume; these will in their turn cumulate progressively. The list is produced by computer-controlled typesetting, so we may envisage that in due course the cumulated amendments will be merged with the basic list to produce the ninth edition. However, as mentioned in chapter 12, it is possible to obtain the updated list in COM form, either on fiche or on roll film. The fiche version occupies about 45 fiche, while on 16mm film it will occupy about 4,500 frames, both at 24x reduction. Each quarterly issue will contain the complete list, with additions and changes for the current quarter indicated; deletions will be carried until the end of the year, and it is expected that new headings and references added each year will increase the size of the file by about five fiche after the deletions have been dropped. It will obviously be extremely useful to have the complete list in one file, though the programme of printed cumulations does mean that one would only have to look in two or at most three places—the main list, the latest annual cumulation and the latest quarterly cumulation—in order to be sure of finding the most recent version. The convenience of following up a series of cross-references in a collection of some 50 fiche would need to be established before one could make a final decision on the relative merits of the two methods. However, at US \$40 a year for fiche (US \$185 for film) many libraries will find it worth while to have at least one copy of the cumulated COM version.

FORMAT

The LCSH contains the complete entry vocabulary of the LC catalogues with certain exceptions mentioned below; terms in the index vocabulary, *ie* headings which are used, are in bold type, while those in the entry vocabulary only, *eg* synonyms, are in light type. In some cases LC class numbers are given to help define the subject area, in others scope notes and cross-references, *eg*

Canteens (Wartime, emergency, etc.)

Here are entered works on temporary establishments which provide members of the Armed Forces and, in emergencies, civilians with food and recreation . . .

Works dealing with employee lunch rooms, sometimes called canteens, are entered under the heading Restaurants, lunch rooms, etc.

Some of these scope notes might be thought to be a little less than helpful; for example, under the heading

Alcoholism and crime

we find the scope note:

Here are entered works on the relation between alcoholism and criminal behavior and the incidence of crime. Works on alcoholic intoxication as a criminal offense or as a factor of criminal liability are entered under the heading Drunkenness (Criminal law)

This might well give the cataloguer pause for thought: is the work in hand dealing with alcoholism or drunkenness, and if the former, is it *as* a crime or *in relation to* crime? Many works published currently deal with both, probably in order to cause difficulties for unsuspecting cataloguers.

1)   **Cant** (*English PE3726*)
2)   sa Canting arms (Heraldry) [Hardly relevant to English literature!]
        Shelta
        Slang
        Swearing
3)   x Argot
        Crime and criminals—language
4)   xx English Language—dialects
        Slang

1) Heading used, in bold type. LC class number given.
2) Related headings, which should be considered in case they are more precise for the book in hand.

3) Make *see* references from these unused headings.

4) Make *see also* references from these related headings to Cant.

It should be noted that sa and xx are in effect two sides of the same coin; under **Slang** we will find a reference sa Cant and another xx Cant. However, this is not always true, since the principle of making only downward references applies; a sa reference under a broad term will be reflected by an xx reference under the narrower term, but there will not be comparable references in the other direction. For example, under **Sun** we will find a reference sa Eclipses, Solar, reflected by a reference under **Eclipses, solar,** xx Sun; but there will not be references under **Sun** xx Eclipses, Solar or under Eclipses, Solar sa Sun. There are also inconsistencies which are less easy to explain, as for example is shown above, where the link **Cant** sa Shelta is not reflected by a reference **Cant** xx Shelta, although the two headings would appear to be of equal rank.

Certain categories of heading are not included; these include persons, family names, corporate bodies, structures such as castles, ships, religious bodies, mythological characters—in fact, any individuals of a species bearing a distinctive name. They may however appear in the list if they are used as examples under other headings, and six names—those of Thomas Aquinas, Lincoln, Shakespeare, Wagner and George Washington—are included to demonstrate the range of subdivisions that may be used in similar cases. One page of the introduction is in fact devoted to a complete list of 'Headings serving as patterns for sets of subdivisions', ranging from Founders of religion (example Jesus Christ) through Universities (example Harvard University) to Crops (example Fruit).

Names of places are included, though the list is obviously very selective (it is not intended to be a gazetteer), and since it is impractical to show under every geographical name in the list *all* of the subdivisions that might be used with it, the introduction gathers these together in two complete lists, the first of subdivisions that may be applied to names of regions, countries, states etc, the second of those applicable to names of cities.

Division by place may be used where appropriate. Originally subdivision by place was indirect, but this practice was changed many years ago: however, indirect subdivision was retained in those cases where it had already been used, so the current list presents a somewhat unpredictable mixture of the two. Headings that may be divided by place are always followed by the words (Direct) or (Indirect) to indicate which is the correct method to use; unfortunately, there are a number of exceptions to the normal pattern for indirect subdivision, and though these are all listed in the introduction, the overall result is still confusing to any but the experienced cataloguer. For example, Art is to be divided directly, but Music indirectly, so we have **Art**—Paris, not

Art—France—Paris, but **Music**—Austria—Vienna, not **Music**—Vienna. However, this does *not* apply in the case of the states, constituent countries or provinces of a number of countries, including the USA, Canada, Great Britain, Australia and the USSR, unless the specific place required as a subdivision is a 'subordinate locality such as a county or city'. So we would have **Music**—South Australia, but **Music**—Australia—Adelaide. To keep the cataloguer alert, some headings normally divided indirectly may not be subdivided by names of cities, but are instead used as subdivisions under the name of the city; for example, **Libraries**—South Australia would be correct, but **Libraries**—Australia—Adelaide would be wrong, and we should use **Adelaide**—Libraries. An instruction is given with each subject heading that is to be treated in this way, but even so, it seems most unlikely that the casual user will be able to predict the correct heading to look under, and the network of cross-references that becomes essential is extremely complex.

Bibliographical forms and common subjects may be used as subdivisions as required, and a large part of the introduction is devoted to a list of these with annotations on their use: these may be very brief, *eg*

MORGUES
> Use under names of cities.

or very lengthy, as for example Dictionaries, under which the instructions for use occupy more than a column of type. Cross-references are used within the list, *eg*

MONASTERIES
> Use under names of cities.
> sa   Convents
> x   Abbey

These annotations are an extremely useful feature of the eighth edition, and help to solve many problems that arise in practice, *eg*

DRAWINGS
> Use as a form subdivision under technical subjects for collections of drawings, plans, etc., *eg* **Forging machinery**—Drawings. Use also as a topical subdivision for discussions of the technique for making such drawings, unless headings for the technique have been especially provided. That is, since **Automotive drafting** exists, '**Automobiles**—Drawings' is used only as a form heading.
> x   Drawing

There is no doubt that this list, and in fact the lengthy introduction as a whole, is a welcome addition to the new edition.

Period subdivisions may be used where necessary under countries or subjects. To make computer sorting possible, these subdivisions are always to be given in the form of specific dates, and phrase subheadings used in previous editions have all been converted; thus

Rome—History—Aboriginal and early period

becomes
Rome—History—To 510 B.C.

As computers have their own rules for filing order, the use of MARC records has necessitated some changes in the filing order of the various forms of heading. These changes have however not yet been applied in the card catalogues of the Library, but are followed in the computer-produced bibliographic records available, so that the two are no longer strictly compatible. The new filing order is strictly word by word, in which 'word' is defined as 'one or more letters or numerals set off by spaces or marks of significant punctuation, such as the hyphen'. Numbers expressed in digits file before alphabetic characters, so it may be necessary to look in two different places for, say, a date—1984 will not file in the same place as nineteen eighty four.

Two other major changes are those affecting headings with qualifiers and headings consisting of abbreviations. Inverted headings now precede parenthetical qualifiers, so that in the example given in chapter 7, we would now find in the computer-produced records:

Pipe
Pipe, Aluminium
Pipe, Wooden
Pipe (Musical instrument)

instead of

Pipe
Pipe (Musical instrument)
Pipe, Aluminium
Pipe, Wooden

Acronyms and other abbreviations without internal punctuation are treated as words, but initials separated by, *eg*, full stops are treated as strings of one-letter words, and thus file at the beginning of the sequece. For example, we find in the seventh edition the cross-reference

Compute (Computer program)

see **COMPUTE** (Computer program)

with COMPUTE filed at the beginning of the C sequence as if it consisted of separate letters; in the eighth edition, it is filed in the normal place as a single word.

It is sometimes very difficult to see any sort of consistency among sets of similar headings; for example, if we turn to Libraries we find

	Libraries, naval
but	Libraries, military *see* Military libraries
	Libraries, Catholic
but	Libraries, Hebrew *see* Jewish libraries

Libraries, children's

but   Libraries, Negroes' *see* Libraries and Negroes

We will also find

Library administration   (*not* Libraries—administration)

but   **Acquisitions (libraries)**

Literature and science

but   Literature and religion *see* Religion and literature.

Cataloguing of moving pictures

but   **Classification—Moving-pictures**

the latter two actually occurring on the same Library of Congress card! (LC 67-12056)

The use of both singular and plural forms of nouns can lead to unsatisfactory separations, *eg*

Plastic films

Plastic sculpture

Plasticity

Plasticizers

Plastics

Plastics—research

Plastics, Effects of radiation on

Plastics in buildings

Plastics industry and trade

where Plastic films should clearly be with the other items on plastics if it is not to be overlooked. It is quite true that the liberal use of cross-references can overcome these problems, but this does not seem to be a good argument for abandoning the attempt to help the reader by giving him immediate direct entry, which is the main justification for the use of alphabetical headings.

Sometimes the noun form is used, sometimes the adjectival, *eg*

Abdomen—diseases

but   **Abdominal pain**

Thorax *see* Chest

but   **Thoracic duct**

Many of the sets of cross-references linking related subjects seem to be compiled by chance rather than by design. There are in effect two such sorts of reference, those showing genus-species relationships, and those linking subjects from different hierarchies or even different basic classes. For example, we find a reference

Insects, Fossil *see also* Thrips, Fossil

but not   Insects *see also* Thrips

Weevils *see* Beetles

Beetles *see also* Sugar-cane beetles

but not   *see also* Sugar-cane weevils (which is an orphan)

Education *see also* Libraries

see also General semantics

but not   see also Museums

though this may well be as relevant as the first and is probably more so than the second. J Daily investigated the cross-references that could be followed up started from the heading Hunting; after finding about 2,000, including one trail that led to Pimps, the search had to be abandoned for lack of time.[4] As mentioned in chapter 5, Daily also found a high proportion of 'orphans' though it is not clear just how serious this is in practice.

We would expect to find a fairly close relationship between the classification scheme used for shelf arrangement and the alphabetical headings used in the catalogue, but in practice this does not seem to be the case. The two systems are treated quite separately, and indeed it is often argued that there need be no connection because they serve different purposes. Even the structure of *see also* references does not appear to be based on the LC scheme; Coates suggests that the scheme to which it bears most affinity is DC!

It can be argued that a list of subject headings should not be tied to any classification scheme, since the freedom to make cross-references in an alphabetical sequence would be hampered by too close an adherence to a classified structure. However, unless the task of making cross-references is approached systematically the resulting network is likely to be less helpful than it might be. This does not mean that subject headings should reflect one and only one systematic approach; BTI, for example, uses a number of classification schemes to help in the generation of its cross-reference network. LCSH, however, does not seem to reflect any kind of plan at all; cross-references seem to be inserted by chance, without reflecting any kind of systematic overview. The main objection to this is the lack of predictability; users do not know whether the cross-references they find are all that might be worth following up, or whether they have to cast about for additional headings under which relevant material might be filed.

It is clear that LCSH and its companion classification are by no means perfect tools. Both suffer from inconsistencies and from lack of specificity, and the user outside the Library of Congress needs to view them with caution rather than the uncritical acceptance with which they are sometimes hailed as being the solution to the problems posed by DC. It is only fair to point out, however, that both show in a very acute form the conflict we have already discussed between keeping pace with knowledge and 'integrity of numbers'. Whereas DC and similar schemes are not tied to any particular collection, LC and LCSH represent the arrangement of some millions of items on the shelves and in the card catalogues of the Library of Congress; though the subject cataloguers are well aware of inconsistencies and errors, the amount of effort that would be needed to remedy these is simply not available.

Indeed, one of the reasons given for changing to LC from DC is that the former *is* tied to the collections and will therefore not be subject to large scale changes. There is no easy solution to this dilemma, as we have pointed out; however, the extent to which we can make good use of LC and LCSH depends on our awareness of the problems involved in the maintenance of such large scale tools. Uncritical acceptance of Library of Congress cards, complete with call numbers and subject headings, will lighten the work of the cataloguer, but we should be aware of the possible pitfalls for the reference librarian.

The start of the MARC project prompted a suggestion that the main catalogue of the library, which now contains over 15,000,000 cards, should be closed and a new sequence begun using a completely revised list of subject headings. LCSH would have remained as the authority file for the old catalogue, with a new list on similar lines, but avoiding the inconsistencies of the old, being used for the new catalogue. However, the proposal was given a rather mixed reception and it was decided not to take such a drastic step. At least the use of computers will make changes much easier in the future, and the proposal is currently being reconsidered.[5]

BIBLIOGRAPHY

1 Coates, E J: *Subject catalogues*. Chapter VII.

2 Haykin, D J: *Subject headings: a practical guide*. Washington, Library of Congress, 1951.

3 Horner, J L: *Cataloguing*. Chapters 9 and 13.

4 Daily, J: *LC and Sears: their adequacy for today's library needs*. ALA Pre-Conference Institute on Subject Analysis, Atlantic City, June 19–21, 1969.

5 Angell, R S: 'Library of Congress Subject Headings: review and forecast.' (*In* Wellisch, H: *Subject retrieval in the seventies*. 1972, p143–163.)

CHAPTER 23

Sears list of subject headings

The LCSH has always been very detailed, and a demand arose for a list which should be less comprehensive and more suited to the needs of small libraries—though as we have seen, LCSH is itself frequently not specific. The argument advanced in the preface to Sears ninth edition is that 'specificity is relative and depends on the size of a library, its function, and its patrons . . . Practicality rather than theory should determine the degree of specificity'. It is not clear that these two statements can be reconciled, but in any case this represents a very different approach to specificity than the one put forward in this text.

The first edition was prepared by Minnie Earl Sears, and was based on the practice found in 'nine small libraries known to be well cataloged'. The headings adopted were edited to conform with LCSH practice, so that libraries using LC cards or wishing to add headings from the larger list would find it possible to do so. This edition contained *see* references with their corresponding refer froms, but not see also references; these were added in the very much enlarged second edition. In the third edition, Miss Sears included the 'Practical suggestions for the beginner in subject heading work' which for many years served as one of the few textbooks on the subject, and still forms a significant part of the work. In the fourth edition the scope was enlarged, and DC numbers were added to the headings; common subdivisions, *eg Bibliography*, were indicated by the use of italic type.

The sixth edition was retitled *Sears list of subject headings* as a recognition of Miss Sears' contribution, the the qualification *for small libraries* was dropped; in order to bring the list more into the line with LCSH practice, x and xx were introduced in place of the more explicit 'refer from' used in earlier editions. The latest edition, the ninth, edited by Barbara M Westby, continues the by now traditional format, with the exception of the omission of DC numbers from the headings; it is very largely in line with LCSH seventh edition, with a few modifications, largely in the direction of popular terminology.

The work begins with the preface, in which the policies followed in bringing the list up to date are outlined, with examples of some of the headings which have been changed, *eg* Spinsters, altered to Single women. Over 300 new headings have been added, and the revision process is to continue in subsequent editions. The preface to the eighth edition follows, giving the historical outline, and explaining the layout and typography used, which is the same as that in LCSH; there are also lists of classes of headings included, *eg* names of the most common animals, and excluded, *eg* names of persons and places.

In total, the ninth edition contains about 4,000 headings, compared with over 36,000 in LCSH. However, it would appear that the pruning has at times been somewhat uneven; there are three headings for varieties of pig (Pigs, Hogs, Swine—some nice distinctions here!) and four for cattle (Cattle, Cows, Bulls, and Calves).

The 'Suggestions for the beginner in subject heading work' are now attributed to Bertha M Frick, who edited the sixth, seventh and eighth editions. These notes must be studied by anyone wishing to use the list, but they also form a useful introduction to the subject generally, though in many ways they are not in agreement with the principles outlined in the present work. They are followed by a brief bibliography of 'Aids to subject cataloging' and by a two page spread showing how the list is to be used. The preliminaries end with a list of subdivisions which may be used, *eg Laws and regulations*, and a list of headings to be supplied by the cataloguer, *eg* proper names.

The list itself is in double column format, but only one column is used; the vacant parallel column is for the cataloguer to add any amendments, so that the list may serve as an authority file without the necessity to compile a separate record. The headings used are, in general, current terminology, and recent techniques, such as Finger painting, are included; however, the list reflects (reasonably enough) its American origin, and some of the terms would need to be altered in British libraries. As well as the obvious differences, such as Railroads, we find such terms as Showers (Parties), and Commencements (meaning a kind of university graduation ceremony). Natural language is used with its attendant problems; we find such headings as Cookery for the sick, First aid in illness and injury. 'Compound' headings are used; by these are meant such pairs of terms as Pilgrims and pilgrimages, Pilots and pilotage, Voyages and travels, as well as phase relationships such as Science and state. Many of the headings are not specific, and double entry is recommended as being frequently necessary. The example of a work on Medieval church architecture, which has to be entered under Church architecture and Architecture, Medieval, has already been quoted; a book on Multivariate statistical analysis for biologists would presumably have to take its chance at the general heading Statistics. At one time, books were not written about such specific subjects; now, they are—but subject headings do not seem to keep pace with the tendency. We find the same inconsistencies with Sears as with LCSH; for example, the excerpts quoted from the LCSH heading Libraries could equally well be quoted from Sears, though the latter contains fewer of them.

Despite its American origin, Sears is probably more widely used proportionately in British libraries than in American, where LCSH is more popular. Its helpful presentation and relative simplicity may appeal to the librarian anxious to speed up the processing of his accessions, but it is doubtful if it is adequate to carry the burden of an intensive exploitation of today's literature.

BIBLIOGRAPHY

1 The readings given for LCSH also apply to Sears.

2 Corrigan, P R D: *Introduction to Sears list of subject headings.* Bingley, 1967. (Programmed text).

CHAPTER 24

Manual systems

The systems we have been discussing so far have been pre-coordinate systems in which the headings used—the index language—have included composite subjects. Many of the problems with such systems arise from the fact that in a heading representing a composite subject, some of the elements cannot be found directly, but must be sought indirectly, through additional entries (multiple entry systems), or through indexes or cross-references. Furthermore, the existence of a fixed significance or citation order may separate some elements of a composite subject that would, if brought together, be of interest to a user; again, it is necessary to follow through this kind of search by indirect means, or make multiple entries using the methods discussed in chapters 6 and 15. The problems that arise in the construction of adequate means of finding the headings which will retrieve the information required to answer a particular enquiry—*ie* of constructing a valid index language with a satisfactory entry vocabulary—and the drawbacks of the various multiple entry methods, have been considered in earlier chapters. As we saw in chapter 6, postcoordination, by eliminating the need for combination order also eliminates all the problems associated with it, by using only single concepts at the input or indexing stage and transferring the act of coordination to the output or searching stage. Advocates of postcoordinate indexing have sometimes claimed that there are no other problems in indexing, but in chapters 5 and 6 we saw that there are semantic and syntactic problems to be faced whatever system of indexing we use, and we must therefore examine the ways in which postcoordinate systems attempt to solve these problems.

A post-coordinate system consists of an input in which the headings used are (normally) single concepts, and an output which enables us to compare the entries under a number of these headings in such a way that we can select the ones which are common to them. Take, for example, the composite subject for which we established a heading in accordance with the principles of Coates: manufacture of multiwall kraft paper sacks for the packaging of cement. Without having to make any decisions as to relative importance, we simply enter this under the relevant terms: manufacture, multiwall, kraft, paper, sacks, packaging and cement. Note that these are exactly the same terms as we used earlier, but instead of making one entry we have made seven. There are some points which need to be considered here. Firstly, none of these entries is a specific entry; there will be a relatively large number of entries under each heading, of which the majority will relate to documents which deal with much more specific subjects than the heading. In our example, everything we have in the system to do with *paper* will be entered under that heading. If we have to rely on these headings as they stand, we may find it necessary to do a certain amount of unnecessary sequential scanning. Secondly, the number of entries in the system will be much larger than if we were using a single entry precoordinate system; it will be the same as the number arising if we use multiple entry consistently. Thus far we are in the same position as with any of the multiple entry systems already studied; in these we also found the need for sequential scanning and a large number of entries. However, the third point is a vital one, and it is here that we see the first major difference: the number of different headings will be relatively small.

We have already seen that one advantage of a synthetic scheme is that it can be far smaller than an enumerative scheme of the same specificity, simply because it lists only individual foci, whereas the enumerative scheme lists many composite subjects as well. A postcoordinate system is exactly the same as a synthetic classification; it lists only single foci. However, in use the synthetic scheme is employed to build up a catalogue in which composite subjects do appear, so the number of headings which may appear in such a catalogue is very large, but in a post-coordinate system the number of potential headings remains simply the sum of the foci available. A simple example will demonstrate the difference very clearly. In the schedule compiled earlier for library science (figure 11), we found seven facets (excluding common facets) containing between them about forty five foci; if we used these headings in a post-coordinate system, there would be a maximum of 45 headings, but in a pre-coordinate system we might have many thousands of different headings arising, for the number of different combinations of facets is 127 (2^7-1), and this has to be multiplied by the number of foci in the different facets involved in each combination.

A post-coordinate system is thus characterized by a relatively small number of different headings, each with a relatively large number of entries under it. At the output stage, we have to be able to select the headings in which we are interested and compare the entries under them; what we do is coordinate single concepts to build up a composite subject, but we do this at the output stage instead of the input. If we think in terms of a conventional card catalogue, it becomes rather difficult to carry out this process of coordination; we cannot conveniently scan two sets of entries, let alone more than this, especially since, as we have seen above, there is likely to be a large number of entries under each heading. The use of a post-coordinate system implies the use of some kind of new physical medium which lends itself to this new kind of searching. Basically, of course, entries remain the same in that they consist of a combination of a heading and a document description, just as do entries in any pre-coordinate system. However, to

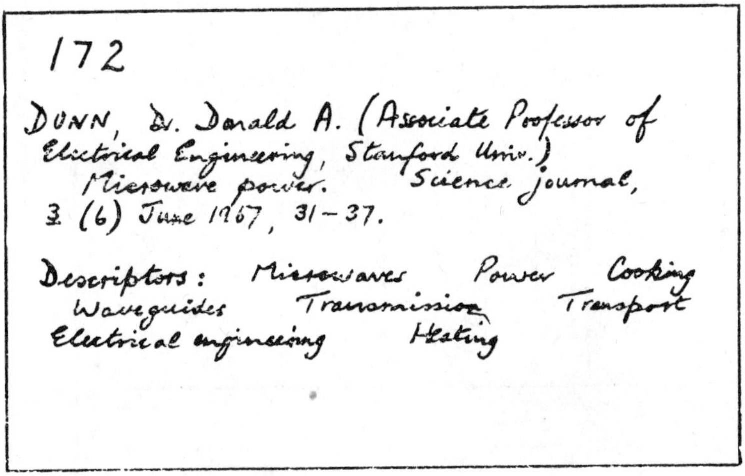

172

DUNN, Dr. Donald A. (Associate Professor of Electrical Engineering, Stanford Univ.)
Microwave power. Science journal, 3 (6) June 1967, 31–37.

Descriptors: Microwaves Power Cooking Waveguides Transmission Transport Electrical engineering Heating

FIGURE 15: A typical accessions card.

facilitate searching, document descriptions are usually reduced to a number, which identifies but does not describe; to obtain the description, it is necessary to turn to a subsidiary file kept in number order. Such a file is an essential part of most post-coordinate systems, and a search through the subject file will yield, not a series of document descriptions, but a series of numbers, which we then have to look up in the subsidiary file. Browsing is clearly not helped by this procedure, and whereas in a conventional card catalogue we can skim through a number of entries quickly, discarding those which do not suit our purpose, we cannot do this with a post-coordinate index, but must instead go to each of the entries in the subsidiary file in turn to establish its relevance. If none of the items found are relevant, or if a change of search strategy is needed to find additional items, we have to begin the new search from scratch; it is difficult to make the kind of alteration of strategy in mid-search which is possible with precoordinate systems.[1]

UNITERM

The simplest form of post-coordinate index is the Uniterm index, introduced by Mortimer Taube in 1953. The name is a portmanteau word, from unit and term, and is intended to emphasize the system's use of single terms as opposed to composite headings. A Uniterm card has a

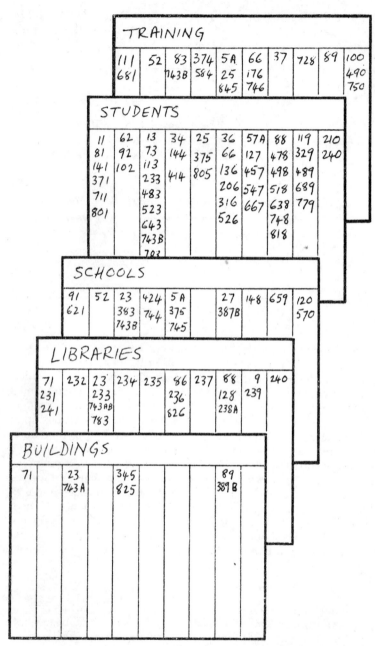

FIGURE 16: A set of Uniterm cards showing the use of links.

space at the top for the headings, the rest of the card being divided up into ten columns. When the terms which are to be used as headings for a given document have been decided, the cards for those headings are removed from the index (or new cards are made out if necessary), and the document number is entered on them, using *terminal digit posting*. This simply means that it is the final digit which determines the filing column: 795 is entered in column 5, not column 7. The method helps to spread entries over the card at random instead of filling it up a column at a time. The cards are refiled in the alphabetical sequence when the number has been entered on them all. Searching is equally simple; once the search terms have been decided, the cards for those terms are removed from the index and compared to see which numbers appear on them all; the card with the fewest numbers on it is taken as the basis of comparison, and first checked against the card with the next fewest, corresponding numbers being jotted down. These numbers can then be checked on any other cards, until we end up with a few numbers which have appeared on all of the cards. We now turn to the subsidiary accessions file to obtain details of the documents.

OPTICAL COINCIDENCE CARDS

Searching a Uniterm file is unsatisfactory in that it relies on our ability to notice matching numbers on the cards we are scanning; it is easy to miss a number, which might of course be a particularly important document. One way of making searching easier is to translate numbers into positions, indicating the presence of a number on a card by punching out a hole at its position; now when we wish to search, all we have to do is to hold the relevant cards up to the light, which will shine through those positions which are punched out on all the cards we are holding. Such cards are known by a variety of names: Batten cards, optical coincidence cards, peek-a-boo cards, feature cards, peephole cards; of these, optical coincidence is probably the best description, but peek-a-boo and feature cards the most widely used.

A peek-a-boo card contains a space at the top for the heading, like a Uniterm card, but the body of the card is divided up into numbered squares. A small card will probably contain 500 or 1,000 positions, while a large one will contain up to 10,000. To enter information into the system, we select the terms we require to describe a document, and remove these cards from the file; then, using a punch of some kind, we drill out a hole in the position corresponding to the document number, and refile the cards. The punch may be a simple hand drill or it may be a much more elaborate electrically operated model; the difference lies in the cost and in the accuracy with which the holes may be made, and the user will normally purchase the cheapest model which gives the required accuracy. When large cards are used, with small holes to give the maximum number of positions, accuracy is important, for inaccurate punching will introduce an element of error. For this reason, large punches will normally go through a number of cards at a time, so that the holes will all be in the same position provided that the cards are properly aligned at the time of punching; this is much more difficult to achieve with a hand punch which will only go through one or two thicknesses at the same time.

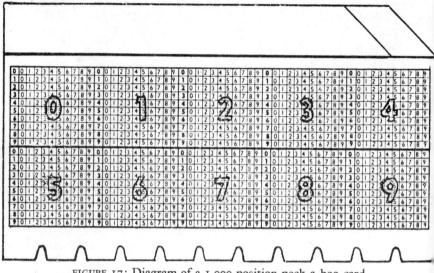

FIGURE 17: Diagram of a 1,000 position peek-a-boo card.

Another useful piece of equipment is the light box. This simply consists of a box containing a diffuse source of light, with one side of the box translucent; instead of holding the cards we are searching up to the light, we place them on the box, and the light shines through from below or behind, which is more convenient than holding the cards up above eye level. There is an additional advantage, relating to search strategy. If we wish to coordinate, say, four terms, but find that when we hold the appropriate cards up to the light that no holes coincide in all of them, we can broaden the search by reducing the number of cards to three; since there are four to start with, we can reduce the number to three in four different ways, by removing each of the cards in turn, scanning the remaining three, then replacing it. With a light box, we can do the same thing in one operation, by stepping up the light power so that light shines through one thickness of card. Some manufacturers are making their cards of translucent material to facilitate this process.

384

Peek-a-boo cards may have certain refinements to make their use easier. For example, a series of notches along the bottom edge fit on to a corresponding set of rods in the bottom of the card tray; these rods enable each card to be stepped in relation to its immediate neighbours. At the top right hand corner, each card has a space for the heading; if a card is removed from the stepped sequence, instead of a heading we see the word OUT, or a row or dots, or some similar symbol to indicate that a card is missing from the sequence. We can refile cards very quickly, without having to search through a set of cards in which we can only see one at the time, as would be the case if the cards were not stepped. There may be room on the card to note items of useful information such as related headings. These refinements do not in any way affect the principle of operation.

UNITERM AND PEEK-A-BOO COMPARED

Although the basic principle is the same, these two methods differ in their case of use and in their cost. Uniterm is very cheap and easy to establish; it requires no special apparatus at all. A peek-a-boo system may involve considerable capital outlay; not only does it require such apparatus as punches, but the cards themselves must be accurately printed on good quality card stock, so they too are not cheap. On the other hand, scanning a large Uniterm index is a very tedious process, and the probability of error is high through the likelihood of numbers being missed; peek-a-boo indexes are easy to use. An interesting compromise is to use a Uniterm system to start with, transferring to peek-a-boo when some experience has been gained in the choice of vocabulary, exhaustivity required and similar factors—or, to use an inelegant but expressive phrase, when the 'bugs' have been ironed out.

Another point of comparison which becomes significant when peek-a-boo is considered is the problem of correcting input errors which are detected. With any system, errors may arise at the input stage; in an alphabetical file, words may be misspelt, while in a systematic file notation may be incorrectly typed or copied. If undetected, such errors, together with any that arise in filing correctly headed entries, will result in loss of recall, and can only be rectified if they are discovered, which will normally be by chance. Highly complicated notational symbols accentuate the possibility of undetected errors through misfiling, but they may arise in any system. What happens to errors that are detected before they become irretrievable? In a card catalogue or Uniterm catalogue, errors can be altered to the correct form without much difficulty, but a hole punched in the wrong place is not so easy to correct!

Withdrawals can also present something of a problem. It is of course possible to stamp Withdrawn on the accessions card, but it would be better not to lead the reader up this blind alley if it can be avoided. One ingenious solution is to have a coloured translucent sheet which is punched out in the appropriate place *when an item is withdrawn;* this sheet is included in the pack of peek-a-boo cards for every search. If a hole shows through all the subject cards but is coloured, the item is potentially relevant and still in stock; if however the hole is clear, it means that the item was potentially relevant but has been withdrawn. If the accessions card is kept, it may be possible to obtain another copy of the item, for example from the BLLD.

CHOICE OF TERMS

This brief discussion of the physical format of Uniterm and peek-a-boo cards has assumed that we knew which terms we wished to use as headings in indexing and searching. As has been shown in the first part of this book, it is precisely this choice which often leaves us in doubt. Early proponents of post-coordinate indexing claimed that to select the correct keywords it was sufficient to read through the document to be indexed and underline the words which appeared to be significant. This procedure is clearly open to several objections; it takes no account of synonyms, and cannot demonstrate any kind of relationship. Though relevance may be high, recall is likely to be low, and the only kind of situation where the results are likely to be tolerable is in a clearly defined subject area with well established terminology, and with readers who can state precisely what they want. If we are to achieve good results under normal conditions, we must use as closely controlled a vocabulary with post- as with pre-coordinate indexing.

The problems associated with the use of words have already been discussed, and there is no need to go into detail again. We have to select a preferred term and refer to it from *synonyms*; we have to distinguish *homographs*; we have to be aware of *semantic relationships*. These requirements imply the necessity of some sort of authority to show usage, just as with a pre-coordinate file; however, to distinguish lists intended for post-coordinate systems, they are usually referred to as *thesauri*[2] (singular, thesaurus). The only difference between a thesaurus and a list of subject headings is that the former normally excludes headings for composite subjects; with some examples, even this is not true, and one is forced to the conclusion that the name is intended to signify a distinction which does not exist. Many lists of subject headings have left much to be desired, and thesaurus constructors have perhaps endeavoured to persuade us (and themselves) that their lists were free from fault. It is certainly true that thesauri in general are more precise in listing relationships to broader and coordinate terms than are most subject headings lists, as we saw in the discussion in chapter 5. The following examples, similar to or expanded from those in chapter 5, will served to refresh the memory on the difference between the two systems.

386

		TEST[3]	LCSH
1)	Preferred term	Thorax	Chest
	Instruction	UF Chest (*ie* Use For)	x Thorax
	Synonym	Chest use Thorax	Thorax see Chest
	(NB choice of scientific term by TEST)		
2)	Preferred term	Forging	Forging
	Instructions	UF Cold forging	x Drop forging
	(broader term)	BT Metal working	xx Blacksmithing
	(narrower term)	NT Drop forging	sa Ironwork
	(related terms)	RT Cold working	sa Blacksmithing
		Heat treatment	xx Explosive forming

SYNTAX

The choice of terms and the establishment of genus-species relationships together provide us with an indexing vocabulary, but we must also consider the other aspect of an indexing language, its syntax. It is possible to use a completely unstructured vocabulary; this may give good recall but is likely to result in low relevance. For example, consider the two subjects: *electrolytic extraction of aluminium from bauxite* and *welding of aluminium beer cans*. In the first, aluminium is the end product, whereas in the second it is the raw material from which another end product is made. A classification scheme would clearly distinguish these two aspects of aluminium by their context; the first would be found in metallurgy, the second in container manufacture. In other words, by placing the concept in a particular context, the classification scheme implicitly assigns it a particular *role*, as we saw in chapter 6. We may use roles in postcoordinate systems, but to do so we must make them explicit; this in the present example we would have two cards for aluminium rather than one, the first headed Aluminium 1, the second Aluminium 2, where 1 = raw material, 2 = end product. By so doing we can improve specificity, while still leaving ourselves the possibility of high recall by considering both entries in our search rather than just one. We can also introduce an element of direction into the relationships shown by bringing together two terms; to quote an example mentioned earlier, if we merely collate Albums and Photographs, we may mean albums of photographs or photographs of albums. By specifying 'end product' or 'raw material' we can make the direction clear. An often quoted but unlikely example is the ambiguous concatenation of blind and Venetian, but the problem is likely to be rather more acute when we are indexing materials in such subject areas as Chemistry, where the direction of a particular reaction is likely to be important. For example, a paper on *the observation of solar eclipses using artificial satellites* would be recalled if we were searching for information on *the observation of artificial satellites* if we did not use roles. If, however, we have more than one card for satellites, according to whether they are end product (manufacture of . . .), or agent (observations by . . .) we can improve the relevance performance of our system. The first EJC Thesaurus contained a list of roles for general use, but these were dropped from TEST following an investigation by Lancaster which showed that their use led to only a small increase in performance to set against the doubling of the time taken to index each document.[4] It seems that roles are only likely to be of value when they are designed for a particular situation, and the set of subheadings used in MESH, described in chapter 26, serve this purpose very satisfactorily.

In chapter 6 we also discussed the possibility of linking together concepts forming part of the same theme. In a precoordinate index this is done automatically as we combine the appropriate terms into strings, but here again we have to make the linkage explicit in postcoordinate indexes by the use of *links*. Suppose that we have a document dealing with two separate subjects, *eg* a description of a piece of research which also describes in some detail a particular method. In a pre-coordinate system we should make two entries, which would be quite separate, but an unsophisticated approach to post coordinate indexing could lead to errors which may be described as *false drops*. For example, a document which dealt with new library buildings, but included a discussion of the needs arising out of the practical training of library school students, might be indexed under the headings Libraries, Buildings, Training, Schools, Students; if we search for library school buildings, this document will be retrieved, although it does not deal with this subject and is therefore not relevant. If we link the elements of each of the two subjects, this kind of false drop can be eliminated. In a Uniterm index this can be done by adding a letter to the document number when it is entered on the cards; in the example above, if we denote the subject of library buildings A, and practical training of library school students B, the document will be entered on the cards as follows (assuming this is document 743) in Figure 16. Now if we search for library school buildings, we shall be warned not to retrieve this document, for Buildings is 743A while Schools is 743B. In a peek-a-boo index, this kind of differentiation is not possible (a hole is a hole!) but it is possible to give a document two or more accession numbers, to cater for as many different subjects as appear in it.

A second example will illustrate the use of links to avoid false drops in a slightly different situation. It is sometimes necessary to split the subject dealt with by a document into two or more parts, even though the document does not itself do this so definitely. Take for example a document dealing with 'The testing of magnesium and aluminium alloys'. This will be indexed under Testing, Magnesium, Aluminium and Alloys, and will be retrieved if we search for magnesium-aluminium alloys, although it may have nothing on alloys

388

containing both of these metals. We have to distinguish *two* subjects here: the testing of magnesium alloys and the testing of aluminium alloys; once we have done this, we can use links to prevent the incorrect association of magnesium and aluminium. Note that in a pre-coordinate index we should have had to make two entries in both this and the previous example; the two composite headings would have performed the work done here by links, by showing which concepts were associated and which were not.

A further use of links is possible within a single subject, but must be viewed with caution, since it may exclude associations incorrectly. Consider the subject 'Plastic coatings for tinplate containers'. If this is indexed without any controls, it will be retrieved when we search for documents on plastic containers, or tinplate coatings. Straightforward indexing of 'Manufacture of multiwall kraft paper sacks for the packaging of cement' means that this document will be retrieved when we search for items on the manufacture of cement, though it may well have nothing on this subject in it. If we link Plastics and Coatings, and Tinplate and Containers, then we shall avoid the false drop of plastic containers, but we shall also at the same time exclude the legitimate associations of Tinplate and Coatings, and Containers and Coatings. If we introduce additional links to show these, eventually we end up by linking every index term to every other—but this is where we started, with simple, unlinked, numbers! It is probably better to avoid this use of links, and employ roles instead in this kind of situation; in addition to the problem just described, the use of a link between Tinplate and Coatings does not give any indication of whether we are dealing with coatings *on* tinplate, or tinplate *as a* coating, whereas the use of roles does.[5]

WEIGHTING

As yet the use of weights in any kind of indexing is in an elementary stage. In conventional catalogues, of course, it has always been possible to make *added entries* for subsidiary subjects; the fact that they are added entries in itself indicates that they are not as important as the main entry, but no kind of quantitative indication of importance is normally given, except perhaps for the number of pages covered by the subject of an analytical entry. In recent years attempts have been made to introduce quantitative weightings, for example those shown below,[6] but it seems likely that their application is likely to be too subjective to be of value in a retrieval system.

Uniterm systems lend themselves to devices such as weighting, since it is simple to add a designation of this kind to the document number; using a peek-a-boo, it is necessary to list the descriptors and their weights on the accessions card if this technique is to be used—it is not possible to weight a hole! Most weighting systems have been intended for use with computer retrieval of information.

Weight	Description	When used
8/8	Major subject	The term is highly specific, and covers an entire major subject of the document
7/8	Major subject	The term is specific and covers most of the major subject of the document
6/8	More generic subject	The term is too broad and covers a major subject
5/8	Other important terms	Terms that would be used in binary indexing but not a major subject
4/8	Less generic subject	The term relates to but is too narrow to cover a major subject
3/8	Minor subject	Includes such terms as relate to results of experiments, intermediate methods, possible uses etc
2/8	Other subjects	Other relevant tags
1/8	Barely relevant	Subjects classifier would not want to use, but feels that some users might consider relevant

A rather simpler system uses only the numbers 1 to 3:

Weight	When used
3	The concept is central to the theme of the document
2	The concept is important, but not central to the theme of the document
1	The concept is worth indexing but is not important nor is it central to the theme of the document

ELIMINATING THE ACCESSIONS FILE

The need to refer from the subject file to a separate accessions file is a disadvantage of post-coordinate systems; it makes searching much more tedious than, say, flicking through the cards in a card catalogue or scanning the entries in a book catalogue. Two methods of overcoming this problem have been suggested. The first of these is to have a master matrix with a micro-image of an abstract of each document at the appropriate position; peek-a-boo cards are superimposed on this, and those images where the presence of holes in all the cards permits it are projected one at a time on to a screen. In view of the very high degree of reduction necessary in the images, and the accuracy with which the holes must be aligned, this technique is likely to remain expensive, and though the development of PCMI (photochromic micro-images) may make it technically feasible, it seems probable that other techniques will prove more practical.[7]

The second method is a development of the *dual dictionary*. Using a computer, it is simple to print out the contents of a post-coordinate index in the form of a series of headings under which are listed the document numbers to which they apply; in effect, the contents of a set of Uniterm cards are transferred to a printed sheet. If two such print-outs are made and bound up side by side, it becomes easy to compare the entries under two headings; the first is found in one printout, the second in the other, and they can be viewed side by side. A dual diction-ary has two advantages over the usual form of index; the first lies in the ease with which it may be scanned, while the second lies in the fact that it is printed and can therefore be multiplied, so that copies are avail-able in a number of places. An additional advantage is found if brief details of each document are printed out in one of the lists by the side of each accession number; now, comparison of the two lists will show not only the co-occurring numbers but also details of the relevant docu-ments.[8] This form of production, with its obvious resemblance to a conventional printed catalogue, should also help to dispel the illusion that postcoordinate indexes are term entry systems as opposed to con-ventional card catalogues, which are item entry systems; both are clearly term entry systems, the difference lying in the selection of terms and the physical format.

BIBLIOGRAPHY
1 There are a number of works on postcoordinate indexing, of which the following is a selection:

Bourne, C P: *Methods of information handling*. Wiley, 1963.

Campbell, D J: *A survey of British practice in co-ordinate indexing in information/library units*. Aslib, 1975.

Costello, J C Jr: *Coordinate indexing*. Rutgers, State University Graduate School of Library Science, 1966. (Rutgers series on systems for the intellectual organization of information, edited by Susan Artandi. Vol. 7.)

Documentation, Inc: *The state of the art of coordinate indexing:* report prepared for the National Science Foundation, Office, of Science Information Services. Washington, NSF, 1962.

Foskett, A C: *A guide to personal indexes*. Bingley, second edition 1970.

Jahoda, G: *Information storage and retrieval systems for individual researchers*. Wiley, 1970.

Jolley, J L: 'Punched feature cards.' *Journal of documentation, 31* (3) 1975, 199–215 (Progress in documentation)

Sharp, J: *Some fundamentals of information retrieval*. Deutsch, 1965.

Lancaster, F W: *Information retrieval systems: characteristics, test-ing and evaluation*. Wiley, 1968.

Reichman, J: *The state of the library art, volume 4*. Rutgers, State University, Graduate School of Library Science, 1961.

2 Blagden, J F L: 'Thesaurus compilation methods: a literature review.' *Aslib proceedings, 20* (8) 1968, 345–359.

Gilchrist, A: *The thesaurus in retrieval*. Aslib, 1971.

Gilchrist, A and Aitchison, J: *Manual of thesaurus construction*. Aslib, 1971.

Lancaster, F W: *Vocabulary control for information retrieval*. Information resources press, 1972.

See also the *Guidelines for the establishment and development of monolingual thesauri* published by ANSI, BSI and Unesco (refs 7, 8 and 9 of chapter 5)

3 Engineers Joint Council: *Thesaurus of engineering and scientific terms:* a list of engineering and related scientific terms and their relationships for use as a vocabulary reference in indexing and retrieving technical information. New York, EJC, 1967. This, named 'First edition' on the title page, is actually a major revision of the earlier *Thesaurus of engineering terms*, 1964.

4 Lancaster, F W: 'Some observations on the performance of EJC role indicators in a mechanised retrieval system'. *Special libraries, 55* (10) 1964, 696–701.

Lancaster, F W: 'On the need for role indicators in post-coordinate retrieval systems'. *American documentation, 19* (1) January 1968, 42–46.

5 Taube, M: 'Notes on the use of roles and links in coordinate indexing'. *American documentation, 12* (2) 1961, 98–100.

Artandi, S and Hines, T C: 'Roles and links—or, forward to Cutter'. *American documentation, 14* (1) 1963, 74–77.

6 Maron, M E, Kuhns, J L and Ray, L C: *Probabilistic indexing*. Los Angeles, Ramo-Wooldridge, 1959.

7 Wall, R A: 'COMP: Computer output microfilm peek-a-boo.' *Library Association record, 74* (3) 1972, 44.

8 Cherry, J W: 'Computer-produced indexes in a double-dictionary format.' *Special libraries, 57* (2) 1966, 107–110.

CHAPTER 25

Computer-based systems

Although some computer-based systems are precoordinate (for example PRECIS, BTI), the vast majority are indexed by postcoordinate methods, or use text searching, and systems which are indexed precoordinately can also be searched postcoordinately by computer. It therefore seems appropriate to consider computer-based systems in this section. No attempt can be made to describe all the available systems; a directory published in 1976 by ASIS listed three hundred and one data bases originating in the USA or Europe, and is in loose-leaf form so that additions can be made as necessary.[1] We will therefore restrict the discussion to a few examples, which may be taken as typical of the vast majority; once the general principles are established, they may be taken to apply to other examples besides the ones studied.

MEDLARS
The MEDical Literature Analysis and Retrieval System is typical of a very large number of data bases linked to the production of a printed index; it was one of the first to develop computerized processing, and the evaluation study by Lancaster (chapter 28) has led to various changes which are mirrored in other systems. It may thus be taken as a model of computer-based services based on intellectual indexing.[2]

The National Library of Medicine (NLM) is the centre of medical information services in the USA, having developed from the Surgeon-General's Library set up in 1879. The library has been involved in the bibliographical control of medical literature, with *Index medicus* as its major index to journal literature (under a variety of names) from its inception, but by the end of the 1950's it was beginning to find that the increasing quantity of literature to index was causing increasingly unacceptable delays. A preliminary project carried out in 1958–1960 explored the possibilities of using a computer to speed up the production; this was successful, but only in its limited objective, and the decision was taken to embark upon a much more ambitious project, which would not only speed up production but would at the same time produce a machine-readable record which could be used for later searching. With the aid of a substantial grant from the US government, the MEDLARS project began in 1961, with the following nine objectives:

1 To improve the quality and speed up the production of *Index medicus* (IM).
2 To make possible the production of other publications.
3 To expand the coverage of IM to include monographs etc.
4 To make possible the prompt searching of five years of tapes for both demand and recurring bibliographies.
5 To increase the depth of indexing.
6 To increase the coverage of journal articles.
7 To reduce duplication in the coverage of medical literature.
8 To keep statistics to monitor the system.
9 To permit future expansion, including new objectives.

Not all of these objectives have been fulfilled as yet, but there is no doubt that the system represents a tremendous improvement on the previous manual system.

Incoming journals are indexed in the normal way, using MESH as the source of headings (chapter 26). At first, journals were divided into two groups, those which were indexed in depth—the key journals—and those indexed less intensively. The evaluation study showed this to be a mistaken approach, and all journals are treated in the same way, with indexers basing the depth of indexing on the estimated importance of each article regardless of source. The bibliographical details and the index terms are then fed into the computer; those terms to be used as headings in IM are marked; the rest (terms of minor significance, or those not appropriate as headings in a printed bibliographical tool, *eg* adjectival qualifiers such as 'animal') are retained by the computer, but not used in the production of IM. Some 2,500 journals are covered (the 1975 *List of journals indexed in Index medicus* contains 2,331 titles), and about 120,000 items are added to the system each year, including some monographs, though the coverage of non-journal literature is not on the scale envisaged in objective 3, and the expansion of journal coverage does not appear to have taken place in the way envisaged in objective 6. However, Lancaster's study showed that coverage of the significant literature appeared to be at about the 95% level, and to improve on this would necessitate an enormous increase in the number of journals scanned which is almost certainly not economically worthwhile.

At the beginning of the project, no suitable equipment for computer-controlled typesetting of the kind required existed, and a large part of the government grant went into the design and construction of GRACE—GRaphic Arts Composing Equipment; the production of this equipment was a major step forward, but so rapid has been the development of computer technology that GRACE went into honourable retirement some years ago and has been replaced by more modern equipment.

The bibliographical information fed into the computer is used to produce *Index medicus, International nursing index, Index to dental literature* and *Population sciences*. It also produces the annual *Cumulated index medicus*, and a series of specialized recurrent bibliographies, *eg Index of rheumatology*, which are extracted from the main file but cover a restricted area of interest to a particular user group. MESH and the various associated publications are also produced from the information stored in the computer: however, the printed bibliographical tools are now only part of the overall operation.

MEDLARS went into operation in 1964, and the full files go back to that date. As part of a cooperative effort, whereby other countries supply entries for MEDLARS in exchange for the magnetic tapes containing the machine-readable files, MEDLARS centres have been set up in a number of countries outside the USA; the first of these was Britain, but other centres are now in operation in Europe, while in Australia the National Library has offered the service for some time. The first service to be offered was a demand bibliography search: users sent in their requests, which were translated into the appropriate search formulations using MESH, and Boolean logic (AND, OR and NOT) as explained in chapter 4. It was this demand search service which formed the subject of Lancaster's evaluation; this revealed a number of weak points, some of which are particularly relevant to this discussion.

The time factor was shown to be important in enough cases to be significant, since even when users do not express any dissatisfaction with the time taken to answer an enquiry, there is no doubt that for *any* user 'the sooner the better'! At the time, all enquiries were batch processed, using programs which were able to handle twenty or thirty enquiries in the same batch operation. In Britain, this meant that the usual turnaround time was a week or more, while at the NLM, with a greater demand, turn-around time might well be two weeks rather than the two days originally hoped for. These delays stressed the importance of online access, and led to the setting up of MEDLINE, discussed below.

Problems arose in the formulation of searches; many failures, both in recall and precision, arose from the fact that the search as carried out did not correspond to the real needs of the enquirer, either because the original enquiry was badly expressed or because it had become distorted by an intermediary—a local MEDLARS centre librarian or an NLM MEDLARS search analyst. This again emphasized the importance of on-line access, so that a wrongly formulated search may be altered as soon as it is seen to be wrong (heuristic as opposed to iterative searching), but since it was clear that on-line access would not be widely available for some years, some other action had to be taken in the mean time, and also to help those users who would continue to use the batch service. This action was the redesign of the enquiry form in order to elicit more information from the enquirer, who is required to write a full statement of his needs, in his own words; guidance is given on this, indicating the kind of information that is required. Any previously known work should be cited, and any limitations on the search should be specified. For example, the enquirer may only be interested in 'experimental' work on 'pathological conditions' in 'rats' in relation to the main subject of his enquiry, in which case he can tick the appropriate boxes. He may only be interested in documents in English, or some other specific language; Lancaster found that 45% of the data base was in languages other than English, but that in general the users surveyed made little use of this material. The request may be for a full search, (high recall with the risk of relatively low relevance), or he may prefer a narrow search (high relevance, and never mind about low recall). To give some guidance to the workers processing the request, the enquirer is also asked how many relevant items he expects to have been published in the previous three years, though it is not at all certain that any answer to this particular question can be anything but a guess for the majority of users.

The demand searches are usually performed on the most recent years of the data base (in Australia up to three years), but can be extended on request (accompanied by a higher fee!) The full data base goes back to 1964, but because of the changes introduced as the result of Lancaster's survey, the base is usually taken to begin in 1966; the ten-year file 1966 to 1975 contains some 2,500,000 references.

In addition to the demand searches, MEDLARS provides an SDI service; users submit a statement of their interests, which is converted into a MESH+ profile (*ie* any of the limitations which may be placed on a demand search may be incorporated) and matched against each month's tape as it arrives. This can be an important service in countries such as Australia, where the printed versions of such data bases may take anything up to three months to arrive (or even more if they clash with the Christmas mail!) whereas the tapes can be sent by air mail and be in use within a few days. This does not, of course, solve the question of the availability of the original articles, but so long as one copy is supplied by air mail this ensures a measure of accessibility while users await the arrival of other copies by surface mail. This problem does not exist in the USA, except in reverse for those journals for which indexing information is supplied from overseas; normally an article will not appear in IM until the original is in the NLM.

Lancaster's report had indicated the need for on-line access, as mentioned above, and in 1970 an experimental on-line system was set up to investigate the possibilities. AIM/TWX (Abridged Index Medicus—Telex) gave access through a number of remote terminals to a limited file of about 150,000 citations from some one hundred journals, selected as being the most important covered by MEDLARS.

The success of this experiment led to the setting up of a full-scale operational service in 1971, MEDLINE,[3] and this is now becoming available in other countries, *eg* Britain, Scandinavia and Australia. Access is normally restricted to part of the total data base (in Australia it is hoped to reach half a million references by the end of 1977), but searches can of course be extended to the full data base if the user wishes by processing them through the batch demand search service.

MEDLINE users can get help in formulating their searches by asking for displays of related terms; the hierarchical lists can also be scanned to suggest alternative strategies. The planning of a search can be quite complex, and it is usual for those wishing to use the system to undertake a short training course in order to be able to use the system to the full. It has proved to be very successful indeed in the USA, increasing the use made of the MEDLARS data base by an order of magnitude, and no doubt it will achieve similar success elsewhere as it becomes more widely available.

ERIC

The Educational Resources Information Center was set up by the US National Institute of Education (part of the Department of Health, Education and Welfare) to serve as a clearinghouse for educational information, in particular the increasing number of reports which were being published, and which were not subject to adequate bibliographical control. It was never the intention to set up a large library on the lines of the NLM, but rather to serve as a focal point for bibliographical activities carried out by a series of specialized clearinghouses run by bodies such as universities. For example, there was a Clearinghouse for Library and Information Science, CLIS, under the auspices of ASIS, and another for Media Resources, run by Stanford University. These have now merged to form the Clearinghouse for Library and Information Resources, CLIR; similar mergers have taken place between other clearinghouses, and a few new ones have emerged, so that at present there are seventeen. Each of these abstracts and indexes journals and reports in its own special field, and sends the entries to the central office, where they are assembled to form the two abstracting services, *Resources in education*, covering report literature from 1966, and *Current index to journals in education*, covering some 700 journals from 1969. Reports are given an Eric Document number, *eg* ED 013 371, and are made available in microfiche form at a standard price, or as hard copy at a price depending on size, through the Eric Document Reproduction Service. The two abstracting services are produced by computer from the data supplied by the clearinghouses; in addition to the normal bibliographical details and the abstract, the tapes include all the descriptors assigned to the document by the indexer, using the ERIC *Thesaurus* (chapter

27); however, as in MEDLARS, only those marked as major descriptors by the indexer will be printed out, so that a search of the tapes will reveal information not available through the printed indexes.[4]

The total file now includes some 250,000 references, with a further 30,000 being added each year. It is possible to obtain various subsets of the full file to serve particular purposes; for example, one can purchase the file for each clearinghouse by identifying the appropriate code, *eg* IR for CLIR. The tape will then include all items issued by that clearinghouse to date. Alternatively, it is possible to obtain all journal abstracts to date, or all report abstracts to date, in each case with a monthly, quarterly or annual update as required. If the whole file is not required one can order sections by quoting the first and last ED number or EJ accessions number, or by supplying a printed list of these numbers any desired subset can be obtained.

A variety of formats is available. Originally, all printout was in upper case only, and this is still the case for reports up to ED 016 144; currently, tapes are available for upper case only or upper and lower case—for the latter the user must of course have the appropriate computer hardware, as some configurations will only handle uppercase. Tapes can be supplied at 800 bits per inch or 1600 bits per inch; again, it will depend on the user's computer magnetic tape readers which is appropriate. The normal coding used is EBCDIC, but the journal and report abstract files are also available in MARC II format in ASCII code. It is obviously important to select the right combination of codings before ordering any of the files!

The ERIC *Thesaurus* is also available on tape, so that the user can obtain in machine readable form all the items necessary to perform his own searches, either in batch mode or on-line. Alternatively, the full tapes are usually available through various other centres, *eg* the National Library of Australia. One final point of interest is that, as with the preparation of the initial input, the ERIC Central office does not produce the tapes itself, but contracts this out to a commercial firm, currently Operations Research Inc.[13] ORI took over LEASCO in 1974.

CHEMICAL ABSTRACTS SERVICE (CAS)
Chemical abstracts is one of the most important abstracting services in the field of science and technology; beginning in 1907, it has gradually grown to become an essential part of almost any reference library worthy of the name. (In passing, we may note that it was not until after the beginning of the first world war that English displaced German as the major language abstracted!) As the years have passed, so the size of CA has steadily grown, as have the problems associated with its production and indexing. From 1907 to 1946 the indexes were cumulated decennially, but from 1947 the increase in size led to a decision to

cumulate quinquennially, and the latest quinquennial index (1972–1976) will occupy over sixty volumes! The number of abstracts has increased remorselessly; at present over 350,000 a year, the figure seems likely to reach the 400,000 mark in the foreseeable future.[5]

By the late 1950's it was becoming clear that the methods which had proved adequate until then were beginning to break down. An article published in, say, January 1957 in a non-American periodical might not appear in CA until the beginning of 1958; the subject indexes to the 1958 volume did not appear until the end of 1960, so that one might have to wait for up to four years before being able to trace an article through the subject index. Obviously steps had to be taken to bring the situation under control, not merely as it stood then, but as it was likely to develop, and investigations into the possibilities of computerization were begun.

The first fruits of these investigations showed in 1961 with the appearance of *Chemical titles*, a KWIC index to a selection of some 700 of the 12,000 journals then being covered by CA. Although this was seen by many as merely an interim stage before the introduction of more satisfactory services, it has in fact proved successful in its own right as a current awareness tool, and is widely used. Progress towards full machine production has been slow but steady since then, and the whole operation is now computer-based once the abstracts have been produced and keywords allocated. There has perhaps been some slight loss; the abstracts are not as full as they used to be, and the claim that they can act as a complete substitute for the original document is no longer made, but any losses of this kind are more than compensated by the presence of indexes in each issue and the prompt appearance of cumulated indexes, as well as the availability of various tape services.

In many ways, the problems facing the editors of an abstracting service in chemistry are the same as those facing the editors of any other service, except perhaps in quantity; there is, however, one problem which is unique to chemistry, and is the root of a great many difficulties: the identification of chemical compounds, especially organic compounds. CAS currently has some 3,000,000 compounds in its *Registry*, but the difficulties do not only stem from the huge numbers involved. A chemical compound may be described in a variety of ways, some of which may be ambiguous; for example, it may have a 'trivial' name such as 'aspirin', originally a trade mark; it will have a name such as acetylsalicylic acid, which will identify it rather more precisely, but does not necessarily give any clues as to its structure; or it may be expressed in diagrammatic form:

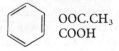 OOC.CH$_3$ One molecular formula:
COOH   C$_9$H$_8$O$_4$—not very helpful

The diagram itself is only a partial description, since it is a two-dimensional representation of a three-dimensional entity. A compound may also be expressed as a chemical formula, giving the atoms of which it is composed and the number of them present in each molecule; we are all familiar with the formula NaCl for sodium chloride, common salt, but how do we express the structural formula shown above? Works published earlier this century, such as Beilstein's *Handbuch der organischen Chemie*, adopted arbitrary systems which enabled the user to locate a particular compound, but did not always distinguish between different compounds, and certainly did not attempt to identify particular structural features. The Commission on the nomenclature of organic compounds identified twelve different kinds of name in its 1957 report, and there have been a number of different systems for the identification of structural formulae without using diagrams yet giving an adequate representation; few of these have survived the strains placed on them by the vast numbers of new compounds synthesized each year. Two of the most successful are the system devised by Dyson, sometime editor of CA, and Wiswesser line notation, and CA uses these in its registry. The main problem is that not only do chemists want to be able to identify specific compounds, they also want to be able to distinguish those compounds which have certain features in common, since these are likely to have similar properties. Any system for indexing chemical compounds must take all of these factors into account, and it is the development of a machine-searchable registry which has taken a high proportion of the effort devoted to the mechanization of CA. The ultimate objective is that each compound shall have a unique registry number which will identify it, and will also through the information stored in the registry be identifiable by as many of its chemical characteristics as is feasible.

At present, CAS produces a variety of tools from its machine-readable records; these include both printed versions and tapes. The major printed tool continues to be CA, now divided into two sections, the first covering Biochemistry and organic chemistry, the second covering macromolecular materials, analytical chemistry, physical chemistry and chemical technology. This is supported by *Chemical titles* for current awareness. Some idea of the complexity of the production of CA is given by the fact that the photo-composition font requires 1400 characters, and special keyboards had to be developed to cope with the input.

Tape services available include: CAC—CA Condensates, in two parts corresponding to the two sections of CA, containing all the bibliographic information and keywords from CA but not the abstracts; CASIA—CA subject index alert, containing the current files for the volume issues of the subject indexes, chemical substance index and formula index, covering the items listed in CAC and giving the registry numbers; Chemical titles; CHEMNAME, giving registry numbers for CA index names, molecular formulae and other synonyms for substances included in CAC; and CBAC—Chemical-Biological activities, consisting of a subset of the whole data base but including abstracts. CAC is available from 1970 (in Australia), and the file contains over 2,000,000 entries, with over 300,000 additions a year; CASIA and CHEMNAME are more recent, with availability from 1973, giving approximately half the current file size of CAC.

MEDLARS is produced very largely by one US government body, the NLM. ERIC involves a number of different bodies, of various kinds, with central coordination by a US government body, the National Institute of Education (formerly Office of Education); CAS is an independent non-profit making body, but did receive financial help from the government to develop its present computer-based operation. The common factor is the very large expense involved in setting up these operations as well as in maintaining them, a point which we shall return to later in the chapter when considering *availability*. They are all geared to the production of significant printed indexes, with computer tapes as a by-product, but as the computer-based versions become more widely available we are beginning to see an increasingly large tape tail wagging the printed dog. The tapes may be searched by the kind of query profile construction described in chapter 4; MEDLARS and ERIC both use closely controlled vocabularies, while CA uses keywords but also titles, and text searching techniques can be used to search these. Logical operators may be used, in fact their use becomes essential for anything but the simplest enquiry.

INSTITUTE FOR SCIENTIFIC INFORMATION (ISI)

In the early 1960's Dr Gene Garfield received a substantial grant to enable him to investigate the feasibility of producing a citation index in science; the first experiments were carried out on a limited number of periodicals, mainly in the biological sciences, but they showed clearly that the principle was both practical and useful, and SCI went into full production in 1964. As the service expanded, it was found that increasing numbers of social science journals were being included, and in 1973 a separate publication, SSCI, was set up to cover this area. The ISI is a non-profit making body set up to administer the two publications and the associated services, with Dr Garfield as President.

SCI and SSCI rely entirely on derived indexing, as stated in chapter 4. The information included in each entry consists of the full bibliographical details (including author's affiliation—not always thought of as important) and the citations at the end of the article. From these tapes are produced the quarterly issues and annual cumulation of the source index, which can serve as an author index to current literature, the citation index listing all the cited articles, the patent number index, corporate author index and permuterm index, mentioned in chapter 4. In addition, there is an annual author listing entitled *Who is publishing in science*, giving each author's place of work. There is a current awareness service, ASCA, which can be searched for individually constructed profiles, in which case the charge depends on the complexity of the profile *and* its success, or for general subject profiles, which are geared to less specific subject areas but are cheaper because the cost is shared with other subscribers.

Since the early 1970's, the weekly tapes have also been available in the USA and Britain for on-line searching on a rolling basis: at any time the latest four weeks are available. They may be searched by author's name or affiliation; journal title; or keywords. The searcher can specify the section of the entry he wishes to scan, and can limit his search to one or more of a very small number (about half a dozen) of broad subject groups. Forward and backward truncation can be used as well as Boolean logic; as usual, in running such a search on-line it is a good plan to work out a detailed search strategy in advance, otherwise it can become costly, though the regular running of a well-constructed profile can be reasonably cheap. (As pointed out in chapter 3, for those linked to the central computer via the telephone network, communication costs can become a significant factor.) SCI now covers some 3,500 journals, SSCI 1,000 with some small overlap between them, so this service, known as SCISEARCH, gives access to a major part of the world's significant journal literature.[6]

AVAILABILITY

The four services considered so far are, it must be stressed, only a small selection of the increasing number of similar services available; no mention has been made of INSPEC (Science abstracts and Current papers. . .), COMPENDEX (Engineering index), BIOSIS (Biological abstracts—service previously known as BA Previews) or many others. Space precludes a detailed study of each, and in fact the four services described display most if not all of the features found in all services. One of these features is cost. Although it is possible for individual libraries to purchase the tapes in many cases (some, *eg* MEDLARS, are only available through official centres), the cost becomes prohibitive for most libraries when set against the benefits. As a consequence, the past few years have seen the growth of processing centres which act as central stores; individual libraries can either send in their requests for batch processing, or increasingly they can link up to the central computer direct from a terminal and carry out searches on-line. In this way, the costs to the individual library can be kept down, and the use made of the data bases is raised to a viable level. There is little point in a library paying, say, £1,000 per annum for a tape that is used for five minutes a week. Machine-readable records only begin to pay for themselves when they are used intensively.

Processing centres are of various kinds. They may be national libraries; in Britain, the BLLD; in Canada, the National Science Library;[7] in Australia, the NLA and CSIRO. They may be based on universities: in Britain, UKCIS, the UK Chemical Information Service, is based on Nottingham University, and the University of Newcastle cooperated with the NLL (now BLLD) in the development of the MEDLARS service; in the USA, the University of Georgia at Athens offers a range of services. They may be linked to professional bodies: in Britain, INSPEC was developed by the Institution of Electrical Engineers; in the USA, CAS has similar links with the American Chemical Society (which itself publishes a substantial proportion of the world's English language chemical literature). They may be commercial organizations: in Britain, Scisearch is available from Cybernet Ltd, a commercial computing bureau; in the USA, Lockheed Information Systems and Systems Development Corporation both offer a range of data bases. The National Library of Australia has recently concluded an agreement with Lockheed making the DIALOG system available to Australian users; the system currently contains some 12,000,000 references (1976). Searches can be sent on-line; the output can be line printed and sent air mail, or received on-line in Australia at a higher cost. Similar cooperative systems have developed in Europe, where the communication problems are less acute. The prospects for the future are exciting but at the same time a little overwhelming; we could run the risk of inundating our readers with a mass of computer-produced bibliographies! It is very clear that as these data bases increase in size, the need for retrieval systems which will give high relevance becomes more and more acute.[8]

LOCAL SYSTEMS

In addition to the large centrally produced data bases, some libraries have introduced their own computer-based information systems, using in some cases information generated within the institution, eg IBM, in others a mixture of information from within and from outside sources, eg ICI. These two firms are typical examples of the feasibility of running one's own computer-based system; both are large multinational firms, with ample computing facilities and a long-standing awareness of the importance of information services.

IBM

As befits the library of the largest manufacturer of computers in the world, IBM information services are very largely computer-based. The whole library is taken as a system, so that the primary machine-readable record is generated when the documents are first received, and serves a multiplicity of purposes: cataloguing, circulation control, stock control, use studies, and information retrieval, including an SDI service.[9]

The core of the collections is formed by IBM technical reports. Each author is asked to prepare an abstract at the same time as he writes the report; these abstracts are written with the advice of technical information staff, to ensure that they adequately represent the subject of the document. Although no thesaurus is now used, the vocabulary may still be said to be controlled to a certain extent, in that all the authors concerned are working on similar subjects, within the same organization. The abstracts are fed into the computer, together with the usual bibliographical details, to give the data base on which the information retrieval system works. Some periodical articles are also included, and this coverage is likely to increase steadily in the future.

To answer a request for information, a member of the technical information staff collaborates with the enquirer in framing his request in the same form, *ie* a natural language abstract. This is fed into the computer, which matches it against the stored abstracts and prints out the results (or possibly a statement to the effect that the enquiry as phrased would yield an undue number of references). This answer is studied to see whether it is what the enquirer wants, or whether the search formulation needs modification. The system is available on-line, so that the user can conduct his own searches if he wishes; the programs enable him to conduct a dialogue with the computer in order to clarify his search strategy. Word truncation may be used, as may levels of coordination, and word co-occurrence, with the user setting the limits at which the words must co-occur. For example, if we are looking for information on chemical documentation, we would want the words chemical and documentation to occur in the same sentence, and preferably within, say, three words of each other; this would enable us to retrieve 'chemical documentation' *and* 'documentation of chemical compounds'.

The SDI system is closely controlled; users receive a print-out of document abstracts matching their profiles, and are asked to return a card indicating the relevance of each item, including a brief reason if the document is not considered relevant. These responses are used to modify the user's profile if necessary.

ICI

ICI has always been in the forefront of developments in the special library field in Britain, and they were one of the first to set out to try to use computers for information retrieval. (Their use of KWIC indexing was described in chapter 4). The Agricultural Division library devised a complete system known as ASSASSIN (Agricultural System for Storage And Subsequent Selection of Information), which is now used throughout the company.[10]

404

The system was intended to serve for both SDI and retrospective searching, and to accept input from within the firm and from outside sources, eg CAC and SCI. The input consists of extended bibliographic references, including such information as the security code— important in a large industrial firm—and source code, together with an abstract and any added keywords. The input is automatically checked against the machine-held thesaurus which can be amended if the indexer wishes to include new terms or amend existing ones. The thesaurus may be printed out, in two forms: alphabetical or hierarchical. At regular intervals the input is matched against user profiles, and SDI notifications are printed out; the batch of input is then added to the main file, normally weekly. From time to time, KWOC indexes are produced; these may be limited by various factors, eg security code or subject descriptors, or could be of the whole file.

The major problem facing such a system is one of size. ASSASSIN was originally intended to hold up to 70,000 items, but as we have already seen, CAC alone includes over 300,000 items each year. The problem is the same as that facing the ordinary library wishing to use MARC records, discussed in chapter 15. The solution appears to lie in programs which allow libraries to select the items of interest to them from data bases held by central agencies, and incorporate these in their own systems; complete reliance on external data bases presents problems for the industrial special library, in which much of the information available arises within the firm and is subject to commercial security restrictions. The significance of this was emphasized recently by the news report that an employee had stolen the company information files from ICI's Dutch subsidiary, and was holding them for ransom!

PROJECT INTREX
During the late 1950's, MIT began experimenting with Project MAC, an on-line system which permits up to thirty users to be in contact with a large central computer at the same time through a network of consoles. The success of this experiment led to the much wider concept of a nation-wide library and information service of the future in which the number of potential users would be unlimited. This project was given the name INTREX (INformation TRansfer EXperiments),[11] and a planning conference was held in 1965 to discuss the scope and aims of such a concept. The major problem is seen as the gradual breakdown through overloading of conventional library services, in particular those intended for the scholar and research worker. The planning conference did not suggest any solutions, but rather served to define the problems. Two main methods of approach were seen: the application of computers and other technological developments (eg those in photocopying) to conventional library operations, and the development of a completely new information network based on computer

stored information, with new documents being entered at source, by the authors, thus by-passing conventional publication procedures.

The logical conclusion of such developments has been outlined by one of the participants, J C R Licklider,[12] who foresees the disappearance of the book—that inefficient means of conveying information—and its replacement by the console, connected on-line to a vast central computer network, with information displayed on a screen in response to the user's requests, and with facilities for immediate interaction between user and computer.

Progress with the development of INTREX has been slow, and by 1969 only one terminal was in operation. However, the main difference between INTREX and the systems that we have been considering so far is that not only does it retrieve references in answer to a request, it also will provide the text of those references thought suitable by the user. The texts of the documents in the collection are not stored in the computer on the grounds that this would be a waste of expensive disk storage; instead, microfiche is used, which can be physically retrieved by the system and displayed page by page on the user's VDU. If the user decides that the item is worthy of closer study, hard copy can be produced from the microfiche.

Considerable doubts remain about the viability of such a system on the scale envisaged in the original report. Communication costs would be high, as would storage, despite the relatively cheap use of microfiche. Computer costs would also be high if the system is to be large enough to cope with the expected number of users; the mind boggles at the thought of thousands of users all on-line to the same computer at the same time! The direction that computer processing is likely to take seems to be rather different, as computers grow smaller and cheaper. Before very long, it seems probable that minicomputers with disc stores will be small enough and cheap enough for nearly every library to have its own, to serve as a store of locally needed information and as an interface to enable the library to link up with larger national centres if necessary. The solution to the provision of documents as opposed to references is one that still remains to be solved, though INTREX may well be pointing the way.

Another point to be remembered is that libraries do not only exist to provide information in response to specific requests. Even in the situation where the reader is actively seeking information we have pointed out the importance of serendipity, but libraries also exist to provide education and recreation. And after a hard day at the office, or slaving away over a hot stove, who wants to curl up in bed with a VDU?

BIBLIOGRAPHY

I Williams, M E: *Computer-readable bibliographic data bases: a directory and data source book*. . . ASIS, 1976. (Looseleaf.)

See also:

Finer, R: *A guide to selected computer-based information services.* Aslib, 1972.

Herner, S: *Selected Federal computer-based information systems.* Information Resources Press, 1972.

Proceedings of Aslib annual conference, 1972: *External data bases. Aslib proceedings, 24* (12) 1972—25 (3) 1973.

Many of the references given for chapters 3 and 4 are obviously relevant, but one may single out:

Lancaster, F W and Fayen, E G: *Information retrieval on-line.* 1973.

Lynch, M F: *Computer-based services in science and technology—principles and techniques.* 1974.

2 Austin, C J: *MEDLARS, 1963–1967.* NLM, 1968.

Lancaster, F W: 'Interaction between requesters and a large mechanized retrieval system.' *Information storage and retrieval, 4* (2) 1968, 239–252.

Lancaster, F W: 'Aftermath of an evaluation.' *Journal of documentation, 27* (1) 1971, 1–10.

Stevens, N D: 'MEDLARS:a summary review and evaluation of three reports.' *Library resources and technical services, 14* (1) 1970, 109–121.

3 Lancaster and Fayen (above) contains a substantial proportion of information on MEDLINE.

4 A brochure ERICTAPES/ERICTOOLS is available from Operations Research Inc, 4833 Rugby Avenue, Suite 303, Bethesda, Md 20014.

5 Batten, W E: 'The mechanization of chemical documentation.' *Journal of documentation, 32* (3) 1976, 207–234 (Progress in documentation).

6 References for SCI have been given in chapter 4 and will not be repeated. For up-to-date information on the whole service, brochures can be obtained from ISI, Philadelphia, or in Britain or Australia from local agents.

7 Mauerhoff, G R: 'CAN/SDI: a national SDI system in Canada.' *Libri, 24* (1) 1974, 19–29.

8 Leggate, P: 'Computer-based current awareness services.' *Journal of documentation, 31* (2) 1975, 93–115 (Progress in documentation).

Dammers, H F: 'The economics of computer-based information systems: a review.' *Journal of documentation, 31* (1) 1975, 38–45 (Progress in documentation).

9 IBM have published a series of technical reports describing their library operations in some detail. The system is known as ALMS—Automated Library Management System.

10 Clough, C R and Bramwell, K N: 'A single computer-based

system for both current awareness and retrospective search: operating experience with ASSASSIN.' *Journal of documentation,* 27 (4) 1971, 243–253.

11 *INTREX: report of a planning conference on information transfer experiments,* September 3 1965, edited by C F J Overhage and R J Harman. MIT Press, 1965.

Reintjes, J F: 'System characteristics of Intrex.' *AFIPS conference proceedings, 34* 1975, 457–459.

12 Licklider, J C R: *Libraries of the future.* MIT Press, 1965.

13 The provision of tapes in MARC format has been discontinued because of problems in converting to this format from the original ERIC format.

CHAPTER 26

Science and technology

Of the indexing languages prepared specifically for post-coordinate indexing, those in science and technology were first in the field, and still preponderate, both in areas covered and in number. There is however, no equivalent of the general classification scheme covering the whole of knowledge; even those lists which cover substantial areas are all within one subject field such as science and technology, education, and economic development. There is also no equivalent to the widespread use of DC, UDC or LCSH; the most widely used post-coordinate scheme is probably the EJC Thesaurus and its near relations, but this is still used as it stands by only a limited number of libraries. Most libraries using post-coordinate indexing methods have tended to generate their own lists, perhaps using one of the major lists as a model. This situation may change in the future, but for the present these two chapters will set out to present some basic information about some of the more important lists now available.

These lists are usually called *thesauri*, though as we have pointed out in chapter 24 they are in fact lists of subject headings. The term thesaurus will be used here to denote such lists, with the proviso that this is strictly speaking a misuse of the term. The only one which fits into the conventional meaning of the word is the English Electric *Thesaurofacet*, for which a new term had to be coined. It is only recently that much guidance has become available for the indexer wishing to construct his own thesaurus, but there are now two publications available from Aslib[1] which should fill this gap very satisfactorily.

EJC THESAURUS

This thesaurus is the most significant work to come out of the US in this subject area, and it is worth tracing its history in some detail. One of the major information handling agencies in the United States is the Defense Documentation Center (DDC), formerly the Armed Services Technical Information Agency (ASTIA). As part of its work ASTIA compiled a list of subject headings, which developed through four editions, the last being published in 1959 as the *ASTIA subject headings list*. By this time the agency was exploring the possibilities of using mechanized methods for information retrieval, and a new vocabulary was drawn up for this purpose, the *Thesaurus of ASTIA descriptors*, the first edition being published in 1960, with a second following shortly afterwards in December 1962. The thesaurus was used for the indexing of the *Technical abstract bulletin*, as well as the internal searching within the agency. With the development of interagency abstracting and indexing services, in particular *US Government research and development reports*, the need for a vocabulary common to the four major government agencies became obvious, and led to *Project LEX*. (The four agencies included DDC, NASA—the National Aeronautics and Space Agency, USAEC—the Atomic Energy Commission, and OTS—Office of Technical Services; the latter was later redesignated the Clearinghouse for Federal Scientific and Technical Information—CFSTI, and has recently changed its name yet once more to National Technical Information Service—NTIS, and is now the main source of supply for unclassified (in the military sense!) US government information in the technical and scientific fields.)

At the same time as the US government was beginning to show interest in the development of vocabularies for post-coordinate indexing, the scientific and engineering societies were also becoming concerned. A significant proportion of the world's scientific and technical literature is published by these societies, and they became aware that—for a variety of reasons—much of this information was not reaching its goal. They therefore set about raising the standards of technical writing, paying particular attention to indexing problems; one of the results of this effort was the improvement in titles, making them more suitable for KWIC indexing, while another was the compilation of the EJC *Thesaurus of engineering terms*, published in 1964. This was based on a rather rigorous selection from about 120,000 terms submitted by a number of societies as well as DDC and other government agencies, resulting in a list of nearly 8,000 preferred terms and over 2,000 non-preferred synonyms or near-synonyms. It is not clear how the reduction was achieved, though a preliminary selection seems to have been made by rejecting terms which were suggested by only one of the contributing bodies—though some of these were later restored in order to maintain a balance within each discipline.

The terms were very largely single concept terms, but did include a fairly high proportion of composite headings, *eg* Oil circuit breakers; Ionizing radiation scattering; Salt spray tests. No attempt appears to have been made to introduce consistency of form, so we find Salaries, but also Salary administration; Electrical measurements, Electrically powered instruments, Electric devices and Electricity. Some phrases appear, *eg* Modulus of rupture in torsion; center of gravity; these correspond to normal usage, and would be difficult to eliminate. The problem with this kind of usage is predictability; the user does not know with any certainty where to look for a particular concept, and it is very difficult to insert new terms with any confidence. Some of the terms have scope notes, though this does not apply to very many; example,

NOISE (SPURIOUS SIGNALS)

(LIMITED TO INTERFERENCE GENERATED
INTERNALLY WITHIN A SYSTEM OR
EQUIPMENT)

Others have a note advising against their use, because of their lack of specificity:

ELECTRIC POWER

(USE MORE SPECIFIC TERM IF POSSIBLE)

The symbol $\neq$ is used to denote a term for which two or more broader terms may be substituted, the converse of this being &; the net result of this convention is rather confusing, especially at a heading such as Electric motors:

ELECTRIC MOTORS &

NT A-C MOTORS &
AMPLIDYNES $\neq$
CAPACITOR MOTORS $\neq$
D-C MOTORS &
POLYPHASE MOTORS   *etc*

Relationships between terms are shown rather more precisely than is usual in subject headings lists, as has already been pointed out. Synonyms are linked by means of USE and UF (*ie* Use For)

BURSTS (MINES)

(EXCLUDES EXPLOSIONS)
UF GAS OUTBURSTS
ROCK BURSTS
GAS OUTBURSTS
USE BURSTS (MINES)

Generic terms are indicated by BT (Broader term), with specific terms NT (Narrower term); related terms, which may be linked in a variety of ways, are indicated by RT:

COLD WORKING &

UF COLD BENDING
COLD DRAWING
. . .
NT DIE DRAWING
METAL POINTING
PLANISHING
BT METAL WORKING &
RT BULGING
CLADDING
DEEP DRAWING $\neq$
etc

The list is produced by photoreduction from computer printout, and is not particularly elegant, though it is certainly usable; preferred terms are emphasized by printing twice to give a bold effect. There are two appendices; the first of these is a short note on information retrieval thesauri, the second a brief account of the Engineers Joint Council action plan mentioned earlier. Following this appendix is a table showing the EJC set of roles, of which the following is an excerpt:

8   The primary topic of consideration is; there is a description of

1   Input; raw material; a material being corroded; energy input

2   Output; product, by-product, co-product; device shaped or formed

3   Undesirable component; waste; scrap; rejects; unnecessary material present

4   Indicated, possible, intended present or later uses or applications

5   Environment; solvent; host

6   Cause; independent or controlled variable

7   Effect; dependent variable

9   Passively receiving an operation or process with no change in identity, composition, configuration . . . or physical form

10   Means to accomplish the primary topic of consideration

0   Bibliographic data, personal names of authors . . . adjectives

These seem to bear some relationship to Ranganathan's seminal mnemonics, though their purpose is of course rather different. In practice, some problems were found with their use and they are not now recommended.[2]

There were a number of critical reviews, particularly by British librarians, who found the list inadequate for a variety of reasons.[3] In the first place, it made no attempt to cover English as opposed to American terminology, or British technical developments; for example, though several types of nuclear reactor are mentioned, gas-cooled reactors are not, though Britain had had several such reactors producing quantities of electricity for several years. Secondly, and more significantly, the complete disregard of any kind of systematic basis for the network of BT-NT and RT-RT relationships meant that these were quite haphazard, and did not in many cases bear close examination. In 1965, a large-scale revision was set in motion, with the intention of enlarging the vocabulary, tightening up the network of relationships, and resolving any differences between this thesaurus and that being prepared by the DDC in Project LEX. The joint result of both projects was the second edition of the EJC thesaurus, now entitled *Thesaurus of scientific and engineering terms*, published in December 1967, and usually referred to as TEST.

One of the first steps was to formulate rules and conventions governing the selection of terms and the construction of cross-references; these rules are printed as Appendix 1 of the thesaurus, and are a useful guide, with, for example, one of the few tables of guide-lines on when to use the singular or plural form of a term that has appeared. Many of these rules are refinements or restatements of rules that have been used by subject headings lists since Cutter, but it is convenient to have them in this concise form.

The terms used were drawn from a total of some 150,000 taken from about 150 major sources and a further 200 lists which were used for reference purposes. From these the final list of 17,810 descriptors—preferred terms—and 5,554 USE references was selected by a team of over 300 scientists and engineers, with a final review by an editorial panel. The resulting thesaurus is a complex and useful tool, though it is still open to criticism, particularly from the point of view of British users—for whom of course it was not intended. There are several improvements over the first edition, notably in the organization of relationships between terms. The printing, carried out by computer controlled typesetting, is also of a much higher standard, though the small type face used for cross-references could be something of a hindrance.

The main list consists of preferred and non-preferred terms in one sequence; both are printed in bold, but non-preferred terms are in italics. In some cases, a single non-preferred term is replaced by more than one preferred term, *eg*

Artificial sea water
USE Sea water
and Simulation

This is indicated under the preferred terms by a dagger, thus

Sea water
UF † Artificial sea water

Broader terms, narrower terms and related terms are shown in the same way as in the first edition, with one additional convention. A dash preceding a NT reference indicates that the narrower term has itself further narrower terms; a useful indication, corresponding to the use of bold type in the relative index to DC to show that a topic is subdivided in the schedules. An example:

Personnel
NT—Craftsmen

though when we turn to Craftsmen it is something of a disappointment to find only two subdivisions:

Craftsmen
NT   Electricians
       Electronic technicians

Scope notes appear, as they did in the first edition; there are also a few occasions where a context note is shown in parentheses:

Microorganism control (sewage)
Microorganism control (water)

Control of organisms such as bacteria, viruses, plankton, algae, and protozoa

There are two other important new features, which represent in effect a recognition of the importance of the classified approach in linking related subjects. The first of these is a tabulation of single terms showing every heading in which they appear in the main sequence; this is called the Permuted index, though it is not very clear why, as none of the terms in it are permuted. A rather confusing difference from the main sequence is found in the type face; terms which are used on their own in the main sequence are printed there in bold, but in the permuted index they are printed in bold italic. Terms printed in bold in the permuted index are those which are *not* used on their own in the main sequence. An example will demonstrate the use that might be made of this index; suppose that we wish to find all the headings in which the term *membrane* appears, we turn to that heading in the permuted index and find:

Membrane
Hyaline membrane disease
Ion exchange membrane electrolytes
Membrane filters
Membranes
Webs (membranes)

Membrane is in bold type; this tells us that it does not appear on its own, but only as a component of the headings Hyaline membrane disease and Ion exchange membrane electrolytes. Under Membrane filters in the main sequence we shall find a USE reference, 8.

Membrane filters
USE Fluid filters
and Membranes

Membranes is used as a preferred term, but there is a reference from Webs (Membranes) USE Membranes. In effect, the permuted index serves the same purpose as the chain index to a classified sequence or the cross-references in BTI, by enabling us to get from a particular term to those places in the main sequence where it will appear.

The second is the Subject Category Index. This is in effect a broad subject classification with 22 major subject fields, each of which is subdivided into groups; the largest group is Biological and medical sciences, with 21 headings, the smallest Atmospheric sciences and Mathematical sciences, each with two. The classification was originally devised by COSATI, the Committee on Scientific and Technical Information, which is part of the organization which exists to advise the US President on matters scientific; it has been modified slightly for use in the EJC Thesaurus. It is discipline-oriented, so it suffers from all of the problems that we have already noted with conventional classification schemes; for example, nuclear propulsion is under Propulsion, nuclear explosions under Nuclear science and technology, nuclear warfare under Military sciences, explosions under Ordnance, nuclear reactions under Physics, and so on. One is tempted to wonder why an existing scheme such as UDC was not used, since there is no basic difference, and not even very much difference in detail. Each category has a two-figure number, and each group has a further two-figure number; thus Computers is group 02 in Category 09, Electronics and electrical engineering. If we turn to 0902 in the classified tabulation we find about 100 terms falling into that category and group. Preferred terms in the main sequence have their group number, giving a second method of finding related headings, *eg*

Computers 0902

The third method is the Hierarchical Index. Any term in the main sequence which has no BT references, but has at least two levels of NT references, is tabulated in this index, showing all the terms related to it directly or at one or more remove by an NT reference. The level is shown by indentation, *eg*

Addition resins
.Vinyl resins
. . Styrene resins
. . . Styrene copolymers
. . . . Styrene butadiene resins

A heading may appear in more than one hierarchy, not necessarily at the same level. We can get to the last heading in the above example through another hierarchy leading to the same level:

Addition resins
. Vinyl resins
. . Vinyl copolymers
. . . Styrene copolymers
. . . . Styrene butadiene resins

Another example shows how the same term may appear at two different levels, though both within the same generic heading:

Vertebrates
. Domestic animals
. . Livestock
. . . Cattle
. . . . Beef cattle
. Mammals
. . Eutheria
. . . Ungulata
. . . . Artiodactyla
. . . . . Ruminants
. . . . . . Cattle
. . . . Beef cattle

A third example shows a concept which occurs at different levels under

different generic headings:
Addition resins
. Olefin resins
. . Ethylene resins
. . . Polyethylene
Thermoplastic resins
. Polyethylene

These three indexes certainly add to the value of the thesaurus by enabling the indexer or user to find related terms in a systematic way, but they call into question exactly what is meant by the term 'concept'. The guide lines inform us that 'a descriptor represents a concept', so it would appear that Radioisotope thermoelectric devices; Target drone aircraft; Marine biological noise; and Microorganism control (sewage) are all 'concepts'. This is clearly not what we have been considering as a 'concept' when referring to facet analysis, for example.

The subject coverage of the thesaurus is reasonable, including some fringe subjects which might be thought to be outside the scope of such a list. Information retrieval is well represented, and there are headings for Religions and Religious buildings, Literature, Musical instruments and Drama, among others. There are problems with American terminology, *eg* Pavements and Sidewalks, just as there are with Sears List and LCSH, but in general the terms used in science and technology are more standardized than those used in the social sciences or humanities.

The revised EJC Thesaurus is clearly a very important tool, and is likely to continue as such for some time to come. One wonders what would have been the result if the same amount of effort had been devoted to the revision and updating of UDC, and the Thesaurofacet shows what can be done with very much smaller resources if a more systematic approach is used.

THESAUROFACET

A number of libraries in Britain have compiled thesauri, but none on the large scale of the EJC or Project LEX, with the exception of the English Electric Company. The EE *Classification for engineering*, which we have already mentioned, was the first large faceted classification devised by a member of the CRG, and reached its third edition in 1961. In the course of the next few years it became clear that a detailed revision was becoming essential, but at the same time the company's libraries were investigating the possibilities of using computer techniques and post-coordinate indexing, and the decision was therefore taken to develop the new edition of the classification scheme in conjunction with a thesaurus. The result, given the rather ugly name *Thesaurofacet*, was published in 1970 (the date 1969 in the scheme proved to be a little optimistic), and is an important contribution to subject indexing theory and practice. The full title: *Thesaurofacet: a thesaurus and faceted classification for engineering and related subjects*, shows that there are in fact two tools here, a classification and a thesaurus, but it is necessary to emphasize that the two have to be used together if the best results are to be obtained; the two are complementary rather than parallel.

The work begins with a detailed introduction in which the construction and use of the list are outlined, and these have also been described by Jean Aitchison, the chief editor, in *Journal of documentation*.[4]

There are several points of interest here. The classification is no longer entirely synthetic, for reasons which are relevant to analytico-synthetic classification generally. There will, in any given situation, be a number of composite subjects which arise regularly, and of which the individual concepts rarely appear on their own in the literature; in such a case it is better to enumerate the composite rather than give the classifier the trouble of constructing a piece of notation each time. As we have pointed out, synthesized notation tends to be longer than non-expressive notation allocated to enumerated topics; the notation used in Thesaurofacet is largely non-expressive, and can thus be used economically in this way. However, there are advantages in synthesis, particularly in providing for the composite subjects which have not yet appeared but which may do so in the future, so provision is made for this in the notation, and instructions are given in the introduction as to when this is to be used. An attempt has been made to strike a practical balance between the advantages of synthesis and those of enumeration, in a way which emphasizes that this is a practical working tool, not just a theoretical exercise.

A classification scheme can only display one set of genus-species divisions; in *Thesaurofacet*, others are shown in the thesaurus, using BT-NT-RT cross-references, and others by cross-references in the schedules, denoted by an asterisk. To use the scheme, the indexer or user looks up a term in the thesaurus; this will give him a class number, but may also give him some related terms. These related terms may come from the hierarchy to be found at the given class number, but they may also be from other parts of the schedules, in which case they are marked as *additional, eg* BT(A). Class numbers derived by synthesis are shown by the use of *synth* and an *S* preceding the constituent terms.

The notation is mixed, using uppercase letters and numerals, and the stroke / to indicate synthesis. Where synthesis occurs, instructions are given, with examples showing the kind of notation that results. The filing order is stroke, number, letter, *eg*

TM	**Cutting (flame)**
TM/TA2	Cutting machine tools
TM2	Arc cutting
TMB	Flame deseaming.

Alphabetization in the thesaurus is letter by letter, so that Lawrencium precedes Law reports. This is in accordance with EJC practice, which has been followed to a large extent.

Some examples will demonstrate the use of the two halves of the system. Suppose we are asked for information on 'thinners'. When we look this up in the thesaurus, we find:

Thinners *use*
Solvents

We turn to Solvents, and find:

Solvents   HXG
  UF   Thinners
  RT   Dispersants
          Dissolving
          Plasticisers
          Solutes
          Solutions
          Solvent extraction
  NT(A) Paint thinners
          Turpentine

If we turn to HXG in the classified schedules, we find:

HX **MATERIALS BY PURPOSE**
HX2   Additives
HXG   Solvents

However, the terms mentioned in the thesaurus may have caused us to realize that what is actually wanted is information on *paint* thinners, so we turn to this, and find that the class number is VGD; by turning to this class number, we find that VGD is a subdivision of VG Paint constituents within VF Paint technology.

In contrast to the NASA list, abbreviations are normally spelled out, so if we look up a,n reactions we are referred to alpha particle neutron reaction; at this heading we find:

Alpha Particle Neutron Reaction
                E8C/E5V/E8E/E5N
Synth
  UF   a,n reaction
S RT   Alpha particle projectiles
S BT(A) Neutron product reaction

When we turn to the classification we find that the notation for this topic is synthesized from E8C, Projectile particles in E8 Nuclear reactions; E5V alpha particles; E8E product particles; and E5N neutrons. The complete notation is enumerated under a heading which tells us:

Classify specific reactions by combining the notation above, in the order Projectile/Type of reaction

Some terms appear in the thesaurus with a class number only, *eg*

Butter VMO
this indicates that the only relationships with other topics to be found
are those at the class number; if we turn to this we find:

VM   **FOOD TECHNOLOGY**
      *Food industries ZKCB
      By products
VM   Food
VMM   Dairy Products
VMN   Milk
VMO   Butter
VMP   Cheese

From this display we see that Butter falls into the BT Dairy products,
along with Cheese and Milk; Dairy products itself is a subdivision (*ie*
NT) of Food; and that if we are interested in the industry we should
turn to ZKCB. If we do this, we find that ZK Industries and its subdivisions are to be used only for economic aspects, not technological.

The whole system depends on the interaction of classification schedules and thesaurus; once this point is grasped, the scheme becomes
easy to use and helpful to both indexer and user. Because of the systematic approach, relationships are displayed more clearly and precisely
than in the subject category lists provided by EJC and similar bodies. In
coverage, the scheme is, not unnaturally, biased towards subjects of
particular concern to English Electric, but a serious attempt has been
made to avoid undue imbalance. In size, it compares with the EJC Thesaurus, with about 16,000 preferred terms and another 7,000 non-
preferred. It is likely to prove a very useful tool, especially in British
libraries, where the US bias of the EJC Thesaurus could be a hindrance
in its use.

MeSH
This list is called by the old-fashioned name: *Medical Subject Headings*, and is published as Part 2 of *Index Medicus* in January each year.
It is, however, a thesaurus in the sense in which the term is being used
here, that is, a list of headings for use in a post-coordinate indexing
system. MeSH is in fact used in two different situations; it is used in
Index medicus, and also in MEDLARS, as explained in chapter 25. There
is also an annotated version for use with MEDLINE. In *Index medicus*,
articles appear under an average of four terms; the headings are not
precoordinated, and in consequence one may have to carry out a fair
amount of sequential scanning in the search for information on a
specific composite subject. However, this is not necessarily a bad thing
in a tool largely intended for current scanning; as we pointed out in
chapter 2, for this purpose it is possible to be *too* precise. For retrospective searching most people now have access to MEDLARS, for which articles are indexed by, on average, ten terms, and it is possible to

perform coordinate searches using the computer; the additional terms tend to increase recall, but the ability to coordinate terms enables us to counterbalance this with a gain in relevance.

The cross-reference network between related headings is worked out in some detail, but uses rather different symbols from those we have seen so far. A typical entry is as follows:

PERSONALITY DEVELOPMENT

F1.752.747
see related

    CHILD DEVELOPMENT

    GROWTH

    SOCIALIZATION

XU INDIVIDUATION

XR CHILD DEVELOPMENT

XR GROWTH

XR SOCIALIZATION

Headings are all in bold, whether preferred or non-preferred, but preferred terms are in large capitals. A preferred heading is followed by one or more class numbers from the Categorized list, which occupies over half of the whole list. See related references correspond to RT in TEST, with XR as the converse symbol: thus in the entry above we are reminded of the related headings Child development, Growth and Socialization, and under each of those headings there would be a similar cross-reference to Personality development. XU is the converse of see under, which is a cross-reference from a specific term not used to a broader term used to include it; in our example, Individuation is a specific term not used, and we told to use the broader term Personality development. A similar example is the cross-reference

FASCIA LATA see under **FASCIA**

A preferred term may have references to it from one or more non-preferred terms, *eg*

MOUTH FLOOR

A14.549.441

    X FLOOR OF MOUTH

    X SUBLINGUAL REGION

with the complementary cross-references

FLOOR OF MOUTH see **MOUTH FLOOR**

SUBLINGUAL REGION see **MOUTH FLOOR**

Occasionally a see reference may lead to the preferred term indirectly, *eg*

MIDWIFE, NURSE see **NURSE MIDWIFE**

NURSE MIDWIFE see under **NURSES**

It is recognized that this is not good practice, but it is linked to the use of MESH in MEDLINE; it is hoped to alter the present computer programs to eliminate it in the future.

As mentioned above, the Categorized list occupies a substantial part of the publication, and contains the 'tree structures' which are the classified form of the alphabetical list; these used to be published separately, with a brief selection only given in MeSH, but it is clearly more advantageous to have both forms of the list together. For example, we find the heading

ERYTHROCYTES

A11.118.413   A15.145.229.413

If we turn to the classified list and look at class A, Anatomical terms, we shall find Erythrocytes under both A11 and A15 in the appropriate place. It should be noted that the class numbers are used as integers (A15 files after A14, not between A1 and A2), and each section is marked off by a point. The numbers appear to be allocated at random, and stress is laid on the fact that the categories do not set out to be a definitive classification of medicine, though each section is supported by a bibliography and is compiled with the help of experts in the field. Within the 14 categories there are 106 groups, ranging from 26 in D Chemicals and drugs to 1 in J Techology, Industry, Agriculture and Food; included are categories for Information science and communication (L) and Named groups of persons (M). To take another example in a little more detail, in the alphabetical list we find:

THEOPHYLLINE

D3.132.956.826   D3.438.759.758.824.751
D15.128.919   D16.116.919
XU XANTHINOL NIACINATE
XR TEA

If we look under Xanthinol niacinate, we find the cross-reference

XANTHINOL NIACINATE see under **THEOPHYLLINE**

Under Tea we find

TEA

B6.510.911   B6.560.895
J1.125.873
see related
THEOPHYLLINE

In the categorized list we find D is Chemicals and drugs, D3 is Chemicals-Organic, Heterocyclic compounds. The four hierarchies for theophylline are:

HETEROCYCLIC COMPOUNDS	D3
ALKALOIDS	D3.132
XANTHINE ALKALOIDS	D3.132.956
THEOPHYLLINE	D3.132.956.826
XANTHINOL NIACINATE*	D3.132.956.826.950
HETEROCYCLIC COMPDS, 2-RING	
(NON-MeSH)	D3.438
PURINES	D3.438.759

PURINONES	D3.438.759.758
XANTHINES	D3.438.759.758.824
THEOPHYLLINE	D3.438.759.758.824.751
CENTRAL NERVOUS SYSTEM AGENTS (NON-MESH)	D15
ANALEPTICS	D15.128
THEOPHYLLINE	D15.128.919
AUTONOMIC DRUGS	D16
BRONCHODILATOR AGENTS	D16.116
THEOPHYLLINE	D16.116.919

In the above example (NON MESH) indicates that the headings are included to complete the hierarchy, but are not used as indexing terms. The asterisk following XANTHINOL NIACINATE* indicates that this is a *minor descriptor*; it is used as an indexing term in MEDLINE and in the recurring bibliographies, but not in *Index medicus,* where THEOPHYLLINE is the index term, as shown by the see under cross-reference in MESH.

Occasionally we find inverted headings, giving a small measure of grouping in the alphabetical section:

NAILS
   A1.835.472
NAILS, INGROWN
   C17.805.506.406
NAILS, MALFORMED
   C17.805.506.506

These are however very much the exception.

There is a list of 68 subheadings, showing which categories they may be used with and giving detailed scope notes on their meaning, *eg*

Nursing (C, E, F3). Used with diseases for nursing care and technics in their management; includes the nursing role in diagnostic, therapeutic and preventive procedures.

These subheadings were developed following the evaluation of MEDLARS by Lancaster, discussed in chapter 28; in effect, many of them are role indicators, but much more precise than the set dropped from the EJC *Thesaurus.*

There is a list of new headings adopted during the previous year with the previous equivalents, *eg*

New	*Old*
STREPTOCOCCUS SANGUIS	STREPTOCOCCUS
TELECOMMUNICATIONS	COMMUNICATION
	RADIO
	TELEPHONE
	TELEVISION

There is also a complementary list of superseded headings and their replacements, *eg*

	Old	*New*
	MYCOPLASMA	UREAPLASMA
	MYCOPLASMA	ACHOLEPLASMA

The annotated list for MEDLINE users mentioned earlier includes various additional headings used for indexing the computer-based file but not *Index medicus, eg* geographical headings, and certain 'check tags' such as 'male', 'female', 'human' etc. These are the kinds of adjectival property discussed in chapter 5, which cannot serve as indexing terms on their own but are very useful in narrowing down a search when attached to the major headings of interest. Another useful tool is the *Permuted medical subject headings* published from time to time, though why it is called *permuted* is a mystery, since it is in fact a KWOC index to MESH headings.

An interesting guide is *Biomedical subject headings*, which is a list of MESH headings (1970) with their LCSH equivalents. There is also a list of subheadings, with equivalents, and a short list of LCSH terms with MESH equivalents not included in the main list, though it is not clear why they were omitted. Terms added during 1971 are listed separately, but the listing is necessarily somewhat out of date now, with the annual revision of MESH and the new edition of LCSH. It should however serve as a help to the cataloguer who can find a MESH heading and wants to know the correct heading from LCSH.

AMERICAN PETROLEUM INSTITUTE

For many years this list retained the title *Information retrieval system subject authority list*, but it now called simply *Thesaurus*, and a note states that it is compiled in accordance with the ANSI recommendations. Like MESH, and in sharp contrast to TEST and *Thesaurofacet*, it is revised annually.

In appearance, the list is rather like the first EJC Thesaurus, being produced by computer printout, with preferred terms emphasized by double printing. The terms included are of course rather more specialized, including may chemical terms, *eg* 2-AMINOETHANOL, (filed by ignoring the 2-) but also names of important firms, *eg* AMERICAN CYANAMID, used for indexing patents only, and place names, *eg* GREECE, GREAT LAKES.

The list is geared to the various bibliographical tools maintained by the API, including their computer-based retrieval system, and the latter influences some features of the list, for example the cross-references. A list of abbreviations is given to explain these:

BT   Broader term (autoposted)
CA   Chemical aspects (autoposted)
NT   Narrower term
RT   Related term (autoposted)

SA   See also
SA*   See also autoposted
SN   Scope notes
UF   Used for

BROADER TERMS are autoposted; that is, in the API usage, they are indexed whenever one of the narrower terms is used. RELATED TERMS and CHEMICAL ASPECTS are also autoposted; NARROWER TERMS are not, and in addition to these and related terms we find SEE ALSO references:

ABSORBER

SN—PROCESS EQUIPMENT
    WHEN CITED ONLY TO INDICATE THAT
    THE EQUIPMENT IS USED, INDEX THE
    PROCESS INSTEAD
BT—SEPARATION EQUIPMENT
NT—ABSORPTION TOWER
SA—ABSORBENT
    SHOCK ABSORBER
UF—ABSORPTION TUBE
      PLUS TUBE

The last of these cross-references is complemented by the entry

ABSORPTION TUBE
USE TUBE
    PLUS ABSORBER

Chemical aspects are used to show the various groups into which a particular compound may fall:

FURAN

SN—ADDED IN 1966
CA—C4 [*ie* number of carbon atoms]
    SINGLE STRUCTURE TYPE
    HETEROCYCLIC
    5 MEMBER RING
    MULTIOLEFINIC
    ETHER
UF—FURFURAN

SA* means that when the related term is used, the term referred from is autoposted:

HYDRODEALKYLATION

SN—FOR MORE COMPLETE SEARCH, SEARCH
    REACTANTS AND PRODUCTS
SA—DETOL HYDRODEALKYLATION*
    HDA PROCESS*
    HYDEAL PROCESS*

If a document is indexed by the term HDA PROCESS, then HYDRODEALKY-LATION is automatically used as an index term also, but the reverse is not true.

Cross-references from unused terms are dated:

ALLERGY 69
USE HYPERSENSITIVITY

Scope notes are frequent, and add greatly to the ease with which the list may be used:

ABOVE
SN—MODIFIER. LINK TO WORD MODIFIED
ADDED IN 1966

INTERSTATE
SN—ADDED IN 1968
NOT FOR INTERNATIONAL, FOR WHICH
USE WORLD WIDE

IONIZATION DETECTOR
SN—ADDED IN 1968. IN 1966 AND 1967
SEARCH RADIATION DETECTOR
BROADER TERM DETECTOR ADDED
IN 1970

HDA PROCESS
SN—ATLANTIC RICHFIELD CO AND
HYDROCARBON RESEARCH INC.
ADDED IN 1969
FROM 1966 THROUGH 1968 SEARCH
DEALKYLATION AND HYDROCRACKING
IN 64-65 USE HYDOGENOLYSIS

INTERMEDIATE, REACTION
SN—INDEX THE MATERIAL PRODUCED
AND REACTING, WITH ROLE I
SEARCH THE MATERIAL WITH ROLES P
AND A

MULTIPHASE
SN—INDEX IF IMPORTANT OR DISCUSSED.
CATALYSTS OR TREATING AGENTS ARE
NOT COUNTED AS PHASES.
ADDED IN 1970

The list of terms is followed by several smaller sections. The first of these is a list of terms added during the previous year, and a (very much shorter) list of terms dropped. These are followed by a list of changes in scope notes; then comes a page of bibliographical index terms, *eg* Glossary, a list of major chemical companies, used for indexing patents (these may also appear in the main list), and a brief list of descriptors for illustrations and data. Chemical aspects fill the next three pages, with scope notes showing how each is to be understood; for example, it is possible to use the descriptor IDE for anions and compounds ending in ide, *eg* chloride, cyanide, etc.

The next page is concerned with links and roles. The indexer is told to use links in five situations:

Chemical descriptors—assign a link so that autoposted broader and related terms will be linked

Chemical aspects—assign a link to all aspects of a chemical compound

Common attributes—link to the descriptor they modify

Materials—link terms from different facets used to index the same materials, *eg* Function and Composition, to the materials

Structure—link descriptors from the Structure facet to the materials they relate to.

Many of these situations are in fact noted in the thesaurus under the appropriate descriptors. There are five roles:

Role A (agent/reactant) = raw material

Role P (reaction product) = end product

Role I (intermediate) is used when a material is both a product of a reaction and the starting point for a further reaction. When the index entries are transferred to computer tape and the dual dictionary printout, this role is automatically converted to A + P; in other words, I is used only in indexing, and cannot be used in searching.

Role T (prior treatment) is used to particularize a material which has been produced as the end product of a process, *eg* for Frozen food one would index Freezing with Role T and Food

Role X (substance determined) is used to index documents relating to the detection or determination of a specific material in a mixture.

The next twenty pages contain four lists of section headings with scope notes explaining their use in *Petroleum refining and petrochemicals, Air and water conservation abstracts, Transportation and storage abstracts* and *API Patent alert*, all of which are products of the original indexing process.

The final section of the thesaurus is headed Hierarchy, and consists of a systematic tabulation of terms in the list based on the broader term—narrower term relationships, with a supporting alphabetical index leading to the appropriate column. The tabulation includes Place and Common attributes as well as the expected Materials and Processes, etc.

The API list is a good example of a thesaurus tied to a particular indexing situation. Like the special subject editions of UDC, it gives a lot more help to the indexer than the more general lists, and it serves as a model in the frequency and usefulness of its scope notes.

CONCLUSION

The four thesauri discussed here do not of course form anything more than a very small sample of the scientific and technical thesauri available, but they serve as an introduction to thesauri as a whole. Each has its own particular features, but they also have many features in

426

common. TEST was devised as a dual-purpose device; it serves to index the publications of the EJC (*Engineering index* and its computer-based version COMPENDEX) and NTIS, but it is also intended to serve as a general purpose thesaurus, for use in a wide variety of indexing situations. Its system of cross-references is used as a model by many other thesauri, as are its guidelines on such matters as the use of singular or plural forms of nouns. *Thesaurofacet* was designed for one specific library, but its combination of classification scheme and thesaurus actually represents a return to the pattern of Roget's *Thesaurus*, and has caught the imagination of a number of other thesaurus constructors; it has also been suggested that the index to UDC might be in this form. MeSH represents the results of many years of experience in indexing medical literature, as modified by the results of a searching evaluation of its performance. The API *Thesaurus* is more specialized and thus smaller (rather more than 5,000 terms) and is notable for its use of scope notes and for the regular use of autoposting.

On examination, we find that each consists of an alphabetic list supplemented by a classified arrangement; each contains some precoordinated terms; and each has a very detailed network of semantic cross-references. *Thesaurofacet* is the only one to provide fully for syntactic relationships, but MeSH has its subheadings, and the API *Thesaurus* has its roles and links; TEST has a higher proportion of precoordinated headings than the others, which introduce syntactic relationships and necessitate a KWIC index (the so-called permuted index) to reveal hidden terms. In other words, they present their compilers with exactly the same problems as the precoordinate systems that we have been examining, with the one exception of combination order—and even that is found in *Thesaurofacet*! The problems of constructing indexing languages discussed in chapters 5 and 6 are quite general, and a change from precoordinate to postcoordinate indexing does not cause them to vanish.

No attempt is made here to discuss the more exotic forms of thesaurus, such as the TDCK *Circular thesaurus*, which sets out to show relationships diagrammatically; readers who wish to explore these byways will find them well described in the works by Gilchrist and Lancaster.

BIBLIOGRAPHY

1 Gilchrist, A: *The thesaurus in retrieval.* Aslib, 1971.

Gilchrist, A and Aitchison, J: *Manual of thesaurus construction.* Aslib, 1971.

Lancaster, F W: *Vocabulary control for information retrieval.* Information Resources Press, 1972.

See also Blagden, J F: 'Thesaurus compilation methods: a literature review.' *Aslib proceedings*, 20 (8) 1968, 345–359.

2 Lancaster, F W: 'Some observations on the performance of EJC role indicators in a mechanised retrieval system.' *Special libraries, 55* (10) 1964, 696–701.

3 See for example the review by D J Campbell in *Journal of documentation, 21* (2) 1965, 136.

4 Aitchison, J: 'The thesaurofacet: a multipurpose retrieval language tool.' *Journal of documentation, 26* (3) 1970, 187–203.

Aitchison, J: 'Thesaurofacet: a new concept in subject retrieval schemes.' (*In* Wellisch, H: *Subject retrieval in the seventies.* 1972, pp72–98).

CHAPTER 27

Social sciences

Thesauri in the social sciences have tended to be even more specialized than those in science and technology; there have also been rather fewer so far, with nothing on the scale of Project LEX; the largest single effort supported by the US Government in this field has been in the field of education.

ERIC

The Educational Resources Information Center Clearinghouses network was set up in 1966 to disseminate information in the field of educational research; one of its key publications is the monthly abstract journal *Resources in eduction*, and the Office of Education Panel on Educational Terminology decided to sponsor a thesaurus for the indexing of this bibliography. The first, preliminary, edition was published in January 1967;[1] this contained just over 3,000 descriptors, and was issued in revised form in 1968 as the *Thesaurus of ERIC descriptors* (first edition). The first edition proved somewhat inadequate for indexing, and a second edition was published in 1969, replacing the first edition, dated 1967, and the supplement dated March 1968. This edition contained over 6,000 descriptors, twice as many as in the preliminary edition and over 2,000 more than in the first edition. It also contained other new features such as the descriptor group display.

The 6th edition, published by Macmillan in 1975, is very well produced, by contrast with the early editions, but in content it remains very similar, though some new features have been introduced.

The thesaurus begins with a twenty-page introduction on 'the role and function of the thesaurus in education', by Dr Frederick Goodman. After a discussion of the significance of the thesaurus as an authority, and its total basis in literary warrant, he goes on to describe the system of relationships used, which are the conventional use/UF, BT/NT and RT cross-references; scope notes and parenthetical qualifiers are also used, though very occasionally in comparison with most other lists, as the cross-reference structure is expected to define a term by its associations. Then follows a rather cautious discussion of the problem of multi-word terms, in other words precoordinated subjects. To what extent is it in order to use these in a postcoordinate system? The thesaurus has a very high proportion of such terms, in fact single terms are the exception rather than the rule. Some doubts are expressed as to whether the proliferation of multi-word terms is a good thing, but it would now be an impossible task to eliminate them or even to reduce them significantly, whether this is thought to be desirable or not. The Cranfield II project (chapter 28) found that such precoordinated headings were a major cause of the poor performance of some of the indexing languages tested. Their use necessitates some kind of listing to reveal the hidden terms, in this case a KWIC index called the rotated descriptor display; inverted headings are not used at all, so all the terms in the thesaurus are in natural language order, and the KWIC index enables the user to locate all the uses of any particular word. Alphabetization is letter by letter, and the usual rules on word forms (singular or plural) are followed.

The terms used are also listed in the descriptor group display, which is in effect a broad classification, though Dr Goodman emphasizes that it should not be considered as a classification in the sense of enabling the indexer or searcher to select the 'right' indexing term, but merely as an aid in showing context. The groups are also used for the arrangement of the abstracts in the other ERIC bibliographic tool, *Current index to journals in education,* whereas *Resources in education* is arranged by accession number.

Users of the thesaurus are next warned that documents may be indexed by *identifiers,* which do not appear in the thesaurus and are not included in the cross-reference network. The introduction concludes with a discussion of the use of the thesaurus and some considerations to be taken into account in attempting to evaluate it. The whole introduction is aimed mainly at people in education who are not familiar with the use of a thesaurus, but does contain some interesting general comments, for example in the section of multi-word headings.

The introduction is followed by a summary of contents, which begins with the rather startling statement that 'descriptors are in bold-face capital and lower case letters (*eg,* **Objectives**)': startling, because it is the reverse of the truth, which is that descriptors, *ie* preferred terms, are in boldface small capitals, while non-preferred terms are in boldface capital and lower case letters! It then briefly lists the other features, which have been discussed at length in the introduction: the summary of contents is evidently intended for the user who is familiar with thesauri and wishes to learn quickly what features to look for in this particular one.

The list of descriptors and non-preferred terms occupies the next 275 pages, and contains between 5,000 and 6,000 preferred terms. It is notable for the very lengthy sets of cross-references to be found under nearly every term, *eg*

ACADEMIC ACHIEVEMENT   Jul 1966
   UF   Academic Performance (Del Jun74)

Academic Progress

. . .

Student Performance   twelve in all
NT   Academic Failure
     Student Promotion
BT   Achievement
RT   Able students
    Academic ability

. . .

Underachievers   twentysix in all

All preferred terms have a date showing when they were first entered into the ERIC system, but unlike the API thesaurus, there are no scope notes indicating what previous practice might have been; one is forced to assume in the light of the comments in the introduction that the subject could not have arisen previously.

As mentioned, some descriptors do have scope notes, though some of these seem to serve little purpose: *eg*

ABSTRACTION LEVELS   Jul 1966
SN   Levels of abstract reasoning reached
     in the process of developing successively
     broader generalizations reflected in
     language usage

CORRESPONDENCE STUDY   Jul 1966
SN   Method of instruction with teacher
     student interaction by mail

(though it is not thought necessary to have scope notes for CORRESPONDENCE COURSES OR CORRESPONDENCE SCHOOLS)

MAN DAYS
SN   Unit consisting of one hypothetical
     average man day

a definition which appears to be circular.

As already mentioned, there are a very few descriptors with parenthetical qualifiers, *eg*

PATTERN DRILLS (LANGUAGE)
ACTION PROGRAMS (COMMUNITY)

(which might surely have been better as COMMUNITY ACTION PROGRAMS?)

ACCREDITATION (INSTITUTIONS)

Occasionally adjectives are used as descriptors, but this is usually in the situation where the word 'people' is understood, *eg*

HANDICAPPED

The alphabetical list is followed by the rotated descriptor display; from this, one may find, for example, that though the word 'addiction' is not used as a descriptor it does occur in the term 'Drug addiction'. This section is the only means of access to words such as this, but it does also include all the single-word terms in the list, eg 'writing', 'zoos', 'botany' etc.

Related terms are brought together in the descriptor groups; there is first a tabulation of the 52 groups with scope notes explaining their significance, *eg*

080 **Communication**

Methods and characteristics of communication, *eg*, Oral Expression, Verbal Communication, etc. For types of communication equipment, *see also* EQUIPMENT.

This is followed by the groups, which are alphabetical tabulations of the terms falling within them. In the early editions, each descriptor in the alphabetical list was accompanied by its group number, *eg*

PARKING AREAS 210

but this has been dropped, and there is now no access to the terms in the groups other than sequential scanning.

The next sequence is the hierarchical display, which is in the same format as that in TEST. Each term is only listed in its place in a hierarchy, *ie* a term which has one or more broader terms above it will only be found under the term at the top of the hierarchy. Terms which have no broader or narrower term relationships are however also listed, *eg*

ACHIEVEMENT
. ACADEMIC ACHIEVEMENT
. . ACADEMIC FAILURE
. . . READING FAILURE
. . STUDENT PROMOTION
. GRADUATION
. LANGUAGE LEARNING LEVELS
. NEGRO ACHIEVEMENT
. READING ACHIEVEMENT
. READING LEVEL

ACHIEVEMENT GAINS

ACTIVITIES
. AFTER SCHOOL ACTIVITIES
etc.

This listing, and the rotated descriptor display, cannot but emphasize the degree of precoordination that is found; approximately 5,400 terms are listed in the descriptor groups, but there are approximately 9,500 entries in the rotated descriptor display, the difference arising from the number of multi-word terms in the list. In the above example we find Negro achievement; but Negroes and Achievement are both descriptors, and in a postcoordinate system one would normally expect to obtain the composite subject by coordinating the two single concepts. All three date back to July 1966, and one is forced to the conclusion that, having started out with no clear principles on the formation of headings, (the *Rules for thesaurus preparation* which now govern the strictly controlled addition of new descriptors were published in 1969) the first set of headings 'just growed' on an *ad hoc* basis. Whatever the cause, the effect is that anyone wishing to search the ERIC data bases must first study the *Thesaurus* very carefully in order to formulate an adequate search strategy.

The final section of the Thesaurus is a bibliography of over two hundred items relating either to education or to thesaurus construction and indexing. Perhaps it is symptomatic of the whole approach that it is arranged alphabetically by author in one sequence, and does not include the *London education classification*.

The thesaurus is updated by the incorporation of new terms at the suggestion of indexers at the Clearinghouses. Any proposals must be made on the *descriptor justification form*, which was included in the early editions but has now been dropped. Full justification must be given for any additions; it must not be possible for the concept to be adequately described by the existing terms; implications for BT/NT and RT relationships must also be thought out. New proposals are examined by the central indexing staff, within the policy laid down by the Panel on indexing terminology, which consists of representatives of both fields, documentation and education. The result of this stringent procedure is that very few new terms are now added; a random 5% sample showed 208 terms dated July 1966, 13 added in 1968, 11 in 1969, 11 in 1970, 5 in 1971, 1 in 1972, 3 in 1973 and 1 in 1974. From this it would appear that over 80% of the terms were in the original edition, while fewer than 5% have been added since 1970. This does not of course take into account changes in the cross-reference network, which is also under constant review. However, it does emphasize that the current edition, though very much better produced, is still very much in line with the original, and one can only wonder what would have happened if a more systematic approach had been adopted at the start of the project, such as is exemplified by the next thesaurus to be described.

INFORMATION RETRIEVAL THESAURUS OF EDUCATION TERMS
As part of the preparatory work for the ERIC project, the School of Library Science at Case Western Reserve University developed a thesaurus of terms; this list was not the one finally used, though it is not clear why, as it appears to be much better than the ERIC Thesaurus as it now stands. Compiled by G C Barhydt and C T Schmidt, with assistance from K T Chang, the *Information retrieval thesaurus of education terms* was published by the University in 1968.

After a brief foreword, there is a very useful introduction preceding the three sections of the list: alphabetical array, faceted array, and permuted list of descriptors. The introduction is more than just an

433

introduction to this thesaurus, it is a very good albeit brief summary of the kind of problems that are likely to be found in indexing or searching for material in a subject field such as education, and the steps taken in the construction to deal with these problems. The original development arose from the indexing of some 7,500 documents and the compilation of a *Semantic code dictionary of education* containing nearly 11,000 terms. (The WRU experiments with semantic coding are described briefly in chapter 5). This list was reduced to a working list of about 5,000 terms by eliminating abbreviations, different spellings and identifiers, *ie* terms which denote specific institutions, etc. Although further terms were added during the development of the thesaurus, rigorous editing and selecting of terms has meant that the final list contains just over 2,000 preferred terms, with cross-references from additional non-preferred terms. However, the compilers point out that because the vocabulary is clearly structured it is relatively simple to add new terms if this is thought appropriate in any given situation.

In addition to straightforward synonyms, which are relatively few, five classes of USE reference are defined, most of which are already familiar:

1 prefer the appropriate grammatical form, dictated in many cases by the facet analysis, *eg* Interviewing rather than Interview, since this falls into the activities facet

2 prefer general terms to trade names

3 prefer normal word order to inversion

4 use one term for a concept and its opposite, *eg* Attendance for Non-attendance

5 use a general term rather than specific terms for subjects of fringe interest.

Scope notes are of six kinds. The first of these is the qualifier added in parenthesis, which could usually be replaced by an ordinary scope note, *eg* Sampling (statistical). Second and third are positive and negative limitation; the former is a kind of definition, the latter serves to exclude concepts which might otherwise fall into the scope of the heading but which in fact have separate headings of their own. Fourth is a straightforward definition, or definition with positive limitation. Fifth is a kind of positive limitation, but applies to terms of rather general meaning which are used in particular sense in the field of education, or where only one meaning of several is of interest in the subject. The sixth kind of scope note is unusual, consisting of an asterisk, *eg* Facilities SN*. These are terms which are unlikely to be used for indexing because of their generality, but which are given because they form a potential link in genus-species division or because the compilers felt that they would, *in a given indexing situation*, become more meaningful.

Broader term-narrower term relationships are shown by use of BT-NT entries in the usual way. Related terms are however given more elaborate treatment. Each descriptor has at least one RT reference leading to the subfacet in which it is to be found in the faceted array, but in many cases this is the only RT references since there are no related terms in other hierarchies. Where other RT references appear they fall into two groups: reciprocal and non-reciprocal. Reciprocal RT references work both ways and are marked with a kind of blob in the shape of a distorted inverted comma; non-reciprocal references work only the way shown, and are not marked. For example:

PRESCHOOL EDUCATION
   SN *
   RT   2012
       CULTURAL DEPRIVATION
       EARLY CHILDHOOD
       PRESCHOOL LEVEL'

This means that we should first of all consider very carefully whether we wish to use this term (SN*); we shall find it in subfacet 2012; and there will be an RT reference to it from PRESCHOOL LEVEL but not from the other two related terms mentioned.

Related terms are hard to define and isolate once we go outside a particular facet; the introduction discusses the semantic aspects, and in addition to whole-part and near-synonymous relationships lists sixteen different kinds of other relationships. Some of these are difficult to distinguish, resting as they do on distinctions so nice as to be almost invisible; on the other hand, in some cases the compilers have taken a pragmatic view and eliminated RT links between terms which file close together in the alphabetical sequence. This useful summary of the problems emphasizes the fact that we are still only at the beginning of the solution to this particular problem.

The faceted array is broken down into 17 facets, with 133 subfacets. Within each subfacet there may be several groups, which are not given any notation because, it appears, of the lack of a suitable computer program; there would of course be no objection to notation for these, but as it stands, order within groups is alphabetical rather than systematic. This is not a hindrance in practice, as the groups are rarely longer than about ten terms and can be scanned easily. Guide lines for thesaurus use, immediately preceding the thesaurus, stress the importance of the interaction between alphabetical and faceted displays, just as in *Thesaurofacet*.

The permuted index is a KWIC index, necessitated by the use of composite headings. These are used because so many of the terms in this subject field are rather general, and to use single terms would require a massive use of links in indexing practice; it was felt to be more helpful to give ready-linked, *ie* precoordinated, terms in a good proportion of cases.

The significant point about this thesaurus in contrast to the ERIC thesaurus is of course the systematic approach. This permits later additions and amendments to be consistent with the original structure in a way that is not possible with a more haphazard first construction. It seems a pity that so many thesauri have adopted the *ad hoc* approach exemplified by LCSH, rather than the more systematic approach shown in this scheme. However, the frequent use of multi-word terms in a list which is prepared along analytico-synthetic lines does serve to emphasize the problems of terminology that arise in the social sciences.

LONDON EDUCATION CLASSIFICATION (LEC)

The LEC has already been mentioned earlier in the discussion of systematic arrangement, and it may seem odd to include it here. However, the second edition,[2] published in 1974 after ten years of experience with the first edition, is in thesaurofacet form, and although in general it conforms to the now established pattern, there are some points of difference.

The new edition was to some extent stimulated by the development of the European Documentation and Information System for Education, EUDISED, but it also reflects developments and changes in education during the decade. The major facets and the citation order have remained unchanged—a tribute to the care that went into their original selection and arrangement, but there has been a considerable expansion of the 'fringe' subjects Philosophy, Psychology, Sociology and History. It was hoped that a classification might be developed for these subjects from which LEC could borrow (the new BC?) but none had appeared by the time the decision to revise the scheme was taken, and in consequence they have been greatly expanded by a careful study of the literature and of other thesauri.

The notation consisted of capital letters for the facets, with two-letter combinations of lower-case letters for foci giving pronounceable syllables. The growth of the subject has meant that this interesting experiment—which was reasonably successful—has had to be dropped, and notation may now include four-letter combinations (excluding *the* four-letter combinations!) and three-letter non-pronounceable groups. Instructions on how to use the schedules are included; each facet and subfacet is clearly labelled to show what the steps of division are. However, we are here concerned with the alphabetical index, which is in effect a thesaurus in its own right. Unlike *Thesaurofacet* and Barhydt and Schmidt, it does *not* require the user to turn to the schedules to discover BT/NT relationships if he does not wish to; these are included in the thesaurus, along with RT relationships. The class number is given with each preferred term, so that the user can refer to the schedules to clarify the context of a term if he wishes. Some examples will illustrate

436

these points.

Brain Drain   Basv
SN Emigration of skilled and
      professional persons
BT Emigration
RT Immigrant
      Immigration

Brilliant
USE Gifted   Tag

Boarding School   Rol
UF Residential School
BT Exceptional Schools
RT Direct Grant
      Hall of Residence
      Preparatory School
      'Public School'   [British terminology!]

Boy Scouts
USE Scouts   Sog

As in the two previous examples, we find some precoordinated terms, *eg*

Administrative documents
Administrative staff
Administrative structure

where the terms Administration of education, Staff and Structure are also included; others have obviously been included because it would involve too much repetition to separate them, *eg*

Training of Teachers
Theory of Thought
Speech defect

A term may appear in two facets of the classification; in the thesaurus, this is indicated by the notation, with the term entered twice with appropriate scope notes:

Salary   Fig
SN Of members of the teaching
      profession
BT Conditions of Service
RT Leave
      Retirement
      Secondment

Salary   Hrs
SN As item of expenditure
BT Expenditure

RT Allowance
   Wage

As might be expected, the terminology is noticeably British as opposed to the American terminology in the previous examples. The list is also much shorter, with approximately 1,200 terms in the schedules; however, it must be remembered that the large number of precoordinated terms in the ERIC Thesaurus necessarily leads to the bulking out of the list. The first edition of the classification was widely used in education libraries in Britain, and it will be interesting to see what effect the new format has.

EUDISED MULTILINGUAL THESAURUS

This thesaurus,[3] prepared as part of EUDISED, also offers some interesting contrasts with the American publications, as well as the linguistic features which particularize it. The intention was to produce a thesaurus which could be used throughout Western Europe and be produced in several different languages; the original languages are English, French and German, but a Spanish edition is in preparation and an adaptation for use in Brazil is being considered. The list is geared specifically to use in Europe, where the ERIC Thesaurus cannot fit satisfactorily into the cultural patterns.

There is a valuable introduction by the editor, Jean Viet, explaining the purpose of thesauri in general and this thesaurus in particular; for example, although BT, NT and RT do not fit languages other than English (eg the French *voir aussi* VA) they are now well known, and to have different sets of instructions in every edition would be confusing.

The list begins with a tabulation of the descriptor groups and subgroups, *eg*

13000	TEACHING METHOD
13100	TEACHING. TRAINING
13200	MICROTEACHING. TEAM TEACHING
13300	DIRECTIVE. NON-DIRECTIVE. GROUP LEARNING
13400	CLASSWORK
13500	DISCUSSION. QUESTIONING
13600	RECREATION. TRAVEL

The groups are not intended to form a classification; they correspond to the ERIC descriptor groups rather than the LEC facets. After this brief listing of the groups, the descriptors are tabulated by group, with the main heading given in all three languages, *eg*

13000	TEACHING METHOD
13100	TEACHING. TRAINING

13110
   EDUCATIONAL PRACTICE
      USE: TEACHING PRACTICE

```
INSTRUCTION
   USE:  TEACHING
INSTRUCTIONAL MODEL
   USE:  TEACHING MODEL
LEARNING OBJECTIVE
   USE:  TEACHING OBJECTIVE
REALITY PRACTICE
   USE:  TEACHING PRACTICE
TEACHING—ENSEIGNEMENT—UNTERRICHT
   UF:  INSTRUCTION
   NT:  AUTOMATIC TEACHING
        BEGINNING LEARNING
        . . .
        TELEVISED COURSE
   RT:  COURSE
        CURRICULUM
        . . .                    [19 in all]
```

Group 30,000 is a list of countries. The question of whether such a list is appropriate in a subject thesaurus is discussed in the introduction, where it is justified in the interests of standardization in a multi-lingual list.

The grouped lists are followed by an alphabetical list in an unusual format. It is in effect a KWOC index, listing each single term, with all its occurrences listed below, together with their group numbers, *eg*

```
ABSTRACTION
   ABSTRACTION   17342
ACADEMIC
   ACADEMIC DEGREE   19720
   ACADEMIC FREEDOM   16120
   ACADEMIC GAME   13340
      USE:  SIMULATION GAME
   ACADEMIC STAFF   20210
      USE:  TEACHING PERSONNEL
   ACADEMIC YEAR   19220
   BEGINNING OF THE ACADEMIC YEAR   19220
ACCELERATED
   ACCELERATED COURSE   19600
ACCELERATION
   ACCELERATION   17200
```

It would obviously be unwise to rely on the alphabetical listing without reference back to the groups, though it could be done, as preferred terms are indicated. The editions in other languages would of course have the terms listed in those languages, but would still have the three equivalents for each major group heading.

The list is produced by straightforward computer printout, and it is hoped that future editions may be produced in a more satisfactory format, with lower case letters and accents—the latter being significant in French, though in German the umlaut can be replaced by E, *eg* Beweisführung is printed BEWEISFUEHRUNG

It will be interesting to see what progress the list makes; the existence of EUDISED is a strong incentive for the development of use of such a tool, which could be the forerunner of other multilingual thesauri in similar fields.

BIBLIOGRAPHY

The general references from chapters 4, 24 and 26 are also relevant here.

1 American documentation, *19* (4) 1968, 418–419 (review). For an account of the background to the ERIC Thesaurus, see:

Eller, J L and Ranek, R L: 'Thesaurus development for a decentralized information network.' American documentation, *19* (3) 1968, 213–220.

2 Foskett, D J and Foskett, J A: 'The London education classification: a thesaurus/classification of British educational terms.' *Education libraries bulletin* supplement six. Second edition, 1974.

3 Viet, J: *EUDISED multilingual thesaurus for information processing in the field of education.* First English edition, 1973. Paris, Council of Europe, 1974.

CHAPTER 28

The evaluation of information retrieval systems

For many years librarians tended to take information retrieval systems for granted; classification schemes were part of the librarian's way of life, catalogues were compiled according to sets of rules drawn up by librarians to meet the requirements of the user as seen by the librarian. In recent years attitudes have changed; accepted ideas are increasingly subject to challenge and to close scrutiny as costs rise faster than funds, and as the providers of funds begin to question whether they are getting value for their money. The development of the computer has added a new dimension to the question: how much of what has always been thought of as intellectual work in indexing can be taken over by the machine? We have already discussed the application of computer production to BTI, and the consequent realization that many of the operations previously thought of as intellectual could in fact be mechanized; we have also considered one of the experiments in the application of computers to the generation of classifications. Librarians have become aware of the need to evaluate the systems they use, with two major objectives in mind: to develop the most efficient and effective systems, and to provide the systems which are of most value to the user. In this chapter we shall be examining some of the major projects in these areas; as with many other aspects of information retrieval, space precludes the consideration of more than a few of the multitude of projects which have been undertaken in recent years.[1] Evaluation is rapidly becoming a branch of information retrieval in its own right, but we have tried to choose those examples which have had the most influence on present-day trends in information retrieval thinking.

THE ASLIB CRANFIELD RESEARCH PROJECT[2]
One of the earliest tests to establish the comparative efficiency of various indexing systems was carried out in the early 1950's by ASTIA (Armed Services Technical Information Agency: now DDC—Defense Documentation Center), to try to establish whether the set of subject headings it had developed were more useful than the Uniterm system proposed by Mortimer Taube. The results of the investigations were inconclusive, though ASTIA did adopt the post-coordinate system; the

difficulty lay in the fact that the two sides were unable to agree on what were the 'correct' answers to the test questions. As has been pointed out in the early pages of this work, relevance is a subjective judgement, depending on the background of experience which the user brings to the collection of documents being tested. The ASTIA test did little to show which system was more efficient, but it did show that there was a need for a more objective test. A great deal of money is invested in different methods of information retrieval, and the amount increases each year; if one method can be shown to be clearly superior to all the others, then that method should be adopted, and its rivals allowed to fall into disuse.

With this mind, Aslib set up in 1957 what has come to be known as the Cranfield Project, under the direction of the librarian of the College of Aeronautics at Cranfield, C W Cleverdon. Under the title 'An investigation into the comparative efficiency of indexing systems' the project set out to try to establish a methodology which would make possible the objective comparison of four systems: a faceted classification; UDC; alphabetical subject headings; and Uniterms. Several variables were taken into account in addition to the four schemes. Three indexers were employed, one with experience of indexing and subject knowledge of aeronautics, the field chosen for the experiments; one with experience of indexing, but little relevant subject knowledge; and one straight from library school, with neither indexing experience nor subject knowledge. Different times were used: 2 minutes, 4, 8, 12 and 16 minutes (though the time was only controlled for one of the indexing methods, each report being indexed by the other three methods without the operation being timed). The whole experiment was run through three times, to see whether the indexers improved their performance as they gained more experience. The material indexed consisted of batches of 100 technical reports and articles on various aspects of aeronautics; thus with three indexers, four systems, five time periods, and three runs, a total of 18,000 items were indexed.

The next problem was to arrive at a method of testing which would eliminate the subjective element. The method chosen was to ask a number of people in different organizations to select documents from the collection and in each case phrase a question to which that document would be an answer. From the 1,400 questions suggested, four hundred were selected by a screening panel of three experts in aeronautical information. These questions were then put to the four indexes, and a search was counted as successful if the 'source document' was revealed. Rearrangement of the subject elements in a search did not count as a new search, but dropping or changing one element did, except in the case of the Uniterm index, where an additional term could be dropped without being counted as a failure if the source document was found.

Both the indexing and searching situations are clearly artificial and do not bear much relationship to real life situations. There was no feedback during indexing, and the indexers were not able to concentrate on one particular system as they would normally. To count a search as a success if one particular document is found but a failure if it is not is to alter completely the nature of searching by subject, converting it to the yes/no situation valid for the factors which identify. There was no feedback at the search stage; a question once framed was permanent, though in real life we would normally expect to modify a question if our first search did not reveal the answer. Despite these criticisms, the results of the experiment are very interesting, and their influence has been considerable.

The first important finding was that all of the systems were of approximately equal effectiveness; to begin with, the Uniterm index was found to give best results, with the faceted classification giving the worst, but a subexperiment run with the latter showed that it could give slightly better results than Uniterm. The main problem with the faceted classification was in fact the fixed citation order coupled with a chain index; as has been shown, this can lead to problems if the users' approach is not a standardized one, and in the Cranfield experiment this was the case. Using the faceted classification as the basis of a multiple entry system, with a simplified alphabetical index, improved the test results—but we are speaking of an improvement of some 10% only. (It is also necessary to remember that this test was not conducted under the same experimental conditions as the main comparison, so the results obtained cannot be strictly compared with those obtained to begin with.)

No significant difference was found between the indexers or the three runs; since we normally find that indexers improve as they gain in knowledge and experience, these findings are unexpected. The other findings were perhaps equally unexpected. There was, it appeared, little point in spending more than four minutes indexing a particular document, for the additional time gave no improvement in results, though to spend only two minutes was inadequate and gave rise to a high proportion of the failures. However, the largest single factor leading to failure was human error: failure to use the systems correctly, or to search correctly, was the cause of about half the total number of errors.

Though the results of the experiment were very interesting, perhaps more important were the developments in thinking to which the project as a whole was to lead. These developments form in fact a significant part of the approach in this text. The concept of two related factors, recall and relevance, was the result of studying the documents revealed by the Cranfield searches, and the quest for factors which might influence recall and relevance led to the formulation of the criteria of specificity and exhaustivity. The isolation of these basic factors has enabled experimental work in the comparison of indexing systems to go forward on a far more satisfactory basis, and has also indicated practical ways in which we can improve the results we obtain in using information retrieval systems in our libraries. It is probably true to say that none of these ideas was completely novel;[3] writers on classification have been discussing the merits of close and broad classification for many years now, for example. However, it has been very valuable to see them isolated and defined, just as it was valuable for Ranganathan to isolate and define ideas which were implicit in schemes such as DC.

A further test of the Cranfield ideas came with a comparison of the index to metallurgical literature compiled at Case Western Reserve University using semantic factoring, with an index to a selection of this literature compiled using the English Electric faceted classification. The major criterion for success or failure was again the performance of the two systems in revealing answers to questions based on documents within the systems, but this time the response was measured on searches of the complete collection, not merely on predetermined documents as in Cranfield I. Although the WRU workers were able to obtain slightly better recall, the Cranfield workers consistently obtained better results as far as relevance was concerned.

We have discussed the WRU semantic factoring system in chapter 5 and it is clearly a very powerful analytical technique, and the document descriptions produced using the system should have been very effective in retrieving documents at both high recall and high relevance ratios. However, the system is a highly complex one, which adds to the difficulties of precise matching, and in chapter 5 we did in addition express some doubts about the fundamental validity of the method of semantic factoring.

Despite these doubts, it is a little surprising that the WRU system did not show up very well in the test, and a number of reasons were advanced by its protagonists to explain their relative failure.[4] The chief of these was the nature of the questions, which were largely framed on the basis of document titles. The WRU system involved lengthy analysis of the subject content of each document, whereas the Cranfield workers tended to take the overall subject as being the most significant factor—indeed, it is possible to do little else if the time needed for indexing is measured in intervals of four minutes—and were thus more likely to match the questions. Whatever the reasons, the failure of the WRU system led to its abandonment by the American Society for Metals, who had been one of its most important backers.

CRANFIELD II

In addition to the factors already mentioned, the first Cranfield project

444

had led to one other fundamental conclusion, which in fact forms the basis of much of Part I of this book. This conclusion was that all indexing languages consist of a basic vocabulary of keywords together with various devices intended to improve either recall or relevance performance. We saw in chapter 5 that semantic links, for example in the form of classification hierarchies, are basically intended to enable to increase recall if our primary search strategy does not retrieve the information we require. In chapter 6, we saw that syntactic devices, particularly coordination, are intended to enable us to increase relevance if our primary search retrieves too much information, or information on too broad a subject. These two objectives are not completely mutually exclusive; semantic devices can be used to improve relevance, by indicating related subjects more closely matching our requirements, and syntactic devices may improve recall by similar means. On the whole, however, the statement holds good, and it forms a solid basis on which to compare different indexing languages.

Many of the criticisms of the first project and the Cranfield-WRU test arose from the fact that the real-life situation led to the introduction of too many uncontrollable variables, and that some of the measures taken to overcome this (for example, the method of judging success or failure in Cranfield I) had in fact made the problems worse. It was therefore decided to make the Cranfield II project a purely experimental one carred out under laboratory conditions, in which the effects of changing one variable at a time could be judged. A more satisfactory way of judging relevance was also sought.

A much smaller collection of documents, approximately 1400, was used. A selection of these were sent to the authors, who were asked to state their reasons for writing the paper; in other words, the problem they themselves were trying to answer. The whole collection was then searched by a team of post-graduate students in relation to every question; the results obtained by these students were then sent to the authors for their judgement as to whether the documents found were relevant or not. We saw in chapter 2 that in real life the set A of documents relevant to a particular enquiry is normally impossible to define precisely; the objective in the project was to establish the set of relevant documents precisely, so that the 'correct' answer was known in advance. In order to remove any possible bias, the original documents were removed from the collection. The answers obtained by using the various indexing languages investigated could thus be measured against a predetermined norm rather than against a subjective judgement; to emphasize this point, the term *precision ratio* was substituted for *relevance ratio*.

Thirty three different index languages were tested. The documents were indexed thoroughly, including themes within them as necessary; from this indexing process, all the single terms were listed to give the

445

basic vocabulary, and the other indexing languages were built up from this basis, making one change at the time. For example, taking the basic vocabulary as the first language to be tested, the second was obtained by merging synonyms; the third was obtained from the first by merging word forms; the fourth was obtained by merging two and three, *ie* by merging both synonyms and word forms. Other vocabularies were formed by merging terms into hierarchies at different levels; another consisted of multi-word terms found in the documents, *eg* axial flow compressor. (For the basic vocabulary, this was broken down into axial, flow and compressor as three separate terms).

From the preliminary work a set of some 221 questions with predetermined answers had been established. Each question was translated into the vocabulary of each indexing language, and a series of searches were performed. Let us suppose that we have a question containing four significant natural language terms, and we wish to use the natural language single term index. A search is performed coordinating all four terms, and will reveal a certain number of documents; of these, a proportion will be among those previously judged relevant to this question. A further four searches are now performed, using any three of the terms only; once again, a certain number of documents will be revealed, of which a proportion will be relevant. Further searches are made using only two of the terms, and finally each of the terms is used on its own. For this question there will be four 'levels of coordination' depending on how many terms are coordinated together for each search. The main problem was to find a performance measure which would make possible the comparison of results between systems, but also of results obtained by changing one variable within a system, for example the coordination level.

Such a measure had been developed by G Salton, whose work on the SMART project is described below. It is known as *normalized recall ratio*, and it depends in the first instance on the establishment of a method of 'ranking' the relevant documents discovered. This rank is given by a formula which links the number of relevant and non-relevant documents revealed at each level of coordination:

$$^cR_n = X_o + (n - Y_o)\frac{(x_o + 1)}{y_o + 1}$$

in which

c is the coordination level at which the nth relevant document is retrieved

^cR_n is the rank of the nth relevant document

x_c is the number of documents retrieved at coordination level c

y_c is the number of *relevant* documents retrieved at level c

X_c is the total number of documents retrieved at higher coordination levels (*ie* before searching at level c)

Y_c is the total number of *relevant* documents previously retrieved

Let us assume that in carrying out the search used as an example in the last paragraph we have found 4 relevant and 58 non-relevant documents by the time we reach the second level of coordination (*ie* taking two terms together); in taking the final step to the first level of coordination (*ie* single terms) we reveal another 2 relevant and 34 non-relevant documents. We wish to find the rank ^cR_n of the sixth relevant document, found at level 1, so $c = 1$ and $n = 6$. The total number of documents found before we searched at level 1, X_1, is 62 $(4 + 58)$, while the total number of *relevant* documents we found before we searched at this level, Y_1, is 4. The total number of documents retrieved at the level 1, x_1, is 36, of which 2 are relevant, y_1. The formula thus gives us the result for this particular example:

$$^1R_6 = 62 + (6-4)\frac{(36+1)}{2+1} = 62 + 2(12\tfrac{1}{3}) = 87$$

The ranks obtained in this way were grouped into seventeen ranges; at the lower levels, from 1 to 5, each range contains only the equivalent rank, but ranks from 51 to 200 were grouped into six ranges, each containing 25. In our example, the sixth relevant document found, with rank 87, will fall into the range 76–100. If we tabulate for each index language the number of the question showing which ranges the relevant documents found fall into, we can build up a cumulative recall pattern for the language as a whole. The normalized recall ratio is obtained by totalling the steps of this cumulation and dividing by the number of steps, 17. For example, we may find the following results with one particular language:

Range (ranks)	1	2	3	4	5	6-7	8-10	11-15	16-20	21-30	31-50	51-75	76-100	101-125	126-150	151-175	176-200
No. of relevant answers	21	24	18	17	13	16	14	14	13	10	10	8	7	7	4	3	1
Cumulative recall %	10	22	31	40	46	54	61	68	75	80	85	89	92	96	98	99	100

This gives us a cumulative sum of the recall ratios of 1146, and this divided by 17, the number of ranges, gives us a normalized recall ratio 67.4%, which may be compared with the similar figure found for other index languages.

It will be seen that the rank is a measure of how quickly a given index language reveals the relevant documents; the more we have to broaden our search strategy, the higher the ranking of the relevant documents found at each level. When the ranks are tabulated for all questions, the more results there are in the lower ranks, the more quickly our cumulative recall ratio will approach 100% and the higher will be the normalized recall ratio. If all our relevant documents were revealed at the first search, with no unwanted documents at all, we should very quickly reach 100% cumulative recall ratio, giving us a normalized recall ratio also near 100%. It should be noted that even with this perfect result, it is not possible to reach 100% normalized recall, as only the first document found can have rank 1; if there are five, they will be ranked 1, 2, 3, 4 and 5, according to the formula.

It is perhaps worth emphasizing that the normalized recall ratio does act as a measure of relevance (precision), not merely recall. Its main advantage is that it gives a single figure of merit, rather than the recall-precision graph, and it is thus easier to handle. Another advantage is that it serves to rank *all* documents in response to a given question, rather than just those thought to be relevant; the user can in fact set his own cut-off point to give him the number of documents that he feels he can conveniently handle.

The results of the experiments were somewhat surprising. The use of natural language single terms gave results which were bettered only if synonyms were eliminated or paradigms confounded, while the worst results were shown by the use of natural language to express simple concepts. Controlled vocabularies gave results rather worse than single terms, but in general much better than simple concepts. It is important here to know what is meant by 'simple concept'; for example, 'axial flow compressor' is quoted as being a simple concept, but this is clearly not what we have referred to in this book as a simple concept. The question is obviously allied to the depth of analysis discussed earlier in this chapter, but it is also related to what we have called pre-coordination; in fact, it appears to be pre-coordination which led to a number of the failures.

Other tests were carried out to study the effects of, for example, weighting and relevance judgements. At the time of indexing, documents were weighted for each index term according to the simple scale:

1	main concepts
2	less important concepts
3	minor concepts

Relevance decisions were also weighted on a similar scale:

1	complete answers to the question
2	high degree of relevance
3	useful as background, or for certain aspects
4	minimum interest, *eg* historical

448

These tests do not appear to have affected the main results significantly.

The conclusion that may be drawn from Cranfield II is that terms taken from documents may be used successfully with the minimum of control in a post-coordinate index; it is helpful to eliminate synonyms and paradigms, but apart from this any measures taken to control the vocabulary are likely to decrease its efficiency. This is a rather unexpected conclusion, and is of course contrary to most of what has been stated in this text; it is also contrary to the experience of large numbers of librarians, who have found that controlled vocabularies are helpful in practice. There is a need for further research to reconcile these differing points of view, in particular to establish the relationship between the artificial experimental set-up at Cranfield and the kind of situation met in real life.

The two factors which seem to have had most effect on the Cranfield results were specificity and exhaustivity. The use of complex concepts, *eg* axial flow compressor, in the indexing language, means that the vocabulary will be a large one, as we have seen in the discussions earlier; on the other hand, we can reduce the vocabulary to a minimum if we group simple concepts hierarchically. It appears that there is a happy medium; in the project, language I.3, containing single terms only and merging paradigms, used 2,541 terms and gave a normalized recall ratio of 65.82%, the highest recorded. This was better than language I.9 with 306 terms representing the third level of hierarchical grouping, which gave a ratio of 61.17%, and much better than II.1, simple concepts expressed in natural language, which used a vocabulary estimated at some 10,000 terms and gave a ratio of 44.64%. (Note that the description 'simple concepts' here refers to what we have called complex concepts, *ie* composite subjects used in a pre-coordinate manner.)

The effect of exhaustivity is shown by comparing the results obtained by the use of titles (average number of terms 7), various indexing languages, and abstracts (average number of terms about 60). Within a particular language, different levels of exhaustivity may be compared by studying the results given by terms with weight 1 only, terms with weights 1 and 2, and terms with weights 1, 2, and 3. In the project, it was found that the best results were obtained with a language using an average of 33 terms per document.

COLLEGE OF LIBRARIANSHIP WALES[5]
A further laboratory comparison of index languages has been carried out at the College of Librarianship Wales. Using a collection of eight hundred documents in the field of library and information science, the complete collection was examined for relevance in relation to the questions by independent judges, who were neither project indexers nor

enquirers. Most of the sixty three requests used represented real information requirements which were posed directly at the time of the test, or had previously been submitted to Aslib or the Library Association. The main tests were of three different postcoordinate indexing languages:

Compressed term: a 'minimum vocabulary' based on a list compiled by the Research department of Aslib. This had fewer than 300 terms, and a structure of related terms was added for the test.

Uncontrolled natural language: single words derived from the documents by the indexers. Some 1,200 words were used, and no related word structure or even synonym control was provided.

Hierarchically structured: based on the CRG Classification of library science. Some 800 facet terms were used, without synthesis at the indexing stage and thus without a fixed citation order; the notation and the hierarchical linkage were retained.

Since the exhaustivity and specificity of indexing in the different languages was kept at the same level, the number of terms used in each gives a very rough indication of language specificity. More accurate measurements of specificity were attempted by means of searches in which the exhaustivity and specificity of searching were held constant, and these showed that the Hierarchically structured was somewhat less specific than Uncontrolled, but considerably more specific than Compressed term. Measurement of the cross-reference structure or hierarchical linkage formally provided in the schedules of each language showed that Hierarchically structured and Compressed term both had nearly five cross-references per term, while Uncontrolled had less than one, derived from the accidentally helpful collocation of terms in the alphabetical list. These attempts to measure specificity and linkage were seen to be an essential preliminary to the main test in order both to advance the understanding of what constitutes the essential differences between languages, and to increase the capability of generalizing research findings by relating performance merit to measures of index language properties.

Test searches simulated real world searching as closely as possible, and searches for each request in each system were designed to give the equivalent of four searches, to cover variants of recall target. For example, a minimum recall target of only one highly relevant document per request satisfied represented the needs of one type of 'high precision' user, whereas a maximum recall target of all the highly or partially relevant documents in the file represented the needs of one kind of 'high recall' user. A time limit was imposed on searches, which were terminated when either the time limit was exceeded or the searchers reached the predetermined recall target.

All three languages easily attained the two variants of low recall target set for the high precision need, but in terms of non relevant documents retrieved Compressed term always performed worst, with Hierarchically structured and Uncontrolled very similar, the latter being slightly worse in individual request differences. However, none of the differences between the three languages was statistically significant. In the high recall cases, Compressed term was best, with Hierarchically structured worst—by 7% recall in one test, a statistically significant result. Uncontrolled lay midway between these two. If, however, we consider the non-retrieval of non-relevant documents in the high recall situation, Hierarchically structured was best, with Compressed term worst. These effectiveness measures were complemented by efficiency measures based on search time and the number of separate sub-programs used in the searches; Compressed term was best here with Hierarchically structured worst, but the differences were small.

Two of the many conclusions arising from the tests of these three languages were that Compressed term was not specific enough, and that lack of structure in Uncontrolled showed no significant disadvantage. The failure analysis in the final report gives some further explanation of these results, and includes comparisons of variations in indexing exhaustivity and specificity.

Limited tests were also conducted on two more index languages. One of these was the Hierarchically structured faceted classification, used in a precoordinate file with a fixed citation order, synthesized class marks and a chain index. Full comparison of this with the postcoordinate version were limited to measures of recall and efficiency; for high recall, the performance was significantly worse (by 11% in one case) in the precoordinate version. This was due at least in part to the longer search time needed; some 35% of the searches were terminated by the time limit, compared with 10% in the postcoordinate system.

In order to determine whether precoordination prevented many false drops which might occur with postcoordination, a controlled test was carried out. This showed virtually no difference at all, with only 10% of the searches affected, and an average 1% loss of recall with precoordination for a gain of 0.1 fewer non relevant documents retrieved. A further comparison was made of the effect of providing a fully rotated chain index. The searchers used this to select and reject the entries they found, as would be the case in many operational situations, and this nearly halved the average number of non relevant documents retrieved for a loss of 14% recall when compared with searching all matching entries.

The second limited test was of Farradane's relational indexing, described in chapter 6. Because of the limited use that had been made of this system previously, some new rules and conventions had to be developed for the subject area of the test. A subset of rather less than 250 of the documents were indexed, and a comparison test using 60 of the questions was completed, by measuring the performance of the system with and without the operators. These would be expected to act as a precision device, improving precision at the expense of recall, but in the event their effect was very slight. Only 13% of the searches were affected at all; of these, 10% were improved in precision, 3% worsened in recall, but the improvement in the suppression of non relevant documents was very small—about 0.2 on average, with a drop of 2% in recall. Although no realistic tests of efficiency were possible, it became very clear that in terms of indexing time the differences between Relational indexing and Uncontrolled were very considerable.

One of the conclusions which arose almost by accident was that context was very helpful in clarifying the use of single terms; this suggested that printed page indexes, such as those produced using PRECIS or Coates' methods, would be a worthwhile subject for investigation, and a grant was obtained to carry out a further project. At the time of writing no results are available, but the report on this project should be a valuable contribution to the literature of index language evaluation.

THE MEDLARS EVALUATION STUDY[6]

The work we have been describing so far has been carried out under experimental conditions, and there must always be doubts about the extent to which the results may be extrapolated to the real life situation; for this reason, the MEDLARS evaluation study carried out during 1966–1967, is of particular interest as the first large-scale project carried out on an operational system and it has had widespread effects.

The study had three major objectives:
to study the needs of users
to identify factors affecting the performance of the system
to suggest means of improvement.

To achieve these objectives, it was necessary to investigate a variety of factors, including the coverage of the system, its performance in terms of recall and relevance, the response time (*ie* the time taken to supply an answer to a request), the format of the output, and the amount of effort that the user was required to put into using the system.

The MEDLARS service operates through a number of centres which serve as forwarding points, and five were selected as being able to provide the range of users needed to make the study representative. From among the organizations served through these five centres, twenty were chosen as a suitable sample on the grounds that during the year they would submit enough requests to give a worthwhile basis for evaluation; requests covering the eight major subject areas covered by MEDLARS; requests representing five major types of organization (clinical research, academic, pharmaceutical, and Federal regulatory);

requests using the three possible modes of user/system inter-action—personal, local interaction, no interaction. The five centres were the NLM, the NIH (National Institute of Health) and three universities, UCLA, Colorado, and Harvard; in addition, a few requests sent in by private individuals were also examined.

The requests were sent in in the normal fashion, but the requesters were then asked if they would be willing to take part in the exercise; if so, they were sent the normal demand search bibliography as printed out, but in addition were sent copies of up to twenty-five or thirty items selected at random from the printed list. They were asked to judge the relevance of these items in relation to their request, and the result of this judgement was taken to give the precision of the whole bibli-ography (eg if eight of the twentyfive were judged relevant this gives a precision ratio of 32%). They were also asked to judge the 'serendipity factor', ie to state the number of items they found interesting though not relevant to their original request, and the 'novelty ratio', ie the number of relevant items previously unknown to them.

To measure the precision ratio was thus not too difficult, but how might the recall ratio be judged? It was clearly not possible to use the Cranfield technique and scan the whole of the data base in relation to each request, as it then contained some 800,000 items; another method had to be found. The method adopted was to establish an answer to the request by other means, eg the NLM catalogue, subject bibliographies, SCI etc, and to obtain relevance judgements on the documents found in this way by submitting them to the requester, after eliminating those not in the MEDLARS data base. The results of the MEDLARS search were then compared with this standard, which was taken to be the appro-priate recall base, ie the set of relevant documents in the collection. Ob-viously the method can only give an approximation by comparison with the Cranfield-type examination of the whole collection, but by careful sampling a statistically valid comparison was possible.

A total of 410 requests were processed, though it should be remem-bered that at the time the NLM was probably receiving a total of about 10,000 requests a year. Of the 410, 317 users were sufficiently cooper-ative to provide the necessary relevance judgements. Of these, 302 were analyzed in detail, but for three it proved impossible to establish a recall base, so the final evaluation was made on 299 requests. The average number of citations found per search was 175, but the range was quite wide, as in some cases the twentyfive chosen for the precision judgement consisted of the total number of citations in the list, while other lists contained several hundred. The system was estimated to be functioning at an average recall ratio of about 58% and precision ratio of about 50%, but the significance of these figures must not be misun-derstood; they represent *average* values, and as Cleverdon has pointed out, what this means is that half the time the results would be better than this, and half the time worse.[7] In fact, the scatter diagram included by Lancaster in his report shows results ranging from 0% recall and 0% precision to 100% recall and 100% precision!

The reasons for failure were very carefully examined in every case, in all 3,835 errors either in recall or in precision, and a number of conclusions were drawn, some of which have led to important changes. The coverage of medical literature seemed to be about 95%; in other words, there was no great need to increase the number of journals being scanned for input to the system. However, items in languages other than English were not popular, though they formed 45% of the data base; this appears to be a reflection of the fact that foreign literature is in general underused in the USA, and a different attitude might well have been found in, say, the UK. The response time reduced the value of the search in 21 of the 302 examined; not an excessively high figure, but high enough to indicate a need for more speedy processing. 6491 articles were retrieved altogether, from 1387 journals; however, 50% of the articles retrieved came from 157 journals, while ten journals accounted for 10% of the articles found—a convincing demonstration of Bradford's law of scattering!

At the time of the survey, some 800 journals were considered to be key journals, and articles from these were given an average of ten index terms as opposed to the average of four for articles from other journals. This led to a substantial proportion of the errors due to indexing, and the system was changed to one in which all articles were indexed on their own merits irrespective of source.

The version of MESH then in use was the cause of a high proportion of the failures. The total vocabulary was somewhat too limited, but much more serious was the inadequacy of the entry vocabulary. If a concept occurs in a document being indexed for which there is no term in the index vocabulary, two courses of action are open, depending on the type of vocabulary we are using; if it is an open vocabulary, we can add a term to denote the new concept, while if it is closed, we can select the most appropriate term from the existing vocabulary (cf Dewey's instruction to class new subjects at the nearest existing heading) *and add any necessary terms to the entry vocabulary to enable us to get to the term used*. If we do not have an adequate entry vocabulary, then we shall not know where to look in order to find information on the new concept, nor shall we be certain of indexing it in the same way the next time it arises. The entry vocabulary in MESH was poor, and this led to failures in recall and in precision. Failures in recall arose because indexers faced with a new concept not covered by a MESH term had not indexed it at all; they also arose when the indexer *had* indexed the concept because the searcher did not know *how* the concept had been indexed. Failures in precision arose in a similar pattern. If the concept had been indexed, and both indexer and searcher used the same term

454

for it, this would normally be a broader term, which would perform its normal function of increasing recall at the cost of precision, while if the indexer and searcher chose different terms, this would lead to a decrease in both recall and precision. Considerable effort has been devoted since the study to improving both the index and entry vocabularies in MESH, which should mean that problems of this kind should arise relatively infrequently now.

Human error led to a number of failures, as it had in both Cranfield projects; poor indexing and poor search formulation both gave rise to a substantial proportion of the failures in both recall and precision. It is perhaps encouraging in a rather depressing way to know that the computer also contributed a small proportion of errors, including one case in which five documents which should have been retrieved were missed on the first run but retrieved when the search was repeated later. Modern computers have very high standards of reliability, and machine performance is unlikely to be a significant source of errors now, though even the best are subject to external sources of error such as failures in the power supply.

Inadequate user-system interaction played a part in 30% of the failures in recall and 40% of those in precision. Unexpectedly, the best results were obtained when there was *no* personal interaction between requester and search analyst. It has always been assumed that the 'reference interview', in which the searcher established precisely what the user wanted, was an important factor in improving the performance of an information retrieval system, but this was found not to be the case. The cause appeared to be that the request became distorted through premature attempts by either user or searcher to 'translate' it into MESH search formulations. The most satisfactory results were obtained when the requester was obliged to formulate the request in detail in his own terms—for example, in a request sent through the mail—and it was then translated into a MEDLARS search formulation by a skilled analyst. This finding led to substantial changes in the design of the request form, which now takes the form described in chapter 25.

The need for improved user-system interaction and response time emphasized the importance of introducing an on-line system, and the result, MEDLINE, has been described in chapter 25. This has also been subjected to various evaluation tests, which seem to indicate quite clearly the improved results that can be obtained using a system on-line in the heuristic situation as opposed to the iterative mode involved in batch processing.[8] The ten-fold increase in the number of requests handled each year is ample confirmation of this, if any is needed. In his chapter on the evaluation of on-line systems, Lancaster also emphasizes a point made earlier in this text: the tendency of users to become intolerant of delays in response. In a library, as elsewhere, users expect to have to wait a short while at least for an answer, but once seated at a terminal they quickly come to regard any delay exceeding twenty seconds or so as quite unacceptable!

SMART

SMART

The work described so far has consisted of tests on collections indexed intellectually; either collections gathered and indexed specifically for the project, *eg* Cranfield and CLW, or operational systems, *eg* MEDLARS.[9] The SMART project developed by Salton (and known to the irreverent as Salton's Magical Automatic Retrieval of Text) is specifically concerned with the effectiveness of computer-based retrieval systems relying entirely or almost entirely on machine processing of text, either as document input or questions in natural language.[10] For economic reasons most of the tests have been carried out on texts in the form of document abstracts, though some experiments have been carried out to compare the effectiveness of titles, abstracts and full texts. The texts are analyzed by a wide variety of methods, including:

a system for reducing paradigms to their stem, giving a document description consisting of the word stems contained in it

a thesaurus, intellectually constructed, to eliminate synonyms and to show hierarchical relationships

statistical procedures to identify similar concepts through the co-occurrence of terms; associations between documents, either in pairs or in clusters, can also be determined

statistical phrase matching procedures, based on the thesaurus terms; these may simply involve the association of terms in a given unit of text, or more sophisticated procedures involving some twenty specific syntactic relationships between the phrase components.

The system is related in some ways to the *General Inquirer*[11] suite of programs developed at Harvard University, where Salton began his work, though the latter is intended for content analysis rather than information retrieval, and relies rather more on intellectually developed dictionaries.

A set of texts may be analyzed by any combination of the available methods, ranging from single procedures, *eg* the elimination of synonyms, to 'the whole works'. Questions written out in natural language form may be treated in the same way, and then matched against the set of documents. Searches may be weighted, for example by the number of times a particular word stem occurs in a given document; this may again be modified by comparison with the *expected* number of occurrences, based on the occurrence of the word stem in the whole collection of documents. This is the same procedure as that used by Edmundson in the weighting of terms for automatic extracting purposes, described in chapter 4.

An important factor in any computer-based system of this kind is the method used to establish how closely a document description matches a search formulation; a number of methods may be used, but the two most important developed by the SMART team are the cosine correlation coefficient, mentioned in the description of Sparck Jones' work on automatic classification in chapter 13, and the overlap function. To obtain these functions, the analyzed query $\mathbf{q}$ and the analyzed document $\mathbf{d}$ are considered as n-dimensional vectors in a space of n terms which represent the total number of potential document identifiers.

The cosine correlation function is given by

$$\cos(\mathbf{q}, \mathbf{d}) = \frac{\sum\limits_{i=1}^{n} \mathbf{d}_i \mathbf{q}_i}{\left(\sum\limits_{i=1}^{n} (\mathbf{d}_i)^2 \cdot \sum\limits_{i=1}^{n} (\mathbf{q}_i)^2 \right)^{\frac{1}{2}}}$$

and the overlap function by

$$\frac{\sum\limits_{i=1}^{n} \min(\mathbf{q}_i, \mathbf{d}_i)}{\min\left(\sum\limits_{i=1}^{n} \mathbf{q}_i, \sum\limits_{i=1}^{n} \mathbf{d}_i \right)}$$

In the SMART experiments, the cosine correlation function was found to give somewhat better results. Both give correlation figures ranging from zero where no matching occurs at all ($\cos 90° = 0$) to 1 where a perfect match is found ($\cos 0° = 1$), but the cosine function is more sensitive to the number of assigned terms. The overlap function corresponds to the kind of simple matching of keywords found in most post-coordinate systems, whether manual or computer-based; a straightforward count of the number of keywords appearing in both search request and document description is taken as the measure of correlation between the two, with the highest figure indicating the nearest match. The superiority of the more complex measure shown by the SMART experiments suggests that computer-based systems could improve their results by using this instead of the simple matching procedures currently in use.

Both measures allow documents to be ranked according to the degree to which they match the search formulation, ie the document which most closely matches the search is ranked first, the next second, and so on down to the document which matches it least, ranked N in a collection of N documents. This enables the user to set his own target in terms of recall by stating a cut-off point, in fact this would normally be the case. (If we may imagine the SMART system used with, say, MEDLARS, we would hardly want the whole of the data base of 2,500,000 items printed out in ranked order in response to every

457

enquiry!) If we assume that the system works perfectly, then if we want half a dozen items we set the cut-off point at 6, and receive a list of the six most relevant items; if we want a more complete list, then we could set the cut-off point at 200 items, with the most highly ranked—and therefore most relevant—items at the beginning, and steadily decreasing relevance as we worked our way down the list.

The ranked output also allowed Salton to develop the normalized recall measure used in a modified form by Cleverdon in Cranfield II, and a corresponding normalized precision figure. Each is based on calculating the recall or precision ratio obtained at each rank and summing the results; if all the relevant documents are ranked more highly than all the irrelevant documents, the result will be 1, whereas if all the irrelevant documents were ranked more highly than the relevant (disaster!) the result would be 0. In practice, of course, the system is not perfect, and figures between the two extremes are obtained; the results obtained using different processing methods to obtain the correlations and thus the rankings can then be compared directly.

The system was originally intended for use with batch processing, but provision for user feedback was incorporated; a user could formulate a request in natural language, which would then be processed by the system and matched against the data base to give a ranked output down to the set cut-off point. The user would then evaluate this, and the results of the evaluation would be fed back into the system, which would then repeat the search as modified by the user's relevance judgements. This procedure is clearly much better suited to on-line than to batch processing, and it has proved to be a very effective way of improving the performance of the system.

The original work was carried out on three small collections of documents. These consisted of 780 items from IRE *Transactions on computer science* 1959–1961, for which abstracts and titles were available; 200 items from the Cranfield II collection, for which abstracts and titles, and also detailed intellectual indexing, were available; and 82 items consisting of short papers (average length 1380 words) from the 1963 annual meeting of the American Documentation Institute (now ASIS), for which the full texts were used in addition to the abstracts and titles. The results showed that abstracts gave better results than titles, but that full texts did not give a sufficiently clear indication to determine whether they would normally give better results than abstracts. (It will be remembered that Cranfield II showed better results for abstracts than for either titles or full texts). In general, simple methods gave the best results; merging of word forms and of synonyms were both superior to the use of the hierarchical relationships in the thesaurus; statistical phrase recognition gave good results; and better results were obtained with weighted terms (*ie* taking account of frequency of occurrence) than with unweighted terms. Overall, the results obtained showed that computer processing compared reasonably well with intellectual processing, using the Cranfield results as the criterion.

Since these early experiments, new techniques have been evolved for the construction of computer-generated thesauri, the system may be used on-line, and further tests have been carried out on larger collections. One comparison of particular interest is that of the SMART system and MEDLARS; a first trial gave unsatisfactory results because of flaws in the experimental design, and a second test was therefore planned to overcome these difficulties.[12] From the set of search requests used by Lancaster in his evaluation, thirty were chosen, and for each one or more documents judged to be relevant were chosen as starting points. From these, sets of fifteen further documents were established for each by searching the 1964, 1965 and 1966 volumes of SCI, eliminating any references found which did not form part of the MEDLARS data base. The collection of 450 documents obtained in this way was then assessed for relevance in relation to each of the 30 questions; for one, no relevant documents were identified, and it was therefore dropped from the test. (The original documents, which would have given *one* relevant answer to the question, were not included in the test collection). The relevance judgements established that of the collection of 450 documents, a total of 284 were relevant to one or other of the questions, while reference back to the MEDLARS study showed that MEDLARS retrieved 127 of the documents, not all of them in the set of 284 judged to be relevant. This set of 127 documents was then considered to be the standard recall base, giving a maximum recall ration of 45% (127/284). It is not quite clear why this was done; for example, for question 9, MEDLARS retrieved 12 documents, but only 6 were among those judged to be relevant, whereas for question 15 MEDLARS retrieved none of the documents, though 13 were judged relevant.

Four comparisons were made with the results of the MEDLARS searches, which had been made using MESH and the usual Boolean logic operators AND, OR and NOT. The first comparison used basic word extraction only, *ie* removal of 's' (to merge plural and singular) or word stem selection (to merge word forms, *including* plural and singular). The cut-off point for the ranked output was set to match the number of documents retrieved by MEDLARS, and the results obtained showed that under these conditions the performance of the SMART system was relatively poor. The comparison was therefore repeated, but with the SMART system set to retrieve 127 documents for the 29 requests, selecting those which gave the highest correlation coefficients. This removed the artificial constraint imposed by matching the actual numbers retrieved by MEDLARS, and led to a marked improvement in the results. From a 30%–40% difference in favour of

MEDLARS in the first comparison, the second showed a difference of only 15–20%; from this, Salton concludes that the Boolean logic normally used in searches of computer-based systems is less satisfactory than the correlation coefficients using vector matching processes used in SMART. In the other two comparisons, the same technique was used with SMART, *ie* the correlation coefficient was used with the cut-off points set to give a total output of 127 documents.

For the third comparison, SMART used a prepared thesaurus, to help with synonym recognition, and a computer-generated word discriminator list. The latter is produced by (i) obtaining a word list from the abstracts, removing 's' suffixes first; (ii) deleting words which only occur once; (iii) deleting words which occur in more than a quarter of the abstracts; (iv) deleting words automatically determined to be non-discriminatory (*ie* those terms which do not help to discriminate between documents—these include words such as 'has', 'among' and 'other'). The first three of these procedures are similar to those adopted by Sparck Jones to improve the performance of her system (chapter 13), while the fourth corresponds to the intellectual generation of a stop list. In this test, both the word discriminator list and the stored thesaurus gave much better results than the simple word stem procedures, with the theasurus giving results comparable with MEDLARS.

For the fourth comparison, the SMART feedback techniques were added, and this produced a significant swing in favour of SMART. Using three iterations, incorporating user feedback in each, it proved possible to obtain results some 30% better than MEDLARS. One may question some of the methodology of this comparison; the MEDLARS evaluation study had already shown that the indexing methods which led to the answers taken as the recall base were in need of improvement, for example. However, it is clear that the SMART procedures worked well, and Salton himself is quite definite:

> no technical justification appears to exist for maintaining controlled manual indexing in operational retrieval environments.

Not everybody would accept this statement, and it does of course ignore cost factors. The SMART experiments have all involved relatively small collections, which are processed by sophisticated techniques; questions must arise as to what would happen if they were used to handle 120,000 requests a year on a data base approaching three million items, as is MEDLINE. No doubt the automatic clustering techniques in the system would reduce the number of items scanned in response to each request, but even so costs—and almost certainly processing delays—would rise steeply. This will change; as Lynch points out, staff costs are rising and computing costs are falling, so that eventually we shall have to transfer more and more information processing to the machine, and rely on techniques such as those in SMART to do what is now done by human effort.[13] Salton also makes the very relevant point that computers are not subject to human error; the question of 'indexer consistency' would not arise in such a situation.

CONCLUSIONS
The research described in this chapter tends to show that many of the ideas regarding semantic and syntactic relationships discussed in this text, and used in the majority of well-established retrieval tools, are open to question. It appears that the most effective systems are the simplest: those using keywords taken from the text, with the minimum of control, perform as well or nearly as well as more sophisticated systems, and cost a great deal less, when we are considering intellectual indexing. By contrast, SMART seems to indicate that sophisticated computer processing, backed by a minimum of intellectual effort in the construction of thesauri, can give better results still. We cannot ignore these results in the hope that they will go away; it is clear that there is a lot of hard thinking to be done before we finally arrive at firm conclusions. While libraries remain open access systems, classification schemes will continue to be used—though it is possible that they may grow more like the kind used in supermarkets, aimed at attracting the consumers to take the goods we offer rather than at any kind of logical order. The computer is with us to stay, and we must grasp the opportunities it offers to expand the services we offer before others move in to take our place, leaving libraries as secondclass citizens to be ignored by the serious seeker after knowledge.

The present author believes that there is still a place for intellectual analysis, and that the librarian with his information retrieval techniques still has a significant role to play in the communication of human knowledge. This is certainly true now; only the future will reveal whether it will continue to be so.

BIBLIOGRAPHY
1 Cleverdon, C W: 'Evaluation tests of information retrieval systems.' *Journal of documentation*, 26 (1) 1970, 55–67. (Progress in documentation.)
See also the chapters in *Annual review of information science and technology*, edited by C A Cuadra, 1966–.
2 A comprehensive bibliography of the project for the years 1961–1965 will be found in the 'Classification' chapter in *Five years work in librarianship*, 1961–1965. The basic reports are as follows:
Cleverdon, C W: *Aslib Cranfield Research Project: report on the testing and analysis of an investigation into the comparative efficiency of indexing systems.* Cranfield, College of Aeronautics, 1962.
Aitchison, J and Cleverdon, C W: *A report on a test of the index of metallurgical literature of Western Reserve University.* Cranfield,

College of Aeronautics, 1963.

Cleverdon, C W, Mills, J and Keen, E M: *Factors determining the performance of indexing systems*. Cranfield, Aslib-Cranfield Research Project, 1966. 2 v in 3. Briefer summaries of the work will be found in several articles and reviews, of which the following is a selection:

Cleverdon, C W and Mills, J: 'The testing of index language devices'. *Aslib proceedings, 15* (4) 1963, 106–130.

Swanson, D: 'The evidence underlying the Cranfield results'. *Library quarterly, 35* (1) 1965, 1–20.

Cleverdon, C W: 'The Cranfield tests on index language devices'. *Aslib proceedings, 19* (6) 1967, 173–194.

3 Cleverdon, C W: 'User evaluation of information retrieval systems.' *Journal of documentation, 30* (2) 1974, 170–180.

4 Rees, A M: *Review of a report of the Aslib-Cranfield test of the index of metallurgical literature of Western Reserve University*. Cleveland, Ohio, Western Reserve University School of Library Science, 1963. 32p.

Rees, A M: 'Semantic factors, role indicators et alia: eight years of information retrieval at Western Reserve University'. *Aslib proceedings, 15* (12) 1963, 350–363.

5 Keen, E M and Digger, J: *Report of an information science index languages test*. Aberystwyth, College of Librarianship Wales, 1972. 2v. Part 3 Appendices, containing such details as the complete indexing languages used, is available as OSTI report 5121, 1972, from the British Library Lending Division (microfiche).

Keen, E M: 'The Aberystwyth index languages test.' *Journal of documentation, 29* (1) 1973, 1–35.

6 Lancaster, F W: *Evaluation of the MEDLARS Demand Search Service*. Bethesda, Maryland, National Library of Medicine, 1968. (Full report.)

Lancaster, F W: 'Evaluating the performance of a large computerized information service'. *Journal of the American Medical Association, 207* (1) 1969, 114–120.

Lancaster, F W: 'Interaction between requesters and a large mechanized retrieval system'. *Information storage and retrieval, 4* (2) 1968, 239–252.

Lancaster, F W: 'Aftermath of an evaluation'. *Journal of documentation, 27* (1) 1971, 1–10.

Stevens, N D: 'MEDLARS: a summary review and evaluation of three reports.' *Library resources and technical services, 14* (1) 1970, 109–121.

7 Cleverdon, C W: 'On the inverse relationship of recall and precision.' *Journal of documentation, 28* (3) 1972, 195–201.

8 Moll, W J D: 'MEDLINE evaluation study.' *Bulletin of the Medical Library Association, 62* (1) 1974, 1–5.

Lancaster, F W and Fayen, E G: *Information retrieval on-line*, Melville, 1973. (Especially chapters 8 and 9.)

9 Sparck Jones, K and van Rijsbergen, C J: 'Information retrieval test collections.' *Journal of documentation, 32* (1) 1976, 59–75. (Progress in documentation.)

10 Salton, G: *The SMART retrieval system: experiments in automatic document processing.* Prentice-Hall, 1971. This work consists of the original reports by those who worked on the project, and in consequence tends to be rather uneven. Not recommended for the beginner, who will find one of the journal articles an easier introduction to the system.

Salton, G: *Automatic information organization and retrieval.* McGraw Hill, 1968.

Salton, G: 'The evaluation of automatic retrieval procedures—selected test results using the SMART system'. *American documentation, 16* (3) 1965, 209–222.

Salton, G and Lesk, M E: 'Computer evaluation of indexing and text processing'. *Journal of the Association for Computing Machinery, 15* (1) 1968, 8–36.

Salton, G: 'Automatic text analysis'. *Science, 168* 17 April 1970, 335–343.

11 *The general inquirer: a computer approach to content analysis*, by P J Stone [and others]. MIT Press, 1966.

12 Salton, G: 'A new comparison between conventional indexing (MEDLARS) and automatic text processing (SMART).' *Journal of the American Society for Information Science, 23* (2) 1972, 75–84.

13 Lynch, M F: *Computer-based information services in science and technology—principles and techniques.* Peter Peregrinus, 1974.

Index

In addition to serving the normal purpose of enabling readers to find specific items quickly, this index is intended to demonstrate the principles set out in the text and discussed on pages 264–266. Certain conventions are used: *def* indicates that a term is defined; + indicates that a discussion covers more than two pages. Bibliographical references are shown by *bib*; full details of a book, in particular those cited in the bibliography for chapter 1, are usually only given once, and parentheses are used to show further citations, *eg*

Vickery, B C *bib* 9(151, 188), 9, 9 (29, 56, 270, 272), 57, 151, 325 indicates that works by this author are quoted on all the pages shown, but that for full details of the work quoted on page 56 it is necessary to go back to page 9. The reason for this is that the bibliography for chapter 1 lists a number of basic works, many of which are referred to throughout the text, and it was thought unnecessary to repeat the full details at every point.

Synonyms are in general indexed fully, but in some cases this would have led to repetitive entries; in such cases, an index entry is made for the main discussion under non-preferred terms, but these are followed by the preferred term in parentheses to lead to the full set of index entries, *eg*

References (cross-references) *def* 27

which leads to page 27, but also to the index entry

Cross-references

where several additional entries will be found.

Filing is word by word; abbreviations are treated as single words; hyphens are elided, so that Cross-references files *after* Crossley. Order is alphabetical within each heading or subheading; *irt* (in relation to) is ignored.

Figures and tables are *not* indexed, nor are spelled out forms of any of the abbreviations listed on pages xiv to xvi.